ESCORT

Mks 1, 2, 3 & 4

The Development & Competition History

SECOND EDITION

Jeremy Walton

Foulis

Haynes

Dedication

This book is dedicated to Patricia Rolfe, Vera Hutchinson and Arthur Allen Walton

A FOULIS Motoring Book

First published 1985
Reprinted November 1985, March 1987 & 1989
Second edition published 1990

Published by:
Haynes Publishing Group
Sparkford, Nr Yeovil, Somerset BA22 7JJ

Haynes Publications Inc.
861 Lawrence Drive, Newbury Park, California 91320 USA

British Library Cataloguing in Publication Data
Walton, Jeremy *1946–*
    Escort Mk 1,2,3 & 4 : the development & competition
    history. New ed.
    1. Ford Escort cars, history
    I. Title II. Walton, Jeremy *1946–*. Escort MK.1, 2 & 3
    629.2222

    ISBN 0-85429-776-6

Library of Congress catalog number 90-81746

Editor: Mansur Darlington
Page layout: Tim Rose & Rob Pattemore
Printed in England by: J.H. Haynes & Co. Ltd

Contents

Introduction & Acknowledgements

FIRST published in 1985 and reprinted later that year, this account of the Escort's evolution from a purely British project to a 'World' car made on both sides of the Atlantic has prospered alongside that Ford's number 1 sales status in Britain. Unofficially subtitled 'Mk1, 2 & 3' by its publishers, it was obvious that the Escort book would require further updating as the 'Mk4' settled into further sales success following its January 1986 debut in right-hand drive (RHD). However, I wanted to do a lot more than just add the story of the later variant...

Of course we update the production story in Britain and America, supporting that costly tale with even more specifications and statistics in the appendices. The more powerful CVH engines for Europe and the later 1.9-litre GT motor for North America are now covered, along with the electro-mechanical anti-lock braking system exclusively introduced for the 1986 European Escorts. In these back pages there are technical descriptions of major Escort models, performance or otherwise, since 1968.

These appendices are now significantly expanded in respect of the performance figures that everyone seems to enjoy quoting. Additional research has uncovered maximum speed, acceleration run and mpg figures not just for the production Escorts, but also for factory race and rally cars, including the Broadspeed and Zakspeed cars that won international and national titles, plus full figures for a sensational 560bhp rallycross champion that set new records in acceleration when *Motor* magazine and I examined its capabilities, which included an electronically timed 0-60mph in an *average* 2.7 seconds, faster than a turbocharged GP Lotus of its era!

The acquisition of knowledge does not cease because a model is out of production, in fact people are often more inclined to tell the truth! For the Escort RS 1600i, a fast appreciating classic these days, that means we have been able to experience a later body and suspension layout. There are also sections of the appendices showing how well the rarer and faster RS derivatives were sold and produced, plus a detailed account of the development and sales life of the 1986-90 Escort RS Turbo.

Because we had over 120,000 words to compress between its covers, the original Escort book inevitably had some solid slabs of unbroken text. We have endeavoured to break these up with many new pictures and substituted some new ones where profitable.

Although it always seemed logical to me that I should write an Escort history, encompassing road and competition models since 1968, there were plenty of people who asked me during the competition research, 'Why do another book on the Escort?' Sometimes this was because they thought I had written Escort books previously. So let me make it clear that I had not written on the Escort for anything other than magazines; my previous Haynes Ford book was concerned with the Capri.

In fact I had always wanted to 'do' the Escort in book form, but was put off by the mass of material already published. Examining those books and receiving comment on *Capri*, plus a more recent volume upon the Audi Quattro (also published by Haynes), I realized that there was plenty of ground to cover with validity, just so long as I used a strictly personal perspective on the RS products from Ford Advanced Vehicle Operations (FAVO), based on my 1972-75 employment, and so long as I endeavoured to put the Escort's sporting achievements in a wider perspective, summarized by a viewpoint from the eighties, rather than as the original rear drive cars were developing.

I also felt it was important to cover comprehensively the non-competition story, because literally millions of Escorts have given such sterling service all over the world. Thus, the two rear drive Escort ranges and the current front drive models are included. I have now included the facelift 1986-90 Escort, in this, our second edition.

Each time I write a book I vow it will be the last, so what personally motivated an Escort tome? Primarily, the number of such small Fords I had driven and owned made me enthusiastic enough to find out more. For the record, I had my own 1300GT estate for much of the seventies; a very special Mexico; drove a 1.3 Sport for a 29 race novice season; completed a number of Mexico races; and enormously enjoyed a truncated rally season in an RS 2000. Said vehicle needed a certain amount of restoration after tangling with a tree stump buried in a laburnum bush, but I still went on unabashed to drive more competition Escorts in the eighties, including Richard Longman's RS 1600i, and the ultimate, so far, John Welch's 4-WD Xtrac Turbo of 560bhp, mentioned before, that was fractionally better to 60mph than the 3 seconds a full blown Lotus 97T Grand Prix car managed in the talented hands of Elio de Angelis!

As I write this, family transport is provided by a 1986 Estate 1.6L Escort. Also from the front drive Escort series, I have run two XR3/3i Escorts over 50,000 miles.

That is the plea in mitigation, ladies and gentlemen. The author claims to have written a comprehensive history of the world's best-selling car nameplate in the eighties from personal experience rather than cynical recycling of existing material. I shall leave you to decide how successful he has been.

The publishers and common usage have brought us Escort in 'Mk 1, 2, 3 & 4' but Ford themselves have used no such badges, so I should explain how UK slang divides up the models discussed. The Escort '1' was the first 1968-74 rear drive model, but for pedants it should be noted that Ford of Britain did use the Escort badge as early as 1955 on a limited-volume estate version of the Prefect.

An Escort '2' refers to the 1975-80 restyled rear drive models. These were made primarily in Britain and Germany, whereas the Escort '3' spread the front drive philosophy and overall style (but *not* parts interchangeability) to many other manufacturing locations. These include North and South America and are the heart of the Escort name's ability to outsell the German-manufactured Golf and Toyota's Japanese base for Corolla output.

Unlike a Golf, but totally similar to Corolla, the Escort badge does not cover one type of small car engineering, the switch from rear to front drive marking a complete break in continuity that was as pronounced in minor details as it was in fundamentals such as the CVH engine and independent rear suspension.

An Escort '4' in slang is simply the 1986 Winter announcement of the restyled front drive Escort. The Escort 'Mk 5', introduced in September 1990 just prior to this edition going to press, has yet to have its own history, so must wait some time before deserving attention.

This is the longest and most complex book I have written, yet it is divided up around a very simple formula to tell the story of the three main Escort models that existed between 1968 and 1989.

The basic idea is that each model – two rear drive types (1968-74 and 1975-80), plus the 1980-onward front drive Escort, and the 1986 update – is described in a pre-set format; one that provides a chapter for development of a model range, subsequent sales and technical development, plus individual chapters to relate the progress of performance and competition derivatives.

Additionally, the scene is set for the Escort's original development in the fifties and sixties as a straightforward Anglia replacement that developed into a European line for Ford of Germany too.

Later on, I recount the multi-million, multi-national steps that led to the creation of the new Escort's American and English CVH power units for the current Escort: a tough motor that proved capable of accommodating 55bhp, 1.1-litre economy, or 132bhp turbocharging for public sale in Ford's first European turbo, the 1.6 Escort RS Turbo.

There are also individual appendices to detail technical specifications in Britain and America, production statistics, performance figures. These include some competition machinery and a detailed account of the road and rally RS1700T Escort that Ford axed in 1982.

I have tried to ensure that privateers in rallycross and Hot Rod racing have received some of their dues, rather than simply concentrate on factory Fords; in this connection mention of the Martin Schanche domination of the 1984 European Rallycross Championship with a 550bhp, 4-WD Escort, plus driving impressions of John Welch's similar Xtrac Escort, seemed appropriate.

As ever, I have included my own race, rally and road impressions of the many Escorts I have been fortunate enough to test, own or operate.

The idea has been to try and do justice to the enormous spread of machinery that has appeared beneath the Escort nameplate, so that economy Escorts are listed with the same care as the hottest models.

A 1985 trip to Brazil underlined for me just how worldwide the small Ford's appeal is, for the XR3 jostles amongst aged hybrids in South America with just the same panache as its GT cousin in Northern America and the European and South African Escorts.

It is no wonder that Ford were able to claim the largest sales under any one name for the Escort of the early eighties. When this was written the Escort was manufactured in: Britain, Germany, Belgium, Spain, Brazil, South Africa, Canada, and the USA, with many more countries receiving, or assembling, partially built Escorts. There are simply so many countries, and customers by the million, all showing enthusiasm for a body that derived a unique, lengthier, look only in the later development stages, that I have been forced to concentrate on the European Escorts, but wherever possible overseas counterparts have also been described.

As a former Ford employee (Public Relations, Motorsport/Advanced Vehicle Operations, 1972-75) it is natural that I should acknowledge the debt I owe the company for most of the information, and much of the photographic material, within these pages. A former employee, however, is not always the most-loved writer of factual material and it is only fair to say that I frequently had to resort to former personal relationships, rather than official Public Relations channels, in order to complete this book. For the second edition liaison was a lot easier and access, even to Escorts still (unfortunately) on the secret list, was permitted so that I can have a complete story when all such derivatives of the 1990s are available.

Ford departments who gave their utmost were primarily the British engineering and styling departments, Ford Special Vehicle Operations and Ford Photographic. Ron Mellor, Ford's European engineering chief when this was first written, fortunately, insisted on providing a personal interview along with Uwe Bahnsen, then styling and aerodynamics vice president. It is fair to say that this really turned the tide, because many others then followed his example.

In such a large company as Ford it would be invidious to further single out individuals in departments for special compliment. Some actually risked their livelihoods in providing facilities that I could not obtain as a journalist; although they must remain anonymous, my heartfelt thanks are herewith expressed. Wherever I have been able to mention an individual, this has been done at the appropriate point in the book. All Ford-owned test cars were supplied by Harry Calton, Barry Simons or Barry Reynolds, who were Warley HQ press officers at different times during the 1967-1988 period. Such cars were superbly prepared by the Ford press garage at Brentford, Middlesex. Additional second-edition specialist information from Warley employees came from Jim McCraw (American Escort guru), David Nash and Martyn Watkins (statistics). Mike Moreton and Bob Howe, both based at Boreham in 1988, updated or detailed some earlier Escort TC/RS knowledge. Graham Robson, also at the newer Boreham offices for part of his 1988/89 working life, was as generous as ever in sharing Escort lore and some fresh production data.

Chief amongst the former Ford employees who have always encouraged my work with solid facts rather than conjecture have been ex-rally team co-ordinator Charles Reynolds (employed currently by Prodrive), Richard Lee and Kevin Cooney. The latter pair were with Ford Advanced Vehicles Operations at the time I was employed, Lee going on to work for Alfa Romeo GB as managing director, before establishing his own marketing agency.

A quite astonishing amount of co-operation was achieved from the Ford-owning public and some of the keener Ford-orientated clubs. Again, wherever it seemed politic, I have mentioned their names, but let me also single out the Ford RS Owners Club and AVO Owners Clubs for their timely reminders of what the cars were, coupled with concours exhibitions of what they can still be today. It was not just the RS products that caught my interest. I hope you will find the contents represent a fair split between normal road use and enthusiast/competition use, so my thanks also to the often long-suffering Ford Dealers/Ford press garage, for filling in the many personal knowledge gaps I suffered on less sporting models.

Performance figures are now from sources other than the old *Autocar* magazine, but I am still happy to acknowledge the co-operation of former editor Ray Hutton and former production editor Debra Stuart, plus the assistance I received in compiling performance statistics from *Autocar & Motor* in its current Haymarket era.

Photographs came not only from Ford, but also a number of private owners like R.P. Nixon, Martyn Castick, plus my own work and the far more professional efforts of London Art Tech, Chris Harvey or Colin Taylor Productions. At Ford Photographic I must thank department boss Steve Clark, Sheila Knapman and photographer Ken Shipton. Additional statistics, save where politically sensitive, came from David Burgess-Wise, familiar to many as an intermittent contributor to *Car* magazine and the author of erudite motoring books.

David is currently working on a monster Ford history with Walter Hayes (who has always been generous with his time to help my work) which should be an interesting counterpart to Robert Lacey's Ford bestseller.

As a contributor to a number of magazines myself I would single out *Motoring News, Motor Sport, Cars & Car Conversions, What Car?* and latterly *Performance Car,* or *Fast Lane,* as useful sources.

So that you can judge personal bias and context, I would add that *Cars & Car Conversions* was my employer between 1967 and 1969, so my initial memories of models such as the Escort Twin Cam come from that era. Between 1969 and 1972 and from 1975 to 1977 I worked for *Motoring News* and *Motor Sport,* with Ford sandwiched between times. Since January 1978 I have worked for myself, but would have starved immediately had it not been for *Motoring News/Motor Sport*'s staff and chairman/owner W.J. Tee. Gerald 'Big Gerry' Marshall made it financially possible for me to write a first book, *Only Here for the Beer,* which was also published by the G.T. Foulis division of the Haynes Publishing Group.

Some photographs of recent advertising campaigns and much-valued overall loyalty to keeping J.W. solvent came from Ford of Britain's advertising agent during 1979-84, Ogilvy & Mather, in London. Individuals I am glad to thank include producer Peter Harrison, his assistant Ann 'Stence' Gardner, and copywriting director Peter Sugden (Ferrari freak and Ford road and race operator). They have all stood up for me in extremely trying circumstances, together with former account executive/RS 2000 rallyist, John Banks, subsequent Young and Rubicam chairman.

Patricia and Suzanne Walton tried to instill some grammar into the biggest manuscript I have ever attempted, whilst son Steven Walton accompanied me on some of the adventures related within. The Haynes professionals on the manuscript were Rod Grainger and Mansur Darlington. The work was started the minute I first drove an Escort Twin Cam and has occupied most of any spare time I could find, for I failed signally to complete a satisfying manuscript in normal working hours.

Jeremy Walton
Henley-on-Thames

Chapter 1

In the beginning

Ford and their new small car, simply coded as the replacement Anglia, grow through the sixties

IT IS hard to recall the sixties accurately today, even if one did live through that frequently-remembered decade as a teenager exposed to all the delicious perils of the cliché – the 'Swinging Sixties'. Looked at from the eighties, the sixties materialize in the imagination as a swirling black and white collage of TV nostalgia images: John and Bobby Kennedy, the Beatles, mini-skirts and a pre-Common Market Britain, repeatedly rebuffed in its attempts to join the European trading pact. Under Edward Heath Britain did join the European Economic Community, but by then the multi-national way of life was established business practice at Ford, for a June 1967 meeting in Paris had led Henry Ford II into the establishment of a far-sighted concept in the car business – multi-national

The estate version of the first Ford type to bear the name Escort. Little wonder that there was antipathy in some quarters to the plan to adopt the Escort name for the 'exciting new model'.

The finished product (centre) with some of the alternatives explored by the British-based styling teams, showing the widely differing approaches made during the long search for an Anglia replacement.

manufacturing. Today, we have become used to hearing that Ford products contain components from America, Germany, Spain, Belgium, Brazil and Britain, but when Ford of Europe was created in 1967 under the direction of John Andrews, it really did mark the beginning of a new epoch. In British terms the effect of that move is best seen from an eighties' viewpoint. In 1983 Ford sold 278,306 cars in the UK that were home manufactured, yet in total their 28.91 per cent market lead, representing 518,048 cars, were made up from 154,958 made in Germany; 48,337 of Belgian origin; 23,770 from Spain and 12,632 shipped from Ireland. Emphasizing Ford's multi-national operation one must remember that gearboxes may well come from Bordeaux in France, CVH engines will be of Bridgend, South Wales origin, so that a car that was assembled in one country still carries a substantial percentage of components made elsewhere.

In the sixties Ford were still building toward those global goals, but the foundations on which the Escort would be built were gradually established. For British customers the most important facility would be the Halewood, Liverpool factory. Purchased in 1959, the year Escort predecessor, Anglia, was announced, the 329 acre Halewood site went into production in 1963 and would become the home of the Escort in Britain from November 1967 onward.

Other facilities relevant to the Escort's development revealed how methods inside Ford altered during the late fifties compared to the early sixties. The Anglia was basically the product of stylists and engineers, whereas the Escort was product-planned in a complete package. Only after some initial features had already been decided, did the Escort proceed, following exploratory engineering work that typified the usual continuous engineering process, well in advance of the first official New Anglia research in 1963. The directors approved the Anglia replacement programme in 1965, at which time the car was still seen as a simple British market job with good export potential.

Ford of Germany had acquired a lot of manufacturing potential in the sixties – as well as developing their R&D centre at Merkenich as a counterpart to Ford of Britain's 1967 opening of the £10.5 million Dunton R&D site – yet Ford in Germany lacked a suitable new small car project to manufacture. They had acquired Saarlouis, close to the Franco-German borders, in 1965, which would be ready to churn out cars at the rate of 700, or more, per day during 1968/69. At least that was the plan, the first complete Escort trundled away from the line on 16 January 1970...

Also relevant to the Escort manufacturing story was the 1962 multi-national move by Ford of Germany. Forced by the uncertainty about Britain's future in the Common Market, and the certainty that the car market within the protection of the EEC would grow rapidly, Ford of Germany purchased 441 acres of land adjacent to the Albert Canal at Genk in Belgium.

Whilst Ford were gathering together the apparatus of trans-European manufacturing, Ford of Britain engineers were making the decisions that would shape the Escort. Prior to the existence of the Dunton R&D centre, this meant working from a site at Aveley in Essex, to which Escort would return in the years 1970-74, when the FAVO RS products were made on a purpose-built line within its sprawling acres.

Perhaps the most basic decision taken about the Anglia's successor was that it would continue Ford of Britain and America traditions such as front engine, rear drive with leaf-sprung back axle. This was to be a disappointment to Ford's German engineers, who had co-developed the 12M front drive Taunus with American engineers for sale in the sixties. Since the model did not fare well in the commercial sense (leading to that urgent need for a small car design to manufacture in the late sixties), any feeling of disappointment at the absence of new technical features in the new design was relatively easily countered, and thus, no great difficulty was had in arguing the new design into continental, as well as British, production.

On the face of it the British Ford engineers just stuck with a proven cost-conscious formula, for the Anglia had had the same power train basics and sold approximately 1.3 million from 1959 to the close of 1967. Yet, when the engineers sat down to make some solid proposals for a low cost Anglia replacement with more passenger space and contemporary styling – the notch rear window of Anglia and Classic series having failed to start a new general trend, whilst robbing some rear seat and parcel shelf accommodation – the way in which the power train should be laid out was not as obvious as it seemed. This was a result of the public in Britain becoming more technically aware of small car design. The Mini had been launched in 1959 and the success of sportier versions was just beginning to help the whole range 'lift off' in 1961. Then there was the exact opposite power train of thought: rear engine, rear drive. That was characterized by the Hillman Imp, which had an advanced SOHC engine in aluminium as well as all-independent suspension as technical counterpoints to the Issigonis transverse front drive Mini. On the streets of the time you could see plenty of other rear engine designs; Fiat and Renault were typical, both the best part of a decade away from the familiar front drive hatchback formula of the seventies and eighties.

Penetrate Dunton R&D in the eighties and you will find that many of Ford's loyal engineers remember experiments with front drive, and all sorts of other power train layouts, even before the Mini was announced. Ford engineers in the UK tend to stick at their tasks; a trait typified by the overall engineering director at Dunton, Ron Mellor, who

The two main Anglia saloon derivatives in 1965, illustrating the individual styling (note the period interpretation of 'notchback' rear window!) and the slim track of the Escort's predecessor. The striped, white Anglia is the 1200 Super, which cost £614 and was propelled by a 54bhp, 1198cc engine to an Autocar-measured maximum of 82.6mph. The monotone 997cc Anglia De Luxe hides a rampant 41bhp (gross) and the Motor-measured capability of reaching 73.3mph in those unrestricted days. The basic two-door model cost £504 in the mid-sixties with the De Luxe at £565.

joined in 1955 and retired in 1987. To Mr Mellor and men from the original development team, such as John F.G. Brace and Tony Palmer, I owe much of this original background knowledge. This education was further expanded by Dunton residents Brian E. Charlick and Mike Brand, aided by previously-published interviews with Peter Fearn, who was working at Ford's KD Operations when I completed this research, but who was the manager of the product planning office when the Anglia replacement was being conceived.

The Ford Research & Engineering Centre at Dunton, near Basildon in Essex has shared the development work of all Escorts and has also acted as home to the Special Vehicle Engineering group who produced so many performance and special option vehicles. By the eighties the site was bursting at the seams with extra temporary buildings and an American-inspired electronics facility. Primary Ford test track and durability facility remained at Lommel, Belgium, under German Ford management.

Those early attempts at front drive were remembered with much merriment from some of the engineers. It was interesting to learn, however, that in a research centre up in Birmingham they had dissected rival designs like the Mini, prior to producing Ford possibilities along the same lines. These prototypes featured both transverse engine front drive and inline North-South engines (as seen in the Mini of the period and the first Renault 5). Tony Palmer recalled, 'We even had rear drive Minis as advanced studies!'

Tony Palmer was also involved in studying the merits of recirculating ball steering, in comparison with more direct rack and pinion layout that has since become the norm in world small car design. Then rack and pinion was acknowledged in British sports cars, and the Mini, for its accurate performance without the sloppiness associated with other more complex steering gear layouts. Ford decided to investigate such steering gear, and the likely extra cost to the customer.

Advanced Engineering Department V324 of Passenger Car Design presented a report compiled by A.E. Palmer and his manager D.P. Stephens on 28 August 1963. The eight sheet docket was based on 'tear down exercises made by Product Planning and costed by Purchase Analysis'. Advantages listed for the then standard Ford recirculating ball layout included: 'Can be adapted with suitable linkage to any specified steering geometry and front suspension' and 'has low reverse efficiency, hence road shocks are partially damped out before reaching steering wheel!' Nevertheless rack and pinion won the day with plus points listed: 'Permits simple and light mounting members' and 'clearance between pinion and rack teeth is negligible, hence lost motion is small'. In other words the rack offered very direct steering, and continued to do so when geared up, whilst recirculating ball (used by many Japanese cars into the eighties) became progressively more inefficient 'the higher the gear ratio, i.e. the lower the helix angle, the greater the lost motion'.

Fascinating was the only word for the analysed cost, with the Anglia's steering system costing £5 2s. 6.38d., and the Morris Mini quoted at £4 5s. 1.13d; the most expensive system was that of the Cortina (also recirculating ball) at slightly over £6. On such painstaking analysis did Ford decide to make the Escort their first rack and pinion mass production model.

Using a similarly exhaustive approach many of the same men, including Tony Palmer, had delved into the 12in. diameter wheel versus its 13in. counterpart. Their 27 January 1965 report concluded, 'the most important of the effects examined, i.e. weight reduction and package improvements, indicate advantages of 12in. over 13in. wheels'. The weight reduction was around 3lb per steel wheel, or 13½lb for a complete set of five. This further analysed as 12lb for wheels and 1½lb for tyres. It was noted, 'the reduction offers more scope for obtaining optimum ride and handling especially over rough surfaces'. The package advantage referred to was significant, allowing 'reduced wheel arch intrusion into the package space, or reduced wheelbase'.

In turn this meant some manufacturing costs could be lowered with a saving of five shillings (25 new pence!) anticipated for a 1in. shorter body, having its wheelbase reduced by 2.5in. These and similar savings, however, were offset by a quoted £40,000-60,000 investment to make 12in. wheels, and sobering extra costs of 12 to 15s. (up to 75 new pence) anticipated by Dunlop and Goodyear for 12in. tyres.

Although the report highlighted the advantages of 12in. wheels – which were a part of all the mass production original Escort range, only the Twin Cam opting for 13in – it said a lot more against than for. Looking back today it is interesting to read of the advantages offered in 1965, by low profile rubber in roadholding, and that Ford engineers were also well aware of the ride penalties to be paid with these lower profile carcases.

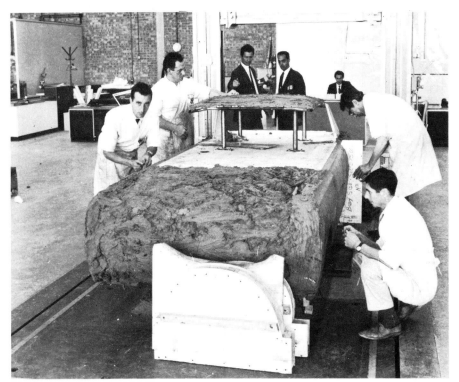

Sticky fingers at work for the Escort cause at the clay full-size stage. This was an era technologically far removed from today's computer-aided progress, although full-size modelling is still a vital task.

Again, with the benefit of some 20 years hindsight, it is also possible to see the wheel diameter facts on Escort as a point in an overall trend toward larger diameters and lower profiles: in the seventies the original design started featuring 13in. diameters more prominently (all FAVO models and mainstream's 1300 Sport) and the Mk2 gradually switched over until the cheapest models completed the process in September 1978. The front drive Escort started life on 13in, of course, and the XR3 took the logic a step further with 14in. diameters and 60 per cent low profile rubber in 1980. By 1984 the Escort RS Turbo had taken wheel diameters to 15 inches embraced by 195/50 tyres.

The Ford engineering study ranged over trim, where they recommended the Luxe level found in the Kadett, and seats, where it was felt Anglia type with 'less liveliness' would be appropriate. The Imp was brought forward as an outstanding example of ergonomics ('excellent whilst inexpensive') whilst on ride the target would be Kadett's road noise insulation: 'boulevard ride at least as good as the Viva or Kadett with better rough ride'.

Naturally the ventilation options were studied and, right from the start, there was to be no help from swivelling quarter lights, so the 'face level ventilation from swivelling nozzles...' with 'large area inlet and outlet required, to ensure good flow' were as specified targets for 1968. Again, Ford really did achieve their objectives, the Escort second only to Cortinas and Capris in their effective ventilation because only dashboard top nozzles were provided, rather than the amazing original aeroflow 'eyeballs'.

NVH (Noise, Vibration and Harshness) was a big Ford of Britain pre-occupation at the time, actively promoted by Harley Copp's engineering overlord role of the time. Ford set themselves at least Anglia standards, thinking little of rivals in this case, and there would be significant changes just before production that were all inspired by the war between effective engineering and premium standards of silence within the car. A prime example was the rear axle, for which the design intention was a pair of location links, *à la* Cortina GT/Lotus layout. Some press cars and a few other originals did have these rear links for the 1300 GT, as intended, but they were discontinued in the cause of NVH and cost for the majority of the production run, leaving only the Escort Twin Cam with this useful additional rear axle location layout.

There was also constant debate throughout development over axle ratios, NVH criteria demanding that a numerically low final drive be installed, whilst a lack of acceleration, compared to the targets set, demanded that models such as the 1300 GT have the 4.125 final drive, rather than the 3.777:1 originally anticipated. In fact the first handbook shows all models on a 4.125 with 3.777 as an option, but most production cars would have been specified on 4.1.

A number of influences, but particularly the then current in-company obsession with NVH, dictated a MacPherson strut front suspension layout with a single transverse lower arm ('TCA' in Fordspeak: Track Control Arm) located by a compression strut *aft* of the TCA. The Ford tradition was, and still is on eighties Escorts, for MacPherson strut, TCA, with that lower arm carrying a jointed mounting for a *leading* front anti-roll bar. Thus the roll bar does a little location work as well as performing the function its name implies; cheap and effective enough with lower power outputs. The original 1968 Escorts did appear without a front anti-roll bar and utilized the compression strut layout, but the Germans insisted – said all the UK engineers with whom I discussed the matter – that the usual roll bar and TCA layout be re-employed, so that by 1969 all Escorts had reverted to Ford traditions once more! Incidentally, the first Ford of Europe design to use successfully the compression strut and TCA layout was the 1976 Fiesta, and such a layout, but with the compression strut always placed in front of the front axle line, was still employed eight years later, even on 'Mk2' XR 2.

The lists of engineering and body objectives for the new Escort ran to twelve typed

Resolving the accommodation package for the Escort involved assessing this salubrious two-seater in 1966-67. Note that the central airflow grilles and instruments are those selected, in due course, as production items.

sheets in the 1965 comparison report, with even the rival jacks and tool kits painstakingly appraised. How well did the Escort perform in its pre-production trials?

Testing, testing

The historic document that encapsulates the multi-national engineering work that went into Ford's new small saloon of the sixties – which had always been designed with the brief that it was to be effective until the 'mid-seventies' – is a silver- jacketed, 12-section report titled *Passenger Vehicle Engineering. 1968 Anglia Programme, Sign-off Status, 26th June 1967*. That simply means that the engineering department – with signatories W.A. 'Bill' Fuke (Manager, Anglia Vehicle Engineering), J.N. Harvey (Executive Engineer, Vehicle Engineering) and J.T. West (Assistant Chief Engineer from the same department) – were saying that development had been completed to the point where the car could pass into production at a specified 'Job 1' date. More work remained to be done, some of it not materializing on cars the public received until after the public launch, but basically the car that would become the Ford Escort was passing from its engineering creators into mass production at this point. In Britain production began at Halewood (Job 1) on 17 November 1967.

Through subsequent talks with those concerned, some of the sheer effort and enthusiasm that went into the Escort can be understood 20 years later, but the report naturally concentrated on facts. As of June 1967 they had completed 243,000 miles on all prototypes, excluding vans and station wagons (sorry, company language again: estates to those in the UK). These were scheduled for approval on 29 September and 16 October (the latter for vans). Also, on later sign-off dates and contributing to the anticipated 285,000 miles covered by the time the first production models were on the line, were Escort 1300 GT (GT Sedan in Fordese!) which went for engineering approval on 10 August 1967, and automatics, which were scheduled for engineering sign-off by January (saloons) and May (estates and vans with automatic gearboxes).

Although Ford opened Dunton officially in 1967, testing for the Anglia's replacement over the planned quarter million mile mark was primarily performed at the company's Lommel Proving Ground in Belgium (about 20 car minutes, north of Zolder race track), whilst accelerated and high-speed durability trials were held at Boreham Airfield – a circuit not unlike Silverstone or Goodwood in terms of high-speed swerves and largely featureless terrain – and the banked tarmac of MIRA at Nuneaton. Cold-climate testing using Finland's chilly embraces for an 1100cc saloon to go through critical cold start tortures, whilst the heated climes of South Africa checked durability, performance and hot weather suitability for prototype 1300 saloon and 1300 GT. MIRA's wind tunnel was used not only to help evaluate the body but also the heating and ventilation system, using a glassfibre prototype initially, and confirming the results with metal bodied prototypes as they became available.

An engineering prototype can mean anything from a slightly changed pre-production car to a revolutionary new concept nestling beneath battered and disguised bodywork. For the '1968 Anglia' the sign-off docket listed four main types used in testing. There were 11

In the following shots are shown a fraction of the many Escort styling alternatives considered in the sixties studies for the original. This very plain two-door has a 'popeye' look and wrap-round tail lights, with ornate wheel trims of the kind found on Corsairs and Zodiacs of the period.

Component Vehicles, all saloons except for an estate. These materialized as 1966 Cortina bodies 'modified as required to accept components for testing and development'. Next were Mechanical Prototypes, nine in all, sub-divided as seven saloons, a van and one estate. These were 'modified 1966 Cortina bodies with 1968 Anglia underbodies and running gear'. Third were Semi-Engineered Prototypes, again nine in all, but this time only five were saloons, supported by two examples of both van and estate. These were really more like the public idea of a prototype with the intended Escort bodywork and running gear united in various states of preparation. Finally, Fully Engineered Prototypes covered just four vehicles: three of them saloons and naturally included running gear and bodywork, plus trim. At the June sign-off point 15 prototypes of all, except the Component Vehicle Cortina first-thoughts, had completed that 243,000 miles, broken down as a 140,000 miles majority for the Mechnical Prototypes in seven variations.

The cost

The cost of such comprehensive engineering work all over the world was considerable by the standards of the sixties in Britain, but was actually less than originally budgeted because one of the inevitable cost-cutting outbreaks had provided £2.54 million as the approved figure in place of the original £2.78 million.

As of 31 May 1967, some £1,951,619 had been spent on what became the Escort; a figure that covered the body, chassis and running gear engineering. Just over £2½ million, however, was still allocated as the final estimate to cover 'lifetime cost'. The biggest sum of money went on body engineering labour (£810,327) and the lowest sum accounted for was just £44 for inspection expenses. At this stage they could only estimate forward costs, as engineeering tests continued with a planned 18 further Escort derivatives, and some accessories to monitor the situation as the car went into production. Such Escorts would be subjected to 40,000 miles general durability or 10,000 high-speed miles, just as in the original testing in some cases, to make sure that 'quality, function and durability of all new items' was checked continuously. All such tests were to be concluded by February 1968, by which time the car would have been on sale less than two months.

Nationalities played a part in the Escort character, too. Perhaps the fundamental point in the way the Escort developed in production was the German influence, for the responsibility for vehicle development passed to Merkenich not long after the Escort's public debut. One Dunton engineer explained: 'In the pre-production stages we worked with the German teams – twice in the early days and then on the car as a Ford of Europe project. There was a difference in attitude; we had tended to "solve problems, and

Considered in late 1967 for the first Escort saloons, was this popular Rostyle-wheel, Cortina 1600E-look with extended tail lights.

November 1967, and the four-door derivative demanded for the German market is rapidly integrated into the main Escort programme, eventually appearing slightly after the original two-door for the UK. Note that the full 'dog-bone' grille is now a feature; compare this with some of the other styling options shown earlier.

bugger the cost" in our approach, whilst the Germans had been brought up on problem solving without additional vehicle on-cost'.

A gearchange to remember

Other key hardware was under development in the sixties that would profoundly affect the Escort. Longest lived, for its principles are with us today in Formula Ford and pushrod Escorts and Fiestas, were the Kent crossflow family of engines. From 1.3 litres to 1.6 litres the crossflows with their bowl-in-piston combustion chambers were intended for Cortina, but Ford also ensured the smaller engines, suitable for Escort and for sub-1-litre applications in Italy and France (responding to prohibitive taxation rates) were also incorporated. The engines all grew from the 105E five main bearing, cast-iron crankshaft, 997cc non-crossflow unit of Anglia and used a common block.

Thus, the Escort engines were all four-cylinder pushrod derivatives of the Kent's separated induction and exhaust type, but the capacities were all based around an 80.978mm bore with a variety of crankshaft stroke dimensions. In Britain the initial capacities were 1098cc (53.289mm stroke) and two stages of tune at 1297cc (62.992mm stroke). The most powerful of these engines was rated at 75bhp; a GT badge denoting the use of high lift camshaft, twin-choke Weber carburettor and fabricated steel exhaust manifold to feed a cylinder head based on the deeper breathing characteristics of the Cortina 1600 GT. Further details are given in Chapter Two's description of the original range.

What occupied much engineering time and received universal applause was the new four-speed gearbox. Unlike the 105E Anglia it had synchromesh on first gear as well as the remaining three ratios. Tony Palmer and John Brace both recalled that it was always described as a German gearbox design, and it was true that the strictly torque-limited four-speeder (1600cc was always reputed to put too much strain on it: 1300 GT was the designed upper limit) did feature Cologne design, although manufactured at Halewood. Mr Palmer, Executive Engineer, Chassis Engineering, at Ford Dunton when I interviewed him in Spring 1983, remembered, 'the Doug Stevens-designed Anglia box was *so* compact and worked well with a three-rail shift, but it was here in Britain that Ken Einchcombe invented the single-rail shift for the Escort box – and that gave a simply supreme shift!'

That Escort four-speed was Ford's first all-metric gearbox in Britain and Peter Fearn summed up everyone's admiration aptly when he said in 1982 that it had 'change quality second to none, even by 1980s standards, I believe.'

The development engineers, however, did have some problems with its externals as

Perhaps the Capri would not have been such a success, had Ford gone ahead with this Escort coupé project? Straightforward side and rear shots show the promise of the project that was aimed at the American and European markets of 1970.

A very different front grille, and wrap-round front indicators were proposed for the Escort coupé; it is worth noting that the earlier Escort saloon studies with extended tail light clusters also had in mind the need to meet American regulations. In the end the original Escort was not offered to the US buyers.

John Brace revealed: 'We had a vibration problem with the casting chosen and the axle ratio for 1100 and 1300 which was worst above 5700rpm. So the first 2000 cars or so had a sand-cast casing, with die-cast casing from then on which was one helluva lot stiffer. The other gearbox problem that a lot more people saw was "the gearlever came 'orf in me 'and" classic. That was caused by the nylon ball seat unscrewing at the base of the lever. We developed a positive locking fix for that, but in the interim an adhesive acted as a temporary cure...'

Escort GT-badged coupé proposal, with neat twin-pipe exhaust. Plus a foretaste of the Cortina Mk III 'coke-bottle' look, originally made popular by GM.

Another look at the aborted GT coupé with a preview of the eighties colour-coded grille fashion. This styling exercise has an overall appearance not dissimilar to Opel's Kadett coupé, pronounced by chrome steel wheels, or an excellent imitation of steel wheels!

Aerodynamic objectives in the sixties

Design studies for the replacement Anglia continued through much of the sixties, under three main influences. Originally, Ford of Britain and Ford of Germany had agreed to co-operate on an ECC (European Common Car). Then Ford of Germany were handed the front drive 12M with much of the development work completed in the USA, so the middle period in the Escort's pre-production life was a purely British project. Finally, the comparative failure of the 12M, a large increase in potential manufacturing capability and the growth of both continental Europe and Britain as car sale markets – in 1969 their combined total of 10.6 million sales surpassed that of the USA for the first time – persuaded the Germans back into the common Escort fold, barely a year before production began. As a result there were some changes, particularly to the suspension, final drive ratios and the adoption of a four-door option that were added very late in the programme. Some German-inspired features, such as the installation of roll bar located front strut suspension, appeared after initial production had started.

Meanwhile, it was to Ford's credit that the eighties obsession with aerodynamics, particularly the drag factor denoted by Cd figures, was an integral part of the original Escort shape. The original objective had been a 0.46 Cd, the figure returned by the Anglia, which was *five* inches narrower than Escort! The Escort was two inches lower in its final form, but still the frontal area was 18.5sq ft instead of 17.5sq ft, so it was clever of the engineers to reduce the Cd to an eventual pre-production 0.43. That may be laughable by the standard of the eighties in which longer production saloons hit 0.28 to 0.30

Here is one Escort we were lucky not to receive! A cramped three- or four-door with coupé hindquarters. Back to the drawing board, chaps ...

Cd slipperiness, and even stubby hatchbacks like the Uno and Peugeot 205 manage a substantial 0.34, but remember that the later, bluff-fronted, Mk2 Escort of 1975 was a step backward from the Anglia figure, rather than a progression from the original Escort...

In fact, Ford could have built a two-door saloon with a coefficient below 0.40 in the sixties, instead of waiting until the 1980 front drive Escorts, for one of the design studies we spoke of was a GTO-badged Anglia with fared in headlamps, but instantly-recognizable Escort Mk1 side panels.

Amongst those earlier Escort sixties design studies there was also a preview of the hatchback look, rejected on grounds of insufficient interior space, and a very upright saloon with almost an Anglia rear window reverse angle and a grille reminiscent of Ford USA's compact cars of the period. Even in November 1967, Ford's Dunton designers were looking hard at the coupé concept for possible 1970 introduction in Europe and the USA, for it was Ford's intention at the time to 'Federalize' the original Escort for the American market. Neither coupé concept nor Escort made it across the Atlantic, but the accompanying pictures are intriguing – and so far as I know, previously unpublished.

The original Escort shape was defined by a team under the leadership of John Fallis, Design Executive, Car Exteriors at Dunton when the car was launched. At the time Mr Fallis described the end result as 'adequacy all round', and added that they had 'got excited about aerodynamics', only to find that fuel consumption gains were noticeable by their absence – although it is only fair to say that the original Escort exceeded the design targets in this respect.

At that time John Fallis and his team were more concerned with cutting wind noise as much as practicable, and that was the primary thinking behind the use of fixed front quarter light panes. One of the key features in production thinking about the replacement Anglia was that it should have the long single-section side panels from front A-post to the end of the rear wing. This was to allow the best quality control of door and window apertures, but that naturally went by the board on four-door variants.

Key styling features that were echoed in most serious design studies and 'clay models' – 'mock-ups so good they could embarrass terribly the unwary body-leaner during boring parts of a design review', in the words of one naughty insider – were the small, fixed, side rear windows and the kicked up body line over the rear wings. The small side glass was purely a styling statement, but the lines of the back wings were justified in some interviews of the period as necessary to clear the vertical spare wheel. The wheel, all 12 inches of it frequently covered by the cross-ply covers that were still current, was mounted upright on the left of the boot (looking forward) and the petrol tank, after much agonizing, drifted into the right-hand corner with its 9 gallon reservoir. Cynics just said the rear wing line reminded them of the Vauxhall Viva of the period...!

Perusing the comparisons and engineering objectives for the Escort makes fascinating reading today. In a report dated 6 July 1965 John Brace, then Vehicle Product Development Engineer, Anglia Range, carried out such a comparison against the Vauxhall Viva, Opel Kadett and the 105 E Anglia, up against the 1968 EC Car – in other words the European Common car that became Escort.

In the eighties, aerodynamic values, particularly drag coefficient, have become as important as horsepower, maximum speed and mpg figures have been in the past. John Brace treated them as of no less importance nearly 20 years ago, leading off with figures that demonstrate how much progress has been made in mass production sheet metal during the past two decades. At that stage the Escort was recording 'Cd less than 0.45' in wind tunnel tests. I believe MIRA (Motor Industry Research Association) was used; certainly there was no Ford in-house aerodynamic test and development facility until the eighties, and then it was built in Germany.

Another coupé Escort alternative featured this American-influenced front grille and another variation on the chopped fastback theme.

That sub 0.45 Cd figure, which became 0.43 for the final production version, looked positively marvellous against the Kadett's 0.55 and the equally bulbous Viva's 0.51! However, the small Anglia's 0.46 was a harder act to follow, given that Escort had to grow to accommodate larger passenger loads and increased customer expectations.

The 1965 survey also set some other interesting objectives for the 1968 EC model: 'Exterior should allow cleaning of vehicle with ease and without scraped knuckles!' From memory I would have said that they achieved that, with the qualification that the front drive Escorts are even better and that the alloy wheels on sporty models were a particular chore in the seventies.

What Ford called the 'package' or interior accommodation, was described as 'borderline acceptable' front and rear for the Anglia. For Escort Ford felt that the front accommodation of Viva was 'good', and engineering recommended that slide seat adjustment be adopted, in place of Anglia's 'restricted' quadrant adjuster, together with an anti-tipping mechanism for the passenger front seat.

The original body is put on the sixties version of the medieval rack, and asked to display a fortitude that was considerably extended in the later stages of practical development.

What's in a name?

Apparently the German influence also extended to the eventual dropping of the name Anglia, which had been used throughout the development period. The official reasoning for the name Escort was that market research had established its effectiveness. In Britain the name had been used for an estate car version of the Prefect as early as 1955. Some cynics thought this reason enough to steer clear of the Escort appellation for the foreseeable future!

Back with our German naming role, a Dunton engineer with a twinkle in his eye and a broad grin told me the unofficial reasoning behind the axe for the respected Anglia name: 'The Germans didn't like it. Said it reminded them of those World War II East Anglian bomber bases!'

The British development engineers and their employers were astoundingly frank in letting me have access to development documentation and background, particularly for these '1968 Anglias'. So much so, that I have had to decide what to leave out, rather than scrape around for engineering background, as is so often the case in marque history research.

Some of the broad problems have already been discussed, but some of the small development details were intriguing. Starting with the body, John Brace recalled that they had recognizable Escorts in 1966 'in plastic because it was so much faster to make than the steel production type body. Even our first full engineering prototypes had fibreglass exterior shell parts for our testing at Boreham'.

Even during the mid-sixties aerodynamic study vehicles based on the Cortina were showing "around 0.35 Cd", so we were not surprised when Roy Haynes over at styling had some replacement Anglia proposals that were below 0.40,' remembered John Brace. These were the GTO-badged design studies that were rejected primarily for insufficient interior space, but Mike Brand, design analyst at Dunton, recalled the 1967 Escort Coupé styling studies, mostly in clay, that were 'planned for introduction in 1970, both in Europe and the USA. They were well down the design process line before they were chopped and would have had 1600 GT and 2000 GT engines in detuned form for the States.' These were the logical successors to that GTO school of thinking, but in production terms the Capri carried all Ford's Anglo-American coupé responsibilities in the sixties and seventies.

So far as the production Escort bodywork was concerned the distinctive 'dog's bone' grille sat above a most revealing change of plan. Brace explained; 'Originally there were four holes cut out in the lower front panels for cooling, but they were not needed, so we used production slots instead. However, if you look carefully at a Mk1 Escort you'll see that the hole cut out for a starting handle remained...even though the starting handle would have needed to pass straight through the radiator to work!' Looking at the original Escort saloons in production trim, that detail is best illustrated on the Twin Cam Escort with its quarter bumpers, both slots and central 'starting handle' hole clearly visible.

John Brace also recalled that the 1000 miles of *pavé* and concrete block testing of the

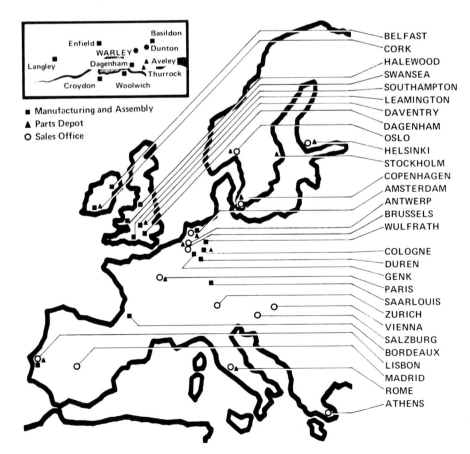

How Ford spread their multi-national presence across Europe. This was the picture by the mid-seventies; it gives a good idea of the location of the various factories mentioned throughout the book.

Home for the Escort in Britain, at least in terms of assembling cars from a worldwide parts supply, has been the Ford factory at Halewood, part of a Merseyside complex outside Liverpool. In 1988 over 10,000 employees could make 1000 cars a day.

type carried out both at Lommel and Boreham had prompted a change in gauge for the body side rails: 'These were strengthened up just before production after we had run five cars day and night for six weeks'. Again the original NVH brief had led to a suspension design – this time of the rear spring hangers – that was abandoned after durability testing, too.

The Bowl-in-Piston (BIP) crossflow engines caused little in the way of development

Halewood's counterpart in West Germany, and the source for most LHD Escorts in Europe, is Saarlouis.

engineering problems, although the dreaded NVH did mean that they ran through at least three sump modifications to find the best damped design until it was 'like a miniature Rolls Royce'. Naturally weight had to be kept under constant supervision with so much body engineering going on. Again, one could see a difference in British and German approaches with the Aveley and subsequently Dunton-based teams the more wary about any engineering solution that added weight. From the sign-off documentation of June 1967 one would judge that all parties had been supremely successful with a target of 1632lb (742kg) matched by an actual vehicle weight of 1634lb (743kg) for the standard saloon! For the De Luxe they reported in at just 4lb overweight at 1640lb (745kg) whilst they hit the bull's-eye on the Super to the pound at 1671lb (759kg)!

Although the engines caused few problems, some of the permutations caused a shudder to pass through present day Dunton denizens. One engineer recalled, 'The 1100 auto was awful: it couldn't pull away on a chilly morning start! We only had to have it because of the 1159 Viva...eventually both were killed'. The 1100 Escort automatic officially ceased production over a year after the Escort's debut: August 1969 in Britain.

Another engine derivative vividly recalled was the ultra-short-stroke 940cc for France and Italy which earned the blunt epithet, 'Bugger-all torque. It had a twin choke carburettor and 46bhp and we did get it up to 50bhp, but it was hard work to drive'. The subsequent motor racing sub-1.0-litre Escorts were torqueless, too, even if they did give more than 100bhp...

The engines emerged triumphantly from trials such as 40,000 miles durability and 2000 miles 'accelerated durability', along with a 1300 GT saloon that covered 10,000 high speed miles at MIRA and the 1300 saloons which tackled 20,000 South African miles, including 3000 miles checking 'off-road durability' mainly over gravel tracks.

In South Africa only the embarrassment of pulling into car parks reserved for blacks interrupted a constant flow of development mileage, while the Finnish cold climate testing around Rovaniemi provided a total contrast with temperatures of minus 30°F part of the daily development diet. Incidentally, when engineers took the fabled 940 to Finland in January and February of 1968 as part of the post-production validation programme it 'burnt out two clutches during drive-aways', according to the report of Brian Charlick, who was then Development Engineer, Corsair Vehicle Group. They eventually fixed the problem with 'automatic transmission fluid in its gearbox which allowed borderline satisfactory take-offs down to minus 10°F'. Not to worry, it was usually warm in Italy and

The completed European successor for the English Anglia was entirely conventional, but appealed to such a cross section of the motoring public that it stayed visually much the same for seven production years. Front and rear suspensions altered over the layout shown here; the front within a year of launch and the rear's inclined dampers went out in 1973.

France, where those cars were destined to spend most of their sales lives...!

Although the general engineering objective of life-lubricated chassis components and even the provision of a gearbox without the need for a drain plug, were achieved, they were a little disappointed over the engine's oil changing needs. The objective had been 6000 mile oil change intervals, but they eventually had to settle for 5000 mile recommendation due to 'mechanical package implications'. That was not amplified, but owners should remember that the rack and pinion, rear axle and plug-less gearbox all had a top-up requirement.

While the rear axle ratio debate centred on getting adequate performance from the 1300 GT via the 4:1 and on achieving lower noise levels on others (via a development programme originally based on 3.77 and extended to a 3.99), there was considerable work to be done getting the gearbox ready for the public. As we know the gear lever's actually coming out in the driver's hand went on to become part of the early car's public performance, but not so well known was a pre-production problem with reverse gear jumping out of engagement. Ford of Cologne had a modification ready for appraisal on 14 July 1967, but extended durability testing went on right until the November production of Escort began.

Quite a lot of development time was devoted to the cable operated 6½ and 7½ in. diameter diaphragm clutches, devoted mostly to the cable size and end fittings. To get the shortest, straightest, cable runs LHD and RHD Escorts had to have individual clutch bellhousings, but this was considered an acceptable expense for the convenience, low weight and cost, of cable operation. Certainly, a very light clutch pedal operating pressure was achieved to complement the sweet gearchange, but cable clutch operation and the word durability rarely belong in the same sentence. Sometimes the cables last forever, but just as often they will be severed at mileages of 10,000 or so – and it still happens on today's front drive descendants!

For the price of a heater

Even with correction for 20 years inflation Ford engineers and stylists provided at remarkably low cost, what they described as 'Full four-seater family sedans, easy and pleasant to drive, with an improved package over competition'. At that June sign-off the engineers simply stated: 'In spite of associated derivative multiplicity the low cost objective of the base car has been achieved'. Even at the estimated £2,501,320 Ford had a bargain which can best be judged by the following paragraph from the 1984 Renault R25 press pack, 'Heating and ventilation has been developed to cope with the most extreme conditions – at a cost of nearly £2 million'. Just the new CVH engine for May 1980-announced Ford SOHC four-cylinder cost, 'nearly £500,000,000 to implement', but that platoon of zeroes did include building Bridgend and re-tooling Ford America's Rouge factory...

Chapter 2

The small car that isn't!

'The small car that isn't'. One could quarrel with Ford grammar, but not with seven years production life...

USING the slogan 'The New Ford Escort. The small car that isn't' for their pan-European advertising and the 17 January opening of the Brussels Motor Show, Ford's first European co-production car hit the public in a blaze of co-ordinated marketing moves. Just how effectively the Ford marketing machine worked can be judged from the fact that Ford of Germany alone made 848, 388 Escorts before the model was phased out of production on 27 November 1974. Exactly seven years and ten days previously (17 November 1967) Ford of Britain started making the car at their £55 million Halewood, Liverpool, site for the home market and for the £7 million-worth of export orders announced at the launch. They were able to report UK sales as 649,092 but they had made around a million, including those exports, when production of the original saloon ceased officially in January 1975, so we're scarcely discussing a motoring rarity!

The press and motor show publicity was the obvious promotional side. As ever, journalists and dealers had to be shown the car in sheltered circumstances. The British press were flown to the Rabat Hilton, Morocco, earlier in January 1968 to drive a 725 mile route with an overnight stop in Marrakesh '...where the cars stood overnight outside the Hotel Es Saadi under palm trees and orange trees laden with fruit,' according to the account from Maurice Smith in a contemporary *Autocar*. Ford had all the basic models for appraisal, including the solitary Escort Twin Cam with shiny Rostyle wheels and a competition number 4 on the door! This model, together with subsequent RS MkI models, is dealt with in the next chapter – and throughout the book we have three 'Performers' sections to deal with the more specialized sports Escorts.

As ever, Ford dominated the motoring columns and magazines as a result of this

Halewood's overhead lines were busy with Escort in 1968, after an initial trickle had been manufactured in 1967.

spectacular PR location, but historically the trouble the company took to establish a European base was far more significant. In December 1967 W.B. 'Bill' Batty had moved up from directing the car and truck group to replace Leonard Crossland as Managing Director, Ford of Britain, effective from 1 January 1968. T.N. 'Terry' Beckett took over as director of sales from Mr Batty (by the eighties Mr Beckett was more familiar as the titled director of the CBI in Britain).

This had an immediate public effect on the Escort, for it was Bill Batty who revealed how hard they had tried to promote Escort overseas. The new MD reported at the Escort launch: 'I suspect that we have put more effort, time and money behind the launching of the Escort in export markets than any other British car ever. Our most important overseas customers drove prototypes of the Escort more than a year ago. They saw earlier prototypes a year before that, and the car incorporates many of the things for which they specially asked.

'We have, moreover, delivered ahead of orders £2 million worth of service parts to Europe alone, and we have trained literally hundreds of European salesmen. No less than 8,000 cars have been delivered to export dealerships by announcement day.'

By comparison it was estimated that about 11,300 examples of the Escort had been built by the announcement day for the British market, a high proportion of them De Luxe and GT models. Production was reckoned to have hit 500 a day in January, but there were always problems hitting the 1000 a day rate predicted for Halewood. Unfortunately for UK manufacturing credibility, similarly equipped plants in Germany and subsequently Belgium did manage to hit peaks of over 1100 Escorts a day. Britain became more competitive at Halewood (the traditional home for UK Escort) in the eighties, gradually getting back the

Power tools with multiple attachments affix four-bolt wheels on the original Escort saloons of 1968, at Halewood.

prestige work – luxury and high performance models – that had drifted to continental Europe in the seventies.

The launch range in the UK

Ford in Britain had made 1,829,612 Anglias, of all types, and had used that model name for 28 years! By comparison Escort was a name given to an estate derivative of the Prefect (used, 1955-1961) and there was a certain amount of cynicism inside and outside Ford directed at the use of a rather utilitarian name for a brand new model, particularly as in that earlier distinction made by giving separate names for estate models, Ford in Britain had also used the Squire badge. Inevitably, the hacks of the day wittily coined the generic term 'Esquire' for such Fords. The thought of naming something the Squire today (Know wot I mean John?) would send shudders through the nattily-attired shoulders of younger Ford executives brought up on aspirant machines with Ghia, XR and generally upwardly-mobile market branding...

In January 1968 Ford prices included delivery, but even so they were derisory by today's standards. Without taxes an Escort DL 1100 started things off at £517, or £635 9s. 7d. in pre-decimal coinage with Purchase Tax and delivery included. Reflecting the changing face of UK motoring in the past two decades was the listing of static belts (the ones that tangled themselves hopelessly around the interior of so many sixties cars, threatening the motoring populace with various degrees of strangulation and general entrapment) at £7 19s. 10d. The more sophisticated inertia reel design, as we find on all eighties UK offerings, demanded £13 4s. 4d.

The rest of the mainstream Escort launch range was priced as follows: 1100cc Super, £666 4s. 2d.; 1300 Super, £690 15s. 10d; 1300 GT saloon, £646 10s. 10d. whilst the rare Twin Cam was over £1,000. Such figures mean little now unless you have some comparisons to place alongside the effects of inflation. In 1968 I was 21 and serving a second year at *Cars &*

Morocco was the backdrop chosen to launch the Escort to the press, early in 1968. Here the 1300 model is driven by Lotus expert and photographic wizard, David Phipps.

Car Conversions with a salary of just over £1,000 a year, adjusted to give about £20 a week; about a fiver below the industrial average of the time. Petrol was available to grades equivalent of five star and cost around 6s. (30p) a gallon. Through Zurich Insurance, Ford were offering insurance from some £40 comprehensive in London and nearly £28 in the country, for the 1100. Road tax was raised by over £7 that year, but one still paid no more than £25 annually.

In round figures the 1100 Super's £666 (plus nearly £28 if one wanted front disc brakes and radial tyres!) compared with £647 for an 1100 front drive Austin, then Britain's best seller; £682 for a similar capacity Fiat; £699 to buy a rear engine, rear drive Renault 1100; some £627 for the delights of Triumph's swing-axle Herald 1200, with very independent rear end and drive; or £606 for the Vauxhall Viva's conventional front engine, coil-sprung rear suspension with rear drive. The Vauxhall was a model that Ford had used for comparison throughout the Escort's development.

Against a motoring background of Britain's becoming acclimatized to the overall 70mph limit of 1966 and the 1967 introduction of the breathalyser, the new Escort gave us a preview of how well Ford had prepared themselves for the multi-national car making role of the seventies and beyond. Traditionally BMC with their innovative front drive Mini and derivative designs were setting the British marketing pace, but on the day Ford announced the Escort, the biggest UK motoring news came from a £410 million alliance between British Motor Holdings (BMC's offspring when combined with Jaguar) and Leyland, whose Sir Donald Stokes emerged as leader of that ill-fated enterprise.

With the benefit of hindsight it could be said that the creation of this unwieldy British mammoth motor corporation allowed Ford to capitalize on their new models to an extent that surprised even the parent American company. By 1974 Ford would have Cortina and Escort finishing 1-2 in the UK sales charts, although it would be 1979 before Ford got to the 28 per cent conclusive UK market lead, following a long scrap with BL through the mid-seventies for overall domination.

Boot of the first Escort saloon shared its capacity with the upright spare wheel (left) and the 9 gallon fuel tank.

Today we take for granted the front drive Escort's number one position in the British sales charts, beating the outgoing Cortina in 1982 and the incoming Sierra for 1983. For the rear drive example it was the exception (such as 1976), rather than the rule, to hold number one in the UK. That privilege went to Cortina for much of the seventies, and on into its final complete UK sales year, 1981. Before we leave the sales subject, it was the overall simplicity of Ford's trans-European operation that was often held up as an example to the struggling BL; by the late seventies, in fact almost exactly a decade after Escort's original introduction, Ford were able to claim a UK market lead not only overall but by category as well. In other words the Granada, Capri and Fiesta were beating allcomers within their sectors, just as did both Cortina and Escort, and Transit for light commericals.

So the creation of Ford of Europe and the Escort's role as the first tangible saloon car result (Transit was the first multi-nationally produced European Ford) was particularly bad news for the British taxpayer, whose money was tied into Chrysler as well as what became BL Cars, and really an object lesson in international thinking from Ford. Just in case they get too smug reading these words, let's remember that GM were teaching Ford a thing or two about multi-national manufacturing and marketing when this was written, staging a UK recovery that was led by the Cavalier's front drive success against the rear drive Sierra.

Ford introduced the 1968 Escort with a few generalities to place it against the background of its Anglia predecessor. The 17 January press-pack highlighted '...more room, 4.0in./101.6mm more shoulder room at the front and 6.0in./152.4mm at the rear. More performance and economy. There is a choice in the range between 36mpg/7.8L100kms and 115mph/185kph. More manoeuvrability. With a turning circle of only 28ft/8.8metres the Escort is easily parked.'

'Yet the Escort is not a big car. The extra roominess has been achieved with an increase of only 3.0in./76.2mm in length, 4.0in./101.6mm in width – and it is 2.0in./50.8mm lower.' Ah! The long lost skills of the sixties PR Ford professional at work, leading with the good news, ...but how did that first range line up?

Full specifications are given in the Appendices, but from the basic £635 Escort

Darlington District Motor Club's Croft Rallycross venue served as a valuable promotion site to Ford. As with the Capri in 1969, the company used Croft's televised sport to tie the Escort and motor sport success together in the opening months of the model's life. Note this 150 plus horsepower Escort's lack of any wheel arch extensions beyond the handbeaten modifications of the standard steel panels. Contrast it with today's Kevlar-bodied, turbocharged, mid-engined, 4-WD recipes needed to attain this kind of publicity in top level motor sport, mid-eighties style.

upward, the principles that emerged from that skilled cost-conscious engineering gestation included: crossflow four-cylinder engines, all with simple pushrod valve operation rather than today's fashionable overhead camshafts; and the new four-speed synchromesh gearbox with 'remote sports-type shift standard on all models'; a complete understatement for many contemporary British sports cars had far worse gearchanges, and lacked synchromesh on first gear. Incidentally, it might be worth noting that the Anglia was Ford of Britain's first four-speed saloon car...

Ford also pushed hard on the fact that servo-assisted disc brakes were available on all models, although they were actually an option at slightly over £15 on all but the GT or Twin Cam Escorts. Naturally, all the press cars (that I can recall) came with discs.

There were plenty of other items, however, that were useful basic equipment throughout the range, including that double fascia nozzle system that served as aeroflow ventilation, and swivelling demist/heater units. For Ford the rack and pinion steering was a new feature as well, the rack mounting across the front engine crossmember with a column that included a flexible joint for safety reasons. Ironic this, for the danger in rallying of an untoward impact disabling that layout meant that the works rally Escorts usually did without the impact-absorbing safety column – and they carried on using a deeply dished sports wheel long after safety tests had proved the succeeding flat spoke design was a lot safer!

Remember all those to-and-fro development arguments about the merits of 12 inch wheel diameters over 13 inch? Well, the range appeared with 12in. diameter on all but the Twin Cam, a 3½in. narrow-rim production item on all but the 1300 GT, where 12 x 4.5in. steel wheel was specified. One could specify the GT's standard equipment of 155-12in. radials and the 1in. broader wheels for the equivalent of just over £12.25p. Naturally, in later editions of Escort, Ford made such largesse available in the standard spec, part of the continuous improvement they refer to in catalogues – or the marketing game, if you are a cynical observer.

The optional discs within those wheels were the same 8.6in. diameter (218.4mm) as for the GT. If you find an Escort with drums from this period you will find that fronts are slightly different between models: both used 8.0in. (203.2mm) diameter, but thickness of the 1.1 drum was 1.5in. (38.1mm) instead of 1.75in. (44.5mm) of non-GT 1300s. At the back they all used 8.0in. drums with 1.5in. thickness.

It seems unlikely that you would find a sixties Escort on the original cross-ply tyre equipment today, but for the record the original factory spec for all but the GT was 5.50-12in. four-ply on the 3.5C rim.

The suspension and back axle of the first cars were likely to change right up to production. As noted in the development chapter, the arguments for and against various final drives, balancing low noise levels and economy against a definite performance requirement (particularly for the 1300 GT), led to a lot of heart searching. They even blew up a prototype 1300 GT with the 4.1:1 final drive as Ford engineers reached for over 7000rpm in fourth on a long incline down to Liège in Belgium!

Finally the 4.125:1 ratio was specified over the original 3.77 and it became the ratio for the SAE 90-lubricated hypoid axle from the slowest 1100 to the 1300 GT, although the handbook listed 3.77 as an option. Engineering also performance – assessed a compromise 3.9 ratio which gave a significant economy gain, but added 1 second to the 30-50mph time of the smaller-engined Escort.

On the suspension side, the story was a similar one of continuous work up to and beyond the production initiation at Halewood. The press kit specified, 'Twin radius arms additional for GT,' but it is thought that fitment went very little beyond the first batch made, including the press cars. The axle links provided some defence against tramp when starting off briskly, but to the Ford of that period NVH and the consequent penalties of extra arms and brackets around the rear axle carrying noise into the cabin, were sufficient reasons to delete those rear axle arms from the specification before production got fully underway. We also checked with Ford Dunton engineering chief Ron Mellor over the fitment, or the original absence, more correctly, of a front anti-roll bar on the original Escort saloons. His recollection – cross-checked in his office by a member of the original development team – was, 'All the German cars had the roll bar up front and not the tie bar we designed. In round terms the tie-bar arrangement lasted in Britain for a year. Incidentally, the Germans specified a front roll bar for extra autobahn stability'.

Another suspension feature that changed during the run, but only in the seventies when they were preparing the floorpan for the Mk2 'Brenda'-coded Escort was the angle of the rear suspension dampers. Colloquially these were often referred to as Escort's 'sea-leg' dampers, because they were on a tilt (60.5°) to the back axle. Later they were mounted in the more efficient vertical style. Although Ron Mellor could not recall if the reason for this was in any way competition-derived, it seems a possibility because Ford at Boreham engineers adopted the vertical 'turret kit' mounting of rear dampers early in the car's competition life; the damper being able to operate more effectively over its stroke action than when inclined. Why incline them in the first place? Maybe to provide some location assistance to the axle under side forces, but there was no perceptible deterioration when the dampers were moved to the vertical stance in 1974.

Naturally, leaf springs survived at the back of this Ford, three of them of a maximum 47in. length originally. Up front, whether tie bar or roll bar was used, the strut and its coil spring/steering function were combined in the traditional Ford MacPherson strut; a design that is now almost universal in eighties front drive machinery, including the Escort. (The preferable front roll bar layout can be spotted easily because the tie bars are mounted

The Escort Estate followed a few months behind its saloon car cousins and offered a very useful, long and flat load platform with excellent access. The same rear end, i.e. past the B-pillars, served for the 1975-80 Escort estates, too.

behind the single lower TCA, and butt into the body just ahead of the front chassis rail, whilst the roll bar mounted in front of that single lower arm). Advantages for the MacPherson system to Ford were cost, combining several functions and using less components than the more sophisticated double wishbone system. Today the MacPherson strut has been developed beyond its original Ford sixties format where front-end 'shimmy' and vibration at certain cruising speeds haunted its use in service. The Escort was not the worst offender in Ford's range for this characteristic, possibly because there was less wheel mass to go out of balance and upset the steering. Incidentally all these mass production 1968 Escorts shared a dinky dished three-spoke plastic steering wheel that was quite small by the standards of the period at 14.9in. In those days Ford were not so proud of the company logo, now to be seen on the boot of every model and prominently displayed within, usually on the steering wheel boss. So the Escort carried just its name in the centre of the steering wheel, unless it was a GT, in which case that fact was recorded 'right before your very eyes' with crossed chequered flags, naturally!

Electrically, remember that the Escort was born in the phase-out age of the dynamo, rather than with today's powerful alternators. The launch range shared a 22 ampere dynamo of two-brush layout with 12 volt negative earth also standarized throughout, although battery specification did vary slightly with 32Ah for the 1100 and 38Ah on 1300s and all export models. Headlamps were used as a point of visual identification. Only the basic De Luxe, the range price-starter of contradictory nomenclature, had the superior seven inch round lamps 60/45 watt sealed beam units. All the rest, including GT, had rectangular 45/40 watt fashionable lighting that was described at the time as semi-sealed beam, which at least meant you could change the bulbs, instead of a complete unit in the all too common case of a failure. Again it is ironic to note that it was the round unit that became glamorous longer term, being used on the works rally Escorts from Monte Carlo 1969 onward, and adopted for all RS Escorts when production began in 1970.

The cable-operated clutch made it through into production after those deveopment worries, but only the 1100s used the 6.5in. diameter diaphragm plate as all 1300s, GT or not, utilized the 7.5in. single plate device. Gearboxes differed in detail, too, the 1100 DL and 1300 Super sharing these ratios: first, 3.656; second, 2.185; third, 1.425; fourth, direct, 1:00; reverse, 4.235. The GT provided the same direct 1:0 fourth but the first three gear ratios were: first, 3.337; second, 1.995; third, 1.418. Reverse was changed as well, GT selecting 3.867. The overall effect was to take advantage of the GT's higher-revving abilities to provide extra initial acceleration.

The production engines

All the small pushrod cousins of the originally Cortina Kent-series crossflow family emerged with five main bearing, iron crankshafts, and bowl-in-piston combustion chambers, meaning that the interior of the cylinder head was no longer recessed to accommodate a combustion chamber. It is a layout that is still used widely today, although Ford were restricting its use to the Fiesta pushrod small capacity descendants of these original Escort units when this was written, the bowl-in-piston four cylinder Ford 1600 (ex-Cortina, originally) is still used for installation as an industrial engine, or more familiarly in Formula Ford, where Ford Motorsport assumed responsibility for its sale and service in 1984.

As noted in the first chapter, all the iron cylinder block Escort engines shared an 80.97mm bore, and were laid out with the carburettor to the left of the compact motor (looking into the bonnet, from the front) with the exhaust system on the opposite side creating the widely used generic name 'crossflow'. To provide 1098cc they selected the miniscule stroke of 53.3mm whilst the 1300s shared 62.99mm for a capacity originally given as 1297.7cc in the press pack, or 1297cc in the first edition of the handbook.

The most common compression ratio in Britain, demanding 97 octane (four star) fuel, is that of the 1100 and 1300 DL and Super of 9:1. There was a low compression (8:1) alternative, for 89 octane, that dropped 4.5 gross horsepower on the usual readings. This did not apply to the 1300 GT which was offered only with a 9.2:1 compression ratio, suitable for today's four star (97 octane) petrol.

To produce extra power the 1300 GT used much of the technology that had been proved on the 1600 GT Cortina, including a more vigorous camshaft that demanded 10° initial, static, ignition advance and an idling speed set about 100rpm (minimum 680rpm) above the usual Escort tick-over. Valve sizes were also increased as part of an overall 20 per cent power boost in the gross figures that Ford quoted in the sixties.

Externally, the extra power implicit in the GT modifications was more obvious, the usual Autolite (a Ford subsidiary) single-choke carburettor being replaced by Weber's twin-choke with progressive operation. Equally obvious externally was the four-branch exhaust manifold for the GT, fabricated in steel instead of the usual cast-iron. The GT

Also engineered slightly in arrears of the main Escort saloon car programme was this van derivative. Again, the back-end served on, even when the front sheet metal went into Mk2 panelwork. 2/9

system also contained two silencers, one in front of, and one behind the rear axle. It was the only model thus equipped, but the system's lifespan was not one of its most attractive features and, in my experience, even the top manifolding could crack up.

Engine & car performance

Power was always quoted by Ford in gross terms, but net readings are also available from some contemporary sources. As these are closest to the DIN methods used almost universally to give a more realistic appraisal of engine horsepower and pulling power (torque) I have appended these net calculations within brackets.

The 1100 supplied a Ford-reported 53bhp (49.5 net) at 5500rpm with 62lb ft (58.5 net) torque at only 3000rpm. The appendices supply all the independently measured performance figures, but Ford did provide some perky figures to whet the journalistic appetite. Just how these were used can be judged from this monthly magazine's introductory words: 'The 1100's time for the 0-60mph standing start is around five seconds quicker than that for the Mk1 Sprite of less than ten years ago – and that was a sports car!'

Ford figures for the 1100 showed intermediate gear speeds of 25,40 and 61mph in the first three wide ratios and an 80mph maximum with 42mpg overall. They reckoned 0-60mph should occupy around 17.3s.

The 1300 Super had a recorded 63bhp (58 net) at 5000rpm coupled to 75.5lb ft torque (71.5 net) at 2500rpm, so both maximum power and torque were delivered 500rpm earlier than with the small engine with a commensurate ease of driving bonus. Ford reported an 87mph maximum speed for the 1300 with the same maxima for the first three identically geared ratios. In fourth both 1100 DL and 1300 Super provided 15.27mph per 1000rpm, so cruising at Britain's 70mph limit demanded an audible 4600rpm. In the eighties we expect our five-speed Escorts to deliver 70mph at a whispering 3000rpm or so, depending on model.

Acceleration claimed for the 1300 Super included 0-60mph in 14.8s (not a bad time for

How it was in the sixties: Escort three-speed automatic on show. A deeply dished three-spoke steering wheel and two dials for the instrumentation were focal points, along with sweaty seating that did not offer cloth comforts until the seventies.

a sixties Mini Cooper 997/998!) and 0-70mph in 20.6s, with an overall fuel consumption expectation of 36mpg.

The 1300 GT had a very slightly different final drive mph/1000rpm figure of 15.13mph, owing to the radial tyres fitted to those broader rims. In practice, it simply meant one needed a hearty 4650rpm of the allowed 6800 GT rpm to attain 70mph. Ford, in their press-pack, put the maximum horsepower at 75bhp (71 net) at 6000rpm coupled to 91lb ft at 3800rpm. Those who spotted the deliberate error will know that the handbook figure of 74.5lb ft (70 net) at a rev-happy 4300rpm was a more accurate total.

Ford reckoned that 93mph with lower gear speeds off 28,47 and 68mph were likely, setting the average mpg figure at a not unreasonable 30. The startling claims were those for acceleration, including a 12s time for 0-60mph and only 22.2s reported for 0-80mph. *Autocar's* co-operation has allowed me comprehensive figures for the Appendices, but meanwhile I note that *Motor* tried the 1300 GT on two different final drives, first in 1968 and then in the Summer of 1971, and they recorded 13.1 and 12.5s to 60mph with maximum speeds fractions apart in the 93mph band and overall mpg figures in the 25 band; a little under the 27-28 being what we used to record in my own (heavier-bodied) 1300 GT Estate in routine use. Incidentally it was the 1968 GT that *Motor* found faster, by almost two seconds, on the longer haul from 0-70mph and over three seconds away from the Ford prediction in the slower example's 0-70mph scrabble.

Inside story

So Ford had produced a small saloon that was in every mechanical way competitive with, (and notably superior in gearchange quality to) its mass production opposition. It allied simple but strong underpinnings with low service demands (5000 mile intervals for all but Twin Cam) and low weights from 1641lb (744kg) for the cheapest Super to 1716lb (778kg) for the 1300 GT. Those weights would be far from a disgrace amongst eighties weight-conscious saloons, but remember they are for the initial two-door, not today's more popular three- and five-door hatchback styles. The closest descendant to 1968's Escort saloon in the eighties Ford range is the front drive, four-door, Orion cousin to Escort: with a 1296cc CVH motor it weighs 1969lb (895kg)...!

Aerodynamically, the Escort was effective for the period, so it was a shame that Ford eventually did exactly as for the earlier Cortina and later the Capri: they produced a 'Mk2' of boxier and aerodynamically inferior style.

Although the 1968 Escort's interior looks very dated today, by the standards of 1968 the Escort's cabin was not a bad place to sit, in spite of the heavyweight plastics featured in the seating, the front seats notably being without any moulding to help locate the driver on their shiny, sweat-inducing, surfaces in this pre-cloth-trim era. The movable ventilation grilles, handy steering wheel size and light controls all made drivers feel at home quickly. There were some complaints from the motoring press that window area, particularly that of the side rear, was restricted, or even dated (this at intro time!) which must have influenced Ford at Dunton heavily in view of the increased glass area that was offered in the original saloon's post-1975 successor.

Basic instrumentation comprised two large dials: a 110mph speedometer balanced by a combined water temperature and fuel contents gauge. The upright fuel tank, on the right of the boot (looking in from behind), was of 9 gallon capacity, with the spare wheel also upright and in the opposite wing on all but the Twin Cam.

For GT and TC models two larger circular dials were again featured, being this time a 7000rpm electronic rev-counter and a 110mph speedo for the GT. Adjacent were four minor gauges, Capri-style, for battery condition, fuel tank contents (still 9 gallons, so a GT

Shot of the 1300GT's definitive crossed-flag steering wheel emblem, 110mph speedo, and 7000rpm tachometer, it redlined from 6500. The same instrument layout, with the minor dials masked partially by the steering rim, was also a feature of later RS products.

could be relied on for little more than 200 miles a tankful), oil pressure and water temperature, both graduated but without specific unit figures, so that they could be used in the UK or Europe without problems. Unlike the Capri of a year later, the UK Escort did not bother with those new-fangled kilometre conversions on its mph speedo, a point some correspondents noted gleefully in Ford's 'European' Escort, and which was later rectified.

Trim levels differentiated the rich from the poverty-stricken in the usual Ford class system, but there was far less difference than we have been used to since the advent of mainstream Ghia luxury and XR sports models. The bottom of the range suffered rubber mats (far more practical than carpets with kids or dogs in residence) but was saved from abject humiliation by Ford allowing the fashion-conscious Fordist 'tough rubber floor covering, colour-keyed to the upholstery scheme'. Oh, the shame of it all!

More seriously, Ford's constant use of the colour-keyed phrase predicted the kind of exterior colour matching that would sweep the industry in the eighties, designs like the Maestro echoing the 'high performance' use of the theme in cars from Quattro to hot Golf GTIs in West Germany. Ironically, Ford were late off the mark on this exterior trend, preferring plastics that looked like add-on cladding rather than integrated panelwork, typified in Sierra XR4i and XR3i's wide use of matt black plastics for the aerodynamic aids.

Back in 1968 we find Ford gave all Escorteers above the rank of 1100 DL 'thick loop-piled carpet', and a thicker 'padded bolster around the edge of both front and rear seats.'

Optional extras from Ford that have not been mentioned included a push-button radio. It had barely passable performance in 1968 (what do you expect for just under £20?) and was usually mounted to the right of the driver in RHD cars, alongside the steering column. It was left to the 1969 Capri to pioneer the Ford built-in radio layout as part of the dashpanel. Metallic paint was just over £6 and one could have had white sidewall tyres (cross-ply only) if one wanted an instant reminder of Ford's past and heritage. It certainly was not an option that was widely taken up, and the company's increasing, and eventually

The Escort Sport arrived in 1971 with an RS look, but without lowered suspension, causing the kind of three wheel delights shown here being demonstrated by the author on a wet Surrey test track. The 1971 Escort Sport derivative demonstrated how the company would mass produce the competition Escort look to an increasing audience at lower cost. The ordinary road car was not as fast as the equivalent 1300GT, owing to unsuitable gearing.

complete, use of radials put an end to such nostalgia. In fact, in the period 1965-1984, I cannot recall ever driving a car with whitewall tyres. Perhaps a rented Mustang in the USA, but otherwise I blush to confess this enobling experience passed me by, certainly so far as Escorts were concerned. One certainly couldn't go kerb crawling without whitewalls, but on the other hand any sterner brushes with kerbs and other roadside objects were always clearly recorded by the sullied white wall...

Public Reaction and Production Changes

As in my other Haynes marque work, the majority of driving impressions are corralled together in a later chapter, where they cannot harm the accidental browser. Here we are more interested in what the public and press felt at the time, plus the running changes and subsequent derivatives that developed.

Perhaps the fairest way of judging public reaction is to see whether hard-earned cash was expended on the new Ford, and here the best direct comparison is between the Anglia and Escort. It took the Anglia eight years to top the million mark; even if one looks only at Escort manufacture in the UK, ignoring counterpart Continental production, it took only five and a half years for the millionth Escort to come bobbing out of the Halewood system.

Ford of Germany began to build the Escort in quantity a little bit behind the UK. They acknowledge they made five new Escorts in 1967 and over 60,000 in launch year, but they did not hit the really big 150,000-plus numbers until 1970, whereas Halewood built a hearty 161,747 Escorts in 1969. The largest Escort production year for the original 'dogbone' grille design was 1973, when the Liverpudlians and their mates constructed 189,873. Well...Mmm, that is actually the Ford of Britain total. The plant I was then working at (though I never did anything so useful as to construct a single Escort), Ford Advanced Vehicle Operations, made 13,037 Mexicos and RS 2000s in 1973, so Halewood actually made 176,836!

The biggest production year for the first Escort saloon in Germany was 1971, and they built 156,958, but they were also just over the 156,000 number in 1973.

However, the surprise from those production figures I have been so fortunate to obtain, is the record of Capri versus Escort, for right from its first full year (1969) in

The 1972 Escort heads a mixed line of face-lifted Capris and van cousins at the completion of Halewood's ministrations.

German production the specialized coupé was ahead on numbers! By 1973, Ford of Germany had made 809,497 Capris versus 772,099 Escorts. In Britain the position was totally different. Ford's biggest production number was the primarily Dagenham-based Cortina, which was made in numbers of the quarter million mark routinely. In fact, the year before Escort came along, the boxy MkII Cortina damn nearly made the 300,000 level, Ford of Britain making 290,972 during 1967.

In Britain Capri numbers were only close even to 80,000 during 1969, and thereafter bore no comparison to Escort, even when the original Escort design hit its 1971 UK low of 128,430 units.

Prior to reading the press accounts, most motoring magazine scanners would have seen a two page colour spread with 'The new Ford Escort. The small car that isn't' copy line. The spread showed a male Escort driver with a rectangular-lamped machine alongside a yellow kiddy's pedal car and began with the line, 'The new Escort might appear to be a small car', and listed reasons for buying, such as the 15cu ft boot, before summarizing the model range with, 'All four have a very modest price; speed, extra room and all ... so you won't feel the pinch either way.'

Judging from the sales figures Ford knew exactly what kind of market they were pitching towards, and with the benefit of sales record hindsight even a writer can see that the 1300 GT Escort and sportier derivatives marked the beginning of Ford's establishment in the socially attractive (and profitable) niche of smaller, sportier and better-equipped mass production cars. Prior to the 1300 GT and its image-building (though numerically rare) cousins of Twin Cam and later even more powerful Escort engine installations, Ford's smallest car – the Anglia – had built its own reputation via the conversion efforts of clubmen such as Ford dealer Allan Allard in South London, or the racing efforts of Superspeed. These activities allowed a 1650cc version of that original economy Ford to be built in surprisingly large numbers for such a specialized conversion.

Looking at the demand for 110mph Anglias with front disc brakes, and the sales BLMC were enjoying with ever more expensive derivatives of the high performance Mini-Cooper S theme, Ford just knew there had to be an even more profitable spin-off market above the sales of their cheapest model. What puzzles this writer, looking back with the benefit of nearly 20 years hindsight, is how Ford spotted the trans-European taste for extra performance and luxury? Today we can see how well placed they were to offer extra facilities – from electric side-glass to central locking – on a range as ostensibly downmarket as Escort. Anticipating such trends shows how the derided market research and searching pre-sale customer clinics can contribute to a manufacturer's knowledge of the public taste, *before* the public know that this is the taste they are going to develop in forthcoming generations.

Press reaction to the new car, particularly in Britain, was awesomely predictable because the motoring press was not then constituted of consumerist hardliners. *Motor* headlined their 1100 Super report, 'Perfectly practical', along with an introductory, 'Smooth, quiet, engine, fussy at high revs. Excellent gearbox. Good roadholding with average ride. Lively performance with modest fuel consumption'. Naturally the enthusiast press went wild over the solitary Twin Cam presented, part of a pre-production run of what was to be a pretty sparse series anyway.

Perhaps the best balanced comment came from eighties *Automotive News* correspondent, then *Motor Sport* cub Richard Feast. He naturally got cuffed in print for his attendance on the trip, by Britain's longest-serving editor, William Boddy. 'In the New Year those journalists fortunate enough to be able to spare the time away from more mundane duties, or having nothing more important to do, depending on the point of view, were flown to Morocco to try Escorts for themselves. About this my PA reports on page 116 – W.B.'

Feast reported cheerfully, 'We covered a route of over 700 miles, almost always at high speed, yet hardly any trouble was reported throughout. One car was found to have an inoperative clutch one morning and three others had their gear levers come out (see the first chapter). However, Ford did not seem to think this problem very worrying and no doubt the fault had been rectified when the cars came on to the market midway through January'. There was a little bit more about the Twin Cam and then Richard Feast (who had turned into something of a European *Autoweek* guru for Ford America-origin executives by the time I attended the 1984 Geneva Motor show) summarized: 'For those who thought the whole trip an expensive public relations exercise, Ford's Barry Gill gave a simple answer: it cost the company no more than it would to place two full page advertisements in a national newspaper.' Ah, the power of the press!

Ford's first official UK move with the new Escort line was the 28 March 1968 introduction of the estate car under the PR heading, 'Big load carrier with full passenger comfort'. Initially one could have only the 53 or 63bhp 1100/1300 non-GT crossflows in this 54cu ft load area model. Dimensions were exactly as for the two-door saloon, save for an increase in overall length to 160.8in., just four inches longer than the saloons. Eventually Ford would offer the 1300 GT/75 gross horsepower motor in the heavier body, but, in my experience, even Ford dealers never believed that combination might be a production combination, until they had to order parts!

Weight was up in almost direct proportion to the extra Estate sheet metal and fixed side rear glass with a third door. The 1100 weighed 1803lb (818kg) and the 1300 some 1815lb (823kg). Ford had to recognize this heavyweight fact of life by inserting a rally-style 4.44:1 final drive in the 1100, although the 1300 remained at the usual 4.125.

Other specific changes for the estate included the use of a 7½in. diameter clutch plate throughout (instead of 6.5in. on 1100 saloons), and wider 4.5C steel rim wheels, still of 12in. and employing 6.00 six-ply cross-plies at announcement time.

A minimum extra 160lb (73kg) was the penalty for a package that gave 'a little better' leg room than the saloons, as well as more than 31cu ft storage, even with all passenger accommodation in use. Seating was in PVC and the air extraction ducts were in the rear pillars, instead of behind the rear window as was the case in the saloon layout.

The Estate's rear leaf spring rates, and those of the conventional inclined hydraulic dampers, were increased to cope with a load capacity that was considerably increased. I carried Cortina engines in mine and a lot of other rally gear in service use (or two children, a companion and enough paraphernalia for two weeks away from the base), without ever feeling the vehicle was overloaded. The rear springs didn't like rally servicing, but from Ford's viewpoint I could say that the vehicle had been through a gateway with the entrance in a closed mode with a previous owner, and that I once left a spare engine in there for four days, before backing it down a 1:3 incline. The vehicle recovered normal ride height in the following week!

At the time Ford described the load space – which applies to the MkII 'Brenda'-coded model as well, for they did not change the load area, or the styling aft of the centre B-posts, come to that – as 'over 5ft in length and completely flat, apart from the minimal intrusion of wheel arches and spare wheel. At floor level the rear loading width is 47in., and even at the wheel arches a minimum of 39in. leaves room for long wide loads'. The spare wheel was lodged in a moulded plastic cover in the left wheel arch, released by three screw-headed devices that worked well until gnarled by age. Today everyone would say that the load area was wonderful in that one didn't have to lift objects over any sill. In practice that worked as well as it sounded, our only worry as parents being that the kids liked to live in the back, right by the sharp hinges. 'Racer's tape' and sponge padding alleviated that worry.

Estate fuel tank capacity remained at 9 gallons, but consumption was inevitably higher with the heavier body, new axle ratio for the 1100 and the usually weightier payloads carried.

Escort derivatives followed at the rate of roughly one a month in this first Spring flush of enthusiasm. On 5 April 1968 the van appeared with tempting tax-free prices (and a speed limit of 50mph in the UK at that time) from £449 for the 6cwt 1100 up to £523 for the 8cwt 1300 model.

As for the saloons the vans succeeded Anglia in Britain, but were nine inches longer and four inches wider for a 112lb (51kg) extra payload, an extra 3in. load platform and 9cu ft bonus load area. A pair of twin, lockable, back doors gave access to the load area, which was heavily ribbed in sheet metal, but otherwise unadorned in this application. The fuel tank stayed at nine gallons capacity, but was mounted underfloor for the van, as for the estate.

Any form of heating was an option. I can remember buying a 1965 basic Mini where the heater was also an option and such a feature remained at extra cost on sports cars like the Spridgets beyond the advent of Escort. Instrumentation was confined on Escort vans to a speedometer and mileage recorder with a fuel gauge, and warning lights for the dynamo, indicators, main beam and low oil pressure.

The load section of the Escort van proved itself in the same way as did the aft section

The 1300E, available in the emotive range of metallic colours that were also featured on the legendary Cortina 1600E, went on sale in 1973. Many such cars were finished at the Ford Advanced Vehicle Operations site in Aveley, Essex.

of the Estate, being passed on to the post-75 Mk2 Escort, the front end changing on the 1975-1980 Escort van. Then the back half and the running gear retained original Escort principles, until the front drive model appeared in February 1981, a little after the main Escort range was launched (Sept 1980).

In May 1968, availability of a Borg Warner three-speed automatic transmission was announced for all models. As noted earlier the engineers were not overwhelmed with the 1100 in auto guise and it was officially dropped on this model from August 1969.

The near £87 Borg Warner Type 35 automatic option was tested in *Autocar*'s pages by November 1968 and they found a 1300 Super in this trim would reach 84mph, cruise from rest to 60mph in just under 20s and return 25mpg. Included was their usual performance testing day at Nuneaton's Motor Industry Research Association (MIRA) grounds. Top gear ratio was little changed, so that a true 70mph cruise demanded 4640rpm and exactly 25mpg. If you want evidence of the mpg progress manufacturers have made, even in automatic transmission small cars, have a look at the equivalent 75mph test figure for front drive Escort with the lock-up automatic: even a 1.6 carburettor 1983 auto managed nearly 33mpg at this constant speed, and the injection 1.6s of the eighties did return 33.6mpg.

Back in November 1968 *Autocar* revealed that Ron Mellor's memory was an excellent guide to that front suspension change-over point from compression strut to roll bar lower arm layout. For *Autocar*'s test car carried a front bar and offered 'considerably reduced' roll angles as a bonus.

Since Ford changed a number of external and internal trim details in time for announcement at the October 1968 Earls Court Motor Show, it is a fair bet that these slightly modified cars would carry the superior front roll bar suspension layout too. The small trim changes for the 1969 model year shown within Earls Court's then-seamy walls included: Super and GT with wood grain finish fascia and instrument surround (usually peeling away nicely after a year's use...) with their colour-coding consciousness now extended to the steering wheel and its shroud, the front ashtray, heater panel and aeroflow vents, all of which took their colour cue from the upholstery specified. The GT, and the few production TCs then made, picked up wood grain finish on the top door interior trim and the 'rear quarter panels'. If the usual black interior were ordered for these performance Escorts, the gloom was completed by a headlining in black; a rather more practical fitting, if the driver or regular passengers smoked, even though the usual perforated white headlining was washable.

There were some minor safety alterations internally. Door handles and window-winders were all designed to break-off under impact, and a non-slip polypropylene pad was attached to the accelerator. It is more important to remember that we are talking about cars from the pre-laminated screen era, so shattered screens were, and still could be, part of early Escort motoring. I had a rather nice tinted and laminated Triplex screen fitted to my Mk1 GT, and immediately sold the car...!

Externally, the October 1968 Escorts had the matt black radiator grille previously applied to GT and TC model, while the Super and GT lost the bright chrome moulding on the drip rail channel, Ford magnanimously providing 'chrome beading' to surround the door and back window. Oh, the sheer big-heartedness of a multi-national's Purchase Department! I imagine it must have been quite difficult to quiet some of the more emotional reporters when evidence of this largesse was offered after the then-traditional large motor show banquets.

By October 1968, Ford had sold something over 200,000 Escorts worldwide, and this date also marked the introduction of a fresh range of body colours.

In November 1968, the Ford chassis numbering system was progressively changed, many of the basics applying for many years afterwards, although the source of manufacturing and some mandatory requirements have complicated things. The post-November 1968 system was: first letter for country of origin (B for Britain, D for Germany); second letter for assembly plant (B for Halewood, or in LHD, B for Genk in Belgium. A for Cologne); third letter for the model (A for Escort); fourth letter for body type; fifth letter for year of production (H for 1968, J for 1969) and sixth letter a random code system, which moved year by year, but was based on a letter denoting each calendar month. At that time there would follow a five-number sequence which was the individual vehicle number. The chassis plate, or VIN (Vehicle Identification Number) plate is normally on the engine bay panelwork closest to the radiator; a Ford dealer's stores

Inside the 1968-69 Escorts we see the Super's twin-dial layout and the GT instrumentation's sextuplets. All of this was placed within a cabin that forms a period contrast to the front drive Escorts produced twenty years later.

department can translate the code for any Escort year of manufacture, the biggest changes coming in January 1981.

In 1969 the range settled down with a Super-trim estate alternative provided in May, news of the bigger, four-door, being held for October's Motor Show. The four-door the Germans always wanted (which demanded a very different manufacturing technique, losing the single side panel principle that had been at the heart of the car's original design brief) went into production in September 1969. Available in Super and DL trim with 1100 or 1300 power plants, the four-door body could also be had with the GT powerplant and trim. A cheaper standard trim 1100 was listed from January 1970, too.

On 13 October 1969, Ford announced uprated spring rates with appropriate damper settings on all Escorts, plus a redesigned back suspension bump-stop and they claimed, 'A substantially improved ride, particularly in the fully-laden condition over rough surfaces'.

Electrically speaking, these Autumn 1969-onward Escorts had seven fuses instead of six and the GT gained the two-speed wipers that had been part of the basic Twin Cam specification originally. Now fuse protection extended from the lighting circuits to coverage of the cigarette lighter, windscreen wiper motor, flashers, horn and heater fan.

Externally the fuel filler cap became flush-fitted in alignment with the back panelwork and a bonnet release mechanism that worked from within the car had now been adopted; the original, which was set into the radiator grille, was less prone to failure at embarrassing moments.

There were some slight internal alterations, too: a black finish to the instrument panel surround introduced for the DL and a second package tray on the driver's side for all models above the rank of the scorned DL.

In engineering terms 1969 had seen some hard and analytic testing carried out on Escort, Capri and Cortina in the USA, plus back-tracking to reference files at Lommel, and within Ford of Europe service records, to see what other usage had produced in the way of product failures.

Such tests began in December 1968 and a final report was submitted on all three models for 16 May 1969. Over 51 specific problems were raised by such rigorous appraisal and some of the introductions listed above, particularly in connection with the electrical system, were a direct result of such background marathons. Unheralded but equally important service actions to improve the car's quality concerned the strength of the cast-iron and silencers within the exhaust system, a sharp increase in bracket strength for

By 1973 the four-door Escort showed that only minor changes had been made to the basic Escort theme of the sixties. Externally, the blacked-out grille and the wheel trim changes were obvious, but all the crossflow engines had been uprated in 1971. Cloth finish for the seating was widely available, too, during the later years of the Escort 1's production

the petrol tank upper support (an 80 per cent failure rate had been reported in Jamaica!), and the battery tray specification was also improved.

One of the most significant service complaints referred to difficult starting, and a splash-shield was introduced for the distributor from 31 March 1969 in the UK and 10 April the same year in Germany, typifying the kind of action Ford engineering implemented in the wake of such thorough research.

The 1970 Escort season was dominated by sports-related announcements, the larger-engined pushrod Escorts used on the World Cup Rally allowing a superb platform on which to launch that year's inauguration of the Ford Advanced Vehicle Operations (FAVO) plant at South Ockendon, Aveley. Initiating production was the aptly-titled Mexico, which formalized the type of 1600GT engine transplant that specialists had been offering almost from the advent of the Escort, as a cheaper alternative with easier servicing than the Escort TC. More about those exciting and durable machines in Chapter 3.

Meanwhile, the mainstream of Escort production in 1970 was dominated by April's 1300GT power for the estate and September's new designation, plus uprated engine outputs, for all models. The estate carried on the matt black grille tradition and had the GT trim, including comprehensive instrumentation, within a cabin that combined Super and GT features. Naturally, the 1300GT's radials, vacuum servo front disc brakes and a fair rendition of the saloon's 93mph performance was provided with the usual (pre-September changes) 75bhp. Unfortunately, no rear wiper was provided in those days, so the back screen used to get pretty muddy, but otherwise this £1,060 GT Estate proved rapidly useful. It came about as the result of repeated requests to Ford's Special Vehicle Order Department, who were used to requests for higher performance estates from the days of Cortina GT. For the record, this was the most powerful engine one could have in an original series Escort estate and was not officially duplicated in the Mk2 range, so one has to come to a front drive 1600 to get a more powerful Escort estate off the production line.

April 1970 also saw Ford revise all Escort prices – along with Cortina, Capri, Corsair, et al. Now the effects of a gathering inflation rate could be appreciated with the range beginning at just over £731 for a basic two-door, and another £34 for the four-door body. The 1300GT two-door, mainstay of the production performance Escort sales figures, was listed at £923 and most of the estates were over £900, too.

The September 1970 changes were packaged beneath new badges. De Luxe went out of the window in favour of plain Escort saloon, sold in two- or four-door bodies, and there was always the possibility of a basic estate. Power would be from the freshly uprated crossflows of 1300 or 1100cc. They were now rated realistically according to DIN terms, thus: 1100, up from 45bhp DIN to 48 (+ 6.7 per cent); 1300, from 52bhp DIN to 57 (+ 9.6 per cent) and 1300GT up from 64bhp DIN (previously rated 75 gross/68 net!) to 72 (+ 12.5 per cent).

The engine changes included new camshaft timing, increased carburettor jet sizes and redesigned combustion chambers within that bowl-in-piston design. In fact the heads strayed a little from the straight Heron principles, taking on slight combustion chambers of their own. Camshaft timing for the non-GT models was 21-55-70-22 with 43° overlap, 256° inlet duration. For the GT, inlet and exhaust duration was extended to 272°, the exhaust duration figure shared with the usual 11/1300s. GT cam timing called for 50° overlap. All models shared the 31.5mm exhaust valve diameter and both 1300s, GT or otherwise, had 38.1mm inlets, the 1100 sucking through a 36mm aperture. Cam timing on the 1300GT was 29-63-71-21. Incidentally the 1300GT cam was timed as for 1600GT, but the lift of 8.6mm inlet and 8.7mm exhaust was identical to the 1.6 motor found in Cortinas and Capris of the period. Not surprisingly the 1.6-litre GT also had larger valves (39.2mm inlet/33.6mm exhaust). Naturally, the GT continued to use the twin-choke Weber carburettor and fabricated steel exhaust manifolding, the 1300 picking up the GT's 9.2:1 CR as well, the 1100 usually being sold with 9:1.

Continuing the trim and badgework offered from September 1970, we find the L provided with the carpeted interior of the Super, a map pocket, two-speed wipers, luggage compartment mat and light, dipping mirror, foot-operated wipe/washer, over-riders and reversing lamps. Grab handles were also proferred for the occupants! XL was the designation now for saloons and estates, these being provided only with the uprated 1300 and having equipment in addition to that of the L which comprised: opening rear quarter windows on two-door models, vanity mirror in the sun visor, cigarette lighter, slightly plusher interior trim, and external neighbour-dazzlers such as 'additional bright metal ornamentation', and rectangular headlamps, the basic versions retaining round headlamp units.

External GT identification remained centred on the matt black radiator grille and rear panel. Matt black was then Ford's status-conscious code for machinery with a little extra virility, although only Capri had to suffer the full matt black bonnet insignia.

September 1970 also saw the first hesitant step toward the fabric trims that Europeans enjoyed, beginning with an extra-cost nylon fabric 'resistant to stains, fade and burns', along with eleven body colours, eight of which were new for 1970. Sales had reached around three-quarter million by this time.

Sport for all

So far as Escort news was concerned, much of 1971 was biased toward the sports side with one announcement deeply significant for the way Ford had decided to take the sporting Escort theme to a wider public, foretelling a future in which enthusiast Escorts would come from the main production lines rather than a specialized facility such as FAVO.

Purists, and there are just as many pedigree assessors inside Ford as at any other car company, did not rate highly the 11 October 1971 Escort Sport. It looked like the products FAVO had produced around the heavy duty Type 49 bodyshell, having flared arches, round headlamps and 13in. diameter wheels, but it carried only 1.3 litre/72 DIN bhp of 1300GT crossflow power and the body was no stronger internally. The gearbox was the GT close-ratio affair, too, but mated to the original 4.125:1 final drive, rather than the 3.900 that appeared quietly in mainstream Escorts from 1100 upward after their September 1970 power boost.

Even with a 4:1 final drive, the Sport was considerably taller geared than the GT, fourth gear giving 16.3mph per thousand revs. Thus, there were the inevitable embarrassments on the acceleration front compared with the original 1300GT – a fate *Motor* also highlighted for the power-boosted GT versus the original, as related earlier. The 165 SR radial-equipped Sport with its 5 x 13in. steel wheels (a real RS product had a minimum of 5½in. rims with greater offset) was greeted with plenty of raspberries. For , in addition to its sluggish demeanour, its handling was pretty odd on GT spring and damper settings allied to taller wheels and grippier tyres. Even in the wet one could lift front wheels with this hybrid.

Inside the £940 Sport, rated by Ford as capable of 99mph and 0-60mph 'in less than 13s', were some more hybrid touches. The original Sport had its tachometer, a tiny Mickey Mouse add-on, mounted to the right of an instrument binnacle that was of L/XL derivation, rather than GT, which lacked the quad minor dials, and packed just the speedo and combined temperature/fuel gauge in front of the driver. The bolt-on tacho lived in a little pod and could read to some 7000rpm, whilst the driver twiddled a heavyweight, padded, three-spoke wheel of similar design to that used in Capri GT models. Incidentally the Sport's weight reflected the generally plusher trim that had been adopted in seventies

Escorts, including the general use of fabric, although the Sport was sold with either PVC or plastic trim originally.

As I said, there were many inside Ford who didn't rate the Sport concept, seeing it as purporting to be something it was not. That slight disillusionment appeared in print when independents like *Autocar* reported 92mph and 0-60mph in 13.8s compared with a near 70lb lighter 1300GT (still on 12in. wheels, remember) running 96mph and 0-60mph in 12.4s, both with 72bhp DIN GT power, of course. For myself the Sport was a godsend, tailor-made for the production Group 1 racing category that was to become popular in 1972. I have to admit that the first move we made was to fit the lowest profile F3 tyres Dunlop could provide, effectively lowering the gearing below even that of the rev-happy GT; but that's a story for the last Chapter.

Production record

Just a week after Ford's Sport was officially unveiled, on 18 October 1971, Ford were able to boast, 'The millionth Escort to be produced by Ford came off the assembly line at Halewood today – only three years, nine months after its introduction. This sets up a new production record for Ford and makes the Escort the fastest selling Ford model ever produced in Europe'.

The part Halewood played in such a record was underlined by the acknowledgement of 555,000 Escorts, made in estate and saloon styles, plus 110,000 vans. The North Western UK Ford plant produced a daily supply of body components for transport to Genk and Saarlouis factories on the continent, which made 450,000 Escorts in the same period. At that time Dagenham was a major engine-supplier to the continent as well.

By this stage the simply laid out Ford small car had attracted business from 77 overseas countries, and that is just the figure for British-built Escort, with further assembly deals done in 12 more countries. The leading customer for the UK Ford of the period was Australia, pursued by Portugal, South Africa and Austria. Including all FAVO Escorts and the 11 October Sport, Ford were offering 21 Escort derivatives!

By October 1972 Escort prices spanned from £820.46 to £1127.37 for the most expensive estate; the GT was not listed in estate form any more, so the 1300XL Estate became the most expensive mainstream product in the Escort line. Incidentally the four-door 1300GT was discontinued by November the following year (1973), but the two-door GT continued to have its following. In October 1972 the GT was £861 basic; one paid nearly £180 in Purchase Tax and the result was a tag of £1040.37. The Sport was a more competitive £1008.96. Since the all-model Escort improvement programme of October 1972 doled out the GT instrument cluster to the Sport, along with two-speed wipers and other range minor improvements, the market now began to favour the Sport over the GT.

The range improvements in that Autumn 1972 offensive included 4½ x 12in. as the minimum road wheel size, the two-speed wipers (important in order to exceed 50mph with any wet weather safety), the floor-operated wash/wipe layout that Ford adored a decade ago (it was all too easy to stamp on it accidentally in moments of stress or confusion!), and a water temperature gauge. All this, even for the sub-species that provided tempting range-starter prices. Black radiator grilles came in for all but the very cheapest model at this point, so it was no good looking in your mirror any more to see if the man behind was trying to drive through the boot with the aid of 70+ bhp, or had just suffered terminal brain/brake fade in a less powerful model!

It was also at this 1972 date that hazard warning flashers began to penetrate the Escort line, offered as standard on all models of L-status and above. Damn it! if you suffered a breakdown in a cheaper version it was your own fault: other road users could recognise you for the cheapskate Ford, back in 1972, obviously felt you were... Electrically, heated back screens and alternators were creeping into the options lists of the mainstream Escorts at this period, though even the Escort Twin Cam had such hardware, before it disappeared in 1971.

For 1973, there were some intriguing marketing moves, beginning with the emotive two-door Escort 1300E. No, E was not for emotive; my meaning was that Ford had deliberately set out to appeal to the same sort of market, but in Escort terms, as they had with a car some Ford freaks still regard as immortal: the Cortina 1600E. Since you may be too young to be overawed by that legend, the Cortina 1600E was an alliance between the Mk2 shell, Lotus Cortina lowered suspension (long after A-bracket unreliability days), the reliable 86bhp 1600GT motor (as found in the Mexico) and some clever showroom appeal via metallic paints (a kind of roman purple and silver or gold, were most common), shiny Rostyle wheels and surprisingly nice woodwork within. It was an easy car for BMW owners to sneer at, but when I borrowed one regularly from the advertising manager of *Motoring News* I discovered it had absolutely staggering appeal to the opposite sex, besides being a lot quieter than most contemporaries, decently roomy, affordable and entertaining to drive.

The Escort 1300E echoed some of those famous features, but is not the legend today that the Cortina became. When the 1300E ('E' for Executive) Escort was introduced in March 1973 Ford's sales director Ron Platt frankly said, 'The thinking behind the new model is essentially similar to the concepts embodied in the Cortina 1600E...More than 60,000 Cortina 1600Es were sold in Britain and overseas and you have only to look at its current resale value to judge how highly it is still regarded by the motoring public'.

Together with the four-door 1300E that followed in April 1974, Ford sold several thousand of these E models, and it gave them a profitable little number to offer during a period when fuel prices became a prime concern, as a result of the 1973 Arab-Israeli war and the ensuing oil crisis changing motoring priorities overnight. The 1300E also presaged the formula which Ford would later fairly exploit for big car profit and luxury within smaller models, although it would be the Ghia badge that made such a practice more widely acceptable.

Whether two- or four-door, the E-formula mated Sport running gear such as 13 x 5in. steel wheels and flared wheel arches with the usual 72bhp motor, close ratio ex-GT box and the usual 8.6in. solid front disc brakes with servo assistance. The 165 SR radial-ply tyre selection was made with the Sport's 4.125:1 final drive.

The 1300Es, however, wore a completely different dress to catch the showroom prowler. Rectangular lamps were adopted, along with similarly squarish auxiliaries with Halogen bulbs protruding from the chrome-edged, matt black grille. The wheels lived

By the Summer of 1974 all models had received the later rear suspension layout with the dampers closer-to-vertical stance. This four-door 1300XL represented the kind of chrome-embellished Escort motoring that was offered, before the advent of Ghia models in the later body. 2/20

beneath bright chrome rings, but still carried the sports steel 'spokes' styled-in from October 1972 onward. Externally, I remember the cars as all purple because the first batch mostly were that metallic shade, and came to FAVO for final finishing in what seemed enormous numbers, but one could get them in gold just as easily. There were pin stripes along the flanks, nose to tail and supplementary indicators just forward of the flared front arches.

Inside, the big bonus was reduced road noise through extra sound insulation, including a PVC-coated mat to the boot floor. Heavy carpeting helped civilize the small Ford, along with traditional wood fascia and door cappings. A centre console of the type optionally available on other Escorts of the period (not the RS design) was standard, along with the useful electrically-heated rear screen, alternator, cloth seat trim and the standardized GT/Sport instrumentation. The steering wheel was the large padded three-spoke of Capri ancestry, while the glovebox was a properly wood-encrusted affair that showed true commitment to the luxury cause.

Prices? They began in 1973 at £1198.67, with 28 April 1974's four-door option at £1420.71. By then a vinyl roof could be yours for a further £17.77.

It is quite possible that a four-door 1300E and an early two-door could have had completely different suspension, for in October 1973 Ford introduced the floorpan and revised suspension – notably incorporating a rear roll bar and a more upright stance for the dampers – to support an outwardly similar original Escort style. In fact the dampers were vertically-mounted and a lot more efficient at their job, working with three leaf springs that were 2.36in. broad instead of 2in. for the four-leaf layout that had immediately preceded them.

As on Capri II, the rear axle was braced by a roll bar that was also intended to provide some torque location. The bar was mounted via top extensions and bolted into suitably bushed location points to the underbody, forward of the axle.

The front suspension looked much the same, but in preparation for an all-radial-tyre line that would feature on the following Escort, a thicker diameter roll bar was employed in alliance with a more progressive action from the bump stop rubbers.

Incidentally, I remember the excitement at FAVO when we got one of these vertical damper bodies in for building on our small line. There were people poking all round the

There was an obvious need for further suspension work in the performance derivatives...!

boot to make sure mainstream had really installed a feature previously always regarded as a necessary high performance conversion via the slang-labelled 'turret kits'.

As Ron Mellor remembered there was 'a much improved ride on those run out Escorts. The damper was controlling the ride fundamentally better, with no stiction. That rear roll bar did some of the jobs that those rear axle links were meant to do on the first GT layout, but those links were always such a pain, you know? They fought against their bush locations and transmitted all the noise into the cabin. No, the roll bar cum linkage, like that of the Capri II, cut noise on both models with large roll bar bushes, and did a number of useful jobs for us'.

Sales records: the £1000 basic Escort arrives

By March 1974 it was becoming hard for Ford to hold prices of even the basic two-door under the £1000 barrier. The standard saloon was retailed at £993.70 with the 1300E four-door taking the mass production Escort line to £1420.71. The Cortina had already blazed the £1000 trail with a noticeable lack of UK resistance to buying Ford. In June and July there were a succession of announcements that quietly and efficiently recorded Ford success, and the price we would have to pay to stay in touch with these marketing maestros.

On 10 June 1974, Ford at Warley advised everyone of the two millionth Escort's emergence. 'An achievement that has never been equalled by any other Ford model outside the USA. 60 per cent of the total were built in Britain. The Halewood plant on Merseyside, which celebrated its millionth Escort last year, accounted for 1,187,675 saloons, estates and vans, while Ford Advanced Vehicle Operations at Aveley in Essex contributed another 13,037 potent versions of the car, like the Mexico and RS 2000. The company's German plants produced 799,288 saloons and estates.' At that stage the Brits had exported 'over 375,000, either built or in knocked down (KD) kits,' with 25,000 more assembled locally in Australia and South Africa.

Just seven days later they hit us with the new, uprated, stiffened and thoroughly unsporty price list, in which the humble 1100 two-door gained nearly £80, demanding £1173.63 to step outside the Ford showroom. By now the upper end of the Ford range, then typified by the Granada GXL, was £2807.

July saw a repeat of the 'Good News, Bad News' technique. First they trumpeted a market share of 26.65 per cent in a year of continuous advance: Cortina was the 11.5 per cent leader over Escort (8.5 per cent), but all models were doing well, Capri II grabbing a 4 per cent market share on its own. Remember that that is the kind of stake that large companies, such as Fiat and Renault, would like to have had with all their models in 1983, and one begins to see how the Ford grasp of the UK market was approaching a peak.

The Bad News followed in six days (18 July) when Ford 'instructed its dealers to replace two nuts in the front suspension top mountings of 20,000 Escorts and 7,000 Capris built at Halewood between 19 April and 10 June 1974'! There was some evidence that the nuts had not been properly locked into position, an action that would 'eventually lead to the suspension piston retracting into the shock absorber casing, leaving front spring movement unrestricted'. Gulp! All Escorts and Capris were offered a free check, on this low profile recall, but there's no way a faulty one could have struggled through ten years service without somebody noticing something awry – is there?

As they galloped through the inflationary closing months of the original Escort's life in the UK there was a 25 November 1974 landmark to highlight. On that date a 1300E became the 1,288,957th British-built Escort, 'beating the Ford of Britain production record for a single model set up in 1967 by the Escort's hardy predecessor, the Anglia'. Production of the Anglia had ceased almost exactly seven years previously, 20 November 1967, when

A word of advice to all owners of our new Escort GT.

Part of the original advertising campaign, featuring 'The New Ford Escort. The small car that isn't', was this use of a policeman and the performance derivative. The same marketing device, now a cliché, was used by Vauxhall in 1984 with the fuel-injected Cavalier.

Go easy.
The new Escort GT is no pussycat.
It has a high performance B.I.P. 1300 cc engine that churns out 75 B.H.P.
If you're unfamiliar with the abbreviations it means it's O.K. when you P.F.D. (Put Foot Down).
It'll zoom you from 0 to 60 mph in roughly 13 seconds. Which is going like the clappers.
The Escort has a top speed well over 90 mph. This is very handy on large airfields, race tracks or if you happen to

own your own private road.
Anyway, it's nice to know the power's there.
The gearshift is stubby, racy and crunchless. The gears are fully synchromesh.
Our engine has a five bearing crankshaft. So it can take the wear and tear of motoring on the quick.
The suspension is conventional and simple. When you've won as many races and rallies as us, you get to know what works and what doesn't.

We've built this experience into every nut and bolt of the Escort GT. But we don't charge you for it. Only the car.
That's why the price we recommend is only £765. And even that includes delivery to your dealer.
Finally, with so much power we thought you should have brakes to match. So we fitted servo-assisted discs on the front.
We'd rather you were pulled up by our brakes than the constabulary.

The new Ford Escort. The small car that isn't.

1,288,956 had been built.

With barely a month to go before the facelift Escort Mk2 arrived, from 16 December 1974 to be precise, all Ford prices were again lifted by over 8 per cent, pushing the 1100 two-door up £90.52 to a total £1296.81. It had been a year when the manufacturers just took it in three monthly turns to be the first to tell consumers the latest effect of inflation on motor car prices.

Over two million Escorts had been sold worldwide from 1968-74, with a further trickle supplied into 1975, but the models everyone seems to remember (frequently as a composite of Mexico economy with RS 16-valve performance, such are the strengths of legend!) formed a fraction of that outstanding output. So let's look at Part 1 of The Performers: Escorts to make production managers keel over, competition managers ecstatic and the public remember with rose-tinted warmth...

Chapter 3

The performers, part 1

The Escort Twin Cam was a cocktail that mixed all that was mechanically best from the Lotus Cortina and crammed it within an Escort shell ... But there were even better hybrids to come, and a specialized factory to build them.

'THIS car is one of those superb, breathtaking, rarities which just doesn't know what a straight line is, unless it's something that has to be straddled with all four wheels as you wag your tail all the way up the road. Taking it from a standing start on wet surfaces, you poke it into bottom gear, let in the clutch and apply right foot: there is a loud slithering noise, the revs go to seven five (beyond which, we gathered, lurks disaster) and whoops, it's time to swop cogs. Except we've hardly moved yet. Oh well, try again. Second now, there is still a loud slithering noise and the revs are climbing like they were charting the ascent of the GPO tower lift. We are still hardly moving – at least, not forward; there is a graceful side-to-side weave which is really quite soothing. Then, suddenly, you get this feeling that you've been parked in the path of a Centurion tank at full chat; as all the urge is transmitted into go in second gear you begin to realise how astronauts feel on lift-off. By now you are moving – not only sideways, but also forwards and then a bit. Seven five in second, it's time to hook third out of the box. The far horizon gets a lot closer – and you suddenly realise that all this previous action has been packed into about four seconds.'

The scene was a rain-soaked Essex lane near the Ford Competitions Department; the car a Ford Escort Twin Cam (XTW 368F) from the factory, complete with a 5.5:1 final drive that gave a quarter-mile gobbling time of 15.2s and the maximum of 98mph at 7500rpm. Its job was to show the two journalists within what 1968's state-of-the-art works rallycross machinery could achieve on 1.6 litres of ex-Bengt Soderstrom Lotus Cortina power – some 153 bhp. This was about half what the roadgoing Quattro Sport 2.1-litre

Antecedents of the Twin Cam Escort included the original Lotus Cortina. Here Grand Prix racer Jim Clark shows Roger Clark pace in the 1966 RAC Rally, in which he was co-driven by Brian Melia.

Turbo offered the 1985 public (or the public who had over £50,000 apiece for such four-wheel drive frolics). Let's give the sixties another nostalgic run through, to see what motoring editors were made of in an era when TC too often meant anaemic Twin Carb, and matt black always stood for motoring machismo!

'And now you're motoring. Seven five in third – all change – up to about six in top. At this speed, says a tiny voice in the small of your back (it used to be in the pit of your stomach, but the acceleration changed all that), the corner which is rapidly approaching is Not On, and you are about to make a tiny alteration to the local OS map. On the other hand any attempt to reduce velocity is probably going to end up with an even larger hole in the fence, so the only thing to do is apply lock and power in third, in that order, and try to look as though you know its going to work.

'Oddly enough it does. The fast-approaching disaster whistles past your right ear; you're not, of course, going where you are looking, but if it's this much fun, who cares? When the road straightens out everything about the car but the front wheels says you are still turning left, only you're not. The tail hangs out to THERE, a bit more power and a shade less opposite, there's a bit of a lurch which indicates to your passenger (he's the chap with the grim face, and a hideous grin, on your left) that you aren't quite as clever as you tried to make out, and wacko, you're accelerating out of the bend like it was never there.'

I was that 'grim face'. The driver-author working up a sweat for the May 1968 issue was editor of the equally rapidly accelerating (in terms of circulation) monthly magazine *Cars & Car Conversions,* Martyn Bourne Watkins, now a Ford PR person.

There could not have been a better introduction to the delights of really rapid Twin Cam motoring, for Ford also laid on one of the first ten 'standard' Lotus SE 109.5bhp Twin Cams that had been Boreham built to give the press a more realistic idea of the road car due for limited production at Halewood: the kind of modified production saloon that could win rallies in the finest Lotus Cortina/Mini-Cooper S tradition. At least 1000 cars were planned, then the number needed to qualify for international competition in Group 2.

The second DOHC Cortina, Ford Cortina-Lotus, provided an immediate test bed for many competition and roadgoing components within the Escort TC. Here former GP driver Richard 'Dickie' Attwood gets a grip on the red and gold Alan Mann example at Mallory Park Ford Sport Day, 1968. This unique competition Cortina was guided by a rack and pinion steering layout that was also used in race Escorts.

At Ford, competition came under the wing of the press and public relations department (PR, actually called Public Affairs then), so the link between media and sport was always rather closer than I have seen at any other motor manufacturer, prior to Renault's involvement in the sport. A good example of the innovative thinking that the publicity department then possessed were the Capris of a year later, equipped with the first Cosworth 16-valve road engines (BDA, Belt Drive A-series; the A referring back to Anglia as the roots of Cosworth's first specialist Ford units). The press were let loose in them to cheer up a Capri launch without the benefit of motors beyond 2 litres! It is relevant to note that the head of Ford Public Affairs in Britain at the time (who returned in 1984 as Vice Chairman, Ford of Europe) was Walter Hayes, former Fleet Street editor. He was the man who was largely responsible for Ford taking the £100,000 gamble on the Cosworth DFV Grand Prix/FVA Formula 2 racing engines that did so much to popularize the use of four valves per cylinder, now an eighties road car technical fashion in the wake of the turbo trend.

Other personalities we should introduce in our Twin Cam casting list were Henry Taylor (Competitions Manager, 1965 – 70); Stuart Turner, Competitions Manager, 1970 – 72; then managing Ford Advanced Vehicle Operations 1972 – 75, before becoming head of PR, Ford of Britain, (in 1983, he was appointed European Motorsport Director); Bill Meade (Rally Engineer) and the mechanical talents of the legendary Boreham mechanics, notably Michael 'Mick' Jones, Ken Wiltshire and Norman Masters. Norman, who died early in 1984, was best known for his loyal association with Roger Clark, although he had built Ford winners as far back as the 1959 RAC Rally winning Zephyr for Gerry Burgess. There were many more who made this small airfield band into an elite amongst world class rallying teams, but that is our cast of principal players.

In 1967, Ford had still to emerge as a winning force in international rallying. True, the Mini was fading fast, but too long had been taken to sort out the Lotus Cortina after a lengthy love affair with the Cortina GT. When I went on my first visit to Boreham, around

The original XTW 368F, with rather crass numbering and stripes, was the introduction to Twin Cam Escort motoring for Moroccan-bound journalists in 1968, as well as being a widely used competition number and an advertising model.

the time of the foot and mouth-cancelled 1967 RAC, the public pre-occupation was with the Tecalemit Jackson fuel-injected Cortina Lotus (i.e. based on the Ford-produced Mk II Cortina TC).

Away from my naïve eyes they were well along the route that would take the Escort and Ford at Boreham to the 1968/9 International marque rally championship title that preceded the official World Championship, a title that Ford won in 1979, with an Escort that still owed plenty to a 1967 programme hidden behind the hardboard-walled sector at Boreham. Even in 1981 David Sutton/Rothmans and the Ford Escort RS provided the world champion driver, Ari Vatanen (a Boreham protégé), and one could still see the basically simple Escort formula in action at all levels of motorsport from quarter mile ovals outwards, and still see it winning, in the mid eighties. In fact British club rallies continued to have a predominance of Escort entries in the top ten during 1984, owing to the wide availability of parts and the still-competitive speed that could be found.

Cortina Precedent

The J25 code for the Escort Twin Cam went back to the 25 January 1967 paper proposal that outlined the concept of Cortina Twin Cam components – notably the 1.6 litre DOHC engine from Lotus (built on a Ford 1500 GT iron block), four-speed gearbox and a Ford mid-range Timken Cortina back axle – mounted within an Escort that could offer light weight and modest dimensions as competition plus points.

So the true starting point for much of what went into production TC and later RS Escorts can be traced back to April 1966. At that point, Ford began to re-engineer the Cortina for production at Dagenham with the Lotus Twin Cam engine in the Mk II shell. The first Lotus Cortinas, made at Delamere Road, Cheshunt, were Lotus Type 28s and they appeared in 1963, the year Colin Chapman's concern first won the GP world title. Then the 'Cortina-developed-by-Lotus' had a 1558cc version of the engine with a Harry

You have just st advertisement fo twin cam mode

Picture.

Now you prob to sleep tonight.

imbled on an
r the new Escort

Specification.

Power
The engine is a modified version of the famous Cortina-Lotus engine.
1560cc 82.55mm bore, 72.75mm stroke.
Compression ratio 9.51:1
Develops 115bhp at 6000 revs. Maximum torque is 106 lb/ft at 4500 revs.
The Lotus cylinder-head with its hemispherical combustion chambers and opposed lay-out is die-cast in light alloy with inlet manifolds.

Transmission
Hydraulically operated 8″ diaphragm clutch acting on 4-speed synchromesh gearbox.

Gear ratios	Overall ratios
1st 2.9	11.225
2nd 2.010	7.592
3rd 1.397	5.276
4th 1.00	3.777

The rear axle is semi-floating type with hypoid final drive. Axle ratio is 3.77:1

Suspension
Front: Independent coil springs with Macpherson telescopic dampers and stabiliser bar.
Rear: Semi-elliptic springs with hydraulic double-action telescopic shock absorbers and trailing links.

Brakes
Hydraulically operated. Servo assisted.
Front: Disc dia. 9.625 ins.
Pad width 2.087 ins.
Rear: Drum dia. 9.00 ins.
Total lining area 68.64 sq ins.
Swept area 285.6 ins.

General
Speed, engine revs., fuel, oil pressure, water temperature, and battery charge are in an easy to read central binnacle.
Two speed wipers, non lift blades. Washer button on floor.
Aeroflow ventilation. Heater and demister.
Fuel feed: twin choke 40DCOE Weber carburettors.
Exhaust: branch free flow system.
Valve operation: twin overhead cam, driven by single stage roller chain.
Ignition; 14mm long reach plugs. Vertical.

bly won't be able

Especially when you hear that most of the early models are heading for the export market. (We're doing more than our share of backing Britain.)
But rest assured, you can still buy the exciting Escort GT, 1300 Super and 1100 Super and De Luxe.
Just pop along to your nearest Ford dealer. *Ford*

The power and the glory.

With the cradle marks hardly off its boot this nipper of ours keeps winning things.

Circuit of Ireland Rally: Outright Winner. International Tulip Rally: Outright Winner. And the Austrian Alpine Rally. And the Acropolis Rally. And again in the Scottish Rally.

Wins made possible by parts developed at the Ford Performance Centre. Parts that you yourself can buy to add sparkle to your own races and rallies. Or to your every day motoring.

If something below catches your fancy, please let us know.

The Ford Performance Centre,
Ford Motor Company Ltd, Boreham Airfield, Nr Chelmsford, Essex. (Telephone Boreham 661)

Rally proven ESCORT extras now available include:—

LIGHTWEIGHT Magnesium sump shield (as 'developed' by Roger Clark). Part No CD 1000/12. £18 P & P 12s. 6d.
EXCITING 6" x 12" Magnesium wheels – stronger and more forgiving than steel wheels and exciting to look at too. Part No CD 1000/7. £17 each P & P 6s. each.
ESSENTIAL Heavy Duty Rocker Assembly – for performance engines where increased rev limits are envisaged. Part No CD 105E 6563. £14 P & P 5s.
ADJUSTABLE Rear shock absorbers. With 22 settings. Part No AT 2225. £10 pair (incl brackets) P & P 7s. 6d.
STRENGTHENING. Steel main bearing caps to eliminate crankshaft whip. Part No CD/6000/1. £18. 10s. per set of five P & P 10s.
A MUST. 4.7 Crownwheel and pinion. The ratio for rally transmission. Part No CD 118 SEE1. £12. 10s. each P & P 7s. 6d.
SAFETY first. Interior roll over bar. Used on all Ford racers. Part No CD 1000/11. £9. 5s. each P & P 7s. 6d.
KEEP COOL. Our oil cooler kit reduces those irritating degrees in the heat of the battle. Part No CD 6600 SR £14. 10s. P & P 7s. 6d.
COMFORTABLE superbly-styled driver seat and frame in cloth. Part No CD 1000/15B. £16. 4s. P & P £1. Also passenger seat (reclining) including headrest and frame in cloth. Part No CD 1000/16B. £37. 7s. 6d. P & P £1.

SPECIAL OFFER for 2 door Mark II Cortina. Light Weight Body Panels. Aluminium outer skin on steel frame, weight saving approx: 40lb. per kit. Kit: N/S Door, O/S Door, Bonnet, Boot, in primer. £35 P & P £2. 10s.

Good examples of the XTW 368F registration at work include the original Escort TC launch spread from a 1968 issue of Cars & Car Conversions *(see preceding pages), and the famous 'yumping' shot as used within Ford advertisements of the period.*

Mundy designed alloy, chain-drive DOHC, cylinder head. At first the Mundy Twin Cam, with classic hemispherical combustion chambers, was destined for use upon the 997/105E Anglia block, but when Jim Clark débuted the power plant, in a Lotus 23 at the Nürburgring in 1962, the block was the Cortina/Corsair 1500 GT unit (116E), then running 1498cc.

From the start the engine provided exceptional performance, Clark pulverizing Astons, Ferraris, Maseratis and Porsches during the early wet laps, before skating off into the scenery when affected by exhaust fumes on a drying track. The Twin Cam was well known to the public even in 1962, for Lotus sold it within their revolutionary backbone-chassis Elan.

The Lotus engine development team, overseen by Steve Stanville, rated the engine at 1499cc with a bore and stroke of 80.96 x 72.7mm. The first 22 engines for the Elan were made at this capacity from October 1962 onward, built by JAP at Tottenham in North London. When international class limits tended toward 1600cc, rather than 1500cc, Lotus followed suit and the Twin Cam finished up in production at 82.55mm bore with the usual 72.75mm crankshaft stroke.

Originally the engine gave an advertised 105bhp at 5800rpm and 108lb ft torque at 4000rpm and that is what propelled the fabled 1963 Lotus Cortinas to 108mph, with 0 – 50mph in less than eight seconds, and an overall 21mpg or so. 'Fabled' because these machines had a specification that called for lightweight body panels, totally revised suspension (including an unreliable but effective A-bracket axle location) fat 5.5in wide steel wheels of 13in diameter, and a gearbox that provided over 40mph in first! Just how many cars were built in this legendary specification is obscure, but Ford had enough to go for Group 2 homologation late in 1963, the limit being set then at 1000 cars per annum.

Even in the late seventies, when researching a Lotus Cortina article for *Old Motor,* I found that everyone at Ford who had been involved with the Lotus Cortina from 1963 – 1966 on the production side tended to shudder at the memories evoked. It was not surprising, therefore, that the company shifted the car under its own wing for the 1967 Mk II Ford Cortina-Lotus.

At that point, April 1966, Ford at Boreham became involved. They took a pair of Cortina GTs that had finished their engineering trials (one LHD) and under Bill Meade's supervisory eye, Mick Jones and Ken Wiltshire began to develop them into what became the production Cortina-Lotus. The engines had remained at 1558cc, but by the time development commenced of the Cortina TC, Lotus had introduced the Special Equipment (SE) specification for Elan. In gross terms this was said to supply another 10bhp, some 300rpm up the rpm scale, an SAE total of 115bhp at 6000rpm. In net terms the 9.5:1 CR Twin Cam with its pair of sidedraught Weber 40 DCOE carburettors was rated at 109bhp and 106.5lb ft at 4500rpm.

Boreham's development mileage with those original Cortinas included the inevitable inversion at Bagshot's rough road circuit and five weeks at Lommel to select springs and dampers. An 8in. hydrostatic (self adjusting) diaphragm clutch was introduced and other transmission changes included the 2000E Corsair remote change four-speed box and a two-piece propshaft, with a 3.77:1 differential that was exclusive to the Cortina-Lotus. This diff featured high tensile nuts and bolts on the differential carrier and had been 'known to cope with up to 140bhp in competition use', according to Mike Cotton's contemporary account in *Motor Sport.*

There were many other detail changes; for example, the engine was eating pistons and their spec was changed, also a massive double barrel air cleaner was fitted across the Lotus-embossed cam covers. Or was this a sophisticated cover-up itself?

The brakes also came from the Corsair 2000 of the period, these having servo-assisted discs at the front. The battery was moved into the boot and all the bodies were to Ford Export standard, which meant the suspension pick-up points had extra reinforcement. These Lotus, or Cortina-Lotus if then current company-speak was faithfully followed, machines were very important. Together they, with the Lotus Cortina, provided the parentage and 90 per cent of the hardware that went into the Escort Twin Cam. Ideas like the radius rod location of the axle, by simple upper arms, could be found with an exact echo in the Escort TC and the later genuine RS products, so that 1966-67 Boreham involvement with the Cortina was exceptionally important.

Legends grow of course, so it is a bit of a shock to look back at the 1967 Cortina-Lotus two-door and find its 2016lb (916kg) took 11 seconds to reach 60mph. Very little quicker than a Mini Cooper 1275S of the period – and 105mph was about all you would get out of the later body. To be fair Lotus power outputs were not all they were cracked up to be, until Tony Rudd had got the 126bhp Big-Valve motor into production, when things improved considerably. We put a BRM Phase III Twin Cam in our *Motoring News* staff Cortina-Lotus (actually Andrew Marriott paid the bill and passed on the wonderful result to me within months!) and that produced a reliable car with many of the attributes of a BMW 2002: capacious, comfortable and quick.

Escort TC development

By Spring, Ford at Boreham's bleatings to anyone in mainstream with the influence to get them the unannounced Escort to try out their Twin Cam transformation, had produced a plastic prototype that they could use for all measurements. Bill Meade and Mick Jones were still with the Company in 1984. Meade was away at Dunton putting the final touches to the Escort Turbo with many of the old FAVO engineering team (who had regrouped under the Special Vehicle Engineering tag), whilst Mick Jones was still very much the practical rally engineer at Boreham, just a little more subdued after the body blow the whole department took when the RS 1700T was scrapped, along with years of promising development work. As ever much of my knowledge of what went on in Escort Twin Cam's day traces back to these loyal employees.

Bob Howe, a key figure in product planning and one of the later Ford Advanced Vehicle Operations factory's first employees, who went on to progress machinery like the eighties RS 200, was an invaluable mainstream ally. He helped Boreham to procure that plastic prototype in March 1967. The team had the car for a long, hard weekend only, but they emerged from a mechanical marathon, with some of the practical problems having receded slightly after tearing out Escort pushrod guts and inserting Cortina-Lotus parts. Unfortunately, these problems were immediately replaced by new obstacles, because in building the TC, Boreham wanted to add a high performance freak to an existing mass

The original Twin Cam road test car for Motor Sport *in 1968.*

production model, one vital to Ford's future profitability. Since the Lotus Cortina and offspring had not endeared themselves to those who had to make them, the Escort's planned TC mutant was given a chilly welcome.

So the Twin Cam was very much the latecomer to the Escort's party, but one could see the basis of Boreham's potent and persuasive argument when one compared a 2016lb (916kg) Cortina TC with the finished 1730lb (785kg) Escort TC, or simply looked at an overall length of 156.6in and 61.8in width for the Escort, compared with 168.25in and 62.5in for Cortina. Their heights were within fractions of 54in. Also, beneath Escort's more modest dimensions and comparative feather weight the same rear track as the Cortina's could be adopted, using the same drum braked axle – an axle which lived on into the RS Escorts which provided a wide-tracked 52in. At the front MacPherson strut suspension could be modified to provide whatever Ford's now extensive sports experience with the system required, but you could have a good 51in. stance, just 2.0in. down on Cortina.

It all sounds quite simple and logical when written down, but to the men cursing and straining over the practical problems of loading that DOHC motor and Cortina running gear into a body designed for no more than a 70bhp pushrod 1300 GT, it was a task that demanded all of what one wag (ex-Cooper Car Co's Ginger Devlin actually) once said was Boreham's prime asset: "they're a race of cross-country tinkers!"

The primary problem was finding enough space for the big-headed engine. Finding an answer left the visible legacy of the engine mounted at a mild diagonal angle across the engine bay: if one looks at the later RS 1600 the squeeze is even more obvious with the cam covers hard up toward the front passenger firewall.

Boreham had to think up new homes for the many ancillaries around Escort's engine bay, particularly the clutch mechanism, which went from the usual cable activation of lesser models to an improvised hydraulic layout for the 8in. unit of Cortina TC parentage. The production brake layout was 9.625in. front discs and 9.0 x 1.75in. back drums (as per the 3-litre Capri of 1969, although the units were common in other high performance Fords), the servo being shifted over to the nearside of the engine bay, alongside the radiator.

As for Cortina TC the battery was banished to the boot, but whereas Cortina had

A superb illustration of how the Escort Mexico, and other 1970/71 Escort RS types, appeared within. The dished sports wheel was very popular with Boreham's works rallyists, and therefore those who sought to imitate such heroes.

The 1968 Escort GT actually foretold the J-plated 1970 production Mexico with greater accuracy than the competition cars used on the London-Mexico World Cup Rally. This autocross prototype typified the way in which many private tuners – in this case Willment, working on a factory-supplied body – inserted the 1600GT pushrod engine into the Escort, long before the company had the capacity to provide a complete transplant themselves.

space to continue mounting vertically its spare 5.5 x 13in. road wheel with 165 SR radial (usually from Goodyear), the Escort's spare in TC guise could only live on the floor, rather than in its designed upright location. Unfortunately, Boreham were unable to do anything about enlarging the 9 gallon wing fuel tank's capacity, so the road car suffered from a limited range as one of the penalties of being a conversion job to an established car.

The gearbox, a traditional remote-control 2000E four-speeder from the Cortina, did not slip magically into place either! Basically the transmission tunnel took some GBH from the weekend workers, and *that* problem *had* literally been hammered out! Works rally cars

The LHD 1973 Escort RS 2000 from Ford Advanced Vehicles offered items such as the four-spoke alloy wheels, and an improved interior, along with 110mph capability.

had gearbox tunnels that were totally re-fabricated in later life, accommodating ZF five-speeders a decade and more before we were allowed ratio quintuplets on the road. Five-speeders were never production options before front drive Escorts of 1982 ...

Originally the competition department had hoped to provide more rear axle location than the top radius links of the Mk2 Cortina could provide, but such sophistication went out of the window in the need to placate production men at Ford in the ensuing struggle to get the car made at all. A similar objection put an end to the obviously preferable use of round lamps. I remember Bill Meade looking quite dejected when we watched Group 6 prototype rally cars under Boreham preparation with round lamps, whilst the road car had to soldier on with rectangular units because the marketing men had built a link between prestige and rectangular headlamp use. So how could the most expensive, and fastest, Escort go back to round lamps? In the end they were allowed to have their seven inch circular units, but the Twin Cam was an established production fact by then ...

Another squeeze was needed to get the wide-track axle and 5.5 x 13in. wheel inside the arches, so the flared Escort arch was born, setting a trend that lasted many years. Both front and rear arch had gently protruding lips that were widely imitated and carried over to both the RS products of the seventies and the mainstream Sport. Ford at Halewood modified those arches, originally designed to cut costs in the wake of those 12inch versus 13inch wheel studies of the sixties, so that they could accommodate vigorously bouncing 13in. wide wheels instead of the usual 12 x 4.5in. maximum of the production Escorts.

Halewood and Ford mainstream also held some other body modifications of similar heavy duty worth to those found on Cortina-Lotus, all originally developed for export markets (over 60 of them in those glorious days, just as destinations for British built Escort). Lumped together under the coding '49' the body changes that would appear in most production TCs as well as all later Mk1 RS Escorts were: flared front wings; quarter bumpers; strengthened chassis rails running from front engine bay to rear crossmember; stronger flitch plates; reinforced front strut top mounting plate; mounting points for rear

Legitimate permutations on an original RS 2000 theme. Shown here are two models, the LHD one with the Scheel seating (with built-up sides) and the RHD one with a more basic RS approach. Both featured tachometers redlined at 6500rpm – rather high for the Pinto 2-litre. Note that the basic Escort 1300GT six-dial instrument layout had survived, the minor dials covering fuel tank content; water temperature; battery condition and oil pressure over unnumbered scale. The two examples share the flat, three-spoke, steering wheel that the RS 2000 did so much to endorse. In safety tests it performed considerably better than the dished RS item featured in the 1970 Mexico picture.

axle radius rods; and a deflector stone guard at the rear. For the later RS products it was fair to claim some higher paint quality standards as FAVO had its own paint booths and a great deal of rectification was carried out to cars after their ride down from Halewood in painted and trimmed bodyshell guise. Cars could be completely sprayed to special order at FAVO too.

Later in 1967 Boreham were allowed a 1300 GT in which to try out their Twin Cam conversion in rolling metal: unfortunately they did just that when a steering failure demolished the Twin Cam GT at the airfield circuit! Just like the Cortina programme then? No, for this was a tarmac accident and it actually helped the programme along a bit as nobody had been that pleased with the way the converted GT was going ... There is some evidence, via Ford AVO Club, that some 25 initial Escort TCs were made on the unmodified Type 48 body; no more than 25 such cars were constructed.

By November 1967, ordinary Escorts were beginning to be made at Halewood and nobody was going to disrupt the vital familiarisation period as workers and management headed for 500 and then the 1000 per day Escort target production level. In the end British compromise and a remarkable man – Dick Boxall, former rallyist and Halewood production wizard (later in charge of FAVO production at South Ockendon) – helped get things moving. The first 25 Escort TCs were built at Boreham during those 1967-68 winter months with some assistance from the Halewood volunteers who would be building cars when production shifted to Halewood in February 1968. Then Boxall bravely supervised as the initial batch needed for Group 3 (100-off) homologation were constructed, right in amongst the tracks full of 1100s and 1300s.

Boreham had demonstrated that a small workforce (never more than 30 men, less than 20 of them mechanics, during this period) could practically develop not only a suitable basis for international rallying, but also a saleable road car.

Escort TC: production

Approximately ten of the new Twin Cam Escorts were built for press and publicity use to promote the new high performance star in the Ford range, which went on sale theoretically from the 17 January main Escort launch date at £1,080 8s. 9d. Actually obtaining such a car was a different matter and Ford used the communications skills of Barrie Gill at Boreham to try and placate the growing list of would-be owners, most of them after some sort of publicity or competition deal.

By the time the Escort did get to Halewood, and Ford had met the demands of machinery for their own rally team and the saloon car racing representatives such as

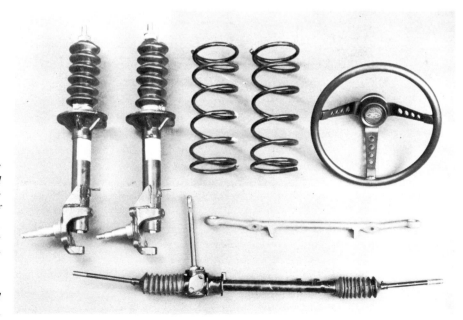

Typical of the huge range of RS equipment offered for the Escort is this useful combination of uprated front struts, increased poundage front springs, quicker lock-to-lock steering (2½ turns, instead of over 3) and the optional dished RS steering wheel.

Broadspeed, Alan Mann *et al*, it was quite a surprise to find that Ford were also able to list 'owners of new Escort Twin Cams', a record which they said 'reads like an international Who's Who? of racing and rallying', and which included then current GP stars John Surtees with All American Dan Gurney.

That was in May 1968, when the Escort had already stamped its Twin Cam performance across the victory podiums of three international rallies, none of them 'Noddy Events'. Around the same period *Motor* got hold of XOO 352F, one of those original Boreham-built predictions of the production TC, and *Autocar* were given XOO 353F! If you want to see how hard Ford worked early TCs, you'll find the same plate (XTW 368F) in use for the Moroccan launch, the inaugural Croft rallycross win (altered to read 6F but one can see space for the 3 and 8 on the front plate), privileged journalists – see this Chapter's opening paragraph – some phenomenally hard yumping miles around Bagshot in pursuit of pictures, plus sump guard destruction. And it went on to become one of Barry Lee's rallycross machines ...!

By the time those two Twin Cams appeared in the pages of *Motor* (April) and *Autocar* (June) one could have been forgiven for thinking the price could accelerate nearly as fast as the car, for that £1,080 launch suggestion had turned into £1,123 3s.4d. for *Motor* and £1,171 1s.9d. for *Autocar!* They had included slightly over £8 for fixed seat belts and honestly listed the extras, which included over £34 for the Ford push-button radio and nearly £30 for the shiny chrome Rostyle wheels popularized on the Cortina 1600E. These, like the fuel filler cap standing proud, the chassis rail front ends built to take compression struts, and the rectangular headlamps, did not make it beyond the 1969 improvements to the mainstream Escorts. The round lamps, however, were not officially offered until the Summer of 1969.

Since Boreham built those first press cars they represented exactly the kind of beautifully-assembled high performance saloon that every Ford enthusiast would have enjoyed. Even though both magazines used MIRA facilities in dry conditions with top wind speeds within 5mph of each other, the results were as predictably different as experienced observers have come to expect. *Autocar* was as conservative as ever; recording 113mph maximum, 0-60 in 9.9s and 0-100 in 33.6s: *Motor* reported a 116.9mph best and equivalent elapsed times of 8.7s (1.2s faster) and 29.5s (4.1s quicker!). *Autocar* returned 21.5mpg overall and *Motor* 23.4mpg.

The cars conformed to the ex-Cortina recipe we have discussed: 109 net horsepower, 3.77:1 final drive, 165 radial tyres on 5.5 x 13in. steel wheels, and a four-speed box, the ratios for which were first, 2.972; second, 2.010; third, 1.397; and a direct (1.00) fourth. This meant top gear mph per 1000rpm was a little more generous than for the 1300s and well chosen; the performance of the distributor cut-out could be erratic, but at 17.8mph for each 1000 revs one could usually reach 6460rpm and 115mph.

All this meant most intoxicating motoring in 1968-9. All the cars I saw or drove were white and looked just like 1100s, unless one had an eye for the Boreham-built car's extreme front wheel negative camber, the wide wheels, a larger bore exhaust pipe and suspension that followed pretty thoroughly the road Cortina-Lotus principles, offering roughly an inch less from the overall ride height, stiffer inserts for the front MacPherson struts, chunky front anti-roll bar and more sporting spring rates from front coils and rear half-elliptic springs. The radius rods made it through into production and the car took off with wheel-spinning smoothness that Toyota had still to emulate with their wheel-tramping 123bhp/16-valve rear-drive Corolla GT of 1985!

No, the Escort never lacked power by contemporary standards, but traction was another matter ... Still the limited grip offered was delivered so flatteringly that one was sure nobody else in the world could get one away in such heroic style. Much the same applied to the hack-proof handling, with tail-out oversteer not quite so freely available as in that 153bhp rallycross winner, which started the Chapter. Yet enough power sliding was available to bring out the beast within every hard Ford driver. In wet or loose surface conditions the oversteer could get a bit much, even with the later sub-90bhp Escort Mexicos, but it was well into the RS era before any significant understeer was dialled into the original settings.

Looking around the Escort TC layout today the simplicity strikes one forcibly. The badgework was particularly restrained by later Ford standards with only a repeater Twin Cam legend scheduled for the right-hand side of the boot lid, but *Motor's* test car just retained Escort script to really puzzle its followers! Under bonnet there was a Lotus sign across the chain drive cam cover, the ex-Cortina TC 'twin barrel' air cleaner obscuring the usual cam cover script. Here the simplicity, compared with seventies and eighties emission-conscious high-tech machines, packed with turbos and fuel injection and diagnostic plug-in points immediately comes across. Just two 40mm Webers to gargle, and a lovely fabricated steel top exhaust manifold to dispose of burnt mixture from those elegantly sculptured combustion chambers, deep within the deeply divided DOHC alloy casings. True, it was all crammed in, the nose of the engine notably favouring the nearside with the radiator top hose running alongside the cam cover and beneath the giant air filter. If memory serves me well, one of the charms of the Twin Cam engine was that one had to wrestle the carbs out of the way in order to get at the distributor, which could get damp of a morning just like mortal Escorts ... Servicing was every 2500 miles and that meant a full oil change job with 36 items listed! Some were not necessary on a pushrod Escort – but it was a bit of a disappointment to find the specification had remained so true to the Cortina era that a dynamo remained on this new high-speed wonder.

History has judged as a classic the Lotus Cortina legend in original Ford body, with as many of the Chapman parts as possible, and damn the maintenance. I think the Escort TC was every bit as exciting and a lot more straightforward to run, particularly given the surprising number of specialists who have grown up around the Elan, turning it into an instant classic with excellent Twin Cam parts availability – and most of the other Escort/Cortina components are available with some ingenuity.

The performance figures were given earlier, but they do not convey what a stunning

*The 1971 wheel options. Left is the four-spoke Ford in alloy. On the right is the legendary Tech Del Minilite magnesium wheel, **the** sixties and seventies Escort sports wheel.*

Front and back of the Ford AVO Owners Club Mexico Registrar's 'Mex' shows how the car could be cared for into the eighties. Note the lack of side striping compared with the original alongside and those shown earlier in this chapter; either scheme is correct. MRO 940L is owned by Martyn Castick from Bury, Lancs, and is a natural front-runner in concours competitions.

effect these little white machines had on performance standards of the day. At less than £1,200 in the Summer of 1968, the Escort TC made MGBs scuttle back into the Abingdon antique cupboard on every performance and handling front line encounter and returned better overall fuel consumption in *Motor* Tests. Both *Motor* and *Autocar* dragged out Cortina-Lotus figures for comparison (the bigger performance Ford was then £1,123 or £1,171, the same price as Escort that year), but all that did was underline the reasons of an all-round performance bonus that had put Boreham on the Escort TC track. The beloved, nay legendary, Mini-Cooper 1275S certainly offered an attractive price-saving over the new high in Escorteering, wearing a price tag of up to £921 when these 1968 comparisons were made. Naturally, the 'Min-Bin' was thriftier on fuel; *Autocar* reckoned over 28mpg, and that seems a fair figure to contrast with an average 22mpg for Escort.

Original badges that speak for themselves on the RS Escort boot lids.

Ford, and the supporters of BMC/BLMH/BL Cars/Austin Rover Group, could argue the merits of the handling of S-type Minis and wide-wheeled Fords for many happy bar-time hours. In fact both systems had their say at the top of international rallying in separate decades. Writing in 1984, it seems as though Teutonic logic – four wheels are better driven than either front or rear separately – may have been right all along!

So with white 1300 GT shells and trim (including the six-dial instrumentation) the Escort TC made it into limited production at Halewood. But there was a better future being discussed for the high performance Escort, one that would clear it of any charge of cluttering up vital production facilities and have the potential to earn excellent profits.

FAVO and the RS era

The choice was simple: arrive exhilarated by several miles of bumpy, curvy, Essex B-road, or drag with the world's known supply of container lorries through the main artery that bisected South Ockendon. Either way one got a good insight into the qualities demanded of any RS Escort – minor-road entertainment and A-road sprinting capability – before one arrived at the concreted acres of what was always called the Aveley site, although the postal address was always Ford Advanced Vehicle Operations, Arisdale Avenue, South Ockendon, Essex. This is an address printed across my brain, even though it is a decade since I used to conduct factory tours as part of my press office duties, working at that site from 1972 to the early months of 1974.

January 14, 1970 was the official birthday of what was initially referred to by many as AVO, until a vehicle instrument maker of the same name started writing to any journalist using such slang, so that, in due course, FAVO became the habit. Inevitably FAVO's existence owed plenty to Walter Hayes, formerly director of Advanced Vehicle Ltd, the company created to build the GT40 at Slough. Equally inevitably, all the motor sport enthusiast engineers and personalities from other areas of the company, especially those who had a reputation for getting things done, were early on the scene.

For example, eighties SVE Manager Rod Mansfield vividly recalls 'being amongst the first three employees. I applied as soon as I heard the rumours!' The man he applied to was next Executive Director, BL plc, and a regular TV subject, Ray Horrocks. Ray ran FAVO with a brisk sales charm and phenomenal optimism from 1970 to 1972, when Stuart Turner arrived from Ford Competitions at Boreham to run the place until it closed as announced on the front pages of *Motoring News* on December 12 1974, by which time it had over 200 employees.

For nearly five years FAVO produced better finished, better-equipped and more powerful Escorts, including the RS 1600, the 16-valve successor to Escort TC, and the Escort Mexico, the 1600 GT Kent pushrod engined machine, which gave the factory an equivalent to a conversion that specialists had been performing with varying degrees of success. Additional to these was the 1973-74 Escort RS 2000, originally available with LHD for Germany only. Both RS 1600 and Mexico were in the kind of limited production (rarely more than a total of 20 cars a day) that FAVO's carousel overhead production line provided from November 1970 to the final months of 1974. By then the RHD RS 2000 was making its impact felt as the majority model in the daily mixture. (November 2 was 'Job 1' day).

I first visited FAVO in late 1970 as production was getting started, with Andrew Marriott on behalf of *Motor Sport* who printed the resulting epic in January 1971: it has re-appeared in a few forms since then, the last straight reprint being in December-January's *Havoc* (Ford AVO Owners Club magazine) in the 1983-84 winter. I also wrote a guide to the personalities at FAVO early in 1974 for Ford Sport magazine and it is interesting to see what has happened to them in the last ten years.

Still engineering in the eighties, but at very different tasks, are former FAVO men like Allan Wilkinson, Rod Mansfield, Bill Meade, Mike Smith and Harry Worrall. The latter three are part of SVE today, but Wilkinson (then celebrating a season as the Motorcraft Mexico racing Champion) left Ford after a distinguished role at Boreham in the 1979 World Championship and the development of a replacement championship rally car to Escort. A.W. departed for Toyota in Cologne (his second tour of duty in that German city, for he played a liaison role in the production of Capri RS 2600 ten years earlier); Audi Sport UK was his next port of call, before commencing development of the Mitsubishi Colt Starion, with former Scottish Escort campaigner Andrew Cowan, under the RalliArt banner in September 1983.

Bill Meade was, and is, a fundamental part of the FAVO/RS product story and Henry Taylor actually conducted me around FAVO that first time. I remember a large blue Mustang V8, part of some improbable FF1600 part-exchange deal, and Taylor's status as Horrock's 'right-hand man' at FAVO, but it was not long before the former Lotus formula car racer settled for the good life in amongst the boatyards of Southern France.

FAVO was structured as a miniaturized version of the main company, so there were five main departments with each department head reporting to the overall manager at the frequent policy and review meetings that characterized life at Ford for the suit-wearers of the seventies. The departments were: Engineering, under Rod Dyble; Production, under Dick Boxall; Finance, the responsibility of Ron Owers; and Sales, which started off under Mike Bennett. When he departed for BL, Graham Bridgewater headed the sales area with some very effective support from overseas sales executive Richard 'Ric' Lee. The latter spoke Italian that baffled even the natives, and went on to become the Managing Director of Alfa Romeo GB in the eighties!

Since I said there were five primary departments, it should be mentioned that the most long-lived was really a sub-sales department in the beginning and very much an ex-Boreham operation. Under the stewardship of Keith Verran and with ex-Boreham parts men Barry Reynolds and Eric Bristowe, the RS parts list began to grow, although even before FAVO they had sold over 500 sets of those bulbous wheel arches that characterized all competition, and some custom build/special order, Mk1 Escorts. Today the RS parts scheme lives on heartily under Charles Mead, a long time employee who has seen the emphasis switch from the original motor sport base to road cars and back to Motorsport as a supply function (together with new 909 prefix codings) in 1984; all from that Ockendon site.

When Ford moved their primary parts store to Daventry in the Midlands it left an enormous amount of space for the embryo FAVO. Just the main production line area was reckoned at 90,000 sq ft; roughly the size of Wembley's ground. There were also long corridors of offices for non-production staff and a separate building complex 500 yards along the road which housed Parts (and, for a period in the seventies, the Ford Sport Club under Charles Reynolds) with Engineering in separate, adjacent, accommodation.

Although ambitious schemes were discussed, and a very wide engineering brief tackled, production at FAVO and the machinery produced was surprisingly uniform. At the beginning they were talking about, and progressing, such exotica as the 4-WD Capri 3.0, even having four-wheel rolling-roads installed to greet emerging production cars before they went out into the wicked world. During my tenure they engineered two beautiful Granada prototypes, one with a turbo V6 (Erich Fuchs was the resident engineering expert on this subject, a decade before such a vehicle was ever produced by Ford of Britain) and another with a South African-sourced V8. Both had bodies produced to Mercedes standards at top management's request, but when it was seen just how much handwork was

Starting our selection of performing engines is this immaculate Twin Cam of rather shinier disposition than my original road test cars...

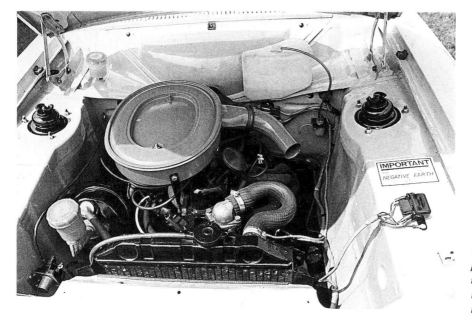

The Mexico's 1600GT
pushrod is hidden away
under the blue air filter
turned to the Summer
intake position.

needed the managerial enthusiasm for this project, or four driven wheels, some ten years before the Audi Quattro made its début, became muted. The engineers kept working on an exciting cross-section of machinery, FAVO doing all the Capri RS 2600 and 3100 work, even though FAVO itself made nothing but Escorts.

All that space and some very clever people produced overheads per car that the company accountants simply found unacceptable, particularly when the fuel crisis struck and performance/competition became very Bad News indeed within the company. This became felt acutely when the outside world featured reactions such as no 1974 Monte Carlo Rally, and the suspension of rallying in Britain, following a 1973 RAC Rally in which the influence of the Arab-Israeli war could be clearly felt at the petrol pump. That FAVO and Ford's Cologne Competitions department were closed could be seen historically as no more than the logical rapid-fire reaction of a company known for its sensitivity to PR image and marketing influences.

Production practice

That FAVO's versatility to make a wide variety of vehicles on the same overhead lines was not exploited remains a great shame. I can fully understand why some company men in the eighties would still like to see such a concern revitalized to make limited runs like the Escort RS 1600i, and it would have been the perfect answer for a high-tech wonder like Escort RS 1700T, which was really defeated by the difficulties of limited production in a mass environment.

Simply put, all Escorts made at Aveley shared the Type 49 body described for Twin Cam, although it should be noted that round, halogen, seven inch lamps were normal equipment throughout RS Escort production. These heavy duty bodies arrived at Aveley from Halewood painted, trimmed in respect of all but the front seats, with wiring loom and instrumentation in place, along with glass, locks and so on. In other words the Escorts arrived ready for all the mechanical components of an RS Escort – suspension, axle, engine/gearbox, propeller shaft, brakes – to be installed from beneath, using hydraulic trolleys with the main assemblies already tied together. The most dramatic stage was lifting

The 2-litre ex-Cortina/Capri engine was such a tight fit within the RS 2000 that they had to put an electric fan on the forward side of the radiator. This RS 2000 bears the sparkling white tubular manifold of a proud owner, rather than the factory's standard cast iron layout.

in the engine, gearbox, front suspension and associated brakes and hubs, about a third of the way around the line.

Unlike the Twin Cam, FAVO Escorts had some civilization within. Sports steering wheels, of two main types, both three-spoke, one dished and the later one a flat safety-conscious design, and better front seating were very common. These items were part of the basic specification by the time the LHD RS 2000 went along the line. When referring to any aspect of a FAVO Escort's equipment it would be an oversimplification to say that a particular model had this specification and that was that. For the Special Order scheme and the July 1971 Clubman Pack, and August 1971 Custom Pack schemes, ensured that a wide choice of interior and exterior equipment could be factory fitted. To illustrate the point, my own factory machine, illustrated in at least two current Escort RS books to my knowledge, was PEV 805K and is shown on Minilite wheels with a quad auxiliary lamp layout. The same vehicle appeared in various ads and promotional material wearing a variety of equipment before I acquired it, when it had two lamps at quarter bumper level and experimental 7 x 13in. FAVO four-spoke wheels. If a concours judge has read both the RS books I referred to he will come away with the impression that the car had been butchered since its factory days, particularly as the paint was a non-standard special order that I never saw repeated (a lighter version of the later metallic bronze). One of these publications has a caption that says, 'strangely enough, no roll cage has been fitted at this stage.' Poor old PEV 805K was pictured with RS 1600 badges, you see, so they thought this Mexico-standard-engined machine (which could barely out-accelerate a 1300 Sport with all this gear on board, including an early Custom Pack and factory-fitted steel arches) was ready to go rallying. The poor thing had a job getting out of it's own way, though it certainly scuttled around corners for as long as Bill Meade could keep me in 195/70 Goodyears for those 7J wheels ...! So, when a man starts lecturing you about standard RS specifications and the like remember: 'Ford policy is one of continuous improvement. The right is reserved to change specifications, colours, and prices of the models at any time'. If the car is a genuine ex-factory model, that could have meant a daily re-equipment schedule for engineering or photographic purposes!

Further to our production Chapter's brief on vehicle identification plate letters and numbers it should be noted that a FAVO-built Escort RS should carry the following prefix: B for Britain; F for Aveley; A for Escort; T for two-door saloon and then it might typically run, N for 1973; J for January. The important parts are BFAT to begin and a five figure ID number, to end with a production date that should certainly not precede November 1970 and is unlikely to run into 1975, although I understand that vehicles were completed in January of 1975. Indeed, I remember that the line was not mothballed instantly, but I do not know if they went to the bother of stamping 1975 on the ID plate.

Much was made at the time of the higher paint standard, and that is one of the reasons still given for the arrival of the 1300E at Aveley for final finishing inside and out. Certainly, the cars were inspected to a severe standard and a lot of paintwork went on, but depressingly often it was rectification of damage incurred at, or on the way from, Halewood. PEV 805K was gorgeous to look at, but I had to respray the area around the front flashers and lamps before the vehicle was sold in 1974. The metallics of the period were generally not a patch (more a flake) on those used by the eighties Escorts.

Production specifications

'The potent Mix' was the theme upon which Ford chose to launch the Escort Rallye Sport 1600 on 20 May 1970. The list price given, with the assurance that 'production of the Escort has now begun at Halewood', was £1,446 11s. 2d., compared with an April 1970 price listing of £1,291 3s. 11d. for the Escort TC.

Ford had said that the RS1600 would be going into production in January 1970 and were certainly well-prepared for the media by May, for in that month *Motor Sport* were able to print a 1000 mile account of life with GNO 420H, one of a small fleet handed out for long term assessment with GNO 400 sequence plates. Such cars were built in small numbers at Halewood with engines assembled by Harper Engineering of Letchworth in Herts, prior to FAVO production beginning on 2 November 1970. Even then the engines were assembled by sub-contractors, arriving at Aveley ready for installation with the four-speed gearbox.

In August 1987 former FAVO employee and current marketing agency director Kevin Cooney recalled one delivery procedure for some of these rare Halewood-built Escort RS1600s.

'Myself and Ric Lee used to enjoy collecting the Halewood cars, going up on the Friday-night train and usually making a weekend of the trip back in the BDA-engined Escorts. We saw some of them being built, and it really was a case of pulling the engine from a Twin Cam, because the Ford production process could not be interrupted, and installing the BDA.

'In fact some of the cars we toured British dealers with in those Potent Mix shows were not BDAs at all, just Twin Cams with bonnets firmly locked to keep their secret! Those were the ones we kept at the back in mass demos ...'

Although details had altered, compared with Escort TC, such as the standard installation of laminated glass, the first RS 1600s amounted simply to BDA-engined Twin Cams. Even the slightly 'crook' engine mounting was retained and my test car actually had TC badges!

Heart of the matter was an engine rated at 1601cc to allow the RS to compete in the larger engine capacity classes that the taller 1600 GT/116E iron cylinder block could provide for, where the TC had a happy capacity stretch limit beneath 1.6 litres. Thus the top tolerance figures of 80.993mm bore x 77.724mm stroke, were chosen for that 1601cc, although any Formula Ford entry, or other application of the same cylinder block and bottom end will normally be at 1599cc. Later in its life (October 1972) Ford released an aluminium block of Brian Hart design – ancestry that allowed 2 litres with ease rather than

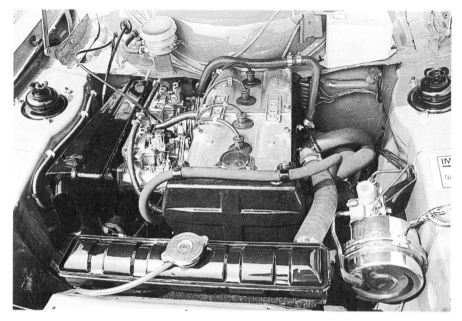

The 120bhp Cosworth Ford BDA was installed slightly angled in the engine bay as a legacy of the Escort TC. For the RS 1600 owner it is very easy to increase power, and this road transport was providing its happy owner with over 140 horsepower in 1984.

the primitive linered or otherwise butchered iron blocks that were needed to try and provide this full 2.0-litre capacity in Formula 2, or rallying.

The aluminium cylinder head was used throughout, but later RS 1600 engines were fitted with a revised oil drainage and crankcase breathing system with a new front cover, modified head casting and additional oil hose; where this is fitted a brass restrictor in the cylinder block face is not present.

The head was the work of Cosworth at Northampton and represented a separate road-development programme to the racing four-valve per cylinder DFV/FVA/FVC series, which all had gear drive for the overhead camshafts, rather than the cogged belt of BDA. In cast aluminium alloy with a separate carrier for the camshafts, featuring five bearings, the head mounted 30.9mm inlet and 27.4mm exhaust valves at 40° included angle. The Monikrom-treated cast iron camshafts provided an 8.76mm lift. A five bearing cast iron tuftrided crankshaft was fitted.

The role of the normal pushrod camshaft was changed, it being modified to drive the oil pump, distributor and fuel pump in this application, picking up drive from the crankshaft by the usual rubber tooth cam drive belt of 54.75in. length and 1in. width. Solid skirt pistons with three piston rings and a specified 10:1 CR were used within.

The announcement spoke of 120bhp net at 6500rpm (115bhp DIN at the same rpm in the workshop manual I have), together with 112lb ft torque at 4000rpm. Based on these figures and the fact that *Autocar*'s test weight for the RS was 1920lb (870kg) for the RS and 1872lb (849kg) for TC with the same gear ratios, final drive and 165-13 tyres size, one would not expect any significant difference in performance between RS and TC versions of Escort. It is to *Autocar*'s credit that the longest 0-100mph runs showed little change, with 33.6s for TC and 32.3s for the RS, although the 0-60mph sprints did require a little further thought. At first sight the gap between the two types looked significant with 9.9s recorded for the earlier Lotus-engined Escort and a second less for the Cosworth combo. Yet *Autocar* kept their car (GNO 425H, although 429H is also illustrated) through 8000 miles, when they recorded an enormous increase in elapsed times: 0-60mph in 9.4s and 0-100mph in over 42s! At that time *Motor Sport* had a fifth wheel, too, and I was responsible for 'figuring' both TC and RS times, recording 9.3s, quoted as 'about half a second' below the

The BDA as it appeared in 1969. An unforgettable combination of Ford 1600GT major components, topped by 16 valves, plus a pair of camshafts driven via the now fashionable cogged belt hidden beneath that black cover.

TC time, while, 'top speed was some 4mph down on the TC when run in two directions and averaging the runs.' At the time and on re-reading *Autocar*'s experience I came to the conclusion that it was the erratic performance of the RS 1600's ignition cut out that was to blame, for it was rare that my test car would reach 60mph in second gear, and *Autocar* suffered the same problem in the second set of runs.

Gear speeds proved to be 39, 58, 82 and 110mph on 'our' example but *Autocar* timed theirs to much the same top speed as the Escort TC:113mph. I got 21.2mpg overall, they managed 21.5 and 23.3mpg, the lower figure for the original road test and the second reflecting a greater percentage of brisk road use. Incidentally we were originally advised that the 16-valver would be happy on two-star fuel, but that was a recommendation swiftly dropped: I ran ours on five-star and *Autocar* settled for four-star and some careful throttle work. Oil consumption was never frugal, even new, and I put in over 4 pints of oil in 1000 miles, *Autocar* also reporting 250mpp consumption.

There is more driving comment on the RS 1600 in the last chapter; here it should be added that the 1970 cars were very much as late run TCs. That meant a pronounced 1½°, front wheel camber, the twin trailing arms for the back axle, 9.6in. front discs and modified MacPherson strut suspension with a thickened front anti-roll bar, uprated multi-leaf rear suspension, still with inclined dampers and the 13 x 5½in steel wheels with plain chrome hubcaps as standard. Again the bodywork was white, but in the case of the RS this was very much for the press and launch stock: later on, as for all RS products, a very much wider colour choice was offered, although by then the RS 1600s being made were notable only for their rarity value!

Inside, those 1970 RS 1600s had standard seats, but the test car supplied did have an optional deep-dish steering wheel with the Ford Sport symbol mounted centrally and a mock leather rim with thumb spats that tended to go walkabout. I think that wheel was made by Springalex and it was a Ford of Britain sporting favourite for many years, before somebody started looking at new safety requirements ... Even then, as noted earlier, rally drivers stayed with them.

The instrument cluster stayed with 1300 GT quadruple minors, but the speedo had been uprated to 140mph and the tachometer was marked to 8000 revs, although the redline remained at 6500rpm. A Triplex laminated screen was production equipment.

Under bonnet, the engine installation was neater than for TC because the air cleaner no longer straddled the rocker covers; there was just a neat, rectangular, cam cover with Ford prominently embossed above each cam bank. The carburettors were Weber 40mm DCOE 48, as for TC, initially, and they were mounted on the same side for the Lotus engine with the large tubular exhaust able to pick up on the previous system below the top manifold. Production carburettor specification did vary, however, and like Lotus, Ford tried Dellorto 40mm side-draught carburettors. So you could find either 40 DCOE 48s or Dellorto 40 DHLAE twin side-draughts fitted. Incidentally, Lotus still fit Dellorto carburettors to their 16-valve 907 engine series siblings today.

Unlike the Escort TC the RS 1600 did not stay relatively unaltered in its production life. Potential owners could find either iron or alloy cylinder blocks; twin or single drain head lubrication; Webers or Dellortos; and anything fitted from the massive list of Ford extras. Underneath, the suspension started off as TC, but the spring and damper ratings were altered, along with other RS products. This produced more understeer in the wake of a successful RS 2000 development, and there was the November 1973 general change-over point from 'sea leg' 65.5° back dampers to vertical mounting, and all the other mainstream changes to consider. By then one didn't often see RS 1600s going down the FAVO line, but if one did the chances were of a LHD export order being fulfilled, sometimes in a batch. The RS aluminium cylinder block and some improvements to the Mexico were announced simultaneously in October 1972. The alloy block, developed by Brian Hart at Harlow (now best known for the 1.5 litre turbo engine that went into 1984 as the motivation behind Toleman GP chassis) was equipped with dry cylinder liners, but offered no particular road customer advantage as official capacity and power output were retained. Obviously there was a slight engine bay weight saving, but no compensatory spring or damp adjustments were thought necessary at the time.

As of October 1972 the following became standard equipment on Mexico and RS 1600. The battery was moved into the engine compartment, allowing the spare wheel to be mounted vertically and carpet introduced as standard (loop pile of course!). The specification also included improved basic seating, hazard warning flashers and the styled spoke steel road wheels of the usual 5.5 x 13in. dimensions.

Prices as winter and the fuel crisis closed in were (now in decimal currency) £1228.87 for the Mexico and £1703.75 for the RS 1600. Both the Custom and Clubman Packs were officially listed, although some of the original items on the Custom Pack list had become superflous; the Clubman option demanded £133.41 and the Custom, £94.66.

I dislike pompous people who say a certain Escort RS *must* have such-and-such specification. Like every other human being, I'm sure I've made my own mistakes and left out many of the month-to-month changes that only practical ownership and the constant search for parts painfully unravels. Any limited production car, be it Lotus or Ford, is likely to change rather more rapidly than the high quantity items where the author has a chance of being right in 99 per cent of cases. Just to underline the point, I remember Marriott's Cortina Lotus had a 1300 Cortina radiator installed from the factory! Try and find that in the spec sheets ... All we can hope to do is say what *should* have happened at a given point.

'The ideal Clubman's rally car'

The above heading was picked to introduce the Escort Mexico, a cocktail of Type 49 shell, 86 DIN bhp crossflow 1600 GT engine and the Escort TC/RS running gear, such as the 3.77:1 final drive axle, big drum back brakes, 9.6in. servo-assisted solid front discs and the choice of 'three distinctive colours: 'Sunset Red, Ermine White and Maize'. The launch price was £1150 4s. and customers could order, 'a special paint scheme based on the livery of the World Cup winning Escort', which basically meant red and white, the red being the decal sector. At least I recall it as a decal, but HAVOC's club mag tells me the first 50 or so were hand-painted, or at least the modest optional side pinstripes were. It was not compulsory to have the side decalling, but most Mexicos are recognised instantly in this finish.

Although the running gear was substantially the same as its high performance

Stripes as worn by the Mexico and the RS 2000 in 1973.

forebears, the Mexico's crossflow engine was mated to a marginally smaller – 7.54in. (19.15cm) – clutch plate diameter instead of the 8.09in. (20.5cm) RS/TC plate. Operation was hydraulic again, but the common brake/clutch reservoir mounted on the engine bay bulkhead was abandoned for separate brake and clutch reservoirs during the production run. This went with a move from the remote servo, mounted in the position originally reserved for standard Escort battery trays, to a standard Escort servo upon an extended mounting bracket fixed to the engine bulkhead. We are told that *all* RS 1600s and early Mexicos shared the remote servo layout.

Because of the politics of motor sport the Mexico engine was also rated at the top tolerance, 1601cc, but one would more usually describe it as 81 x 77.6mm for 1598cc, as Ford did for many other models. It was often rated at 98 SAE bhp, but 86 DIN at 5500rpm is a more realistic figure today with 92lb ft torque at 4000rpm. As ever there were five main bearings for the cast iron crank and the earlier GT camshaft timing of 27-65-65-27, allied to lift figures like that of the 1300 GT/Sport Escort: 8.69mm inlet and 8.56in exhaust.

On the road it meant a tough and untemperamental RS Escort. Ford reckoned, 'a maximum speed in excess of 100mph and a 0-60 time of 10.5s'; *Autocar* recorded 10.7s to 60mph, 99mph maximum and a creditable 27.5mpg overall. That was very nearly the best Mk1 Escort mpg figure they returned to cover all testing and road use: the 1100 managed 27.6mpg! So, a reasonable performer with excellent economy and durability that Ford originally planned to offer with a number of further performance kits as package options. At the Boreham launch I tried one such prototype that had 10.5:1 CR, a pair of sidedraught Webers and Minilite wheels. Not surprisingly, this 109bhp offered very similar performance to that of the original Twin Cam. At that launch Ford also laid on a Brian Hart-rebuilt RS 1600 with another 20bhp, which not only showed itself to be 5mph faster than the standard car, but also a lot more refined in engine manners. However, nobody ever accused the body booming four cylinders in the Mexico or RS of over-refinement, the RS 1600 continuing the Twin Cam legacy of performance delivered to the harsh gargling of four chokes and the babble of components used to life at 6000rpm and beyond.

Both Mexico and RS shared safe braking, slick gearboxes and handling biased toward the original tail-out oversteer of the firmly sprung chassis (100lb front spring rate; 97lb rear). The nervous, sensitive response of rack and pinion steering was allied to pronounced negative camber front suspension. By the time the Mexico arrived, however, even the summer-time RS 1600 specification featuring dynamo electrics had mercifully passed away, it being launched with a 15 ACR/28 amp unit that was swiftly replaced by the 17 ACR 36 amp TRS model. Lamps showed a distinct improvement over the original Escort, sealed beam circular, units rated at 75/50 watt.

Alloy wheels for 1971

January 1971's Racing Car Show in Britain saw the debut of a four-spoke wheel design exclusive to FAVO that would form the mainstay of FAVO/RS fancy wheel production in the seventies, its outline passing on to production models like the Capri S, as well as later sporting Escorts, such as the RS 2000.

The Ford-designed four-spoke was developed with manufacturers GKN Kent Alloys Ltd and was significant in cutting down the enormous price gap between the basic 13 x 5.5in. steel of Lotus Cortina ancestry and the works rally car Tech Del Minilite magnesium items. The latter were close on £160 each, when I checked in 1984! The FAVO wheels were first optionally available on the Escort RS product from March 1971 and were later engineered in 6 and 7in. rim sizes of 13in. diameter, all secured by four forged nuts to the standard hubs.

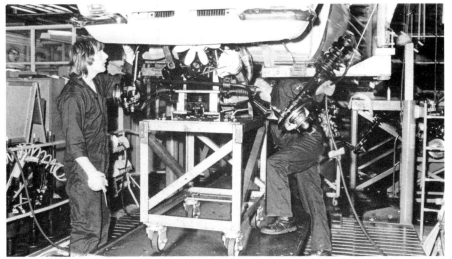

In the following six pictures, taken the month that Ford Advanced Vehicle operations was given its closure papers, Colin Taylor Productions have captured a slice of Ford Escort performance history. The office block shot gives an idea of the size of the Aveley site, but only a fraction was utilized for the miniaturized production-line and Admin centre. The parking space closest to the 'guardhouse' was reserved for Stuart Turner and was usually filled with the most interesting cars as 'the guvnor' assessed both sporting Ford and rival products in his daily routine. Offices, including the one shared by the author, were confined mainly to the front of the ground floor.

The other shots of exceptional clarity give one a good idea of daily production life at FAVO, which was very much an assembly, rather than manufacturing plant. As was by then normal Ford practice, the engine, gearbox and front suspension, with associated braking assemblies, were offered-up to the RS Escorts from beneath. You can see the sub-assembly process that took place prior to line installation, with a corner of the main engine ancillary assembly area and a more detailed shot of the men putting together an RS 2000 with the Escort's exhaust system. Note that the top manifold was the standard cast-iron one in production for the first RS 2000s (tubular steel was used for Mexico Twin Cam/RS 1600), the 'beak nose' model carrying modified iron manifolding.

Overall, it was a factory that provided a vision of Ford at work in a more thoughtful and less hectic manner than most visitors expected...but the manpower and space allocated were way beyond the company's normal expenditure per car produced. What a home it would have made for the RS 1700T, RS 200 and the 4-WD Sierras of the eighties! Production was from November 2 1970 to January 24 1975.

Ford killed the Escort Twin Cam officially in a release dated 9.6.71 and said that FAVO were then building 'more than 100' Mexicos and RS 1600s every week, or something over 5000 cars a year.

In July and October 1971 the optional Clubman and Rallye Sport Custom packs were announced, along with a £17 reduction in the RS 1600 price to £1496.25 after inflation had carried it the wrong side of £1,500. The October reduction was attributed to 'rationalizing the interior trim' with the Mexico and referred to basic cost; Ford actually conceded a little more on the tax-inclusive price.

The Clubman pack was the July débutant. It could be added to all line-built RS Escorts and comprised: two quartz iodine fog lamps paired with similarly-equipped long range auxiliaries on the bracketry usually found on works rally cars; a simple cage hoop bar; competition seats; and a map reading lamp. Mechanically, they installed Bilstein gas-damping front and rear along with a stiffer front coil spring rating. I had a car equipped in this way and the roll over bar was just a hoop, the map reading lamp a flexible type as seen on early Capris (Butler?), and the seats a wrap-around bucket type made in UK, rather than the grand Scheel or Recaro offerings of later RS products in the wake of the RS 2000. The Rallye Sport Clubman Pack cost £145.24 inclusive of taxes and one could then specify other options such as the extra lamps for about £53, or a sumpguard at £49.02, or convert the headlamps to QI bulbs for £15.34. There was a sump shield and oil cooler alternative at £67.36, and 165-13 chunky tyres were £17.30.

Those Clubman prices were revised within two days of the original press announcement, overtaken by 'the Chancellor's latest Budget', and they lumped in both the sump shield and all weather tyres to a £139.06 package on top of the Clubman Pack described.

The Custom Pack was revealed to the press on 16 October 1971 at £86.75 (£108.44 with PT). It comprised an effective sound insulation kit using panels of sound-absorbent materials at known reverberation points; deep pile black carpet; and cloth finish to improved seats, the cloth trim extended to the rear squabs. A small centre console, map-reading light and electric rear screen were also part of the deal. By October 1972 all models had this carpet feature, so it was dropped as an option, and in November 1973 the map light went, as part of the RS Clubman pack at least. Incidentally the RS 2000 was not offered with a Custom Pack, the interior being of considerably enhanced value anyway.

By April 1972, FAVO was a busy place; staffing was then officially reckoned at 250 with an output of 'over 130 Escort RS and Mexico models every week'. It was said that over 30 tons a week of spares were being sent out and there were certainly over 500 dealers listed for RS products, usually over 70 of them in Britain and of markedly varying quality. To quantify how that performance parts business had grown in the train of Escort's incredible motor sport success (see next Chapter) Ford told us that in the first full year of parts sales from Boreham the volume had been 'less than £14,000.' By April 1972 the counterpart figure from FAVO was 'running above £350,000'.

Also in April, FAVO told the World that it would take orders for Special Build with everything from a close facsimile of a factory Ford Escort rally car, to an individual road car with items like the wheel arch extensions, wide wheels and tyres, uprated suspension systems, and individual paintwork (often black). They started off with three machines, two Mexicos and an RS 1600, for some Nigerian rallyists.

The first RS 2000

Negotiations with the ambitious German counterpart to FAVO, a small unit within the main Cologne factory complex, produced a real surprise £2 million order for 2000 new twists to the Escort theme. Announced on 4 July 1973, the Escort RS 2000 was by far FAVO's best recipe yet and a tantalizing preview of what this smaller factory unit could achieve.

Until 11 October 1973, production remained in LHD for the German market, who had demanded a more sophisticated and civilized RS Escort and had gone overboard with enthusiasm when Stuart Turner organized a prototype preview for the Germans at Brands Hatch. The initial 1973 UK price was £1441.82 with the option of spending a further £200 plus on either a race or Rallye Pack. The first RS 2000 would go out of production with demand still healthy for this unusual cocktail of Cortina 2-litre power and revised RS Escort technology, despite a tag of over £2,075.

Squeezing the engine in and testing the results at high speed were tackled with enthusiasm by the Aveley engineers, who managed an astonishing number of detail changes to produce a charming combination of 110mph pace and 27mpg, even under duress. The 90.82 x 76.95mm ex-Cortina/Capri/Granada unit was then quite fresh to the UK market, arriving with the Cortina III in August 1970 (well, that was the theory, they had a protracted strike around that time: cynics said it was so that Ford could get the car right!) and of substantially different basic design to the other Escort engines we have discussed. For a start it had a belt-driven single overhead camshaft and for another the original concept had come from the USA as part of the Pinto Compact saloon programme, thus the common 'Pinto' nickname for this four-cylinder Ford family, which you can still find, albeit in uprated specification, within Sierra, and Scorpio-Granada.

For the RS 2000 this four-cylinder engine's bulk ruled out a normal mechanical fan and water radiator in one compartment, so FAVO squashed in an electric fan in front of the radiator. It was said this saved 2bhp.

Thus, Ford quoted 100bhp at 5700rpm and 107lb ft torque on only 2750rpm. Other ancillaries were changed too, including the provision of a baffled cast aluminium sump with central oil pick-up point. Cast aluminium was also chosen for the bellhousing that mated a cable-operated (*not* hydraulic as for RS16/Mexico) clutch with an 8.5in. diameter plate to a new Cortina four-speeder. This box had 'a raised pivot point for the single-rail shift mechanism to reduce gear lever movement', according to the release I wrote a decade ago. The gear shift was good; positively excellent, in fact.

Ratios for the new RS 2000 were totally overhauled, for the final drive was 3.54:1 instead of 3.77:1 and the gearbox ratios were (with the earlier RS/Mexico/Escort TC in brackets): first, 3.65 (2.97); second, 1.97 (2.01); third, 1.37 (1.40). Both had direct 1:1 fourth, meaning 17.8mph per 1000rpm in top on the earlier quick Escorts, and 18.7mph on the RS 2000. Thus you needed only 3750rpm for a 70mph motorway cruise, compared to over 4700 of original Escort 1300 GT and 3950rpm plus for Escort TC/Mexico/RS 1600. No wonder the fuel consumption was worth writing about; even with performance testing *Autocar* got 26.6mpg overall.

Ford did run an original batch of XVX 300 sequence-registered LHD launch and initial press test machines even in the UK, but by October the first batches of RHD specification were coming through. Complete with the inclined rear dampers these would be something of a rarity, for the mainstream suspension change to vertical back dampers during October and November 1973 swiftly saw the RS 2000 thus equipped.

The spring rates however, were different to any other RS product at the time, as racing rather than rally driver, Gerry Birrell, had sorted it out with a classic blend of understeer manners and some rear axle traction translated for him by many of the men who serve SVE so ably today. In cold figures the front spring rate ascended from 100lb in. to 130lb in. and that of the rear dropped from 97lb in. to just under 85lb in. Put another way, the multi-leaf, top radius rod, rear end now carried rates six per cent *softer* than a mainstream Escort, but

A decade after production ceased, this was the kind of devoted crowd the Ford AVO Owners Club were attracting to their annual Summer gathering. Maybe Ford threw away more than they realized when they shut that Aveley plant...

note that the single leaf rear spring layout was a competition homologation at this stage, not standard wear.

The brakes were different, too. Those dear old 9.6in. solid front discs stayed, but the space where RS and TC servos had lived originally, was now occupied by the large battery, and the back brakes were completely fresh to RS products. These were 8.0in van units with 1.5in thickness instead of being 9.0 x 1.75in. I was told at the time by the RS engineers that German homologation needs, particularly in regard to the safety of using snow chains, had forced this upon them, but there is no doubt in my mind today that the smaller rear brake produced a much better balance, rather than the rally driver's tendency to have an over-braked rear to promote tail-out motoring at will, power or no power. Since the RS engineering team was composed almost entirely of racers, their backgrounds covering Lola, Brabham and even the Dino Clubmans car, plus the influence of Gerry Birrell (who died in June 1973, weeks after the car was launched to the UK press preview in LHD form), such influences were enough to ensure that the early rally settings drifted out of sight for a while.

In fact, if I had a mean streak in me I would say it took Ford until the *front drive* XR3 before we saw such oversteer again from Ford, but one always thought that must have been a power-off mistake. Then they gave us RS 1600i. Twitchy? I'll say that it was twitchy! It made the first FAVO Escorts look like stately limousines in comparison ...!

Internally the six-dial instrument pack of GT parentage lived on, but the three-spoke flat steering wheel was introduced from the first LHD models onward. These also had the large Scheel front seats with cloth trim, but the soft-bummed Brits squealed about their hardness, so FAVO made up a British equivalent that looked almost as good and still represented a hundred per cent improvement over the awful standard PVC type that one could still find in a GT, until that model was discontinued in November 1973.

Standard equipment retained those 165-13in. radials on 5.5 x 13in. steel wheels, but these were now styled items that were effective enough to be used on the 1974 Tour of Britain, where the RS 2000 appeared in rapidly-homologated twin carburettor Group 1 form, finishing first and second on their first appearance. Obviously you could buy the FAVO four-spoke alloy in the same dimensions and many people did.

Standard RS 2000 equipment *did* include an electric rear screen, inertia reel seat belts, halogen headlamps and hazard warning flashers from the start. There was also an option list, particularly with sport in mind, that was as long as you would have expected of Britain's favourite competition saloon choice of the period.

The Race Pack we mentioned earlier included a full roll-over cage, fire-proofed rear bulkhead, oil catch tank, two master switches for the electrical system (one interior, the other exterior), Bilsteins, and four-point safety harness. I don't know how many Race Packs actually went out of FAVO's doors but the £300-level Rallye Pack certainly attracted a few orders with many of those race mandatory features, like the switchgear and seat belts, roll-over cage and fire proof bulkhead; plus a map light, sump shield and slightly modified suspension: dear old Bilstein again.

Other RS 2000 options of the period included limited-slip differential, push-button radios, centre console, wood trim for the fascia with a glove box, rear fog warning lamps, metallic paint and head restraints for the recliner front seats.

The car was very well received by the press and public for its alliance of an independently measured 111mph, 0-60mph in 9s and 27-30mpg economy, with likely durability from proven parts and a large, under-stressed, engine. At the time its strongest opposition came from the £1869 Triumph Dolomite Sprint with its ingenious single overhead camshaft, 16-valve four, which provided over 115mph and 0-60mph in under 9 seconds. In fact we all went off to Boreham to see how 'our' RS products compared with the Triumph one afternoon, for an enjoyable session. Amongst others, FAVO also had the 'Droop Snoot' Vauxhall Firenza that appeared in our Aveley car park for assessment.

Research I did in 1987 leads me to conclude that some 5334 original RS 2000s were made in a wide range of variants. This represented over a quarter of the total for the beak-nosed Mk 2-based successor that was exciting us all so much at Aveley when the closure order came through as a pre-Christmas message of comfort and cheer. Exactly 3759 Mk 1 RS 2000s were sold in the UK, representing 70.5 per cent of all sales of that model.

The Mk1 RS 2000 certainly made it into 1975, while they mopped up supplies and was retailed literally until stocks ran out. The last price list of December 1974, shows the Mexico at £1854.48, the RS 1600 at £2528.94, and the RS 2000 at £2075.67.

Research in 1988 revealed that the official Ford Advanced Vehicle Operations shutdown of production occurred on January 24 1975. My contacts inside the company gave permission for a full record of RS 2000 production to be published, and this November 1981 survey revealed German LHD-only manufacture of the first RS 2000 at Saarlouis, as well as in Britain. Thus do we go on learning even when a model is obsolete. Figures are in Appendix II to replace UK sales statistics in our first edition, but it is worth commenting that an aside to the main output statistics showed that the 1979-1980 period had resulted in 1818 base RS 2000s versus 4121 custom models.

Now we will shuffle through the reams of racing and rallying success scored by the original Escort, a truly international story or: have you heard the one about the Englishmen, the Finns and the Germans who took their ideas to Darkest Peru? Read on, you will hear the rest, all too soon!

Chapter 4

The great competitor

'Simple is efficient'. The Ford advertising slogan of the eighties Escort applied with equal force to a new competition era of Ford international race and rally success that arrived along with the 1968 Escort

BORN to compete on a solid foundation of Lotus Cortina technology, the Escort Twin Cam – in common with Escort derivatives with many other power plant variations – established a winning record in its first year of production life and simply never stopped winning thereafter. The Twin Cam was front line equipment only until 1971, when the Cosworth-developed RS 1600 cocktail took over for most races and rallies, rapidly progressing through 1.8 litres with an iron cylinder block to a full 2-litre aluminium unit during 1972. Whilst the TC brought Ford the European International Rally Championship title – predecessor of today's World Series – in 1968 and 1969, it was a 1.8-litre stretch of the pushrod Kent crossflow that captured first, third, fifth, sixth and eighth places on the London-Mexico World Cup Rally of 1970; a result that helped BL in their decision to withdraw Abingdon from further factory competition!

That left Ford very much as the standard-bearers for UK international rallying aspirations, and through the seventies the RS Escorts, both Mk1 and the post-'75 Mk2, kept clocking up the results. Indeed Ford commissioned a book by France's José Rosinski called *The Car that won't stop Winning,* a title that was no exaggeration, because even the factory records I then kept (as part of my Ford PR duties at the time) had no hope of keeping up with the scope of Escort's wide ranging success outside the factory entries.

So far as International rallies were concerned, it was much easier to say what the Escort did not win! 'The one that got away', was the Monte Carlo classic, although the later, Mk2, models for Bjorn Waldegard should have won in 1979 and the 1973 assault

Courtesy of Tony Jones at AVJ Developments, a former Broadspeed employee, we unearthed this Team Broadspeed picture from the days before Escorts roamed UK circuits. In 1966, operating from their Birmingham base, Broadspeed ran this Ford Anglia 1-litre for John Fitzpatrick and won the British title. This Roger Johnson picture from 14 May that year shows John lined up at Silverstone. Following three class wins already that season he was expected to do well, but on this occasion netted only fourth in class.

Spiritual and actual home to so many competition Escorts: Ford at Boreham. The same premises were still in use during the eighties era of turbo 4-WD rally winners.

produced a fourth for Hannu Mikkola. That result duplicated the previous best placing of the late Jean Francois Piot and present day Talbot Sport supremo, Jean Todt. They were also fourth during Escort's first Monte Carlo mission in 1969.

The East African Safari (including the first win by a European: Mikkola, 1972), the Acropolis rally in Greece, New Zealand, Finland's 1000 Lakes, Portugal; all was winning terrain to the factory Escorts over the seasons. The straightforward Fords showed speed enough to be competitive on specialist sorties such as San Remo (Escort's first overseas international in March 1968: Ove Andersson was third in a TC) and even Corsica's 'Rally of 10,000 Bends,' which could easily be confused for a road race, featured Escorts in the top five during the later cars' competition life. Corsican Escort factory finishes however, never equalled Ari Vatanen's 1980 second overall on San Remo, in a Rothmans Mk2.

Rallying Escorts and Ford at Boreham were intertwined to such an extent that the British performances of Escort simply crushed any vestige of home-based opposition. From 1972 to 1979 the Lombard RAC Rally, Britain's qualifier in the World

Inside Boreham. No, it is not a Ford picture, but one from Colin Taylor Photographic in December 1973. You can see how the race and rally cars used to be built alongside each other in the days of the first Escort competition saloons.

Championship series, was won by no other make and model than Ford Escort, all of which were RS Escort derivatives. Britain's premier rally series, authorized by the RAC, which metamorphosed into the present day Home International format, always had an Escort-driving incumbent from 1971 to 1978, GM's Vauxhall interrupting the flow in 1979, before Escort returned as the British Champion's choice in 1980.

The Escort's home international supremacy was well expressed by the 1973 Scottish Rally, where works and privateer descendants of that original Escort J25 project filled the first ten places! I had been asked to cover the rally for the Press Association, the domestic Fleet Street arm of Reuters, and I can remember the copy-taker and desk sub-editors coming back repeatedly with 'Are you sure there were not any other makes in the top ten?', or 'Does it look like another make will get in there?', as the story of Ford's domination unfolded. In the end even the cynics of Fleet Street decided that Ford's competition press officer was telling the truth, though it says something for Ford's slick PR reputation at the time, that they suspected we could control the results of an established international event!

Naturally, such success produced imitations galore of the basic Ford recipe. Other makes to build 200 bhp-plus 16-valve rally cars during the seventies, hitching their version of the Cosworth 16-valve DOHC head onto their favourite four-cylinder production block, were: Fiat, Nissan-Datsun; Toyota; Chrysler Talbot; Vauxhall (with Lotus, ironically); and BMW. The ingredients would include a five-speed gearbox (frequently by ZF, as for the Ford); heavy duty axle (also frequently to Ford specification); and a rigidly-located live rear axle, usually with four long links and a Watts Linkage, or Panhard Rod. One would usually find MacPherson struts up front, too, along with Mr Bilstein's dampers ... In fact, the whole world and British rallying situation echoed Formula One's kit car phase, where a Ford-Cosworth V8, Hewland gearbox and various fashionable chassis ideas (wings, inboard or outboard brakes; torsion bar suspensions, etc) were also widely imitated. In rallying, it should be said, the honourable exceptions to the British formula rule came initially from France (it was a team of nimble rear-engine Renault Alpines that put paid to any Escort win on the 1973 Monte) and from Fiat-Lancia's all-time supercar classic, the Stratos. That Ferrari-engined device was indeed a noble sight, but just like the Escort it had event blind spots too: a Stratos never won the RAC, nor the Safari; but catching one in

Competition début involved three drivers at Croft Autodrome in North Eastern England. Note the lack of wheel arch extensions over the traditional Minilite magnesium wheels.

The Escort's international rally début (March 1968) was in the subsequently World Championship status San Remo. Swede Ove Andersson was navigated by Britain's John Davenport to an impressive third place in a machine that lacked any development by the standard of later rally Escorts.

Corsica or around San Remo, or during that other Mediterranean World Championship event, based in Monaco ... That was a different matter – Horses for Tour de Corses ...

Racing? Although Ford of Britain's competitions department was headed at that time by a man who had competed at Grand Prix level, Ford set their racing style – as in the days of the GT40 – on sub-contracting such work outside. Their German competitions side did not open until 1969, and that was concerned with circuit racing.

The German priority was the Anglo-German Capri RS 2600 in the opening years of the Escort's circuit career. However, Ford Köln Motorsport was headed by former Porsche factory racer Jochen Neerpasch until 1972, and then by another former circuit and hillclimb competitor, Michael Kranefuss (who now heads Ford Motorsport worldwide, from a Dearborn, USA, base), so the prowess of the circuit Escort was not neglected. They brought on their own stars – notably Jochen Mass and Hans Joachim Stuck Junior – and the Escort played a supporting role to the Capri in the European Championship assaults of 1971 and 1972. Noted Escorteer John Fitzpatrick told me in the late seventies that the Escort was actually held back in its track performance, having the potential to outrun the Capris comfortably in 1971!

When Ford's Cologne competitions department had to be closed, as a counterpart measure to the axe that fell on FAVO at Aveley in December 1974, Cologne had already taken steps that had yielded the 1974 European Touring Car Championship for Hans Heyer's 2-litre RS 1600 and the German title of that year for another German RS 1600 *Meister,* Dieter Glemser.

Those steps led to Zakspeed. Ford in Germany imitated the very successful earlier UK sub-contracting of race needs, by going to East German refugee turned Ford car and truck dealer Erich Zakowski. After six straight class wins in the fuel-crisis-abbreviated 1974 European series, plus a fabulous outright win in that home market show-piece, Nurburbring's 6-hours, Ford had every reason to be equally proud of Escort's record in racing (which also included the 1968 British title with an Alan Mann Escort TC) at every level.

One of the key aspects to Escort racing was the way in which the car also infiltrated the low-cost ranks, with the highly spectacular Escort Mexico Challenge thrilling British crowds from 1971 onward, drawing international attention when Jody Scheckter won several rounds of that inaugural season. Subsequent Mk1 Mexico racing champions were all pretty talented too: Gerry Marshall in 1971; Andy Rouse in 1972; FAVO engineer Allan Wilkinson in 1973; Vandervell heir and Formula 2 flyer, Colin Vandervell in 1974. There was also a rallying Mexico Challenge that assisted careers of Tony Pond and Russell Brookes.

When Group 1 racing started to take off in Britain, eventually replacing Group 2 as the premier RAC title series, the Escort RS 2000 found the 16-valve Triumph Dolomite and the 3-litre Capri too much to cope with long term (never mind the American 5.7 litre Camaros that were allowed in 1974/75) and the racing accent slipped firmly to Zakspeed in Germany with low profile Cologne support. The Escort went on winning in Germany,

From a time gone by: British Saloon Car Championship racing, 1968. The ex-works Cortinas of MkI and II bodywork are attacked by the second Alan Mann Escort TC (XOO 346F) of Peter Arundell. Also representing the Escort, John Fitzpatrick's fuel-injected 1300GT (XOO 342F) from the Broadspeed stable. You can see how close fought the battle with Cooper Car Company's Mini Cooper S type team was, here represented by John Rhodes...

initially clothed in a Mk1 shell even in 1975, but eventually Zakspeed and Ford developed the Mk2 square-rigger into the radical forerunner of the 180mph Capri Turbos ... Ford drivers won the German title every year between 1972 and 1976, but Stuck and Glemser's 1972/3 reign was at the wheels of Capris, so 1974 was the first Zakspeed Escort title; a tradition carried on by the 2-litre/275bhp RS 1600s in 1975 and 1976 for 1984 TWR Jaguar driver Hans Heyer to take the title of *Deutsche Rennsportmeister* in those latter two years.

Quite a racing and rally record! Now remember, we have discussed only top-line international results with works assistance or entries. Even four years after the last rear wheel drive Escort had rumbled off the production tracks, Escorts were still adding to their tally of a motor sport success at national and club level, built around the solid foundation of straightforward engineering, low weight, good parts availability and simply astonishing performance per pound spent. One could still find RS 2000s, usually shorn of their later beak noses, winning international rally classes, too, despite the advent of the RS 1600i and a whole new breed of hot hatchbacks ...

The people

How did the car develop into such a competitive proposition?

The Escort was delivered by creative competitions people for some of the most talented drivers in the world to exploit. Of course, the high profile people we have mentioned – the Walter Hayes, Henry Taylor, Stuart Turner breed – played their well-publicized roles along with mechanics known and unknown at Boreham, Cologne, Broadspeed and Alan Mann, but a lot of other personalities were involved.

Central to the Escort's continuing competitiveness in the seventies was a member of Boreham's shop floor engine building cell. Lancastrian Peter Ashcroft had raced 500 Juniors for himself and worked in between spells at Boreham for the Peter Sellars racing team, but his wizardry – and that of companions like David Wood, now a consultant – was in building better all-round engines, rather than just going for peak bhp. You could say Peter Ashcroft blossomed along with the Escort, for he started his involvement building 140bhp Twin Cams for the first works cars and ended up as competition manager during 1972. He still holds a Ford of Europe motor sporting brief in

All-Ford leaderboard: Frank Gardner used Cosworth FVA power in the UK in 1968 to put the Escort ahead of the 4.7 litre Falcons on twisty circuits such as the Brands Hatch GP layout.

the eighties, and was in charge when they took the 1979 World Title with an Escort II.

With his racing and rallying interests allied with practical preparation experience, hawk-eyed Ashcroft assembled some first-class people around him over the seasons. Perhaps the vital role at Boreham was that of effective number two for the competitions manager, or rally adminstrator as the job often became. Originally, Bill Barnett (life-long Ford employee of the loyalist and shrewdest kind), was the perpetual number two for Taylor and Turner. When Ashcroft swept to the top, 'Billy' B went to the parent PR organisation at Warley, where he was to be found casting those friendly but perceptive eyes over accounts of varying credibility, including those for competitions!

'Billy' B was not directly succeeded, because it simply was not possible to find instantly, a man with that much all-round company and competition knowledge. Tony Mason, frustrated comedian and ex-K Shoes luminary from the Morecambe CC, was drafted in by Stuart Turner. Tony became known as Roger Clark's co-driver whilst Jim Porter was taking his annual sojourn at the organisation of the RAC Rally. In the author's view however, and eventually in fact, they did find another Bill Barnett in Charles Reynolds. Mad keen rallyist, erstwhile co-driver (sometimes seen with John Taylor until car sickness ended a promising partnership), Charles came to Ford from Fiat as the secretary of FordSport Club, moving up to Boreham permanently in the late seventies in time to slave through those classic Fiat-Ford fights of 1978 onward. Charles left Ford for the Porsche/Toivonen/Dave Richards/Rothmans alliance at Silverstone in 1984.

Some of the other Boreham personnel were mentioned in earlier development chapters, but in case you think there were just men at that bleak airfield it's worth recalling that Pam Goater has been at Boreham for more years that she'd probably care to remember. Her distinct laugh and hard work played just as effective a part in Boreham's daily routine as did some of the well-heralded names. In the late seventies, former Thomas Motors of Blackpool bright spot Jill Owen arrived at Boreham, and it was often her voice one encountered first, until she joined the RACMSA in 1984.

Outside Boreham there were the talents of a number of sub-contractors and their gifted staffs; non-Ford facilities that were made increasing use of, even on the rally side, as the Escort's glory seasons rolled by. For example, that engine building group at Boreham

Frank Gardner, running a BMW saloon car racing team in Australia by 1984, shown here scoring a 5 May 1968 début victory for the Escort TC at Zolder, Belgium. In the hour-long race, Gardner averaged over 85mph, set a new record, and finished 10.9 seconds ahead of Richard 'Dickie' Attwood in Mann's back-up Cortina-Lotus.

with men like Peter Ashcroft, David Wood and Terry Hoyle within was gradually disbanded, so that the works Escorts all ran Brian Hart-built BDAs through the seventies. Terry Hoyle went on to set up a very successful engine building enterprise of his own at Maldon in Essex, supplying the Rothmans team of David Sutton that won Ari Vatanen the 1981 World Championship for drivers with a Group 4 Escort RS 1800. Another Terry, Samuells, also left Boreham to set up his own business in the seventies – many of these moves were prompted by the staff reductions that were made in the wake of the 1973 fuel crisis – but this Terry concentrated on ZF gearbox and Atlas axle preparation work. Again he became a regular competition Escort outside supplier.

Another specialist company that became famous by association with the Escort was Safety Devices at Cambridge. When the works stopped preparing their own shells, Maurice Gomm at Woking got the work. Safety Devices, Cambridge, made roll cages and became favoured with work from Dealer Team Vauxhall and many others. In David Sutton's case, Gartrac were the Surrey-based specialists who did much of the body preparation and fabricating work. That has a certain irony because the men behind Gartrac, who also received some Boreham work in their time, were David Bignold and Bill Payne, former Alan Mann employees, who set up on their own in 1969.

Thus, the general pattern of outside work on factory Ford Escorts became ever more pronounced throughout the seventies, the vehicle's straightforwrd specifications making it possible for Ford to run and win entirely on the basis of outside suppliers. For example dealers and outsiders ran the Escorts on the 1978 RAC Rally, when a strike threatened even participation in the event. The Escort simply went ahead and scored its seventh outright victory on Britain's premier rally.

The crews

Of course, it was not just the preparation people who made the Escort the legend it became. Certainly, it was a good car, the best at various points in its career, but it went on winning

One for the model-makers, and a reminder of Alan Mann preparation standards in an age when many Formula 1 cars were not this well presented. For British events in 1968 over 200 FVA Formula 2 horsepower could be employed for the Escort. Such power, coupled to the large rear Goodyears, ensured that Mann's boys spent an awful lot of time trying to get the rear axle shafts to last... The picture is one of many in this book from the Chris Harvey collection, which includes the work of many sixties and seventies photographers.

Vintage Escort/Clark action! Roger Clark and Jim Porter slither to 1969 victory on the Circuit of Ireland with 1.8-litre TC power.

long after its technical peak, and it often won against more experienced or sophisticated international opposition, because the quality of the drivers, particularly the rallyists, was simply astounding. The Escort's simple nature meant that the real heroes could make it perform impossible stunts and turn them into routine victories.

In Britain the Escort legend grew through Leicestershire's Roger Clark. Deserving the adjective 'burly', Roger Albert Clark MBE was a sportsman who grew out of swimming and rugby into a naturally fine competitor, who showed other Britons the true meaning of Scandinavian sideways motoring. Many imitated him in Cortinas and then Escorts, but they just hadn't got the sheer balls and balance to produce consistently better times during the original Escort era. There was Tony Pond, but he wasn't ecstatic about becoming just another Escort clone in Roger's wake, and Ford didn't need to go chasing aspirants at that stage. Tony did win a Tour of Britain for the RS 2000 in its original shell with some vital components and a lot of telephoned help from Mick Jones – and he did finish seventh on the Scottish in a factory Ford at the first attempt – but to everyone's loss the two sides were too proud to try wholeheartedly to make an alliance that might have given us a few more British wins and achievements at the wheel of an Escort outside Britain.

Of course, the Escort rallying legend was really synonymous with those Flying Finns. The car was just made for them to do battle. A host of them took to it with a vigour that would have done credit to a top team of Visigoths sighting a beach-full of defenceless maidens ...

Swede Ove Andersson (now boss of Toyota Team Europe in Cologne) and John Davenport (his eighties counterpart at Austin Rover until 1987) scored the Escort TC's first overseas international placing with third on the San Remo in March 1968. Andersson's fellow countryman (and the 1966 Lotus Cortina RAC winner) Bengt Söderstrom was the first to win outside Britain with the Escort TC being first overall on the May 1968 Austrian Alpine.

The Finnish name that would keep coming back, and the one that scored many of the really big wins, was the world's most successful championship driver, Hannu Mikkola. In eighties conversation, and for that José Rosinski booklet, Barnett recalled for me how he

By 1969 the Escort's grip on the British club competitor was growing stronger, event by event. Here Jeff Harris contests the 1969 Player's No 6 Autocross final at Woburn Abbey in his 1600GT with the cheerful mixture of Magna alloy front wheels and widened steel rears. By this period competitors tended to go either with Mini Cooper or Escort in British competition, leaving little other variety in club entries up and down the country.

met Mikkola on the beaches that form the relaxing background to the Acropolis.

'He had been going like a bomb in his old Volvo, but I seem to remember him, too, doing improbable things with a ruddy great Datsun that looked like a taxi! Anyway, during the 1000 Lakes I asked him if he was interested in driving an Escort for Ford in the 1000 Lakes event in his own country? We offered him the princely sum of £250, plus his expenses – and were glad to secure his services so reasonably. But he hadn't foreseen that he was going to cover 9000 kilometres reconnoitring the route! As a result his expense account was a bit steep ... Anyway, we had no cause to regret it, because Hannu drove superbly and won the rally in the Escort, finishing well ahead of all the other Flying Finns!'

It would be 1970 before the best known of those other Flying Finns came back to employment within a British works team. Not long after Stuart Turner arrived, so did Timo Makinen, both men intent on doing for Ford what had already been done during their legendary liaison at Abingdon. If you gather a group of current and ex-Ford men together and want to wind everyone up, try dropping Makinen's name into the agenda for violent, and contrasting, reactions. The big Finn was an established star with a hard living, hard-drinking image to support and there's little doubt, in retrospect, that the genius of Mikkola was over-shadowed, and prevented from reaching its full potential by the early seventies inclusion of Makinen. Yes, Mikkola did a lot of winning, but talk to him today, Audi's 1984 World Champion, and one realises that 'Little Finn' is fitter, happier and probably just as quick as he was a decade ago in Escort; a fitness he attributes to a drastic cut in alcohol consumption. Then there was some serious drinking to be done and, notably in the 1973-74 season, the saga of 15in. diameter wheels to follow. These were adopted on Escort and stayed there largely through the personal enthusiasm of Timo Makinen, whilst all around were cursing their expensive presence as an irrelevance. Judged as motoring history, Makinen was absolutely correct: larger wheel diameters, 16 to 18 inches, were common Lancia wear in 1982 and *did* become an engineering trend – in alliance with ever lower profile tyres. In 1973/74 with narrow forest tyres, that was not the big wheel carrot. The Escort eventually went back to 13 inch diameter wheels for its successful life after Makinen – but, just when the Makinen moaners were having their heyday with Turner's protégé, Timo's reply was the most effective any driver could produce for a British-based international team: three straight wins on the RAC Rally!

That other Finnish Mini legend Rauno Aaltonen did swipe a third place for Ford on the 1970 London-Mexico, but Rauno's career post-Mini has really been built around Opel and selected saloon car racing/training film exercises for BMW. Another third place, this time 1973, was far more spectacularly scored by the young Ford Finn who got away, latter day Lancia and Subaru star Markku Alen, who took that placing with his loyal co-driver Ilkka Kivimaki. That Escort was Motorcraft sponsored in red and white and spent some time rampaging through saplings. Otherwise, the result for a then quietly-thoughtful Markku with little English and little inkling what Italy had in store for him, might well have upset the established order even further. Although Alen had scored a terrific second place in 1973's edition of the 1000 Lakes with a Volvo, by 1974 he was beginning his decade of sporting service with Fiat-Lancia and notching up the results.

In 1975 another Finn starred heavily on the Scottish ... but he was then in an Opel that looked as though it had taken on unaided a Russian tank squadron! With divine talent and supreme self-confidence in his driving – actually quiet and shy away from the wheel with the sharpest and driest Anglo-Finnish humour to be found – Ari Vatanen impressed immediately. One would stand on a 1975 Highland stage and watch Roger Clark come through in the new Cossack Red Mk2 on track for a Ford victory blitz that included five works-assisted Fords in the top ten. Clark, Coleman, Brookes, Makinen and John Taylor would all drift into view, more or less on the same line. Then came Ari, with (later) Rothmans Porsche mastermind Dave Richards rolling around the hole-infested, battered floor, usually out of view. Whether Richards was racked with mirth, or whether the seat had severed its mountings once more, was difficult to assess, but the speed, the sheer dedication to flying that old wreck into the results – even if it meant popping into view from a ditch and disappearing into another one on the theoretical accidents-only exit line to a corner – was clear for even the most blasé hack to see. Opel were not able to hang on to Ari in the face of Ford's interest, so it was no surprise when the man who really made his name via the Mk2 came to live in and around Boreham for the 1976 season, starting an asociation that would only be terminated by the eighties axe of the RS 1700T. The co-drivers were an equally interesting assortment including Henry Liddon for Makinen, John Davenport, Gunnar Palm and Arne Hertz for Mikkola's two separate Ford spells, and many other Men-of-the-Maps.

So that is a list of some of the characters you will encounter in Escort rallying. Who were the racers? Like the top rallyists today, saloon car racers tend to have a long competitive life and many of those 1968 onward Escort stars are prominent in the eighties, too.

In terms of initial results, and in securing the British Championship for the Escort TC in 1968, pride of place must go to Australia's Frank Gardner. Famous for his quick wit, Gardner came up the hard way, earning money with his fists before making motor racing a career based on mechanical perception and beautifully paced aggression. Mind you, the men around him were no slouches either: team boss Alan Mann was finishing in the top three with a Falcon V8 as late as 1967, and had originally come to Ford's notice when he was a salesman for a Brighton Ford dealer, driving a privately prepared Cortina 1500 GT with rather more results than the factory were gaining at the time. Mann's name lives on in racing lore, however, because of the West Byfleet, Surrey, business that he founded and which ran such Ford activities as the GT40, Monte Carlo Falcon Sprints, Lotus-Cortinas (in the USA and Europe) and the ill-fated 1969 F3L sports prototype with DFV Cosworth V8 power. If you have seen the film *Chitty, Chitty, Bang, Bang*, then you will have witnessed another profitable Mann sideline, the preparation of special vehicles for the sixties film business.

One doesn't see Alan Mann at eighties race tracks in a professional role, but he still has an immensely successful Surrey-based business, at Fairoaks Aerodrome, outside

Club racing Escorts abounded in the UK, with all sorts of motivation. Here John Bloomfield's David Wood (he of Austin Rover competitions in the eighties) BDA Escort scrabbles round the Brands Hatch of 1971. Colin Hawker's immaculate V6 Escort is in aggressive pursuit.

Chobham. In 1970 this site was used as home for Frank Gardner's gorgeous Boss 302 Mustang, but these days the only Mustang one would be likely to find would have over 2000 horsepower and the prefix P51; a stark military single-seater contrast to the private light aircraft and helicopters that are more normal Fairoaks fare, and Mr Mann's personal pride and joy.

The other fast man around Gardner and the Mann team was Keith Greene, who one will find at race tracks today. Following a sixties racing career that touched on F1 (Peter Ashcroft worked for the Gilby-Climax family team) Keith set out in a managerial role that has left him one of racing's most experienced and respected team managers. At Mann's the mechanics remembered, 'He often used to warm the cars up for Frank when we went testing, and he was often quicker, too!' Keith would always clamber into any kind of racer and did put in the occasional seventies outing when he went from Mann to Broadspeed. The Greene expertise has also applied to Gordon Spice, Chris Craft and the Rondeau and de Cadenet Le Mans teams. In 1983 he could be found at the Fitzpatrick Porsche 956 sports racing équipe in Group C.

The Broadspeed team were based originally in Birmingham and made their name with Minis; John Fitzpatrick, John Handley, and proprietor Ralph Broad's brimming confidence, allied to a self-depreciating sense of humour that was delivered at a steady 10,000 words per second. Ralph's flailing hands and bird-like visage behind the obstructive spectacles led to a legion of stories about the Broadspeed boss, either behind the wheel of some unfortunate tin-top protruding from the race- or rally-side shrubbery, or investigating mechanical mayhem with 'a varaflame lighter stuck into a dry sump tank. You wouldn't have believed a man of his experience would do it, but he did and even managed to laugh when he had a white ring where there used to be hair,' recalled former Broadspeed engine builder Tony Jones (now sole prop. AVJ, Pershore in Worcestershire).

Ralph's Escort drivers were Fitzpatrick (1966 British Saloon Car Champion with a 997 Broadspeed Anglia) and Chris Craft. John was a well known long distance sports car driver although most of his international wins had been in BMC, Ford or BMW saloons, prior to winning the European GT Championshp and the Porsche Cup with a 911 in 1972. 'Chrissy' Craft was really a Ford-bred personality of much under-rated speed for he did have lowly jobs at Dagenham and Boreham in the sixties, which seemed to consist mainly of tormenting service barges at improbable spares-delivery speeds. Chris tried his hand at most branches of motor sport: F3 to Grand Prix Brabham and a host of sports cars, winning the hard-fought European 2-litre Sports Car Championship in 1973.

The Cornish-born Craft will, however, probably be best remembered for Ford saloons, beginning with an Anglia and graduating to a Cortina that the BBC cameras caught aviating and replayed each week as the introduction to a popular series! From Superspeed Anglias to Broadspeed Escorts was a natural step, with larger-engined Escorts following on from there. Chris was famed for lousy race starts and incredible lap speeds and was more widely admired than his race record might have led you to believe. In the seventies his continual persistence in the de Cadenet Lola-based Le Mans machines won over a new sector of loyal British support.

Later Escort top runners received Ford support in terms of parts and dealer backing rather than as the direct works team sub-contractors of the sixties. When Fitzpatrick became ever more involved in the German scene, first with an ex-Broadspeed Escort within the Cologne Capri team and then with Porsches, Ralph had bred a superb successor in 1972 Escort Mexico Champion Andy Rouse, but Broadspeed also fielded Yorkshire financier David Matthews in 1300 RS BDA Escorts as well as in 2-litre RS 1600s and a variety of Capris. Another David, this time Berkshire-domiciled D. Brodie of club racing *Run Baby Run* Escort 2.1-litre TC fame, also featured internationally with a works-backed RS 1600 2-litre from 1972 onward. Brodie and Matthews were both involved in that enormous Silverstone accident of 1974 when Brodie's Escort and Matthews' Capri became embroiled in a fracas with a Mini to be lapped, vaulting off the track at the flat out Abbey left. Matthews did race again, but not consistently: Brodie was still contesting the British Saloon Car Championship with a Mitsubishi Colt Starion turbo in 1983-85. Most success, however, went to Andy Rouse. He had become a quadruple British Saloon Car Champion by 1988, creating and driving the Kaliber Sierra RS Cosworths of 440 to 500bhp.

From Croft it started ...

'The Escorts of Roger Clark, Tony Chappell and Barry Lee were all going like dingbats, the

Enough to defeat V8 Chevrolet power, John Fitzpatrick and Broadspeed's RS 1700-engined Escort of 1971, one of the most entertaining and efficient alliances ever fielded under the Escort badge. There is more about the 138mph Escort in the last chapter...

Twin Cam of Clark appearing to have things well sewn up at the end of the second runs, but alas, he was unable to turn out for the final outing and therefore didn't figure in the results. Barry Lee likewise didn't appear for his third run; Dagenham honour was upheld, however, by three stirring drives by Tony Chappell, who finished second overall, a mere 1.2s behind John Rhodes in the Vita 1.3 Mini-Cooper S' – John Higham's *Autosport* account of the 3 February 1968 World of Sport televised rallycross at Croft, Darlington.

The above is a part of motorsport history, for it recounts the first appearance of the works Escort TC, a pair of them in fact; in a branch of the sport that at that time commanded the attention of eight million Saturday afternoon TV viewers. I was at the meeting and can testify just how quick those early Twin Cams were: but then everything did look rapid when one was trying to qualify for one's first ever TV rallycross in a 998 Imp with a frozen engine!

Looking back to those 1968 TCs one is constantly surprised by their standard looks. Wheels that then looked like the ultimate broad-rim magnesium alloy technology, now would have less girth than many a road-going Ford's latest low-profile rubberwear. Then a 7inch Minilite was a big deal, now one buys a Sierra RS with 7 x 15s as production equipment.

Although Boreham's staff had covered over 15,000 miles in road-proving trials for the Twin Cam, traversing surfaces that varied from a snowy MIRA to 10,000 endurance miles at Lommel and some useful road mileage over Belgian *pavé,* actual competition, like war, speeded development to an ever quicker pace. The slightly over-bored 1598cc Lotus-Ford TC engine was persuaded to give over 160hp as routine, whereas 140 and 153bhp were reported for those Croft débutants. They were using Boreham's in-house engine-building team and the latest technology from Cosworth (particularly camshafts), in association with forged-steel crankshaft and connecting rods statically and dynamically balanced to ensure that 8000rpm was safe.

Power wasn't the Escort problem though. Bill Meade and other prominent staff members could be seen watching with some concern, rear-engined Imps and front-engine

In 1972, Ford supported Davids Brodie (behind) and Matthews in 2-litre RS 1600s with excellent results. Both men raced these Group 2 Escorts as well as Group 1 Capris in club events.

(and drive) Minis getting the jump on Escort from a standing start, knowing that radical engine repositioning was simply Not On, however tempting! Things came to a head at the Escort's début International Rally, San Remo in March 1968.

In the José Rosinski book, *The Car that Won't Stop Winning*, published by Ford toward the close of 1974, Meade recalled: 'During reconnaissance I asked Ove [Andersson] to give me a ride. I huddled down in the back of the Escort. He's a fine driver; possibly the best of the lot, and definitely the most sensitive mechanically. He complained about the roadholding of the rear axle, but couldn't describe clearly what was happening – that isn't his strong point. Climbing the hills was an interesting experience, but it was *nothing* to the descent! Ove drove very smoothly, so I wasn't afraid; but good God! Didn't he go *fast*! Apart from that, I had definitely felt the rear axle hop of which he was complaining. Obviously the damping wasn't powerful enough. However, during the rally everything went well, except for some shock absorber trouble. Ove and his co-driver John Davenport finished third – which was more than encouraging for the Escort's first major event – while one direct technical result was that we decided to modify the layout of the rear dampers and mount them vertically.' Thus was created the vertical damper mounting that featured in the widely-sold 'Turret Kit' meaning that the top damper mountings in the boot would be remounted from the standard 60° 5′ to a far stronger and more efficient turret insert of 90° damper angle, to use all the damper stroke. Hugo Emde of Bilstein recalled for me in Spring 1983 just how long the association between the German gas damper kings and Boreham had run: 'Even in 1968, when they had to use the Lotus Cortina until the Escort could come, we did some testing work with them. I remember well working with Henry Taylor and Bill Meade from those days, when the first settings we did after some Geneva tests were called 'the Chambéry settings'. Another thing I remember from 1969 was that when we went testing the team was so separate; the people who had always been there sat together to eat, but Piot and Mikkola, they had to sit on separate side tables'.

The Bilstein link characterized sporting rear drive Escorts and reached a wider

History for Escort and Europe: In 1972 Hannu Mikkola (seen practising and at the victorious finish) took the RS 1600 to the first East African Safari Rally win scored by a European. His partner (in dark shirt) was Gunnar Palm, who runs Ford Public Relations in Sweden today.

production audience when such dampers were specified as a Mexico option from the RS factory at Aveley. 'That FAVO business built up to 2000 shocks a month', recalled Emde, continuing 'Even today we ship 400 of our shock absorbers to Ford every month'. This despite the fact that the production link was severed in October 1982, when the XR3 came into manhood as the XR3i ...

Back in 1968, Ford at Boreham were as flat out as their drivers, for the Safari had to be tackled with three Lotus Cortinas (basically the GT model with the Lotus Ford installed) whilst Roger Clark/Jim Porter were sent to the Circuit of Ireland 'with a lone Group 6 [i.e. prototype] Escort Twin Cam, which was developing 152bhp', according to the *Autosport* account of Paul Stephens covering the 12-16 April event. The opposition included the most competitive international driver (in terms of results) the UK has ever produced, Paddy Hopkirk, in a Weber-carburated Cooper S. The Mini recognized the inevitable and broke its diff whilst behind the Ford, which went on to a massive winning margin over the ex-works S-type of Adrian Boyd. The reporter concluded 'Clark had taken a brand new model on to Hopkirk's own soil and beaten him very, very comprehensively. This Clark/Escort combination is going to take a lot of beating.' Perceptive words, and very few drivers, even Escort-mounted, could beat Roger and the Ford over home ground in the ensuing decade. It took Eire's Billy Coleman until 1975 to relieve Roger of the British RAC title in a season-long fight, but only Clark proved capable of twice winning the RAC Rally against the overseas best ... Writing in 1990, another Briton has still to win the event, even once, since Roger's last 1977 victory.

So that circuit marked the beginning of the Escort era, *not* that of Roger Clark's winning ways, for he had won his first big international, the Scottish, in a Cortina GT during May 1962. It seemed to open the floodgates for the new Ford, which promptly went and won the Tulip, Acropolis and Scottish for Clark; Sweden's Andersson taking second place on Acropolis and the then prestigious UK Gulf London. Söderstrom won the Austrian Alpine and new recruit Mikkola contributed the first of three consecutive 1000 Lakes victories (by 1983 he had won the 'Finnish GP' a record-shattering *seven* times: four for Escort; once Toyota, twice Audi!) Truly an internationally competitive début year ...

Racing results in 1968? Certainly! The Broadspeed and Alan Mann cars were presented to the press at Brands Hatch on 7 March 1968 and on 5 May Frank Gardner had notched up the small Ford's first European Touring Car Championship victory at Zolder in Belgium. For Europe, Mann used a Vegantune Twin Cam of some 170bhp to comply with strict Group 2 regulations. In Britain the liberal Group 5 rules meant that the Escort could compete with the pukka Cosworth Ford 1.6-litre FVA engine of F2-winning ways. Owing to homologation delays Gardner had to use the rack and pinion-equipped Lotus Cortina from Alan Mann for the March opening rounds of the RAC British title hunt, but by 3 June at Crystal Palace X00 344F was lined up complete with Len Bailey-drawn wheel arch extensions and ready to put 210bhp to good use in a 15-lapper.

It was a fitting début ground for an FVA Escort, for Jochen Rindt was using the same engine in the back of his Brabham BT23C to humiliate allcomers in the main F2 event at the London circuit. Unfortunately, the red and gold Ford TC could not maintain its initial startline advantage over the Malcolm Gartlan-owned 4.7 litre Ford Falcon, so ably conducted by the late Brian Muir. The sparkling Escort TC finished 4 seconds adrift, but a clear class winner.

The Len Bailey chassis formula for the Escort TC proved very ingenious: he threw the back axle's leaf springs away and substituted torsion bars, a four link location and Watts Linkage. I went along to see Mann's works at the close of 1968 and found that, 'The real star of the rear suspenders show is the twin torsion bars fitted across the boot, lying one above t'other and individually connected to the leading edges of the axle', in the house style words of *Cars & Car Conversions*. That visit also established that the Lucas fuel injected FVAs were rated at 217bhp by the end of the season with an 8500rpm regular limit. For 1969 the Group V FVA was outlawed so their European experience with 170bhp Boreham long distance TCs or up to 188 Vegantune horsepower was to prove vital.

In Britain the 15cwt/1680lb Mann Escort TC finished the season as outright British Champion, the second time Frank Gardner had taken the title in a row, but the European outings were nothing like so successful. In Britain the Escort FVA managed to beat the thundering Falcons outright on occasion, including at the 20 July Brands GP supporting race.

The regal purple and silver Team Broadspeed Escort 1300 GTs for Craft and Fitzpatrick started life with just the front flared arches installed, but were every bit as sophisticated underneath. The pushrod four was equipped with a down-draught cylinder head, designed by Broad along old 1-litre F3 lines and cast by Ford, with Tecalemit Jackson of Plymouth fuel injection stacks to menace the unwary invader of under-bonnet privacy. Compression was fixed around 12:1 with Hepolite slipper pistons, and Vandervell bearings to support the steel crankshaft and connecting rods up to an officially quoted 145bhp at 9200rpm! Maximum torque was said to be just 95lb ft at 7200rpm, so one had to keep the engine buzzing with the aid of a Hewland five-speed, non-synchromesh, gearbox. In fact, like Alan Mann, they experimented with several transmission layouts, but they needed five gears where Mann could get away with four on the TC model. I gather from ex-Mann mechanics that the weak parts of the Escort TC were all related to transmission, including the rear halfshafts.

Just ten days after they were presented to the press, (17 March, for the Guards Trophy race support event to the Race of Champions), one Broadspeed Escort and an Anglia 1.3 were ready for battle with the demon injection Minis of the day. Frank Gardner appeared for Mann in CTC 24E, the Cortina with coil sprung rear end and rack and pinion that stood in for the Escort TC until homologation was completed, also utilizing FVA power on this occasion.

The 1.3-litre Escort did not conquer the Minis during that 53 mile first round grudge

Monte Carlo victory persistently evaded the Escort, but in 1973 Hannu Mikkola was paired with Jim Porter to provide some relief from an Alpine-Renault A110 victory parade, finally finishing fourth in this 2-litre RS 1600.

match. Fitzpatrick's expired with low oil pressure in the first heat, while Craft split the Minis up with seventh overall, a spot behind John Rhodes in the Cooper Car Co. entry, with the Anglia – which also expired in the second heat.

At first, Ralph's Escorts were a bit fragile, but the potential was always there. At an early Silverstone round Fitzpatrick had a 9 second lead after 12 laps and only lost the class when the diff 'started melting' on the last lap, leaving Rhodes to win once more. On that occasion, however, rising F3 driver Mike Walker brought a BG3 Broadspeed-kitted 130bhp GT through into third place to emphasize that these Broadspeed kits would soon be more widely available, and effective! In fact, the three stages of tune offered by Broadspeed were retailed through the Ford RS system, their official début being in January 1969 at prices from £45 to £100, but those really were road mods.

So the 1300 GT Escorts did not even win their class in the first year's British Championship, although they did take first half a dozen times in the sub 1.3-litre category and frighten Minis onto 12in. diameter wheels for 1969! One very successful outing was to support an entry by the Mann TCs at Nürburgring in July for the annual 6-hr classic. This time the red and gold Byfleet bombers racked up two non-finishes, even with men like Neerpasch and Gardner in the team. The 1300 GTs for Craft and Clark (Roger, out on parole for a weekend full of merriment) plus Fitzpatrick and Trevor Taylor, were ninth and tenth overall, with clear class honours as a bonus. At this time you'd quite often see Roger Clark out racing, something people forgot about until he defeated Gerry Marshall in the battle of the bulges around the 1974 Tour of Britain ...

The path to 16 valves

By late 1968 Peter Ashcroft and compatriots had the dry sump lubrication system available to add another reliability dimension to the TC engine. The works had begun to field prototype Group 6 Escorts with improved lights and the wheel arch extensions. Memory tells me the proper works layout was pop-riveted aluminium but that glassfibre was also offered to the public before steel became the general public offering at RS dealers.

Bleak and grey are the impressions of a winter 'clubbie' at Brands Hatch, but the white hot battle between Gerry Marshall's DTV Vauxhall Firenza and the late Nick Whiting's locally-prepared Escort cheered up much of the 1973 season. 4/19

The 1969 season saw further use of the Group 6 category to prove rallying tweaks from Boreham, but the cars still ran to 1.6 litre Twin Cam specification in classics such as the year-starter at Monte Carlo, where they entered three cars and came away with that fourth place for Piot. Andersson continued his luckless Ford way – it took a 1970 move to Renault Alpine to put him back on the winning track – but Mikkola contributed two good 1969 wins, his second 1000 Lakes and the Austrian Alpine. Tony Fall, with present day Ford of Sweden PR Gunnar Palm, won the Rally of the Incas, as Ford's new competition boss, S. Turner, became more engrossed with the challenge presented by the 1970 World Cup Rally.

Four-wheel disc brakes and the first heavyweight axles of Taunus extraction (later more familiar from the Transit and 3-litre Capri) were also tested in action as well as privately along with the ZF five-speed gearbox and even the 2.3 litre ex-Taunus MRS/Capri 2300 GT V6 appeared in futuristic Group 6 Escorts during 1969, too. Those bigger axles carried ZF limited-slip differentials as a matter of natural modification and it was the ZF gearbox that also found favour long term, despite its chattering idle and the immense amount of development work that was carried out before it became the easy-to change (well under 10 minutes) unit with quick release housings and modified selectors/bearings that is familiar today. In fact it served some of Ford's rivals right that when they came to pick up bits of the Escort recipe, they often found they then had to spend quite a lot more to adapt the technology to rallying their car. Nobody really knew the enormous extent of modifications that had been carried out to the rallying Escort ZF until others started using it.

Ford had their own gearbox answers such as the Rocket or Bullet four-speeders based on Cortina casings that were quite suitable for the earlier sub-160bhp power units. Or there was a choice of five-speed racing ratios from Hewland, but long term the only answers had to come from far stronger five-speeders. That meant shopping amongst outside suppliers, for we were light years away from Ford engineering their own mass production five-speeds for Escorts.

During 1969, bigger capacities became reliably possible outside the legendary club racing 1650cc because Ashcroft managed to bully a thickwall iron cylinder block through the Dagenham foundry system. Complete with 85.6mm bores (a useful dimension if you want Cosworth pistons because they have a complete engine family built around such a bore size), this would provide the familiar 1800cc dimension – actually 1791cc – that could cheer up both TC and the now developing BDA in its original iron block format.

The big Twin Cam engine had its first taste of success inside Clark's second successive circuit win for the Escort in Ireland over Easter, although that example was closer to 1850cc.

The 1969 season brought Ford, (this time Ford of Europe rather than Ford of Britain was the entrant), a second international European Rally title as champion marque and four national saloon car racing titles: Germany, Belgium, South Africa and Denmark. Ford's European thinking extended to ensuring that overseas sales companies could plug into the Boreham system, first through Stuart McCrudden (co-ordinator of both Escort and Fiesta racing series in later life) and then through Martyn Watkins. Such programmes – later collectively known under the ESO initials (European Sales Organisations) – were effective in securing many championship titles for the Escort on track, or rallying.

Racing in Britain for 1969 saw the Mann Group 5 Escorts out for their last season: in the eleven rounds recorded Ford Escort success was widely spread. At the end of the year the small Ford had won three classes – Craft, Crabtree and Gardner in the 1300 GT, 1.6 TC and the Mann 'fan-charged' TC for Frank in the over 2000cc class. The latter Escort had a heater blower placed in some trunking leading to the Boreham built Twin Cam of perhaps

180/185bhp: there was a fragile genuine turbocharged Escort, confined to testing, but it was the trick fan device that did the racing. Anyway, all three Escort class victories counted for little in the end as Alec Poole's 1000cc Mini ran away with the title, which just shows the stupidity that drives so many manufacturers away from this category. Ask Stuart Turner about the British Saloon Car Championship and he would say, 'What's the point of winning something where you have to advertise and spend more money to tell people what it is you have won! And then they won't understand all those classes anyway ...!'

Although the Broadspeed 1300 GTs didn't voyage to Europe in 1969, that did not prevent them enjoying a considerable success in one championship round. For the Brands 6-hours in June, BMW brought a trio of their 2002 models, including two of the first European racing turbocars with comfortably over 250 horsepower. Pole position went to BMW on 1m 46.8s, but a 1m 50.4s from the well balanced duo of Fitzpatrick and Trevor Taylor's 1300 GT served notice that the slick Broadspeed outfit might expect some long term reward. With half an hour of the race remaining the little 1300 GT was whizzing around at 9000rpm with watch-like precision and with the small crowd praying that the impossible might happen, for the little Ford was leading outright!

Finally Dieter Quester and Hubert Hahne made it to the chequered flag with the princely lead of 7.6s after 21,600 seconds racing, or 6 hours, if you prefer. The Broadspeed legend was carried back to Germany and Erich Zakowski freely admitted that his early racing Escorts were all based largely on Broadspeed cars, parts and technology, although they later confined UK imports to just the necessary Cosworth components.

World cup fever

The 1970 Escort rallying season saw two separate paths successfully followed on the engine development front. For the 16,000 mile London-Mexico World Cup Rally (to finish in the Mexican City capital that was hosting the fabulously media-soaked football extravaganza), Ford at Boreham developed a twin Weber carburated '1850 GT'. In other words, one of the thickwall blocks was used to provide maximum capacity, without need to install a long stroke crankshaft. It was topped by the ordinary overhead valve crossflow head with modifications and a camshaft that would not be unfamiliar to clubmen using Holbay 1600 GT motors in the seventies. Power was deliberately restricted to the 140bhp level with the accent placed on servicing needs, for when Ford tackled the London-Sydney Marathon of 1968 with Cortina Lotus TCs it was a cylinder head problem that proved impossible to rectify, robbing Roger Clark and Ove Andersson of likely victory in Australia.

In the end seven World Cup Escorts, with their distinctive roll cage extensions down to the front struts, were entered on that trans-continental event. Of 96 cars that set out from London on 19 April 1970, just 24 made it to the finish, climbing heights of 15,000ft as well as tackling 17 daunting speed tests over enormous loose surface distances en route.

There was a lot of background moaning about the money and effort Ford had to devote to this marathon, effectively robbing them of the chance to compete whole-heartedly in other 1970 events, but Stuart Turner's typically bold pursuit of 'The Big One' and attendant publicity really did bring home the goods. For these big pushrod-engined Escorts thundered home with five placings in the first eight, including victory for Mikkola and Palm. They won the Team Manufacturer's Prize with first, third, fifth, sixth and eighth; plus the National Team Prize for Finland, amongst innumerable other honours!

There were plenty of dramas on the way, but Gunnar Palm's account of how Hannu Mikkola wrestled stark naked with Argentinians invading their South American hotel room in retribution for an earlier baulking incident, and subsequent honourable fisticuffs, typifies the wild adventures that every successful crew had to endure to reach the end. Mr

Dave Brodie presented a number of shiny and effective racing Escorts. This 1973 example is cleverly detailed with spoiler-mounted engine oil cooler and flexible spoiler extension.

Turner summed it all up when he said, 'Success depended just as much on men's capacity to endure the strain of high pressure driving for very long periods, as it did on the mechanical durability of their cars. Fortunately, both lived up to our expectations.'

The second engine development of the 1970 season was the emergence of the Cosworth BDA 16-valve in competition trim. The engine was homologated in October 1970 but once again Roger Clark was entrusted with some prototype development in the public eye and he appeared on 26-30 March 1970's Circuit of Ireland with most of the formula that was to become so Ford familiar throughout the seventies. For FEV 5H, a black-bonnet, white body Escort with the definitive round headlamp front end, extended wheel arches and Goodyears adorning fat Minilites, had the first of the works RS 1600 motors packed underneath and mated with the ZF five-speed and Taunus rear axle.

It was reckoned that this 1.8 litre BDA, 'was never troubled, and, with 180bhp at his disposal, Clark was able to relax once he had established a big lead, and in fact surprisingly was only fastest on half the 60 special stages.' The words are those of *Autosport,* then priced at about 12.5p (!) in April 1970. Roger did not enjoy such success with the RS-Escort (TC-badged) hybrid on that year's Scottish. John Davenport revealed in *Autosport* that even then Brian Hart had built the engine. Unfortunately the car did not finish another international that year for various reasons.

In British racing the BDA made its first appearance outside the British Championship series that 1970 season, Frank Gardner swopping 5-litres of Mustang V8 for a chance to frighten a V8-mounted opposition at Thruxton in August. He took pole position but the back axle failed before any fairy tale race result could be obtained.

In 1970, the September issue of *Motor Sport* reviewed the switch to Group 2 rules in the British Championship and commented of an old class battleground: 'The next division also suffered this year as British Leyland no longer back the tyre-smoking 1275 Mini-Cooper S types which used to battle with the works Escorts in the 1001-1300cc class. Now John Fitzpatrick in the sole Broadspeed 1300 GT used soft compound 350 Dunlop tyres and nearly 150bhp to such good effect that Gordon Spice in the Arden Cooper S has very little opportunity to get within grappling distance, unless the track is wet, in which case the Mini seems to be supreme. Arden have developed a light alloy eight port cylinder head for the S-type, but unfortunately this was not homologated until later in the season, and the BL engine is still not giving enough power to prove competitive once more. Even with the 12in. wheels (homologated in 1969) the Mini still has problems in transmitting power effectively to a dry track ... it is easy to see there is a big gap between the Escort and the Mini now.'

In the 1301-2000cc category Broadspeed fielded Chris Craft with a Twin Cam, following the closure of Alan Mann racing for the 1970 season, and *Autosport* reported a good 160 mile, two-heat thrash resolved between Gardner's Mustang and Craft's giant-killer Escort when the latter won the second of their two encounters when the Mustang broke a damper. Overall, Gardner maintained the lead over allcomers that he would keep all season, and Craft had to settle for second in the 180bhp, TC with its Lucas injection and single leaf spring/radius rod and Watts Linkage layout. There were plenty of other Twin Cams in the class that year – including Rod Mansfield's under-powered but accurately-conducted example – but all they did was rob each other of points whilst Bill McGovern got on with the job of giving the Sunbeam 998 Imp its first of three consecutive British titles.

The highlight of the Touring Car racing year came at the Silverstone TT on 27 June. Ralph Broad fielded his 10.3mpg GT for Fitzpatrick in both two-hour heats and the 9.3mpg TC for Jackie Stewart and Chris Craft. Without the chicane these 1970 saloons returned the kind of lap times we would expect from Group A machinery in 1984 at the same circuit. Pole position went to Muir's Camaro 5.0-litre Z28 on 1m 38.2s, half a second faster than Gardner, and only a row in front of Rolf Stommelen's 2.4 works Capri GT and Mr Stewart's Broad TC (1m 43.2s), which lacked only 3.4 litres on the 'Big Yank Tanks' ahead! Stewart finished fourth in that first heat after a sturdy battle with another works Capri, but Craft did not have a happy session, his problems including a spin before retiring with a broken valve spring.

For the RAC Rally of 1970 Clark's non-finishing RS 1600/1.8 was rated at 200bhp at 7500rpm, but neither this useful machine (the same Escort as was used for that Circuit début) nor the other two works cars finished, so it was left to John Fitzpatrick to close the British season on an Escort high note. John won the final round of the British Championship in October with the Broadspeed TC, closing that model's participation in the UK's premier racing series with a fine victory over the scattered big banger league.

For 1971, Broadspeed concentrated their efforts on a white RS 1600 with Castrol

This is the style that netted both Rod Chapman (seen here) and John Taylor the title of 'Terrible Twins' in seventies rallycross. At this 1973 Lydden, Kent, European Championship finale, Taylor wrapped up the European title.

stripes and with John Fitzpatrick to conduct its primarily Cosworth components. They began the year with an outright win for the 235 horsepower BDA, but seconds were the best thereafter in the UK, although JF definitely gave of his best right up to the last Brands Hatch round, where he and Mr Gardner (by now in massive Camaro) worked each other off the track at over 100mph and left Gerry Birrell's works Capri a surprise win, whilst all the bodywork was drifting back down to earth.

Broadspeed also prepared an equivalent car for Cologne to use in the European Touring Car series. One that totally justified Fitz's stated faith in the machine as compared to Capris of the period, for it nearly won the opening Monza 4-hour round and *did* snatch victory outright for Ford at the closing, Jarama, Spain, event of torrid heat and appalling driving standards. Since no development work was done between the time that this Escort won its class and finished fourth at Monza to that end of season win – which John shared with Jochen Mass – these were worthy Escort achievements indeed.

The 1971 season of international rallying naturally saw the RS 1600 gain more widespread works use in its usual 1.8-litre iron block form, but the results were the worst I can recall for the Boreham team with non-finishes a speciality. In fact the only overseas outright victory was on the island of Cyprus and that was hardly against the cream of world rallying, whilst six works-built cars for Safari came back with a fourth overall as their best result ... At least, by the close of the year, they could get a quartet of 1.8 RS 1600s to finish the RAC, although, again, fourth was their best placing.

It could be said with hindsight that the abortive GT70 project drained off some of 1971's rally potential from the works, but in 1972 the factory rally Escorts came right back to form using a 2-litre siamese bore aluminium block from Brian Hart, which Roger Clark used from June onward in the UK. This saved about 40lb (18kg) and allowed Hart to start providing a reliable basis for Formula 2, particularly the Surtees machinery for Mike Hailwood. Mike-the-bike took the 1972 European Championship using Hart prepared BDAs, although these were not the aluminium versions, which were débuted in Japan during October for single-seater purposes.

The rally alloy 2-litre débuted internationally overseas with a fighting second place from Timo Makinen/Henry Liddon in August 1972's edition of the 1000 Lakes. 'Fighting' because, to quote Gerry Phillips in *Motor Sport*. 'The engine mountings of Makinen's Escort would have been fine for a steel engine, but the threads in the aluminium block were not strong enough to cope. The bolts loosened and eventually stripped the female threads. With typical ingenuity mechanics Gordon Spooner (Boreham) and Raimo Haarta (Helsinki) set about cutting blocks of wood and hammering them into place around the engine block to hold it in place, wrapping each block in a rubber sheet.' The primitive bushmanship worked, although Makinen apparently suffered some loss amongst the claimed 220bhp, that did not help his pursuit of Lampinen's victorious lightweight SAAB.

Even the original iron block BDAs, however, seemed to find winning form in 1972, although one could always mention the half shaft Achilles Heel if anyone from the factory looked too smug. Most prestigious win of the year was Mikkola heading three team mates in the top ten home to victory on the East African Safari, which had never been won by anyone outside Africa before. Roger Clark was notching up an increasing tally of outright British championship wins: Mintex Seven Dales, Granite City, Welsh. In the Welsh Barry Lee esq. took second overall: it made a change from his new career in hot rods. Lee also enjoyed more than 140 events in that original launch Escort XTW 368F, which Barry auto-and rally-crossed with various power plants and some sort of success in over 130 of those outings! Clark came second on the Scottish behind Mikkola, who had journalist Hamish Cardno navigating. Of course Clark won the British title that year with the Manx and Burmah Castrol also going his way in one mighty season.

Finest hour for the Boreham-built LVX 942J in a plethora of national success, was this 1972 win on the RAC Rally for Roger Clark/Tony Mason. Even a last-minute rear axle problem on the way to the finish could not prevent the first 'home win' since the unexpected Ford victory of 1959 (Gerry Burgess/Zephyr 6).

But the news came from November's RAC Rally. Here Clark lined up with a 2-litre alloy engine, a feature only shared by team mate Makinen, for Mikkola and Cowan in the remaining works cars had iron block 1800s. Roger's machine broke new Boreham rallying ground in that it also featured Lucas fuel injection. Power? About 235bhp in a car built to be slightly under 2200lb (1000kg) complete with an ever growing list of rallying equipment and complex instrumentation.

In the event only Roger's legendary LVX 942J, the Esso-backed white and blue Escort that never seemed to lose an event in its career (it did, but it spent a lot more time winning for R. Clark!) occasionally stuttered on its way to the first win by a Briton since the event had gone into the forests for the sixties. I do remember it was the first rally I had ever seen and it seemed a shame to get such a beautifully prepared machine so filthy. Then, when they cleaned it up, ready for the run back to York, it seized a rear wheel bearing on a road section, not far from Harewood hillclimb. Fortunately Andrew Cowan, or 'Marathon Man' as Mitsubishi nickname him these days, was following along dutifully in his repaired works car. The offending vehicle had soon been restored to natural vigour with the aid of a works Escort vital organ transplant!

The 1972 season was a very busy one so far as rally development was concerned, for the 1977cc engine was only part of a specification that improved all round with the introduction of the durable triple plate clutch and the initially controversial hydraulic handbrake. The latter item caused some scrutineering bothers because regulations and the Road Traffic Act called for a mechanical linkage for handbrake operation, but a number of ingenious linkage disguises ensured that the now widely-accepted hydraulic action became part of the works specification – and later duplicates built outside Boreham.

By the close of 1972 the specification was reaching a peak that has been the basis for so many Escort rally cars, whether clothed in Mk1 or Mk2 shells, ever since. Many of these elements have also appeared with championship winning success in European Rallycross and some of the basic running gear – not the engine – found its way into Hot Rod racing via Barry 351 Lee and thus to World Championship honours in a branch of motor sport that has seen the Anglia and Escort as its backbone over three decades. Even now top Hot Rodding Toyotas carry Escort components beneath their Japanese bodywork.

The definitive RS1600 in 1973-74 would have been built around a craftsman-constructed body with rather more steel components than were allowed in earlier Escort days. For example, in 1972 they had to adopt glass side windows instead of Perspex and the bonnets were of steel production origin, rather than the lighter plastic and alloy parts found for bonnet and boot in earlier times.

The body would certainly be the work of Maurice Gomm at Woking in a typical example, but outside contractors were sometimes called in at times of peak preparation stress, such as the World Cup year. The bodyshell would naturally start life as the HD Type 49 with the vertical turret conversion installed at the rear and a mass of minor fabrication

Pictures of a 1974 co-operative Escort success. Working in co-operation with Ford in Germany the Zakspeed concern ran 2-litre RS 1600s with European Championship-winning reward in 1974, even beating the 400 horsepower BMWs and Ford Capris on home ground, at the Nürburgring that season. Here we see the cars at the beginning of the season at Monza, car number 35; and during that historic Nürburgring outing (27). The most successful Escort driver of this Zakspeed era was Hans Heyer, to be found winning similar European events a decade later in the TWR Jaguars.

work to mount items like the rear suspension long links from floorpan to axle, or to produce a boot that would house progressively bigger bag fuel tanks. In 1971 the works spoke of 12 gallons at Monte time; by 1973, 20 gallons was the quoted figure for the foam-filled safety tanks, which usually had a dipstick to read level, rather than cockpit fuel gauge. Also in the boot you would find the alloy dry sump tank with Castrol as major backers for many years, although Shell was contracted as the major supplier in 1972/3. Tyres showed the same changes in affiliation, for Goodyear were the original sixties equipment but by 1971 Stuart Turner had also changed the rubber contract to Dunlop, a link that lasted through the factory rear drive Escort days, although development of the axed RS 1700T was based on Pirelli's abilities with all independent suspension systems.

The cast magnesium sump shield developed by Bill Meade, and developed with some camera-catching yumps by Roger Clark at Bagshot with that hard worked original Twin Cam, lasted the pace and remained a feature of the RS 1600 in the seventies. The degree to which the body was strengthened, besides that fabrication work needed to mount new components and the bracing effect of the bolted-in roll cage of steel, was never made publicly clear. The problem was wording in the regulations and company politics; for both these reasons Ford were not keen, nor were their exceptionally loyal employees, to go blathering on about the precise degree of extra welding and local strengthening that went into a works shell. Later on precise details were given in a booklet by Mick Jones and Charles Reynolds. This is available from RS Ford dealers and has sold over 30,000 copies.

Body strength altered according to the class of event for which that body was originally built, but some works cars were so long-lived that they tackled an enormous variety of terrain. Perhaps the most obvious extremes were Escorts built to tackle Monte Carlo and those for East African Safari. A purpose-built Monte car, complete with low riding suspension and wide wheels to accommodate the racing tyres that would be necessary for dry stages, was obviously a very different original build proposition to the heavily-braced, high-riding Safari machine with a host of extra equipment, biased toward keeping on the move through mud and fending off wild animals.

Early in the Escort TC's competition life Ford tried building coil-sprung Mann-type rear suspension into the Escort for extra Monte speed and during the Mk2's life the

If Roger Clark was not sure which way a racing circuit went, he simply put the car sideways until the truth was revealed! Roger leads temporary Ford team member Gerry Marshall to a fine 1-2 victory on the 1974 Avon Motor Tour of Britain. Naturally, Ford stuck to their Dunlop tyre contract and also surprised the opposition with some demon homologation extras late in the preparation period prior to the event, including twin downdraught carburettors.

descriptions 'Forest Spec' and 'Tarmac Spec' were liberally applied to differentiate between extremes. Boreham, however, stuck to multi-leaf rear axles for the more numerous forest type, and later tarmac Escorts went for a single leaf rear suspension layout, ultimately with a long strut rear damper layout; but that is after our period in this chapter.

Inside the factory Escort of this era there was really far too much information displayed, the result of pandering to a wide variety of works drivers. The key features were a mechanical tachometer with telltale from Smiths and minor instrumentation from the same company: oil pressure, water temperature, ammeter and a supplementary fuel gauge being likely, but some examples would also bombard one with information of oil temperature and of fuel pressure from the boot-mounted high pressure fuel pumps.

Switchgear was a nightmare for the stranger with over half a dozen flick switches and pull knobs, and the navigator's side would have the mechanical Halda Tripmaster of the period, plus a brace of mechanical stop switches. I remember a debate once about the increasing cost of works cars, revealing that the instrumentation of a Boreham Escort was accounting for the best part of £1000. So the Mk2s did have a far more production-biased layout.

Seating was a matter for the individual crews in this period. I seem to remember Roger C carrying on with a perch that had served him from Cortina days, whilst others would demand the latest and greatest, initially from outfits like Restall and Contour in those unsophisticated days without Recaro £500-a-time carnal knowledge! A four-point harness with quick release buckles was usually supplied by Willans.

The typical running gear beneath a factory forest Escort would include four-wheel disc braking, the rear ones being solid disc and those at the front, ventilated units creeping in from Monte influence, but the back axle saw a host of changes within. The Taunus unit and ZF differential were OK, but Mick Jones spent literally hundreds of man hours grappling with the halfshaft problem. Even in 1972 they hadn't the complete answer, and in 1973 I vividly remember following Mikkola through a Scottish rally night with 'his' supply of halfshafts in the boot of the Commanders Cup Consul GT, while the other factory cars were serviced with a different specification. Mikkola came by us on a road section and disturbed our snooze by converting the hapless Ford into a trike that demanded service, *now!*

There were an enormous number of final drive ratios available in the end for that axle,

In contrast to that Cadwell Park racing shot of Clark and Marshall on the 1974 Tour, this illustration of Marshall tidily on course over the classic Eppynt rally territory of South Wales shows the kind of terrain racing drivers had to master if they wanted success on this unique event. Only one racer ever won, that being James Hunt in a Camaro, in the days before so much typical rally mileage was introduced to the Tour.

Last works victory of the Mk1 on the RAC. Timo Makinen and Henry Liddon won this 1974 edition of the Lombard-backed World Championship round; the same crew won the RAC for Escort in 1973, '74 and '75!

but rally cars for forest use were usually set up with 5:1. That meant the vehicle was unlikely to stray over 110mph unless the pilot ignored the recommended 8000 to 8500rpm BDA limit. The engine specification provided by Brian Hart began with some 200bhp at 7500rpm and grew to a reliable 245bhp for forest use in the period we are discussing; by 1976 he could provide 260bhp and you could leave it ticking over happily – if audibly – at 1500rpm; far from the cold start plug-changing days of late TC and early RS!

A typical alloy block BDA of 1972-73 measured 90mm bore by 77.2mm stroke giving 1977cc and had forged steel crankshaft and connecting rods. Compression would be around 11.5:1, carburation by twin Weber sidedraughts with Cosworth BD3 camshaft profiles. At the time John Griffiths, former Weslake engineer, who succeeded Peter Ashcroft on the engine side at Boreham when Peter was elevated in 1972, reckoned such a unit would be 'quite potent. Giving about 240bhp at 8000rpm and 160lb ft torque at 6750 revs.'

Aside from Roger Clark's victorious 1972 RAC machine (subsequently widely used in British Championship rounds), fuel injection was not a public fitment during the early seventies Escort career and the Weber 45 DCOE sidedraughts, larger in later life, typify the works Escorts in Mk1 and 2 guise. Valve gear and cam profiles, along with the majority of components within the BDA, came from originators Cosworth and were assembled by Brian Hart's small factory. Engine reliability was generally excellent although, during this period, the cry 'head gasket' in various Scandinavian or Leicestershire accents often assailed the unwary inquisitive journalist surveying a steaming factory Ford.

Externally, the back axle usually wore a brace that was originally developed within a week during the World Cup intermission, but the vast number of ZF changes tended to be internal, save for the modified bellhousing to get that five bolt quick release speed.

The front suspension was always Mac Pherson strut on the examples I saw for forest use (whereas at the back, some forest cars did vary from that leaf spring routine I referred to earlier, and experimented with coils and Watts Linkage), but for tarmac use a compression strut might well be a feature of a works car in this period rather than the thick front anti-roll bar and replacement TCA normally employed.

Just in case ...

Ford quoted 2016lb (916kg) weight for the RS 1600 works rally car, which came complete

Although the shape was then obsolete, Tony Pond received a good deal of unofficial help from Ford at Boreham in getting this RS 2000 prepared to win the 1975 Avon Motor Tour of Britain. Pond's race circuit performances defeated many of the acknowledged aces of the day, using about 160bhp from Racing Services.

with a small spares box that provided as basics, radiator hoses, spark plugs, brake pads and fluid, a roll of tape, locking wire, useful nuts and bolts, spare wheel nuts and necessary spanners. One would also expect to find a torch and possibly high pressure cylinders to inflate tyres in an emergency. Under-bonnet, there was usually a second fan belt, throttle cable and return spring. Ford were also conscientious about fire extinguishers – I cannot imagine Boreham would have put up with the spate of fires Audi suffered on the Quattro, but then it was an era of steel panel work and normally aspirated engines, not turbocharged plastic temples to technology. In Ford's competition Escort one would find a Fire-eater automatic system on board with nozzles covering boot, engine bay and cockpit.

It's one hell of a job to summarize such a seven year span of successful motor cars, but so far as the front line went the Escort forest car with 2-litre aluminium engine, heavy duty body and transmission was the most successful rally car formula ever. The key elements were duplicated for sale through the FAVO system and by outsiders, and the proof of its worth is in the works results for the period (a tribute and record of the outstanding achievements is given within the appendices) and the continuing use of mechanically similar cars by the majority of British club competitors even in 1984 Top Ten entry lists for many national rally championship rounds. If you built the thing conscientiously, around what the works had proved from Machynlleth to the darkest corners of the South American and African continents, you had the basis to show what kind of rallyist you were, often against opposition that was similarly equipped. From top to bottom the Ford Escort rally car went through it all to emerge as the best thing in rallying since our creator sent Stuart Turner to dwell amongst a bewildered rallykind.

In racing terms the Escort came with all sorts of power units and none of the overall prestige that attached to rally results at World Championship level. In October 1974 Ford could announce perhaps the best overall results for a circuit Escort, culminating in the Zakspeed équipe's Hans Heyer winning the 1974 European Touring Car Championship for drivers. The Escort was never beaten in the 2-litre class and, as recounted, it managed to win outright at Nürburgring (Hans Heyer/triple Le Mans victor Klaus Ludwig at the wheel) besides never finishing lower than seventh *overall* against regular 3.4/3.5-litre opposition with 400bhp in the BMW and Ford camps. That year Ford also scooped the ETC makes title, the German Championship, and were winning races all over Europe, particularly in Sweden and Belgium.

Scoop! Paul Newman, Superstar, drives race Escort in 1974. The alliance was not a major plank in Newman's now solid racing platform of experience, and I understand the sound of crumpling metal and broken glass interrupted Ford's best shot at featuring the Escort as 'The Ford Superstars prefer'. The machine was an RS 1600 prepared by former Broadspeed mechanic Carl 'Tivvy' Shenton when he ran Spec Fab at Pershore in Worcestershire.

*It climbs hills well, too!
Marc Cramer with his
Escort 1300 in
opposite-lock mood at
Prescott hill in 1984.*

In Britain the Escort's record was strongly tied to the continuance of Group 2 regulations, the RS 16-valve concept and Broadspeed's ability to assemble familiar Escort components, including those of Cosworth for the engine. The 1973 season was the last for Group 2 and tradition in Britain; it saw Ford win three classes with the Escort: Les Nash (1.0 litre), Vince Woodman (1.3 litre) and Andy Rouse (2.0 litre) with Frank Gardner emerging as a worthy overall champion once more, but with the benefit of Mr Chevrolet's V8 Camaro.

The 1972 season had seen Bill McGovern take his last 1-litre Imp title, but Ford had not been properly represented on the 1300GT Escort front and present day West Country Ford Dealer Jonathan Buncombe had taken a Richard Longman Mini-Cooper 1293S and grasped the class title for the Mini – the last time that was done with the legendary S-type, though racing Metros live on, of course. So, for 1973 Ford and Cosworth had the obvious answer: an ultra stroke 16-valve 1300RS for the Broadspeed 1300GT chassis! It was driving such a car that Ford VMW Motors proprietor Vince Woodman won back the class in 1973 after some stirring battles with the similarly equipped 1300RS of Yorkshire's former F3 ace, Peter Hanson. In fact Hanson and Woodman quite often ventured to the lucrative Belgian series and grasped pots of Belgian francs from exporting their expertise!

The aluminium 2-litre proved just the job for a man like Rouse to continue Ford and Broadspeed's domination of the 2-litre class, and the Escort could appear in Belgium too. Typical result for 1973 in Britain was the last Group 2 round, October's Motor Show 200, in which Rouse finished second overall with Woodman also inside the top ten and a class winner once more.

Zakspeed specification

As to specification, the equivalent to a works championship rally car was really the 1974 Zakspeed 2.0 RS 1600, the first machine to bring Ford a European title since Sir John Whitmore's epic drives in the 1966 Lotus Cortina from Alan Mann.

Zakspeed used some of the same components as the rally cars of course, but their five-speed machines weighed in at 1807lb (821kg). They carried about 22 gallons (100 litres) of five-star fuel and usually managed 10mpg in longer races, where revs were held down. They finalized on an alloy block BDA providing 270bhp at 9000rpm and it was reckoned this would provide 150mph along with 0-60mph in 4.6s! Externally the Castrol-striped machines with good publicity support from the Radio Luxemburg RTL organisation looked as you would expect a racing Mk1 to look, with the biggest possible wheel arch extensions and integrated front spoiler. It is worth remembering that even at that stage their Dunlop-shod BBS split rim alloy wheels were of 15inch diameter, rather than RS/TC's

Ten years after it went out of production the original Escort saloon was still providing club racing fun and a way of annoying Austin Rover product loyalists! Doug Broad's RS 2000 lifts a wheel at Snetterton in the Summer of 1984.

13inch, or the original 12inch. (See Appendix VI for further details.)

Incidentally the first Escort produced by former miner Erich Zakowski under the Zakspeed label was hillclimbed in 1968 by later Ford of Germany and worldwide competitions director, Michael Kranefuss.

The RS 2000 in action

The 1973 announcement of the RS 2000 gave Ford a new competition option and it was one they investigated along two primary development paths before settling for Group 1 (the car eligible for Group A on a transfer basis from 1983 onward).

Mark Lovell/Peter Davis pose with the turbocharged Group A Escort that failed to fulfil its 250 bhp promise.

This gentleman chose Escort Sport for his 1984 honeymoon!

First option to be publicised was that of enlivening the RS 2000 power unit without much thought of international regulations. There was a turbo version – promising for many sports applications from hot rods to formula cars, but it failed to realise that potential – and a longer term Pinto engine development programme by Holbay. This included a 16-valve head layout and a full formula programme that did not directly lead to a new standard in Ford sporting engines. The RS 2000 and its twin Weber 45 DCOE carburettors that Roger Clark was given to (just) win the 1974 Mintex Seven Dales was more relevant. The idea here was to offer clubmen a more affordable link between Mexico and RS 1600, the modified 2000 running about the 160bhp output of the first factory Twin Cams, plus a strong torque curve.

Former BMW engineer Otto Stulie conducted some engine research in Germany, too, and the results could be seen internally with 10.8:1 Mahle pistons, Tuftrided crankshaft and steel connecting rods with 0.060in. larger inlet valves and new external manifolding both for the exhaust and for the double twin choke carburettor layout. A four-speed Ford-based gearbox and Salisbury LSD were installed in a chassis that was far simpler than a full factory RS 1600: the back brakes were Mexico's 9inch drums with ventilated fronts and spring rates were set around 130lb front and 120lb rear. Bilstein dampers and rose-jointed radius rods were featured along with vented front discs, and the complete car in Boreham's then traditional white and blue created strong interest when it somewhat belatedly appeared. It was almost the victim of the Fuel Crisis which caused rallying to be suspended for the opening months of 1974 and strongly influenced Ford to produce less radical rally cars.

At the start, the RS 2000 for Group 1 turned the clock back to a strictly production base, too. Subsequently the changes came thick and fast for the car was immensely popular and competitive from the time that Roger Clark/Jim Porter and Gerry Marshall/Paul White (now with Talbot Sport) had flown the first two factory examples to a paralysing victory against their keener Group 1 opponents at Vauxhall and Chrysler in the 1974 Avon

Motor Tour of Britain. As a result the Mk2 – with and without 'beak' – became the epitome of a competitive Group 1 machine with many major components replaced.

Those 1974 Tour cars went through Birmingham scrutineering on production of a telex from FISA in Paris that basically said everything was OK ... there just hadn't been time to get the forms back to the UK! The specification, which surprised the hell out of outfits like DTV, included the German-developed twin Solex 40/42 downdraught carburation kit on an alloy manifold, and WC 30 camshaft. A new twin downpipe exhaust system was also part of that first RS 2000 Group 1 spec, which was reckoned to provide 138bhp instead of 100bhp, when built at Boreham.

Those 1-2 winners on the Tour also included a four-speed Rocket gearbox; 4:1 limited slip Salisbury differential; the usual Bilstein replacement of dampers; and a brand new single-leaf rear spring layout for the axle, a single-leaf rear end being part of the 1970 Capri RS 2600 specification. The wheels were standard steel 5.5 x 13in. items and carried Dunlop SP4 road tyres, throughout an event run over everything from Cadwell Park race circuit to Eppynt and Snetterton.

I had to summarize Roger Clark's performance for the Dunlop house magazine after the RS 2000s had trampled the rather startled opposition into the ground with these new weapons, machinery backed by the fearsome alliance of Clark and Marshall as drivers; a line up Stuart Turner quipped was simply, 'Ecurie Beer Gut!' My inter-company propaganda for Ford to Dunlop said: 'Circuit racing is often said to bore Clark, but you wouldn't guess it from his track style. Up to the Tour of Britain this year I fell into the category of enthusiasts who thought that Roger Clark was a very quick race driver, but too fond of travelling sideways, and therefore enjoying himself, to beat the best in saloon car races.

'Roger took particular pleasure in proving myself and a lot of other pundits wrong. Clark set new records for the angles at which an Escort can be cornered.

'Yet, with the steering on full lock and Gerry Marshall nestling his identical Escort on Clark's rear panels, Roger simply motored away from the opposition, using SP4s to beat the best over tarmac, grass and gravel.

'What was noticeable in Clark's performance was the way in which he could win on a track like Cadwell Park (which he had not raced before: rallycross is no help in this respect) by sliding sideways, torturing the tyres until he could see a clear way through the corner.

'In stark contrast, Clark's performance at Oulton Park, which he knows and likes as well, was neat and controlled, many of the audience mistaking Clark for racing driver Marshall.'

It was a true master's performance – I liked the bit where Clark outmanoeuvred some of the Snetterton night racing opposition by extinguishing the lights until he was past! – but I should add that Marshall showed great restraint when they were in very close company and neither car suffered panel damage at any time. Perhaps a little nuzzling, but no heavy petting!

The RS 2000 was an established winner on the Tour throughout its existence and Tony Pond used a Mk1 version (TFR 8) and a lot of assistance from Goodyear and Ford at Boreham to repeat the victory in 1975, despite some fraught engine bay fractures over Eppynt. During that outing Mr Pond displayed the circuit flair that saw him winning races outright for Rover in 1984. Some nine years earlier he was beating renowned circuit dicers Alec Poole and Colin Vandervell, all three Escort-mounted.

Of course, there was a lot more the Escort did in motor sport within the original body, but let's leave the subject with the thought that from an 1100 drum-braked 79mph and near 40mpg economy to 274bhp and 150mph from 2-litres of RS 1600, the Escort proved a simple car could be all things to all men ... Could the Mk2 maintain such a broad appeal?

Chapter 5

A new suit for 1975-80

Much the same mechanical recipe went into the square-rigged Escort II developed under the codename Brenda for sale in 1975. Generally there was more of everything: bigger engines (1.6 litre Ghia and Sport), more luxury, more weight – and more purchase price expense in an expanded range of considerable extra comfort.

PRODUCT letter ER-2 dated 2 December, 1972 may not have the ring of romance associated with an emotive sports machine that is the product of a lonely genius slaving in a draughty attic, but that letter – listing all the qualities Ford wanted in a replacement, interim, Escort – had an enormous impact on the lives of over two million who purchased the previous Escort. For here was a distinctly more comfortable and civilized choice – at a profitable price, of course!

There was nothing deeply significant in the Brenda coding, Ford just settling at the time for girls' names to code future projects. Thus, the previous year's Capri II was Diana within Ford, the original Granada MH was replaced by Granada coded Eva and the front drive 1980 Escort gestation period was under the code Erika. By the way, a lot of writers, including myself, tend to write Escort I, Capri III and so on for purposes of quick identification, but only Capri II actually carried that writer's shorthand onto the flanks of a Ford.

Ford at Dunton chief Ron Mellor was generous enough to let me have the 2 January 1973 'Firm Engineering Timing Plan' that sets out the myriad tasks to complete what seemed a fairly simple reskin to an outsider. Under 12 main headings, from overall design to detail parallel activities such as electrical engineering, the blueprint predicts with quite astonishing accuracy the completion dates for thousands of personnel dealing with every thorny problem from homologation to German official tests in respect of every aspect of

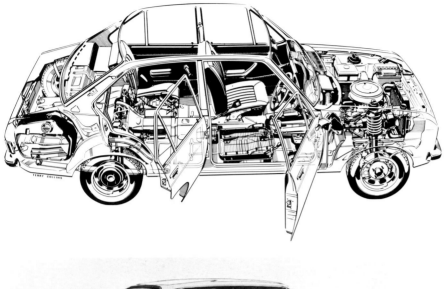

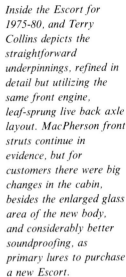

Inside the Escort for 1975-80, and Terry Collins depicts the straightforward underpinnings, refined in detail but utilizing the same front engine, leaf-sprung live back axle layout. MacPherson front struts continue in evidence, but for customers there were big changes in the cabin, besides the enlarged glass area of the new body, and considerably better soundproofing, as primary lures to purchase a new Escort.

Brenda-coded Escort, the way the stylists saw it ...

the car's specification and performance, literally down to what your bottom might think of the new product! How so? Well, February 1973 was the deadline for getting the revised 'seat contour approval'...

As a tribute to the way in which Ford pulls together the activities of many nationalities in precisely costed and targeted schedules to achieve a product aimed with tremendous accuracy at the consumer, this blueprint left me with enhanced respect. This branch of modern engineering may lack the glamour of tooling up a new Ferrari, but affects the lives of a lot more people! Today Ford concentrate more on quality than on meeting target production dates, most of the cars that I monitor missing their predicted débuts.

The timetable for the 1975-1980 'Brenda' Escort foresaw the construction of 8 mechanical prototypes, 19 full engineering prototypes, 7 suitably finished bodies for crash testing and a June 1974 Sign-Off date for the two-door saloons, with other derivatives given that go-ahead from August 1974 onward. They would begin to assemble pre-production parts in July 1974 and build bodies in white during September, these amounting to trial assemblies of what had been approved for production. Training workers to assemble the cars for mass production pace would begin in November 1974 and the first production cars (Job 1) were scheduled for manufacture on the 13 January 1975 for two-door saloons; February 1975 for 4-doors and 24 February on estates and vans. Just how effective their programme prediction was can be judged from the first production Mk2 Escorts leaving the Ford of Germany lines on 2 December 1974. Furthermore, they made over 2300 new Escorts prior to the close of 1974 – before they had been anticipated to make *any*. In the

A 1973 clay model of the squared front-end for a new Escort body.

first year of full scale manufacture (1975) they built a record 215,738 Escorts. In Britain it took them longer to build up to the really big numbers, well up on the original model incidentally, constructing 188,303 in 1976.

So the Escort revamp was entirely successful from an engineering production point of view; to underline the point, note that from December 1968 to January 1975 (6 years 1 month) Ford of Britain sold 649,092 of the original Escort saloon and derivative designs. In just 5 years 4 months the Escort's reskinned successor sold an almost identical 647,289 copies during its 1975 to 1980 UK sales life.

What the customers saw ...

Although the new Escort looked bigger than the 1968-74 models, it was actually a very similar size with rather more internal space and comforts. Dimensionally the 156.6in. (3978mm) length was identical and only fractions separated the track, wheelbase and official height figures, viz: Escort II was officially built on a 94.8in. (2408mm) wheelbase whilst the original was given as 94.5in. in the handbook. Similarly Escort II had a track of 49.3in. (1252mm) and the original 49.0in. at the back there was the same 0.3in. track discrepancy in the official description, but not enough to be significant. Height was originally described in laden guise at 53.0in. (1346mm) for Mk1 and unladen for Mk2 at 53.8in. (1366mm).

There were, however, important body changes. The width was down from 61.8in. (1569mm) to 60.5in. (1537mm) in the later model yet passenger room – particularly with an extra *two* inches rear legroom claimed – was improved. Glass area, and therefore total body weight, were sharply increased. Ford claimed 23 percent 'more glass area' and there was no doubt that visibility was tremendously improved with a raked centre (B-pillar) to assist the driver's field of vision when joining motorways and the like.

Boot space was said to be up 10 per cent at 10.3cu ft instead of the old figure of just

Clay modellers work on the LHD Escort fascia in 1972.

over 8cu ft. The fuel tank remained a 9 gallon vertical unit in one wing with the spare wheel placed opposite, but loading was slightly easier than in the original as the back sill height was reduced by two inches.

What Ford did not detail too precisely at the time was the increase in body weight – 'around, or less than, 100 lbs' was the usual quote. There were two other body minus points. The increase in glass area not only boosted weight, but it also made the vehicle body structure inherently weaker, a factor that was immediately apparent to the works rally team. Ron Mellor, however, naturally prefers to say: 'The Mk1 was probably too strong! Actually we did have the odd customer involved in 1972/73 where the bulkhead behind the rear seat would pull out, so before the Mk2 came along we deleted that feature. In fact both Escorts were extremely strong and torsionally stiff: there was an occasional problem with the bottom of the front pillar (A-pillar) cracking at the lower end in exceptionally hard use [a typical sign of a well-used rally car ...], but we reinforced that up the inside prior to launch.' As far as the author is aware, the new crossmember to pick up the top of the vertically aligned back dampers for all Mk2 Escorts and 1974 model year (say September 1973 onward in manufacturing date) original models was a major improvement in durability of the ordinary Escort for rugged uses such as work along farm tracks and the like. Not only was the damper able to give 'improved ride on those run-out Mk1s and all the later models,' in Ron Mellor's words, but durability of that crossmember's attachment to the body in rough use was also improved.

Why did they have the inclined or 'sea-leg' dampers in the first place? From replies given by Mr Mellor it seems that the primary reason was the hope that some sideways location would be developed by such damper angles, but that didn't really seem to work out in practice, so all saloons went over to the revised location. Ron Mellor emphasized that 'wagons stayed with it'; estates obviously not needing intrusion of a crossmember at damper top mounting height into precious cargo area!

Aerodynamic back-track

Aerodynamically the replacement rear drive Escort was inferior to the original. and this

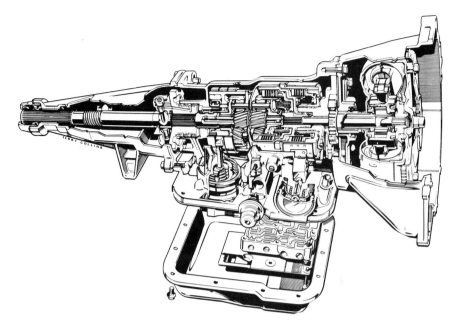

Ford's new European automatic transmission was offered with the new Escort for the first time, mated to 1300 or 1600 engines.

was a point Ford naturally did not highlight at launch time either. Much the same had happened with Capri II: improved creature comforts, extra space, more visibility, but at the penalty price of extra weight and increased aerodynamic Cd (Co-efficient of drag) values. The extent of the aerodynamic backward step in pursuit of comfort and a new showroom look was revealed when the front drive Escort came to the market. In a booklet entitled *Escort, The Technical Story,* Ford's press office recalled, 'The new Escort was to have a clearly identifiable visual character of its own and at the same time achieve a low drag coefficient of 0.40 – a reduction of 12 per cent on the prior model.' Put the Casio to work and one finds that meant Brenda was far from the slippery kind of Escort girl: the Mk 2 Escort averaged out at 0.448, a few percentage points worse (about 5 percent actually) than the original.

Diplomatically, nobody at Dunton discussed the above with me, one senior executive merely commenting mildly, 'I expect you are right', whilst Uwe Bahnsen, Vice President-Design at Ford of Europe pointed out, 'I came to this job in Spring 1976 and in the middle of 1977 responsibility for aerodynamics, too, was assigned to our area. So there is a fundamental difference in the way we work now.' More about that with the front drive Escort description, but it is worth pointing out that German-born Mr Bahnsen had been with Ford 25 years when I interviewed him in 1983 and Ron Mellor had joined Ford in August 1955, so both men were particularly valuable in giving an overall view of the way products arrive in our showrooms from Ford – and their length of service says something about company stability and loyalty too ...

Meanwhile, back inside that Mk2 body we find fundamental improvements that customers appreciated a lot more than percentage points on drag factor. The ventilation system was totally overhauled and went back to the highly effective original Ford Cortina system of disposing separate 'eyeballs' for air flow at each end of the fascia. The front seats were new and the instrumentation was simply superb in respect of clarity, winning Design Council Awards for its black on white messages from beneath a single viewing pane; an idea popularized by BMW, although I believe Rover actually offered it first. Either way it is a feature we take for granted amongst modern mass production saloons and was particularly welcome in the Escort after years of small circular dials, with increasing

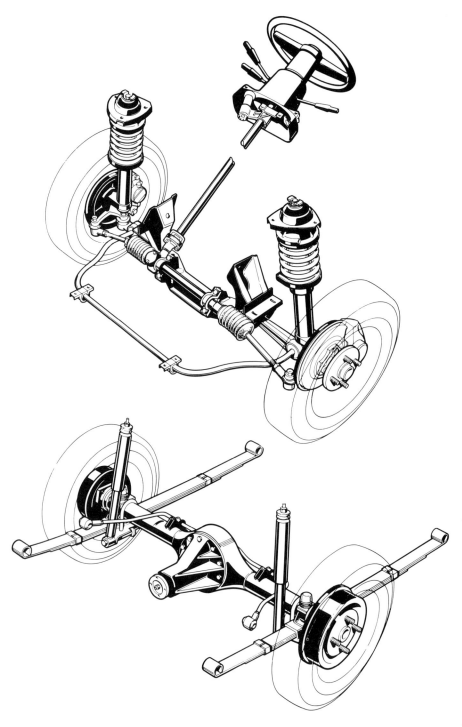

Front and rear suspension systems for the 1975 Escort were altered in detail from the previous model, including three wider leaf springs per side at the back (note roll bar/location linkage, too). The front anti-roll bar thickness was increased, with extra progression allowed in the bump stops, and softer mounting insulation. The illustration of the rear axle amply demonstrates the way in which late model Mk1 Escorts and the 1975-80 models used a near-vertical telescopic damper layout, both dampers mounted ahead of the axle on the U-bracket attachment plates.

amounts of information to impart once Ford had crowded the speedometer with km/h markings as well as mph. The new layout was bigger and 100 per cent better for imparting information faster, even if the scope of information given was censored compared to the originals. For the Mk2, even in Sport or Ghia guise, a water temperature and fuel gauge

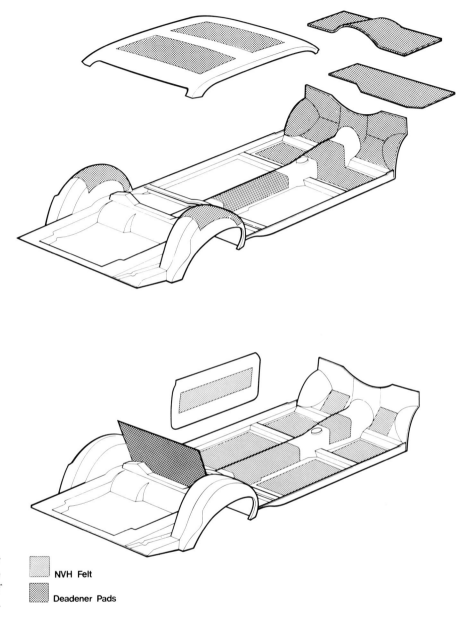

Extra soundproofing was copiously applied to Ford's smallest car of 1975.

NVH Felt

Deadener Pads

was the extent of minor instrumentation. The later RS derivatives did add three minor dials placed between the usual large speedometer and tachometer.

A change of name

Writing of interiors and general equipment reminds one that the biggest change to come on Mk2 was that the mainstream operation took luxury really seriously and introduced the name of Ford-owned styling subsidiary Ghia, in Italy, to the model line in either two-or four-door saloon bodywork. Even in November 1974, Ford were going to call the lesser luxury Escorts by the previous XL designation, but that went in favour of GL before the cars actually reached British showrooms in March 1975. Similarly the old E for Executive snobbery disappeared in favour of the new In-Crowd at Ghia.

The 1975 model range covered 19 basic models. In two-door bodies you could get: an 1100 for £1440; 1100L at £1529; 1300L cost £1591; 1300GL, £1721;1300 Sport, £1803; 1600 Sport, £1933; 1300 Ghia, £2011; 1600 Ghia, £2609. Remembering that it was also significant that it was the main Ford Motor Company who was making sports versions of Escort now (FAVO at Aveley closed at the tail end of 1974, so that plant never produced the revised bodies: see the next Chapter for details of the later RS 2000, Mexico and RS 1800) we now look at the four-door line up. This was basically as for the two-doors, with a price penalty around £50 at the bottom end of the range. No four-door 1300 Sport was offered and it was not long before Ford started juggling around with the two-door range to find a substantially cheaper starting point.

The four-doors, which were first announced with the rest of the range described here for a traditional Ford Brussels début (24 January 1975) and were made available on 4 March that year instead of the originally predicted 19 March – owing to that swift production build-up we described earlier – had the following prices and initial availability. A basic 1100 for £1497; the 1100L with four doors cost £1586; 1300L was £1559; 1300GL, £1777; 1600 Sport, £1999, 1300 Ghia, £2086; 1600 Ghia, £2125.

The Escort Estate was detailed by Ford a little later than the saloon (31 January 1975) as befitted a slightly later engineering schedule. Prices and models, however, were detailed right from the start. The basic 1300 and 1100 models were £1619 and £1701, with a 1300 L at £1790 and 1300 GL for £1920. There was no equivalent to the 1300 GT Estate that had been offered in the earlier seventies Escorts.

We should also note at this point that the Estate (Wagon in Fordspeak) was a very clever amalgamation of Mk2 square front (to the centre B-pillar) and the original long-side window/77.4cu ft rear end. A remark that also applied to the Mk2 Escort van in its second rear drive generation, although its lack of trim increased load area to 82cu ft. *All* Escort estates came with radial-ply tyres, but as on the main saloon car range, you had to pay extra for front disc brakes, unless you had the 1300, in which case they were standard.

Sparkler show accompanied new Escort's assembly at Halewood. Note the lower inlet panels that still remained hidden behind the bumper at the front.

To put the later Escort range in price perspective it's worth noting that in the Spring of 1975, when the cars first appeared on the UK market, the £1440 starting price, with Ghias just bumbling over the £2000 mark, was considered expensive. The Vauxhall Viva started at £1354 and one could have substantially the same car, but called a Magnum with an SOHC 2.3-litre motor, for £1935. Austin offered the hapless Allegro from £1458 to £1982 for a 1750 HL and the Hillman Avenger was priced from nearly £100 cheaper than the new Escort. So it was no surprise when Ford dived beneath the £1300 mark for the replacement Escort by dint of the Popular stripped-out derivative, less than three months after the later Escorts had become available in the showrooms.

The mechanical story

The new body was the visible difference in the second Escort breed, but a Ford PR staff briefing of the period reminded all concerned that, 'In all, the new Escort contains over 15,000 new parts'. What else had been done?

Rather more than originally anticipated was the answer! For Ford eventually crash tested for the safety tests, double the number of cars predicted and constructed 27 test and durability prototypes of various kinds. A lot of practical work went into the suspension. As recounted, the revised layout was produced for the late 1973 and all 1974 Mk1 Escorts. This meant the vertical dampers and the introduction of the anti roll bar/axle location linkage over the back axle, but just how fundamentally Ford has changed the layout was spelt out when the new body was introduced.

Compared to the original Escort suspension, only the track control arms and the front anti-roll bar clamps were the same. The anti-roll bar size went from 0.787in to 0.886in (20mm to 22mm) to increase roll stiffness by 20 per cent. The hydraulic dampers had new valve settings to provide an increase of 80 per cent in bump action and a phenomenal 150 per cent in rebound. Such changes were aimed at extra ride control and side wind stability,

New Escort and Capri II share the Halewood facility in the opening months of 1975.

a feature the Germans had never been too enchanted with, and that was before the previous Escort was slackened off in one of those perpetual Ford damper/spring rate changes that haunt the production life of Escorts and Capris.

The new spring rates showed a distinctive dive toward firm control on all models. All except the Sport shared a 96lb in. rate spring up front (not far away from previous RS model figures) with the Sport over 10 per cent harder at 109lb in. The rear leaf springs were substantially altered too. The vertical dampers allowed a three-leaf layout instead of four that were 1.97in. (50mm) broad instead of the new trio's 2.362in. (60mm). Compared with the quad leaf damping, the replacement vertical dampers allowed 14 per cent extra rebound action and 20 per cent bonus on bump. The theme of extra roll stiffness was extended through the rear roll bar, up 30 per cent compared to the pre-vertical damper arrangement. Rear spring rates were 105lb in. on all non-Sport saloons and 116lb in. for Sports and all estates.

Although much of the suspension work did appear in late model Mk1 Escort, there was considerable fine tuning before the later Escort appeared. A Ford briefing revealed: 'This rear layout was introduced a year ago on the previous Escort to give us service experience, before the new model was launched and to ease the production switch. Since then it has been refined and developed for the new model; combined front and rear suspension tuning had reduced understeer by 75 per cent and roll by 23 per cent. Total cornering power is improved by 10 per cent [some attributable to tyre changes and dependent on model] and there is significantly less fore and aft pitch'.

Mmmm: to reduce understeer by 75 per cent suggests there was something awfully wrong before! And 75 per cent of what? I'll never know now, but the writer was perhaps the best technical author working in Britain today, according to editors I consulted on the subject. We do know that one of the big factors in the fight to improve stability and cut understeer was the reduction in geometric toe-out owing to suspension movement in the previous layout's front end. The stiffer front settings and roll bar were said to have reduced this variable toe-out (where the rear of the wheel and tyre runs further outward than the front) by 60 per cent. Again, the figure does not speak volumes for the Escort in its earlier seventies guise!

It should be noted, however, that Ford were now discussing a model range entirely equipped with radial tyres which involved a number of basic changes to cope with their steel-braced characteristics. Much of the increased cornering capability could be traced to the fact that 4.5 x 13in. steel wheels with 155 SR radials were now fitted as minimum equipment to all models, save for the drum-braked 11 and 1300s (you could specify servo-assisted front discs at extra cost) which returned to the original 12in. rims, but again with a 4.5in. ledge to carry 155 RS-12 radials.

The Sport and Ghia were specified with 5in. styled steel wheels in 13in. diameter, Ghia using 155 radials as standard whilst the Sport – with an average ride height half an inch lower than the rest of the range – was allowed 175/70s as standard. Originally, only the Michelin or Uniroyal 175 section tyres were approved by engineering. Michelin ZX or Semperit were specified in the smaller size of steel braced radials, and the textile-braced Dunlop SP68 or Goodyear G800 were also endorsed by engineering, although the car had been specifically developed around the new breed of steel-braced rubber.

Wider engine choice

Now the mass production plants in Britain and West Germany could offer customers a choice of power plant from 1097cc/48 DIN bhp to 1598cc/84 bhp, the bigger Kent engine previously restricted to the FAVO Escort or larger mainstream Fords of the Cortina/Capri

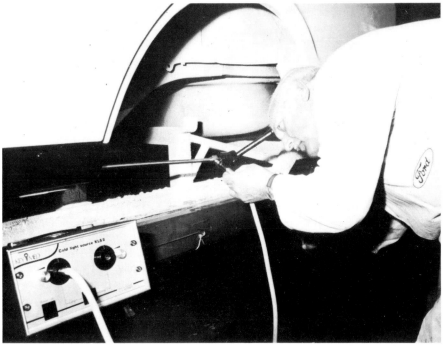

Steps in the fight to reduce corrosion included the wax spray being applied beneath the later Escort, and a fibre optic probe to check wax application within enclosed body areas.

ilk. When the latter two Fords could be offered with SOHC 1.6-litre derivatives of 2-litre SOHC Pinto, then selling a 1600 Sport with Kent engine became a very attractive proposition for Ford to dispense with this long-lived and durable power plant at maximum profit.

So the Mk2 Escort used all crossflow Kent engines with cast iron bores of 80.98mm, all produced on the same tooling. To obtain capacities of 1097, 1297 and 1598cc the cast nodular graphite iron crankshaft had a stroke of 53.29mm, 62.99mm and 77.62mm respectively. The pushrod OHV fours had a 9:1 compression in largest and smallest models, whilst both versions of the 1300 motor had the slightly elevated 9.2:1 CR. Carburation was by single choke Motorcraft-Ford on the 1100 and 1300 Escorts with both Sport and Ghia models taking Weber twin-choke carburation, along with new inlet and exhaust manifolding, plus the traditional GT camshaft with 272° inlet and exhaust duration to pep up their outputs.

Now Ford quoted all German DIN power figures, showing a slight loss over some earlier quotes. The 1100 was rated at 48bhp at 5500 revs and 54lb ft torque at 3000rpm. For the 9:1 CR 1300 they quoted 57bhp at the same rpm and 3000rpm was also peak torque for the 1300 at 67lb ft. In GT/Sport/Ghia trim the 1.6 motor delivered a claimed 84bhp at the common 5500rpm peak and 92ft lb torque at 3500 revs. The 1.3 now spoke of 70bhp for a motor once rated at over 80 gross SAE horsepower, this produced at 5500rpm too. Maximum torque was 500rpm further up the rpm scale for 1.3 Sport/Ghia at 68lb ft at 4000rpm. All should run with no bother at all on four star, but you might find a fleet model that would take two star on an 8:1 CR, when buying secondhand.

There were important transmission changes for the new Escort as well. The automatic option became a lot more efficient than the old BW-equipped cars, Ford introducing their own modern Bordeaux-built C3 three-speed with its own oil radiator – using the transmission oil that needed no service changes – built into the bottom of the engine front water radiator. Automatic ratios on all Escorts for which it could be optionally specified (not for Sports or 1100s) were: 2.474:1 in first, 1.474:1 in second and 1:1 in third, coupled to a 2.111:1 reverse. A torque convertor was used as the basic principle in the automatic box with a maximum ratio multiplication of 2.30; axle ratios were left as for the equivalent standard car.

There were some changes in all four-speed synchromesh manual gearboxes at this point. Basically the 11 and 1300 models stayed with the original launch ratios whilst the GT-engined Sport/Ghia line adopted a stronger, closer ratio gear set. The uprating steps include a 7.5in. diameter clutch plate on all models – they had started off being 6.5in. on 1100 – and went on to cover, 'shot peening of the gear set and the use of high capacity ball bearings and modified needle bearings for the gear cluster,' according to Ford in 1975.

The ratios for Sport/Ghia (with ordinary 11/1300 in brackets) were as follows: first, 3.337 (3.656); second, 1.995 (2.185); third, 1.418 (1.425); reverse, 3.868 (4.235). All Escorts shared a direct 1:1 top gear ratio, but the final drives were a far more varied bunch than in 1968 (when there were subsequent changes in production anyway). In 1975 the Escorts were given the original 4.125:1 to share on 1100 and 1300 GT-engined Sport/Ghia whilst the ordinary 1300 got a 3.89:1 rear axle and the 1600 GT motor within Sport/Ghia was asked to pull a 3.54:1 final drive ratio.

On the road this meant the 1100 and GT-motivated 1300s should have 16.3mph per 1000rpm in 13 inch wheel specification: over 4000rpm at 70mph. The most relaxed figure, 19mph per 1000rpm for 1.6 Ghia/Sport meant 70mph demanded just 3700rpm, with consequent motorway cruising comfort and mpg benefits.

Sound deadening and increased passenger appeal were primary objectives in the replacement Escort's design brief and Ford made a lot of progress. Deadener pads or felt were applied to the floor panels, inside the doors, rear bulkhead and back pillars. The GL had extra insulation over the rear transmission tunnel and within the wheel arches with 'a sandwiched foam material applied to the engine compartment on the cowl top. The latter is also on the Sport, which otherwise is equipped like the Base and L-models,' said Ford in a contemporary briefing.

Naturally the Ghia models gained extra sound deadening treatment. A felt sheet was

Rear of the later Escort continued the squarer body line. The reversing lamps were now built into the wrap-round rear lamp clusters, and this Ghia model proudly incorporates a wide, and useful, variety of protective bumper and side strip inlays.

New interiors were warmly received by press and public, both for the use of extra glass to rid the rear of a slightly claustrophobic atmosphere, as well as for the improved efficiency of the control and instrumentation layouts. This Escort also marked the reappearance of the legendary, and extremely efficient, Cortina MkI aeroflow 'eyeball' to supply ventilation, in place of the original central outlets. This 1975 Escort Sport shows how the flat three-spoke sports wheel of RS parentage was adopted for a wider audience.

applied to the roof panel and a perforated headlining added, along with padding behind the instrument panel, to reduce the noise levels of higher performance engines, as well as the usual wiper and heater blower fan disturbances.

Fundamental engineering also improved Ford's self-imposed NVH standards. Both the rear engine mount and modified exhaust hangers, along with the revised rear suspension, 'directed the firing frequencies of the engine at around 5000rpm into the side rails of the floorpan, where resonance is less likely,' reported Ford. All this work was aimed at reducing or eliminating the motorway drone that is likely to affect any four-cylinder saloon with a weight-conscious steel body between 4000 and 5000rpm in top gear. The Mexico in Mk1 shell with 1600 GT power was a particularly bad offender and these new moves meant one had to be travelling well beyond Britain's legal limit before the resonance problem reappeared, whereas the Mk1 Mexico could drive one insane at a sustained 70 or 80mph. Much the same went for the first 1300 GT and later E models, which had to work hard to provide a legal motorway pace and consequently let the owners know all about such labours.

Call for weight watchers!

'Weight conscious' I said of the Escort's body construction, and I earlier recorded the Ford quote of around 100lb for increased body weights when comparing the 1968-74 Escort with its successor. To make a fair comparison I selected the 1968 and 1975 launch weights for various Escorts and found the penalty was almost double what was anticipated in 1975. On the basic 1100 there was a 202lb gain (1642lb for the Mk1 versus 1844lb) and for the 1300 the original was booked at 1647lb versus 1872lb in 1975. There was a more understandable 225lb increase for the 1.6 Sport versus the original 1300 GT (1716lb versus 1941lb) and the 1.6 Ghia was the fattest of the new lot at 1987lb, compared to 1844lb of the basic model.

Ford had provided a very much more civilized machine as compensation, but did performance suffer?

In connection with the Mk1 and Mk2 Escort my weight theory is partially substantiated. When *Autocar* first tested an 1100 it tipped MIRA's scales at only 1704lb; the stripped out 1975 Popular and the Mk2 1100 L were 1845lb, some 141lb heavier. For 1300 models the *Autocar* tests showed over 130lb difference.

Against the watch? One could make the figures prove anything! In the original range one finds 12.4s and 13.8s reported as the 0-60mph capabilities of the 1300 GT (on 12 inch wheels) and Sport (on 13inch), whilst for the Mk2 brigade one had to have a 1600 Sport to produce 12.3s for 0-60mph, with the Ghia 1300 GT/Sport-engined Mk2 Escort managing 13.5s for the same sprint.

Top speed? In the 1100 capacity there was really no difference. Around 80mph was it for *Autocar*'s samples, but they did show a two second 0-60mph advantage over the original 1968 model, because those crossflow engines were uprated in the seventies. Amongst the quicker derivatives the fastest mainstream Mk1 was the 96mph 1300 GT of 1971 (uprated engine) whilst the quickest of the 1975 bunch was the 1600 Sport at just 97mph. Truly that should be compared with the original Mexico, which managed another 2mph, underlining that the first car definitely did have a slightly superior shape and weight, for the test Mexico sprinted from rest to 60mph in 10.7s compared with 12.3 for Sport with the same power plant specification. RS Mk2 models are described in the next chapter.

Fuel consumption? Here *Autocar* figures showed a substantial bonus for the later model: in 1100 guise it was 32.1mpg overall versus 27.6, and the 1300 returned 27.6 against 26.7mpg. For the 1.3 GT-engined Escort Sport/Ghia, *Autocar's* overall figure was a creditable 29.3mpg compared to 25 and 25.4mpg of the earlier Sport and 1300 GT.

Equipment

The fuel crisis and its full impact came after the point at which we have seen Ford froze the replacement Escort's specification. Thus, all due credit to the researchers and marketing men who predicted so accurately that people might trade down in car size, but they wanted at least the same, prefereably more, luxury features than had been installed on their larger cars.

From Ford's viewpoint there had always been an internal feeling that little cars meant little or no profit. I suspect that the loss-making activities of Leyland with their technically advanced front drive Mini/1100/1300/1800 family added rather too much weight to the arguments against front drive inside Ford. Today the technology of front drive cars is so well known and proven that full cost advantage can be taken of multi-national mass production prices; in fact, most of the majority who now make front drive feel that this

Also announced in January 1975 was the estate version of the new Escort, but it was only half as new in body terms, retaining the original back section of 53 cu ft. Only 1100 and 1300 engines were offered, the bigger motor automatically earning disc brakes up front.

system has a price and weight advantage inherently, because of the lack of rear propshaft and driven back axle as additional cost and weight components.

Ghia operations in Turin, guided by Filippo Sapino and Tom Tjaarda, were the key to Ford's extra profitability in the small car sector. Beginning with Capri II and graduating to Granada, Ghia had shown that it was possible for Ford to compete against the traditional middle class marques for custom. In Britain BL's ageing Triumph models with mandatory wood dressings were prime meat for a Ford attack that proved ever more effective through the seventies.

For the Escort, a Ghia badge gave the following features: wood veneer fascia and glove box; vinyl roof; tinted glass; unique plush and easily marked cloth trim; reclining seat backs with handwheel control; and a carpet that Ford described as shag pile, and on which I can make no decent comment. Carpeting also extended to the boot on Ghias, while more plebian versions stuck to a mat. The steering wheel on Ghia was the basic two-spoke range design – just the Sport had the flat three-spoke tiller – but for Ghia it had a 'soft-feel wheel rim', i.e. it was of a plastic and looked and felt a bit like leather!

From the start even the cheapest new Escorts had an alternator, two-speed wipers with electric screenwash, and radials, but items like halogen headlamp bulbs, reversing lamps, interior carpeting and a dipping rear view mirror were reserved for GL, Ghia and Sport purchasers. In fact the L marked the beginning of standard heated rear screen fitment and it did have carpeting, the dipping mirror and reversing lamps too; at this point one got hazard warning flashers as well.

As ever the GL marked a good compromise between Ghia prices and a reasonable level of standard equipment, sharing items such as the vanity mirror, reclining seat back rests and the square halogen headlamps. Once again lights were used to differentiate the model range, only GL and Ghia having the large rectangular units, whilst the Sport had halogen units in the traditional circular lights, and L and beneath got what they were given within round units, too. Both Sport and Ghia shared auxiliary long range lamps on rust-prone brackets. The Sport was also given a minor and tasteful striping job; the Ghias had a heavy rubber side moulding that saved car park damage when they were finished in the almost inevitable (but optional) metalperlic paints. Note that in 1975's launch range,

Photographed in 1974, the Escort Sport was effectively a new body resting over old Mexico mechanicals. As such its 1.6-litre Kent engine, as still used to supply FF1600 today, saw off the more expensive new Mexico with SOHC 1.6-litre engine ... but only in terms of commercial success. The later Mexico was the better all round enthusiast transport.

having a Ghia model did not automatically entitle you to in-car entertainment or a sunroof, features we now take for Ghia-granted.

Street life

The press were taken to Portugal's Algarve region to preview the latest Escorts and were treated to uncharacteristic wet gales – which at least gave them a reasonable idea of how the new Fords would perform in England! The late John Bolster in a March edition of *Autosport* gave his readers some accurate insight into the qualities of the boxy Escort.

'The new cars have a very different personality from their predecessors... As regards performance, the basic 1100 feels a bit underpowered to the enthusiastic driver, though there are many British motorists who would find it adequate for their needs. It has a smooth wee engine but for very little more money you can have the 1300, which is a better all round car and seems to use no more petrol ... The 1600 Sport is a really lively car, but less refined. However it is far better than the old Escort in this respect, because the main boom period has been shifted up to the top of the rev range, instead of occurring right in the middle of normal cruising velocities. It has a harder ride than other Escorts, in the interest of sporting handling, and as always, the gearchange is superb. The new Ford automatic transmission was also sampled, my sole criticism concerning the kickdown to bottom gear, which can only be performed at rather low speeds.

'The ride of all models, other than the Sport, is enormously improved. There's a marked absence of pitching and rolling and the cars ride very level. During normal driving, the handling is much as before, with a moderate degree of understeer, but when pressed to the limit, the rear end break adhesion, though controllability remains excellent; indeed some drivers prefer a car which tends to hang out the tail. One is conscious that the car has a live axle of course, but the compromise chosen is a very good one, giving praiseworthy steadiness under heavy braking on wet or dry roads.

'In everyday driving, the greater improvement is in the reduction of boom periods, which are now only noticeable on a trailing throttle; that irritating driveshaft backlash seems to have been totally eliminated, too. Very high marks must be given for outstanding stability in side winds,' said Bolster with typical British reserve of a launch lashed by 'gales of unprecedented severity', a conclusion I remember my then colleagues reporting back and concurring with heartily. Mind you those representatives had also enjoyed a number of lighter diversions, including a naked midnight chase and the consumption of a candle to follow an innocent bowl of flowers...!

The new Escort could be driven by the press in the Spring of 1975. Over Portuguese roads impressions were favourable and the consensus was that Ford had done a good job in further refining their product, without blazing any new trails. This is the four door, 1.3 Ghia.

Returning to the reception accorded Escort in March 1975 the consensus was typified by an *Autocar* test conclusion: 'It is not obvious on paper why Ford should have replaced the old Escort with this one. On the road it is obvious at once. The new car is altogether nicer to drive, and one can point immediately to improvements in handling, noise level and driver visibility to justify the change.'

Later reviews all pointed to interior comfort – particularly improved ventilation and clean instrumentation – as reasons enough for buying the Mk2 over the original, along with the efficient disposition of stalks on the steering column to control lights, wipers, horn and screenwashers. There were some reservations over a back seat described as 'a bit cramped' in some quarters, and it is fair to say that the 1980 front drive models did offer a substantial bonus on this point.

Production life

The Escort was advertised under the heading, 'The New Ford Escort. A Change for the Better'. Inflation, however, and the growing effectiveness of the imported car representatives within the UK market, soon had Ford of Britain Managing Director Terry Beckett (as he was then known in official releases: later it was Sir Terence Beckett CBE, B.Sc (Econ), C.Eng, F.I.Mech.E, of the CBI) standing up at a 30 June 1975 London press conference to introduce, amongst other moves such as restricting their car price increase to an average 2.3 per cent, the £1299 Escort Popular. Details were embargoed until 1 July when we could see why Beckett said, 'We believe we have dealt inflation a blow today. Incidentally we have also put the economic boot in a bit amongst the importers'. That's right, you tell 'em Tel ... It was time for the men of Essex to strike back with Beckett promising, 'We are going to have a go. At least it's better than sitting on our backsides wondering what the next tide is going to bring in'. The Escort, which Ford then described as 'the best selling car in both Britain and Europe', was to be sold 'at a price which met head-on even much smaller imported cars,' said the Ford conference report.

Re-introducing the Popular badge was brilliant in a price-fighting stance, but what did they do to the basic model to justify what was effectively a discount on a model that had only been on sale for three months across Europe?

Ford said in 1975, 'The only cost saving on specification has been achieved by giving bumpers, door handles and window surrounds a black finish instead of chrome; removing the sound insulation from under the moulded rubber floor mats; not offering a passenger's parcel shelf, and specifying plain 12in wheels, with hub caps, fitted with 6.00-12in cross-ply tyres'. Back to Square One ...

Looking back it seems obvious that Ford pitched their new model a little too high on the price scale initially, but as with other Ford launch mistakes the marketing and advertising departments, acting on the company's superb feedback from the market place, swept in to counter the problem with lightning reactions for a multi-national juggernaut of a company.

Mechanically, the Popular had an economy-biased engine as 'Ford market research indicates double the interest in consumption compared with two years ago'. As an interim measure engineering provided the usual 1.1 high compression four with carburation biased toward leaner mixture (more air, less fuel) with a limiting stop on the throttle opening. Ford's publicity people reckoned an independent test had shown economy gains of 'up to 15 per cent with touring consumptions of over 44 mpg'. On the road the Popular returned 32.1mpg for *Autocar* who predicted typical mpg at 35 ... They measured constant speed consumption, which makes an interesting contrast with today's machinery, from a maximum 56.3mpg at 30mph to 30.8mpg at 70mph.

Ford offered the Popular derivative in 1100 and 1300 versions (the smaller engine rated at 41bhp) in two-door saloon style only, but the £1399 Popular Plus could be had in either two-or four-doors. The PP put back some of those cost-cutting Popular features so that there was an underfelt and carpet; cloth seat trim, reversing lamps, radial-shod 13in. wheels; dipping rear view mirror; and restoration of the parcel shelf. Mmm: discounting by

In September 1978, the Escort L gained some of the features previously reserved for the GL and Ghia models. Extra equipment included squared-off tungsten bulb headlamps, sports wheels of notably greater offset, and the Ghia's side rubbing-strip. Internally a two-spoke steering wheel and the standard adoption of an intermittent wiper sweep facility were new.

any other name! At this point the unlabelled base Escorts were dropped.

If you buy one of the Popular or Popular Plus derivatives, the chances are that it will be a very basic machine originally purchased for a fleet, but the full range of Escort options was available. So, you could find servo-assisted front disc brakes instead of drums, halogen headlamps, or even automatic transmission with the 1.3-litre four.

Also in July 1975, Ford upgraded standard Escort equipment specifications, ensuring that all L offerings had front disc brakes, 13in. wheels and reclining seat backs. Such Escorts were identified now by bright metal window surrounds, twin coachlines and black-sprayed sills. The GL gained the steel sport road wheel of 5in. rim x 13in. diameter and pronounced body side-mouldings.

The 1975 introductory year was notable for the number of model names and adjustments made, particularly as the RS 2000 and RS 1800 also made their comeback to the line with the Mexico joining them in 1976: all events covered in the next Chapter.

Even with this Popular and Popular Plus initiative, inflation soon regained its ground and typical 1976 prices ranged from the 1100 Popular at £1678 to the 1600 Ghia four-door at a boggling £2986. Even that would look cheap in 1980 ...!

During 1976 very few changes were made. February marked the adoption of the 41 bhp 1100 economy-carburated engine with its flaccid 52lb ft of torque at 3000rpm as the standard unit for 1.1 Escorts. The trouble was that most reps and similar professional motorists on the move thrashed the things so hard in pursuit of any sign of response that overall economy dropped back to beneath 30 mpg.

Just how clever Ford has been in responding to 1975's inflationary conditions was revealed in the Summer of 1976 when they reported a 1975 post tax profit of £7.8 million, compared with £2.4 million in the previous year. Escort had played its role well – and in July 1976 Ford underlined their marked strength with the biggest market share for 15 years. The Escort was No.1 in the UK that month with 14.2 per cent of all sales versus Cortina's 12.3 per cent. Overall they had plenty to crow about. As they said at the time, 'Over the

The Escort Sport was retrimmed in September 1978, gaining this Chevron-patterned fabric in place of the original Cadiz stripes. The MW/LW radio became a standard feature at this point.

September 1978 revised estates included this L model which shared the blacked-out grilled, square headlamps, wider wheels, hounds-tooth fabric trim, improved sound proofing, two-spoke steering wheel and intermittent wiper setting of the L saloons.

seven months to date this year, Ford has edged into outright leadership for the first time ever by taking 27.1 per cent of the market'. It actually did mark the arrival of Ford at the overall lead it maintained in the eighties.

By June 1977 Ford were able to offer a special version of the Escort 1100 Popular for the disabled, the DHSS announcing that it would be supplying 250 such Fords to disabled ex-servicemen. At this stage over 60 per cent of all Ford vehicles converted by specialists Feeny & Johnson were Escorts. The estate models were also used for this purpose, equipped with a steering column extension up to a foot longer, and a single push-pull handlebar control for braking and acceleration. These were supplied to bodies such as the Thalidomide Trust.

Major suspension changes

It took until October 1977 before Ford engineering's latest Escort suspension thinking for the mainstream product was revealed, and then it harked back to the RS 2600 Capri of 1970! Now the rear axle was controlled by a single leaf spring on each side, a feature that had previously been exploited in racing (sometimes only as a vestigial glassfibre spring to meet the regulations, whilst a coil or torsion bar did the work!) and had proved an exceptionally popular feature when included as a homologation component within the tremendously effective Group 1 competition Escort RS 2000. At least, it was originally intended only for competition but like so many other Escort sporting features from flared arches to 16-valve engines, a much wider public was subsequently found ...

For October 1977 Escorts onward, the single-leaf layout was introduced to counter, 'complaints about the firmness of Escort ride and in step with longer term weight saving objectives,' said Ford at the time. It was pointed out that the single leaf eliminated totally, 'the interleaf friction which hambers small suspension movements ... The primary objective was to soften initial suspension movements front and rear, to remove the joggly feel over surfaces with small irregularities and increase the total refinement inside the car,' felt Ford Engineering at Dunton.

Although the Escort Ghia was a common sight on these alloy wheels (also a feature on Capri Ghia), they were actually an option in 1978. Standard features were much as before, concentrated on extra trim items, but a remote control door mirror was included.

Simultaneously, they offset the top mounting for the front struts, reducing side loadings on the damper piston and, it was hoped, preventing the 'stiction' that they had been aware of in the Mk2 from the start, and had endeavoured to sort out with special damper fluids in 1975. Once again dampers were recalibrated all round, this time with a bias toward a softer ride, and roll bar diameter was reduced for the combined axle linkage and rear axle bar.

There was some engine work on the 1300 at the same point to make public with, 'a redesign of the Ford carburettor to give better mixture control under part throttle operation, which gives better performance and economy. The acceleration from 0-60mph has been reduced from 16.5s to 15.5s, while DIN touring consumption is improved from 32.5 to 34.4mpg.' Ford were obviously a lot happier about their fabled corporate image by now, for it was in October 1977 that the Escort adopted the blue Ford oval badging front and rear, a rather neater solution than years of straggling FORD chrome capitals. Also at this point we started to see the engine size badged on the near side of the boot. Estate cars at last picked up a rear wash/wipe system, standard for GL and optional otherwise.

The 1977 sales year saw Ford pull a slight but permanent lead over BL Cars with 25.7 per cent versus 24.3. At that time imports accounted for 45 per cent of British sales (in the eighties the figures were usually another 10 per cent up) but Ford could be quite John Bullish about Escort for 'nearly 92 per cent of all Escorts sold in the UK are made at Halewood in Lancashire, only the Ghia and RS derivatives being sourced from Saarlouis in Germany. Output at Ford's Merseyside plant has been very much on target in recent months [as at Autumn '78], averaging well over 900 cars per day'. So far as individual Ford model leadership in Britain was concerned the Escort had to give up its 1976 Number 1 spot to Cortina until the front drive models came along.

In March 1978 the Poles cheered Escort production along at Halewood with an order for 500 Escort Sports worth £1.3 million. On 13 September of that year Ford unveiled the last substantial changes on the rear drive Escort line, a lot of them cosmetic to follow the classic Ford marketing recipe of withholding tempting trim morsels until a model had aged sufficiently in the market place to require further cheer. Then said tidbits can be popped into the inclusive price of 'new' showroom models.

All 1979 Escorts except the Ghia went to a matt black radiator grille at this point, the

Ghia retaining a chrome surround. The soft-feel two-spoke steering wheel appeared on all but Sport and RS Escorts and the offset 5.0 x 13in. steel wheel was adopted from September 1978, too, boosting front and rear track by 1¼in. Again this applied primarily to the mainstream models, although Ford at the time only excluded RS 2000 specifically.

The wheel advantage

In line with the new wheels, which really did give the car a far less top-heavy appearance, the basic Popular gained 5 x 13in. steel rims with 155 SR 13 tyres. Perhaps the most important thing to remember about Escort IIs with the 13in. diameter steel wheels is that the increase compared to the original car did allow larger brakes within: 9.6in. front discs with 8.0 x 1.5in. back drums on all but the Ghias, which were originally specified with a slightly larger back drum of 9.0 x 1.7in. For the all drum-braked cars the Mk2 had provided an extra ¼in. width, 8.0 x 1.75in. front and the usual 8.0 x 1.5in. backs, which were self-adjusting throughout the range.

For September 1978 the individual model changes were: Popular Plus, heated rear window and side coachlines; Escort L, Tungsten bulb square headlamps; side protection moulding; silver road wheels in steel, houndstooth fabric check trim (ex-Fiesta), a perforated headlining and sound deadening for the roof panel. The latter two moves took the L-models, best sellers within the Escort range, toward original Ghia specification. Simultaneously Ford introduced the intermittent wiper arrangement for L-trim Escorts.

The GL gained a Diamond fabric trim, MW/LW Ford-branded radio and all the uprated interior of the L. The Sport was also retrimmed, this finish known as Chevron and gained a cross between L and GL trim in that it also had the improved sound deadening and headlining treatment, along with an MW/LW radio. The black grille suited this model well as it also wore black stripes and bumpers, which carried on the quarter section tradition begun by Lotus Cortina in 1963. Standard features of the Ghia had remained substantially unaltered over the years but most examples now had the optional eight-spoke alloy wheels, often also seen on Capri Ghia. Amongst the items listed as standard that were not mentioned specifically in the original Ghia press descriptions were a push-button radio and remote control driver's door mirror. Naturally, the Estates shared in the general improvements, so an L-level wagon would now come with the square headlamps, heavily

The October 1979 Escort Linnet was based on the Popular Plus, but included a radio and some GL items for a special price of £3385.

offset steel 5 x 13in. wheels and the rest of the trim changes, all most likely to be found on a T-plate onward example in the UK.

From an ownership viewpoint the post September 1978 Escort was not just about showroom tinsel, for the larger service schedule was now to be performed at 12,000 mile intervals with an abbreviated 6000 miler (which still demanded an oil and filter change for the engine). Ford then had 1200 UK dealers – the official figure in March 1984 was 1241 – and 5300 in Europe. The company reckoned the new Escort was cheaper to run: 'One of the cheapest cars in its class to maintain,' was their justified boast. Ford felt this was because of features like self-adjusting front and rear brakes with inspection apertures at the back; maintenance free wheel bearings; transparent battery, brake fluid and washer reservoirs; life lubricated suspension and steering; printed circuit instrument cluster with easy access; excellent engine accessibility; and a body designed for cheap accident repair.

The Specials

The final full year of Escort rear drive production was 1979 and it was broadly characterized by a number of Special, or Limited Edition Escorts to assist sales in the UK. Something achieved with singular success so far as production was concerned, for Halewood made the second largest total number of Escorts since production had started (185,525), although Saarlouis continued to reflect a drop in Continental Escort manufacture, reaching 83,205 in comparison with the 1975 peak of over 200,000 and a 1976 output beyond 160,000.

Some routine changes were made. In Britain the complete mainstream line benefited from viscous fan coupling. This simply meant that the fan drive – which produces a drain on engine power with consequent slight mpg/power penalties, was not engaged until needed at slower speeds, usually under 2500 engine rpm. A brake fluid warning light and carpet for the base estate were also introduced at this April 1979 date. By September 1979 the Popular, Popular Plus and all basic estates were provided with hazard warning flashers and inertia reel seat belts. The Sport also took on a cigar lighter and centre console in Autumn 1979. That console, designed for a mono radio and 7 watt speaker, was also optionally available, as was another design for stereo units, or combined cassette/radio layouts, together with storage space for ten cassettes.

The Escort Harrier was not so much a run-out special as a celebration of the company's World Championship victory in rallying. It combined Sport motivation with an improved interior, standard alloy wheels and the fitment of a rear spoiler. My next door neighbour referred to it as 'the gasman's car', because, like so many examples, mine was in company corporate colours of white and blue!

The Goldcrest arrived in the closing months of Escort sales in Britain. It was based on the 1300 L saloon and cost £3877.

From October 1979 onward the Special Edition ploys marched forward. On 16 October they took the 1300 Popular Plus four-door and dressed it up with GL seats, head restraints, push button radio, body tape side stripe, passenger door mirror and three-spoke sports steering wheel. That was priced at £3385 and called the Linnet. This compared with the typical 1979 range-starting Escort cost of £3003, ranging to £4700 for the 1600 Ghia four-door.

Very heavily promoted from its 26 December launch onward, including a TV ad, was the white or silver Escort Harrier. The white and blue model was designed to trade on Ford's 1979 World Championship Rally title and cost £4330, with the silver finish an extra £35.83. The Harrier was based on a 1600 Sport and had a planned production run of 1500 units, all with the 80bhp plus 1.6 Kent crossflow and suspension settings to set one's eyes wobbling. Or was that the sensitivity of the Recaro front seats in transmitting every bump? Anyway it was fair value with those super seats allied to 6 x 13in. FAVO four-spoke alloys carrying 175/70 SR radials; the soft rubbery rear spoiler; tinted glass; remote control driver's door mirror; and a push-button radio within the black 'Beta Plus' black-trimmed cockpit.

Earlier in 1979 there was a very limited, geographically-speaking, special Escort. This was the May Capital-badged Escort for Londoners in red at £2995 or orchid at £3023, both based on the four-door 1300L.

In May 1980 came the final nationwide Ford Special Edition Escort, Goldcrest. This was based on the 1.3 and 1.6L four-door saloons, with the wheel colours coded to the main body hue. Equipment included those GL seats and head restraints with Ghia valances; Ford M32 radio and clock in the centre console; a side stripe beneath the usual moulding protection; rubber inserts for the bumpers, swiped from more richly endowed Escort brethren; passenger door mirror; and the faithful three-spoke sports steering wheel.

By August 1980 it was widely known that a front drive Escort was on the way that Autumn and the last price span made interesting reading in reflection of some of the most inflationary years the British economy has ever known. Remember Escort II originally started at £1440? In June 1980 the cheapest Escort was the Popular Plus two-door at £3276, and the 1600 Ghia had reached £4726 in manual four-speed form, or broke the £5000 barrier at £5112 with the Ford C3 automatic option.

It's time to head off into the performance section again ...! Victim of this journalistic assault is an original Ghia Escort. I had just been told that the new Escort 'doesn't oversteer at all'.

If you take only the full production 1975-79 years of Escort II, British and German production was well-balanced with Halewood contributing 840,404 and West Germany, 848,388 for a total of 1,688,792 Mk2 Escorts in those years.

The second range of Escort saloons, estates and vans had done a good workmanlike job for company and customers alike, but by 1980 there was already a front drive small Ford (Fiesta in 1976) and it was only a matter of time before Escort followed suit. It had been a good act, selling over three million rear drive Escorts in total, but the new front drive generation for the eighties would offer a better all round deal for Ford and its customers ...

Now let's see what the sporting Escorts materialized as in Mk2 guise.

The 1.6-litre Escort Sport effectively replaced the previous Mexico in engine power, but there was still a need for the RS engineering improvements detailed in the next chapter.

Chapter 6

The performers, part 2

The second generation of RS Escorts – the 1800, 2000 and revived Mexico – were generally more refined than the originals, but only the RS 2000 was a commercial success.

WHEN the Ford Advanced Vehicle Operations factory at South Ockendon was closed (or 'mothballed' for later obliteration of the overhead production line, to be pedantic) the most exciting RS Escort derivative yet was on its way through the development treadmill. 'Exciting' because this was the first high performance Ford to be produced on the mainstream lines with a substantial bodywork change, namely the second RS 2000 programme, approved on October 9 1974 by the parent company in America.

The model was the embryo of the Mk2 RS 2000, the derivative with the most commercial potential after the Mexico concept had effectively been plucked from FAVO's jaws with the mainstream Kent-engined Escort Sport. Ford stylists with willing practical co-operation from FAVO Engineers – who had conceived this Ford answer to the 1973-announced, 1974-produced Vauxhall Firenza "Droop Snoot" – engineered a deformable polyurethane nose to transform this RS Escort's full frontal aspect. To accommodate its soft beak – which had the wonderful quality of self-repair, even if you attacked bridge parapets, the front wings were cut back 3.94in. (10 cms) and an extra 20lbs of quad headlamp snout grafted into place.

In September 1985 I learned that Advanced Vehicle engineers Allan Wilkinson, Mike Smith and Harry Worrall were actively involved in the RS 2000 right up to the first production examples. Allan told me, 'We bent up a bit of sheet steel to make the first beak-nose RS 2000 prototype and cut back the necessary metal on YOO 470L. It did all the testing at MIRA and in Italy. We even went over to Saarlouis to the pilot build area and converted some of the first cars in a little hut, away from the main production lines. When

Inside and out, the rare Escort RS 1800 was powerfully different to its RS 1600 parent. The 1.8-litre BDA allowed a flexible 120bhp from a single carburettor. For little over £3000 it provided 1985 Hot Hatchback performance in 1975. This example, and another for 1980 World Hot Rod Champion Mick Collard (using a Mk2 Escort), benefits from the conscientious craftsmanship of Colin Beverley . . . and the trim restoration patience of his wife!

that was done, I went off up to Boreham to work with Bill Meade on the 1975 RS goodies before I got the rally engineering job; Mike and Harry went over to Dunton with a lot of other staff.'

For a time the hardcore FAVO/RS men were split up: for example Rod Mansfield worked within the Public Affairs Department, as did former FordSport man Charles Reynolds before becoming Boreham's team administrator. Even Stuart Turner was left to twiddle his thumbs in South Ockendon solitude before assuming his role as Public Affairs boss for Ford of Britain in the later seventies.

Radical and successful though this model proved to be, however, it was some time before it could be produced in Germany (at Saarlouis, like all Ghia and Sport models of the 1975-80 era) so the first of the new RS types to meet the public, and the rarest road car, was the RS 1800. This was previewed in the original January 1975 launch of Mk2 Brenda

Escorts and officially available from June 1975, and was quietly dropped in the latter half of 1977. It was a true Anglo-German product with what amounted to a slightly heavier duty Mexico body built to fully trimmed and 'rolling chassis' state in Germany, before transfer to Britain for insertion of the alloy block big bore version of the BDA and a four-speed gearbox of American antecedents. It is possible that one might find an RS 1800 with British chassis plate. This would be either the common competition 'MkI-mechanicals-into-MkII shell', or UK-built on a Sport shell, but I would expect a production RS 1800 to have a German chassis plate identity.

The second generation RS with BDA power reflected a lot of detailed engine development work by liaison between Peter Ashcroft, Brian Hart and the men of Cosworth and it actually had the potential to develop into a very effective, but too expensive, alternative to Triumph's 16-valve Dolomite Sprint. Indeed, Peter Ashcroft could see the 1.8-litre RS trimmed to Ghia standards and competing effectively for such custom, but the accountants and the attractions of the RS 2000's cost-conscious running gear ended the

*The RS 2000 for the late
seventies takes shape ...*

worthy aspiration of building the RS 1800 as a freely available, high quality, sports saloon.

Thus, we have to remember that in the RS 1800 we talk of a road car of which *Autocar* remarked in April 1978, 'we doubt if there are more than 50 RS 1800 *road cars* in Britain'. My Ford and SMMT information was that 109 RS 1800s were registered in Britain between 1975 and 1978. In other words a vehicle built purely to satisfy the company's continued sports aspirations for the later Escort. It was not until the Renault 5 Turbo (mid-engine) and Audi Quattro came along in the eighties that the British learned that a vehicle intended for rally success does not have to be an unloved, under-estimated 'homologation special' sold in numbers that make Aston Martin look like mass manufacturers. Chrysler UK, BMC and Ford were all guilty – and Vauxhall were ill-rewarded when they tried to do a decent quality build of the HS 2300; as with Chrysler's Lotus Sunbeam Talbot, the cars tended to appear long after the competition model was a familiar sight! They proved a tough assignment for general dealer sale, even with the 400 required of Group 4, rather than the 1000-off demanded by earlier seventies Group 2 sporting regulations.

The extra capacity BDA within the RS 1800 was arranged via an 86.75mm bore in place of the RS 1600's 80.97mm, but the cast iron crankshaft retained its 77.62mm stroke. My Casio and its stumbling operator make this 1836.3cc; Ford described it as 1840 and *Autocar* 1845cc, or with *Motor* it was 1834cc. You take your pick, I'm sticking with Japanese technology! Incidentally *Motor, Autocar* and myself (on behalf of *Motor Sport)*

The 16-valve RS 1800 was a much better road car than its predecessor, the RS 1600, its single-carburettor 1.8-litre engine providing flexible power. Ford did not try to develop its basic appeal as an advanced road car: production ceased in 1977 and less than 110 were registered as new car sales.

In action for Motor Sport *the RS 1800 provided some memorable miles with acceleration that many 1986 'hot hatchbacks' were unable to match. Price, February 1976, was £3049.*

all had the same car, the white JJN 981N.

The engine used the same camshaft profiles as previously but a Weber 32/36 DGAV downdraught twin-choke carburettor replaced the RS 1600's twin 40mm twin-chokes. At first, Ford predicted 125 DIN bhp at 6500rpm with, 'a maximum close to 120mph and swift acceleration from rest to 60mph in approximately 8 seconds'. In fact the unit was rated at 5bhp less then RS 1600, totalling 115bhp at 6000rpm, but with an unsurprising torque bonus of 120lb ft at 4000rpm, instead of the RS 1600's 112lb ft at the same crankshaft rpm. Compression ratio was considerably lower at 9:1 for the now more prevalent top grade four star fuel; the RS 1600 had boasted a 10:1 ratio.

The gearbox used the same casing as you would find on the first RS 2000 and subsequent models but the gears themselves were considerably stronger and were contemporarily described by Ford as having Pinto or Ford Mustang 2.3-litre ancestry. The ratios were: first, 3.36; second, 1.81; third, 1.26 and fourth a direct 1:1. I found such ratios listed for the 108bhp Ford Granada 2.3 V6 for 1974-75, along with the 3.370 reverse, so it seems these gear sets must have been built in Germany for those American models: by 1977 neither American nor German Fords offered these manual four-speed ratios.

All the Mk2 Escorts shared the same 3.54:1 final drive, 175/70 HR13 radials (Pirelli CN36 on test cars) and 18.6mph per 1000rpm top gear capability. The rear axle traced back to that first shoehorn job of installing Escort with Lotus Cortina power, and therefore to

Inside the show LHD RS 2000 of 1975 was a rather generous interpretation of a centre console, and the basic reclining seats.

the earliest Cortinas of Lotus and GT parentage. The same unit was also fitted to the Escort Sport, and carried the same ratio in 1600 guise, or the original Mk1 range choice of 4:1. All shared the 8.5in. diameter single-plate cable-operated clutch.

The second generation RS Escorts shared a lot of other running gear, too, which the RS 1800 previewed in 1975. The brakes were the non-RS 2000 original RS units of 9.63in.-solid front discs and 9 x 1.75in. rear drums with Girling vacuum servo assistance. Although there were obvious differences in engine weights between the alloy block BDA and the cast iron SOHC units in the later RS 2000 and Mexico, the cars were all developed to run the same 130lb in. front, 115lb in. rear spring poundage. As before multi-leaf rear springs and top radius rods were fitted, rather than the mainstream Escort's combined anti-roll bar cum axle linkage.

The front end castor was decreased compared to the original RS range and more understeer deliberately dialled into the chassis with Armstrong front and Girling rear dampers specified for the Mk2 RS range in 1975/6; only a front anti-roll bar was specified throughout the range. Present day SVE engineers, the survivors from FAVO who managed to reform after a rather dodgy existence following FAVO's closure, tell me that the bias towards understeer, really came about as a result of racing drivers like Birrell and Tom Walkinshaw exerting their daily influence (along with FAVO engineers who raced, like Rod Mansfield and Allan Wilkinson). The oversteer bias of the original Lotus Cortina-Lotus and Escort TC programme was the work of Boreham rally engineers. The tail would slide in the later RS models, particularly in the RS 1800 and Mexico, with their lower engine weights, but in general there was an extra degree of stability, less 'nervousness' and steady understeer was most likely in the RS 2000 – unless severely provoked on dry roads, or more moderately assaulted over damp tarmac.

The RS 1800 also showed us that the heavy-duty body mods would be less comprehensive than the originals, confined to a strengthened mounting to the top front strut mounting points and a, reportedly, beefier crossmember to carry the near vertical back dampers. Obviously the RS 2000 had its individual mouldings to incorporate up front, but the RS 1800 and the later Mexico both carried front and rear spoilers, the front

The early RS 2000 show car featured a colour-coded rear spoiler, as well as the production polyurethane nose section and quadruple Cibie headlamps.

ones being in wrap-around glassfibre of body colouring. Only the RS 1800 of the press demonstrator RS fleet carried a body-coloured back spoiler, previewing the eighties fad, but a later demo RS 1800 (ONO 804P) reverted to a matt black back spoiler, along with the usual RS 1800 matt black quarter bumpers. Along each flank the RS 1800 also carried the shades of blue that were Ford Motorsport colours of the period; as far as I know all RS 1800s came originally in white, unless the owner specially ordered another colour at extra cost.

The RS 1800 was offered in two versions initially, the £2825.15 basic model of which retained some of the usual Mk2 soundproofing and a loop pile carpet and 'special lightweight competition bucket seats trimmed in black cloth'. Basic equipment also included a revised version of the single pane award-winning instrument cluster with ɟe 7000rpm tachometer matched by a 140mph speedometer; no redline was indicated but I was recommended by Ford to use no more than 6500rpm when we did our fifth wheel tests. A triangle of minor instrumentation was inserted between tacho and speedo to cover oil pressure, water temperature and fuel contents, the tank remaining at nine gallons and the oil pressure gauge having segment strokes but no figures, so it could be used in Britain and Europe with the same scale. Incidentally the standard bucket seats had no recliner mechanism and had a hefty amount of padding under the knees. For the £2990.12 RS 1800 Custom, Ford described the deal thus: 'Fully trimmed doors and rear quarters [!honestly, that is just what they said on 10 June 1975], reclining front seats fitted with head restraints, a glove box pocket and clock, plus lidded glove box and deep centre console unit, a boot carpet and inertia reel seat belts'. It is worth pointing out that both RS 1800s shared seven inch diameter Halogen headlamps by Lucas and included the mainstream Escort's two-speed wipers with intermittent facility, electric screenwashers and hazard warning indicators.

The most widely seen option was that of 6J x 13in. four-spoke alloy wheels which were £117 by the close of 1975. Later in the life of the RS range 7.5 x 13in. became freely available and was seen in a number of X-pack conversions, normally on RS 2000 equipped with 225/55 or 60-series tyres, according to contemporary Ford RS advertising. Plenty of RS Escorts wore 205,195 or 185 rubber on the 6 or 7J four-spoke alloys, mostly on Pirelli P6 60-series by the late seventies, or 1980 close of RS 2000's production life. The RS 1800, however, came as standard on the 5.5 x 13in. spoked steel wheel, wearing the 175 rubber that was still specified even if you opted for the 6J alloy.

Other options of the period that Ford proffered for the RS 1800 included tinted glass, rear fog lamps, black vinyl roof (the first demonstrator had one, the second was simply all white), opening front quarter lights, remote control driver's door mirror and a choice of AM and AM/FM radios.

RS 1800 performance

Ford quoted a Walter Mitty touring consumption figure of 32.5mpg, perfectly reasonable so long as you drove with a restraint unnatural in an RS customer! They reckoned on 112mph and 0-60mph in 'only 8.3 sec'. *Autocar* were too gentlemanly to sound disappointed with the 9.0s they got, but they recorded an absolute best of 114mph at 6150rpm as compensation. *Motor's* figures were slightly better, 'despite an intermittent and untraceable misfire,' breaking the 9s and 115mph barriers. In fact JJN 981N's performance, at around the half minute to 100mph and a standing start quarter in the 16.5 to 16.9s bracket, was very similar to that of the flyweight Honda CRX I tested for *Performance Car* in the Spring of 1984, just about nine years after the RS 1800 reached the press. The comparative figures I got with the aid of a fifth wheel for *Motor Sport* with all three second generation RS types are reproduced herewith.

MPH	RS 1800 seconds	RS 2000 seconds	1.6 Mexico seconds
0-30	3.2	3.0	3.2
0-40	4.7	4.9	5.5
0-50	6.5	6.9	8.1
0-60	8.6	9.8	11.1
0-70	11.3	13.2	16.2
0-80	15.4	19.2	23.0
Standing ¼ mile	16.2	17.0	17.8
Fuel economy (mpg)	21.24	23.6-27	26.3-28
Prices (£, inc taxes)	3049	2857	2443.50

(Data courtesy of Motor Sport)

In fairness to Ford I should point out that both *Motor* and *Autocar* returned over 26mpg overall – in fact both got the 26.5mpg overall and pointed to a potential for close to 30mpg, whereas my experience was for 21 to 24mpg as the norm. On reflection I think this was because my commuting route to the office could contain an hour through city traffic, travelling through central London.

The rest of the new RS range arrives

Although both the RS 2000 and Mexico were formally launched and priced on 14 January 1976, the RS 2000 had been a familiar motor show sight since its 13 March debut at Geneva's annual salon. Then there were some pretty startling figures for the beak-nose job including, 'made from the same polyurethane plastic as is used on the anti-damage bumpers fitted to Capris exported to the USA, the nose reduces drag by 16 per cent compared with a standard new Escort. An integral air dam below the front bumper cuts front end lift by 25 per cent, and a boot lid spoiler made of the same flexible material (different to that of RS 1800) reduces rear end lift by nearly 60 per cent'. Those figures simply reassure me that all the rude things I thought about the Mk2 Escort shape were true...!

Working on the Cd figure of 0.448 given in the previous chapter for the standard car that meant RS 2000 came out at 0.376, very similar to a 3-litre Capri S of the period and the much later XR3, and very much better than I credited it with at the time in a comparison test of all three new RS Escorts for *Motor Sport* February 1976 . Then I said, 'The new front ensures that the 2000 is the only new shape Escort to have an aerodynamic drag factor

A clay model of the second Mexico revealed that Ford were thinking in colour-coded terms for the back spoiler. Some press demo RS 1800s had this feature, but it was not widely adopted until the company decided the XR3/3i tailplane could be integrated into the RS 1600 Turbo of 1984-85.

The other side of the 1975 Mexico clay revealed the standard steel wheel look, and the careful grille detailing that did not survive to production.

that is as low as that for the earlier Escorts'. That was certainly true, but the statement did not reveal the full worth of the RS 2000 profile because the engineers could not afford to draw too much of an unfavourable comparison between old and new shapes. On reflection it also seems possible that the front and rear spoiler layout of RS 1800/Mexico may well have brought them down from a good 0.45 (remember the wider wheels) close to the 0.43 of the standard original Escort saloon, but I have no proof of that supposition. Ford themselves claimed a 0.383 Cd for the RS 2000 at announcement time.

Together with the beak nose, RS 2000 offered quadruple Cibie $6^{1}/_{8}$ inch quartz halogen headlamps. In 1976 I said, 'At night the 2000 has a clear plus over the single headlamp units (fitted to RS 1800/Mexico). Mr Cibie provided definition and range, while Jo Lucas manages as good a dip beam, but a rather woolly main beam'.

A laminated screen was standard equipment, protecting a cockpit that contained largely black-trimmed finish, including that of two large front sports seats. These had cloth facings but plastic external panels to the reclining backrests and built-up sides of the squab. Backrest adjustment was via the convenient handwheel mechanism. Instrumentation was as described for other new RS products, with the large speedo and tacho flanking minor dials for oil pressure, water temperature and fuel contents in the usual 9 gallon tank.

These strange black X-pack arches did not really catch on for the RS 2000, but a later squared off Zakspeed-look proved very popular on many different sporting Escorts, as on this white Escort seen at the annual Ford AVO Owners Club gathering.

The flat three-spoke RS-developed steering wheel was fitted (only on the test RS 1800 did it come with a leather rim, normally it was a leather lookalike) and the Escort three-stalk switchgear for wipers, lamps, indicators, dual horns, electric washers and two-speed wipers. There was a separate switch to provide intermittent wipe 'for the first time...with a delay of about 7 sec', said Ford.

There were optional seat designs from the start through the then 71-strong RS network in UK, but the interior with a glove box and unique centre console was original equipment in the January 1976 quoted price of £2857. The last prices I have for what became a two-model RS 2000 range are at June 1980, when the cheapest model was £4995 and the Custom £5650, so the RS 2000 certainly kept up in the inflation stakes. As noted the Custom was more popular than the Base.

The engine carried on as the contemporary Cortina SOHC-derived iron block 2-litre, but the ancillaries changed from the first RS 2000 specification. The new Escort's engine bay allowed accommodation of a mechanical radiator fan to replace the previous electric cooler and they claimed an extra 12bhp for the unit with a new exhaust system. The top manifolding was still in cast iron, but it was less of an agricultural device than the original Cortina/Capri layout and hitched up to, 'large bore pipework and absorption type silencers.' The induction remained that progressive twin-choke Weber on the usual manifold, so 12bhp seemed a bit much to claim with no compression, cam or valve changes noted.

Ford now claimed a total 110bhp at 5500rpm and 121lb ft torque from 3750rpm. In Cortina the engine was rated at 98bhp, whilst the first RS 2000 provided 100bhp at 5700rpm and 112lb ft at 3500rpm. The claimed extra muscle had to propel an RS 2000 that was 6.3in. longer than the original (the nose added over 6in. to Mk II's length as well) and weighed an extra 39lb according to Ford figures, the second RS 2000 weighing in at 2057lb (935kg). That compared with 1980lb (900kg) for the alloy block RS 1800 and 1991lb (904kg) for the later SOHC Mexico, which was also officially unveiled in January 1976.

As explained, the gearbox of the RS 1800 was unique to that model, the RS 2000 and new Mexico sharing the German-sourced four-speed with cable operated 8.5in. diameter clutch that we had seen as an arrival on the RS scene via the first 2000. Ratios remained as before: first, 3.656; second, 1.970; third, 1.370; fourth, direct 1:1 with the usual 18.6mph per 1000rpm on the 3.54 final drive and standard steel wheels wearing 175/70 radials. The 6 x 13in. four-spoke alloy was an option, offered with the same tyres originally.

Braking, via 9.6in. front discs and 9in. rear drums was as outlined for the new RS range earlier, but it should be noted that the vacuum servo assistance unit was an inch larger at 7in. than that of the normal Escort. MacPherson strut and link-located rear axle were also as outlined earlier and the cars of this period had multi-leaf back springs.

It should surprise no potential owner, however, to find a single leaf adorning the rear end and a ride revealing considerably uprated suspension, for the Group 1 inspired competition parts were widely fitted by more enthusiastic owners. In this connection it is relevant to point out that a Group 1 RS 2000 would have all its main features substantially altered: there was the high ratio rack to remove about a turn from lock-to-lock's standard figure of 3.5 turns; a close ratio Rocket gearbox, still with four speeds; ventilated front disc brakes (not unknown for an adjustable balance bar to be built in with the bias knob hidden under the fascia!); uprated chassis with those single leaf springs; and an engine featuring twin double-choke Weber carburettors, downdraught rather than the side feed units of Escort TC days. Obviously new manifolding would go along with these changes and there were a number of camshaft developments over the years at Ford, including a roller bearing shaft that had the side benefit of getting over the intermittent camshaft lobe lubrication problem that afflicted Cortinas and a few RS 2000s of the late seventies. One *could* find a road car that had more power than a Capri 2.8i, for 160 to 165bhp was, and remains, perfectly possible from these 1993cc (90.80 x 76.95mm bore and stroke) four-cylinder engines equipped with RS parts originally designed for Group 1 production car competition. Such a specifiation could be delivered with a perfectly flexible engine for road use, and some were used just on the road (perhaps to compliment an X-pack), but the car is more likely to have had a competition heritage.

The standard second generation RS 2000 performed with startling effectiveness in press road tests, both *Motor* and *Autocar* returning very close to the Ford predicted 0-60mph time of 8.5s, and to within 0.5mph of each other on a 112mph maximum at MIRA. Both returning excellent 23.7 and 24.7mpg overall results, including test mileage. Having seen the painfully honest way in which both magazines collect their data I am

Both flat-front and beak-nose Escort RS 2000s proved very popular in motor sport, usually with some 160-165bhp provided by an engine builder using a number of Ford homologated parts for the Group 1 category. The beak-nose is driven with flair that was later seen applied to GM equipment by Ulster's Bertie Fisher. The photograph, showing equal talent, is from Maurice Selden.

happy to quote such results (from two different cars: LHJ 935/3P), but when we had RS 1800 and RS 2000 (ours was LHJ 931P) at the track on the same day the RS 1800 was consistently quicker, not the case for *Autocar* or *Motor*. That was borne out by a figure of 8.6s from rest to 60mph for the RS 1800 compared to 9.8s for our demo RS 2000 in our trial with the gap widening beyond that mile a minute point. For *Autocar* it was 0-70mph before the RS 1800 showed any advantage over the 2000 (0.3s) and even from 0-100mph the gap was only 0.7s in favour of the RS 1800. So there was no practical performance reason for buying the more complex, more expensive and less comfortable 1800 rather than the 2000, and one had to pay a petrol premium into the bargain!

Mexico reborn

In the eighties I learned that the second generation of Escort Mexicos was purely a

Back end of the RS 2000 shows the correct soft material for the black back spoiler and distinctive badgework. Concours RS provided courtesy of Steve Rockingham.

British affair, and it would not have existed at all if the leading RS dealers, such as Haynes of Maidstone, had not bullied later Ford of Britain Chief Sam Toy (now retired) into this additional model. The RS connection was formally badged on the steering wheel, and in specialist magazine advertising, whereas the original carried 1600GT or Mexico badge allegiances. Annual UK sales of 740 in 1977 and 702 the following year were sufficient to please the RS outlets, but the RS 2000 was stronger still and eventually prevailed as the only rear drive RS Escort to make it to 1980.

The Escort Mexico also came back into our lives officially in January 1976, but to a far more apathetic reception than the reborn RS 2000. For now there was a 1.6-litre Escort Sport from the main production outlets at just under £2000, even the Mexico's overhead camshaft alternative with a claimed 95bhp versus 84bhp, was not enough to attract the punters at the intro. price of £2443.50. By September 1978 at a final listing of £3632 it was gone. This defied the journalist who said, 'many readers will wonder if the overhead camshaft, better seating, suspension and braking are worth having? I think they will prove worth every new penny to anyone who enjoys his motoring. Comparing the Sport to the Mexico is about as fair as assessing the Mini Cooper S and the Mini 1275 GT for sporting appeal!' Guess who made the prediction that buyers ignored by the thousands? Blush, blush...

What did one get for £2443 in a 1976 Mexico? 'It is powered by a 1600cc single overhead camshaft engine similar to that used in the Capri 1600S. The single overhead camshaft is driven by a toothed rubber belt, and the special Mexico exhaust system boosts the power to 70.9 Kw (95bhp) DIN at 5750rpm with 124 Nm (92lb ft) torque at 4000rpm,' said Ford. This 87.6 x 66mm cast iron block Ford of 1593cc was normally rated at 88bhp at 5700rpm and exactly the same torque in Capri guise, so Ford were claiming only 7bhp from this exhaust conversion, which once again left the induction principally unaltered. This meant it used a Weber 32/36 DGV downdraught twin-choke instead of the RS 2000's similar choke size Weber DGAV. In both cases the standard of 9.2:1 CR was employed.

The transmission, including single-plate clutch with 8.5in. pressure plate and the ratios mentioned for the RS 2000, was exactly as for the larger-engined model with an identical 3.54:1 final drive and 18.6mph per 1000rpm quoted. Also the same were the suspension, braking, 17.8:1 steering rack ratio and standard issue 5.5 x 13in. steel wheels with an alloy 6in. option.

Fitting the overhead camshaft 1.6-litre engine and uprating the running gear to traditional RS Escort standards was not enough to prevent the Escort Mexico becoming a commercial failure in its second edition. The mass production Sport 1300 and 1600 alternatives just offered too much of the basic idea at an attractive saving ... The 1.6-litre Escort Mexico was a fine car to drive, better than the contemporary Sport or subsequent Harrier, but its slim power advantage and a lack of marketing support ensured that it soon slipped from the public's mind. It was launched at under £2000 and went out of production in 1978, when the cost was over £3500.

The January 1976 Escort Mexico featured a different, and rather more sporting, seat with no backrest adjustment. The three-spoke steering wheel and three minor dials for the new Escort's award-winning fascia remained as for the RS 2000 and 1800. Some 1442 Mexicos were built during 1977-1978

Internally the test Mexicos I drove lacked the centre console and clock of the RS 2000, but they had a simple bucket seat design, the three-spoke wheel, a lot of matt black trim and the five-dial sports instrumentation, including rev counter and oil pressure gauge. The black headlining and intermittent wiper action were included in the deal, too.

Ford claimed, 'around 106mph and acceleration from 0-60mph takes just over 10 sec'. In those back-to-back *Motor Sport* tests we recorded 11.1s and 26.3 to 28mpg, but maximum speed could not be accurately measured at that track, which was sufficient only for fifth wheel timed runs to 80mph from rest and which prompted the remark, 'the Mexico is very hard put to exceed 100mph'.

Street life

13 September 1978: the complete Escort line is revamped with wider offset wheels and

When I began to research the Escort book, pictures of smartly kept RS 2000s abounded amongst the inquiries as to this book's precise contents. This is one of the nicest RS 2000s amongst the bunch: Richard P. Nixon's yellow machine, kept in Shropshire. Richard is one of some 5000 members of the RS Owners Club.

The Mk2 RS 2000 was the most successful of the RS-branded Escorts in pre-front drive days Production details are in the Appendices, showing yearly output until production ceased in 1980. From November 1975 some 25,638 were made in Germany, of which over 17,300 were exported. Sales exceeded 10,000 in Britain.

other changes noted in the earlier chapter. Ford have an obituary to write of their seventies Mexico love child: 'The Mexico derivative of Escort was sired by the Boreham-built car which won the World Cup Rally in the hands of Hannu Mikkola. It enjoyed success as a road car in both MkI and Mk2 forms but would be too similar in specification to the improved Escort Sport, hence it has been discontinued for 1979. Instead Ford's seventy or so Rallye Sport dealers will be offering a pair of smart RS 2000 models.' Since the RS 1800 had already been dropped, that left the increasingly popular RS 2000 as the sole inheritor of the RS/FAVO legacy.

I said 'increasingly popular', but figures for these RS products show minor sales, maximum prestige and market research as more convincing reasons for the existence of such sporting Escorts in the seventies. To illustrate the point the first RS 2000 sold around 3700 copies in the UK, 10039 in the beak-nose, Saarlouis-manufactured 1975-80 guise. Saarlouis made over 25,000 RS 2000s (see Appendix III), but that was not the grand total.

Some 2400 sales were achieved by Ford Australia with 'the top of the line sporty model RS 2000'. Nearly 50 per cent (1013) were sold in New South Wales. Shown on optional alloys these Escorts were locally made, but 50 examples of earlier European RS 2000s were imported.

Tom Chaplin of the Australian RSOC wrote and told us that one type of RS 2000 was locally made in 1979-80. A total of 2400 were Australian-manufactured and, unlike the European model, two- and four-door bodies were offered along with automatic transmission. Australia also saw the RS 2000 imported, 1975 allowing 25 Mk1 models and 1976 the same number of beak-nose Mk2s. Later the XR3i front drive performance successor to the RS 2000 sold over 20,000 units a year, just in the UK!

The replacement RS 2000 line in September 1978 comprised the steel wheeled model with Mexico's 'functional trim', in Ford's words, but reclining seats were offered rather than the bucket units I referred to previously. The Custom RS 2000 came with, '6in. alloy wheels, the superb hip-hugging Recaro seats so often specified by Capri S owners, bronze-tinted glass all round and a remote-control driver's door mirror,' reported Ford. Prices were officially released a day later with confirmation that the RS 2000 Custom seats included those rather obstructive mesh head restraints; in addition, the 2000 Custom had a luggage compartment light, centre console, glove box, carpeted boot and fully trimmed door panels along with the obvious four-spoke 6 x 13in. alloy wheels. It was priced at £4415.73. The straight steel wheel RS 2000 cost £3901.68 in September 1978. To put that in perspective the 1100 Popular Escort then commanded £2253.36, the 1600 Sport running gear within a four-door Ghia-trimmed shell was £3663.71 and the highest specification estate you could buy, the 1300 GL, was priced at £3310.63.

The RS 2000 and its costlier Custom brother continued on offer at dealers' showrooms even after the front drive Escort appeared in September 1980, with only minor changes. In April 1979 they fitted the brake warning light and by the end of that year the 'RS2' as enthusiasts often referred to it was over £4700, even in its cheapest form. Incidentally, perhaps surprisingly, the later RS 2000 did not go over to the mainstream single rear leaf layout in Saarlouis production, retaining the original multi-leaves, top axle location rods and no rear anti-roll bar.

There was considerable sadness at the passing of RS 2000 from Ford showrooms and the process was elongated at very satisfactory prices for many specialists who realized this was the last rear drive small Ford they were likely to be offering at affordable prices. In November 1980 the front drive successor to the RS 2000's niche (and to a completely new breed of Ford XR customer), XR3, was listed at £5123. Yet a look in the back pages of

Motoring News, even in December, revealed the last rear drive RS 2000s still on offer as brand new cars 'from £5300', at outfits such as Brundall Service Station, Norwich. Specialists such as City Speed at Gloucester had really low mileage RS 2000s on offer just below £5000, and the number of advertisers wanting the fabled RS Ford seemed to have increased, if anything. Even in 1984 there were seven adverts in the wanted columns of MN specifically demanding RS 2000s with the promise, 'highest prices paid,' a testimony to the commercial and customer effectiveness of the last rear drive survivor of the Escort Twin Cam and Cortina heritage.

The RS 2000 was a fitting end product to the era of high performance rear drive Ford Escorts. The balance between initial cost, performance, mpg, service practicality and useful carrying capacity was right. So was an overall flair born of the beak nose, comfortable interior and exciting driving manners. The RS 2000 was in the mould of classics such as Mini Cooper S, Cortina GT, BMW 2002 and Golf GTI: the right blend of sporting practicality at exactly the right market time.

Through the eighties the enthusiasm for the RS 2000 showed little sign of abating. This is Steve Rockingham's concours car in 1988.

Chapter 7

Champion of champions

The second Escort body proved just as competition versatile as the original, and did not let cessation of production stand between it and more world titles. In world class rallying it took the driver's title twice and the manufacturer's title once. A trio of European Rallycross Championships also went the Escorts II's way, along with two German national wins in a row and a succession of Hot Rod world titles. From New Zealand to Canada the straightforward Escort kept winning, and, away from the international limelight, it is still defeating the opposition today ...

ALTHOUGH there was nothing inherent in the engineering of the basic car that rendered it more suitable for competition than its illustrious predecessors, the Escort second edition proved every bit as capable of winning at every motor sport level as the previous model. It was still a particularly popular choice in British club rallies of the eighties, over eight years after production ended.

Internationally speaking, my most colourful memories are strongest of the black and gaudily striped Group 5 Zakspeed Escorts in 1977. Then their 2-litre BDAs of 275bhp were becoming dated against a new wave of turbo Capris and BMWs that took over the title-winning honours in the smallest class of the German Championship. The earlier Group 2 Zakspeed Escorts had taken every title from 1973 onward, only the 1976 final Escort *Deutsche Rennsport Meisterschaft* series victory scored by the Mk II.

Yet the world class honours and the spectacle remained firmly with the British Boreham-built and David Sutton (Rothmans, Eaton Yale) Escort IIs. A veritable host of world class drivers rallied these chunky Escorts with their carburated 2-litre alloy BDAs, traditional ZF five-speed gearboxes and four-wheel disc brakes. The rear brakes were mounted on the most formidable rear axle, one reinforced with clear civil engineering construction aspirations in the Severn Bridge league.

Batman! Just as the Escort was reborn in new clothes for road and competition use, so it gained a significant new driver in the late seventies. This classic from LAT's Maurice Selden shows Ari Vatanen at his inspired best, engaged in a full-scale assault on the 1976 British Open Championship in the first year that it was open to foreign nationals. Ari's co-driver for the season was Peter Bryant, and Vatanen duly won the title, including a win on this Snowman Rally qualifying round. Note the squared-off RS 1800 wheel arch extensions and the use of similarly chunky Dunlop A2 tyres, then the 'tweak of the week!'

Recently Ford have promoted the link between Jackie Stewart and the 4-WD RS 200, but even in 1978 JYS had left his triple GP world titles well behind whilst grappling with the Escort. This autumn 1978 photo was taken at Snetterton.

Bodily, the Escort in its new guise offered circuit racers absolutely no aerodynamic advantage. In fact the Capri was soon picked as the better long term bet when turbo power arrived at Zakspeed. Nor was there a weight or strength superiority as an integral feature of the latest small Ford; for both aspects slightly the reverse was true, for extra glass allowed Joe Public a better view out, but was heavier and not so rigid in resisting torsional forces as the previous claustrophobic steel structure.

I said the Escort's rally drivers were world class. Look through the list of achievements and one realizes it was the perfect partnership between a simply robust machine that could be made to do *anything* at a split second's notice, and supreme Scandinavian talent. Yes, Roger Clark did a great job by British standards – winning another RAC and contributing

Shown at the Dorchester launch of the 1975 Escort was this mock rally car, which later became the real thing after also appearing at the March 1975 Geneva Motor Show.

to Escort's tally of six Welsh Internationals, four Internationals in Scotland and a trio of Manx wins on the home international front, plus a Cypriot victory. National advertising from Cossack hairspray ensured that we never forgot the bright red Escort II and its (at only 36) silver-haired British rallying top dog. Yet the World Championship honours, and even Escort RS 2000's win on the home International rally/racing melange they called Tour of Britain, were owed firmly to British recruitment of Swedes and Finns.

Longest-serving and loyalest Escort supporter, until it threatened his career, was also the youngest: Ari Vatanen. The name conjures up the contrast of a quietly spoken and drily humorous rallyist; an atheltic six footer who transformed from God-fearing Finn to demonic talent, once his considerable height was coiled within the confines of a works Escort, or one to very similar specification from David Sutton. There is simply nobody like Ari in modern motor sport: intensely modest on a personal level, but with supreme arrogance behind the wheel that demands fate co-operates with his frequently impossible demands on the laws of gravity. As a leading Ford executive commented to me in 1984, long after Ari had established himself as the force behind the wheel of a totally dissimilar 4-WD Peugeot 205 Turbo 16: 'I've spent a lot of my life travelling beside fast Finns, but nobody, NOBODY, flies into corners like Ari. He knows he can sort it all out ... most of the time! His entry speeds must be 5mph up on anyone. With the Escort, comparatively low-powered by today's turbo 4-WD supercar standards, he could get away with it.'

Photographically, we can recall the 1000th of a second moments from Ari's career, and the parallel development of the Mk2 Escort, from the days in Allied Polymer's black and white British home International title winner (during a difficult début year 'living in' at Boreham) to the final throes of Escort's world class rally career with Vatanen fittingly scoring a second overall on the 1981 RAC Rally. That summarizes the facts of continuous success, but not the spirit of a man like Vatanen and the frequently tattered Ford fighting on to the end. One can picture the incredible sideways angles that all top Escorteers used routinely in this brilliantly manageable little saloon. Only a Barry Hinchliffe film, or memory, brings back the colours, the varied conditions, frightening speed, and snarling sounds of a Cosworth being banged along on the rev-limiter in the cheerful way rally drivers have of using their eyes for covering the next near accident, rather than for boring

Hannu Mikkola had two separate contracted spells as a works Escort driver, both supremely successful.

Hans Thorszelius (left) co-drove the first ever World Champion rally driver, Bjorn Waldegard.

race details like 9750rpm shift points.

This attitude was reflected by Ford at Boreham's switch to increasing use of standard instrumentation within the Mk2, replacing the complex cockpits that grew out of the sixties Minis and the like. Always there had been the large yellow dashboard bulb to plead with

Timo Makinen

Mike Broad

Arne Hertz

Henry Liddon

Tony Mason

Ari Vatanen

Russell Brookes

Billy Coleman

John Taylor

John Brown

Donal O'Sullivan

Peter Bryant

Some of the names who made Escort and international rally success routine, pictured in 1975.

Roger Clark and Jim Porter scored a sixth Scottish victory in the 1975 International using the shining red Cossack Mk 2.

the animal behind the wheel to switch off before the engine became smelted metal, but now such 'idiot lights' were seen as the more realistic way of communicating with a man who might be gliding in from a 30ft yump at 95mph.

If Ari was impressive, then the results amassed by Ford and Mercedes team mates of the 1977-79 era, Swede Bjorn Waldegard and Finn Hannu Mikkola were enough to develop a cult following amongst Ford executives. Transparently honest with each other, and experienced enough to travel truly quickly without wanton car damage, these aristocrats amongst Scandinavian rallying gentry, contributed the bulk of the Escort II's world class wins. Naturally both were assisted by high-calibre co-drivers, usually Hans Thorszelius for Bjorn and Arne Hertz for Hannu.

For the record the World Championship total included one East African Safari in 1977; four, yes *four* Greek Acropolis rallies; a 1-2 victory in Portugal; two wins on the Finnish GP of 1000 Lakes, and single championship victories in new Zealand, Canada, Brazil and the Swedish. The closest they got to Monte Carlo gold was second in 1979, when Bjorn was frustrated by the stage-obstructing boulder incident that left Bernard Darniche's Chardonnet Lancia Stratos a narrow victory.

Vatanen underlined the occasionally overlooked Escort potential for gobbling up Mediterranean stages (usually over tight tarmac twists but also with a significant percentage of loose going) on San Remo with a 1980 second place. In fact Ari damn nearly prevented the historic first woman's win in a World Championship round in 1981, when effectively challenging Michele Mouton/Fabrizia Pons in the Quattro with his Rothmans Escort II. A characteristic challenge that ended in a rocky brush-off.

Rallycross to rods

The Escort's unique combination of freely available speed parts and inherent simplicity was suited particularly to the non-works teams, or those run with Ford support but pursuing their own goals without Ford personnel in attendance. The truth of that statement can be seen in the mid-eighties, where the rear drive Ford is still competing honourably in privateers' hands.

The later shape Escort proved equally versatile in racing and rallycross. The Group 2 racer is that of 1975 German Champion Hans Heyer and the car set something of a wheel arch extension fashion that was widely copied. The rallycross machine is the one taken to a brace of European titles by Norway's Martin Schanche, seen here in subsequent owner Martin Welch's hands at a 1984 Brands Hatch rallycross. The car used turbocharged BDA power, originally of Zakspeed Capri origin, but modified by Schanche and Gartrac to meet the needs of instant response in rallycross.

Pentti Airikkala took this David Sutton Cars/Team Avon Tyres RS 1800 to second place on the 1976 1000 Lakes Rally.

Rallycross is a sport which had its televised roots in Britain, but which flourished under the missionary skills of roving Brits such as John Taylor, Rod Chapman, the late Ronnie Douglas and many others who were eventually able to earn enough at venues such as Valkenswaard in Holland or the rallycross circuits that suddenly sprouted in Belgium, Austria, France and Sweden to become the sport's semi-pros. 'Semi' because they usually had substantial business interests outside the sport, not for any lack of speed. Rallycross demands sprint racing techniques over a variety of treacherous rally surfaces.

Of the semi-works efforts the most money and support went to Zakspeed for saloon car racing, but the 'team' that would earn Ford European Rallycross Championships of the seventies was the loyalty of supporters toward that Norwegian one-man band with a slight Brummie accent: Martin Schanche. Possessed of an incurable wanderlust and an ingenious aptitude for practical mechanics that echoed that of a Boreham rally mechanic, Martin was also precisely the kind of tenacious driver who would not acknowledge defeat, even when the big money équipes arrived in rallycross.

The Escort, of course, had its début in rallycross with Roger Clark, Tony Chappel and Barry Lee amongst its Boreham-run pioneers. Gradually it grew through the 1800 Twin Cam stage and blossomed briefly in large capacity (around 1.8 litres) pushrod form following the World Cup Rally's release of enlarged pushrod, crossflow, technology. Traction was always an Escort need, the Imp and the Mini highlighting its comparative absence on wet days for the Escorteers. When 4-WD arrived in rallycross, a decade *before* Audi stunned the World Championship Rally scene with Quattro, the Escort's days again looked limited.

However, the Mk1's fanatical following included John Taylor and an absence of 4-WD specials in its European early days. Thus, in the Autumn of 1973, driving with the forcefulness that made panel beaters ecstatic and the exploits of Attila the Hun pale in comparison, 'JT', future architect of the British Junior Rally Team, took the first European Rallycross Championship. The Ford wore the usual blue, white and black livery that bedecked equally loyal Escort supporters, Haynes of Maidstone.

Ari Vatanen took the Group 1 RS 2000 to a win on the circuits and stages of the 1976 Texaco Tour of Britain. The co-driver, not carried on circuits, was Peter Bryant.

Biggest international win for Roger Clark (inset) and Cossack came with the factory's RS 1800 win on the 1976 Lombard RAC Rally. It was Roger's second RAC win; we were still waiting for another non-Scandinavian to win, in 1990 ...

Bjorn Waldegard tackled the 1977 Finnish 1000 Lakes Rally for Ford and brought the RS 1800 home third. Another factory RS, for Kyosti Hamalianen, won in a surprise result for the previously unrated Finn, a man better known for his Group 1 Escort efforts.

The rear- and mid-engine brigade from the newly inspired rallycross Euro nations dominated the title hunt for the next four years, including the debut season for the Mk2. In 1974 and 1975 Porsche-dependent VW Beetles scuttled back with the championship for Austrian and Dutch drivers. By 1976 that Austrian, Franz Wurz, had big money backing for a Lancia Stratos supercar. According to the records I have, this was a 3-litre stretch of the 2.4 litre Ferrari V6, but whatever capacity its door-wedge body held, it was enough to take that 1976 title. The following year a full rear-engine machine – Alpine Renault's A310 – won the Euro spoils. Not a promising precedent for an Escort campaigner, but Martin Schanche was not a man to listen to theorists.

The Norwegian's initially conventional BDA Escort Mk2s became wilder and wilder, but that is to take nothing away from Schanche's fearless fight against increasingly sophisticated opposition. Schanche's square-rigged Ford grasped both the 1978 and 1979 titles. In 1980 the well-financed Volvo 343 Turbo team, including popular Swedish former rallyist (you may remember him in Volvos, or the Chequered Flag Stratos) Per Inge Walfridsson mopped up more points than anyone ... but Schanche returned!

Ultimate Mk 2?

For 1981 Schanche had an ultimate Escort II. Complete with huge rear wing to frighten opponents, as well as to anchor the Escort to the earth during all-terrain combat sessions, the front engine, rear-drive, Escort with rear radiators packed a turbocharged BDA punch. It was usually billed as a straight Zakspeed Capri powerplant, which meant 500bhp on a racing power band from engines between 1.4 and 2.0 litres, during this era. Schanche, however, working from his usual engineering base in Britain at Gartrac in Godalming, Surrey, ensured this was no straight racer.

Gartrac co-founder and owner, David Bignold, told me: 'Sure, it was the BDA base and KKK turbo similar to that used in the Capris, but the camshafts were changed and it

Another of Maurice Selden's personal photographic favourites is this study of Roger Clark/Jim Porter heading for second overall on the 1977 Acropolis. The event, part of a year long war with Fiat, was won by the works RS 1800 of Bjorn Waldegard.

The Ford Escort RS won the Safari rally again in 1977, crewed by Sweden's Bjorn Waldegard and Hans Thorszelius.

ran at 1.8 litres when the Zakspeed Capris were 1.4s mainly. On 1.5 bar (21 psi) it gave around 470bhp, but the big thing was that boost was available from 2500 revs with this layout. We used the usual Atlas axle at the back, but we had a huge variety of gearboxes. We ended up with a Hewland five-speeder, and that began the link with Mike Endean that gave us the 4-WD Mk3 for Martin using the Xtrac system.'

Martin Schanche took that Sachs-supported Mk2 into what will probably have been the 2-WD Escort's last European Championship Rallycross victory in 1981. The 1982/83 titles were won by 4-WD Audi Quattros, but by September 1982 Mike Endean, then still at Hewland, Dave Bignold at Gartrac and Mr Schanche had concocted the Mk3 answer mentioned above ... but that's another story.

Hot Rod racing has a very strong British base but nevertheless runs both World and European Championship series that are promoted by Spedeworth International – who run the Ipswich World title – and the National Hot Rod Association, who succeeded Spedeworth in running the European Hot Rod Championships, a series which has culminated at a number of tracks in Germany, Britain, Ireland and, for 1983, Belgium.

The regulations for Hot Rods might have been written for Escort, and the model was used almost exclusively for success until the more adventurous started using the Vauxhall Chevette or Toyota Starlet, beneath which you would usually find familiar Escort motivation! For the period we are discussing the 1700 pushrod Ford crossflow engine was the norm with excellent torque from engines tuned to tackle oval racing around typically quarter mile stadiums. Peak power started around 140bhp from the twin Weber 35DCOE powerplants, running compressions in the 11.5:1 region and a camshaft profile modified from the Cosworth A6 to give excellent second, or possibly third, gear response at crankshaft rpm up to 8000.

The Mk2 Escort began to collect Rod titles in its 1975 début year – the first being the Wimbledon-based European Championship for Barry Lee. Even in 1984 *Cars & Car Conversions* publisher Terry Grimwood, a man with bravery levels that encompass destruction derbies in the USA, drove a Norman Abbott Racing Mk2 that was recognizably based on the same mechanical principles as had served the rear drive Escort so well in both bodies throughout the seventies. By then you could have a low tune Pinto 2-litre or the still more popular 1700 crossflow, in a rather more advanced tune than was allowed a decade earlier, although twin double-choke carburettors still fed the sturdy pushrod from the sidedraught position. By 1984 power outputs in the 175bhp region were reported.

What had changed by the eighties for Escort Rods were the standards of preparation and presentation. Barry Lee had always paid attention to this aspect and his undoubted success with sponsors and results gradually helped Hot Rod saloons of all kinds to smarten up their act in what is normally a no contact sport: fat chance with so many saloons crammed into so little space!

T. Grimwood discovered that the 1984 Escort Rod had tried and true underpinnings. The uprated MacPherson struts featured adjustable spring platforms to trim ride heights, and the suspension was properly located with rose joints. The front roll bar was a separate unit, rather than linked into the strut's lower arms, as in production. At the rear an A-bracket was used, usually fixed to the lower side of the axle, but some ran it above with radius rod axle location. Four wheel disc brakes and slick-shod alloy wheels up to 10 inches wide were normal wear in the eighties, by which time Barry Lee had pioneered a turbocharged alternative that suffered all the teething problems you would expect in a sport where instant overtaking power response is crucial.

Although opposition in the carefully regulated Hot Rod ranks had increased sharply during the Mk2's competition life, its record is unmatched. In World Championship terms

They started reasonably tidily, but rarely finished without scars! The 1975 Escort Sports were run out of Brands Hatch and cornered at fantastic sideways angles on crossply tyres.

it had stopped winning by the time this was written, at least so far as the title itself was concerned, in 1980 with pig farmer Duffy Collard's collection of the World title. Prior to that year a Ford had won every single year from 1972 onward and, it was always an Escort, with the exception of 1976 when folk hero George Polley proved the Anglia could do the world title job. For the world series at Ipswich, the Escort II began to win in 1977 and racked up 1978 (second year in succession for Barry Lee) and 1979 for Jersey-based Midlander Gordon Bland, followed by the Collard victory, also with Escort square-rigged outline. Since then it has been about men like Ormond Christie in the Ford-powered Toyota.

In that European series Lee scored the first championship for the Mk2 in 1975. A Mk1 came out top the following year for Pete Winstone, who changed to the later shell that has gone on winning in every year since then, bar 1981. In 1979 Gordon Bland took both world and European titles and Mick Collard repeated the feat for the later Escort shape in 1980. When this was written, Pete Stevens Mk2 had won the last two European Championships, 1982's Irish event and the 1983 title fight in Belgium, where they run races the other way round to compensate for the usual use of LHD. At least that's what Linda Keen told me at *Motoring News,* but then she was probably suffering extreme boredom through trying to educate me beyond the enthusiasm generated by last watching the sport at a special 1981 Rothmans-backed promotion for rally and top rodders, on the Isle of Man. Boy, is it ever *quick* now ... and the spectacle of so many trying to use *that* piece of road at 65 to 70mph is worth seeing ... And they usually hold meetings where you can get under cover without a mortgage, with refreshment readily to hand!

The multi-million pound turnover success of the Ford Motorsport parts operation in the eighties owed a lot to ads like this. Capitalising on Roger Clark's famous red and white Cossack hair spray RS 1800 they offered to sell everything from T-shirts spoilers and magnesium wheels. Ford market research, published in 1988, showed that Clark and Paddy Hopkirk were still Britain's best known rally drivers to date.

Chapter 8

Rallying worldwide, Mk 2 style

On the tarmacadam or more earthy terra firma, the later Escort conquered the world, and continues to surprise, even at national championship level ...

SCANNING through Mick Jones's conscientious file of every Boreham-built competition car from September 1971 onward, I find that December 1974 saw Robin Vokins and Gordon Spooner constructing the first Brenda-coded Escort show rally car, later registered JJN 974N. That machine appeared, in pristine white with decalling appropriate to an RAC Rally, at the press launch of the Escort II.

That number one Brenda-coded factory Ford was equipped with a Hart 2-litre BDA with the usual alloy block and ZF five-speed transmission and subsequently became a winning machine for Gilbert Staepelaere in European championship events. History shows us the Escort continuing to rack up the British victories at home international level in either bodyshell that début year. Roger Clark was equipped with a new Escort for April's Granite City, which he won before adopting Cossack's red livery to repeat the winning act for the new Ford on the Welsh and Scottish of 1975. Missing the presence of a now South African-based Mick Jones, I can only conjecture that this famous car, HHJ 700N, was actually the original show car, re-prepared from 10 March onward by Norman Masters for Roger Clark's UK programme. It then changed identities again and emerged with Staepelaere in Europe as a winner too!

Clark's car was of the tried and tested Hart BDA and ZF layout, but the basic Escort, on which the winning Ford was based, had changed considerably in Mk2 guise (see Chapter 6, Part II of The Performers) for sound regulation reasons. Instead of the RS 1600 and 1.6 litres we had a basic capacity of just over 1.8 litres, coupled to a stronger four-speed gearbox. This was in order to compete more effectively in Group 2, and proved important

The way rally Escorts will be remembered? The combination of Rothmans money and background support from Ford for the obsolescent Escort kept the car alive in World Championship rallying after the factory withdrew in 1979. These David Sutton-built machines are contesting the 1980 San Remo World Championship round. The one on the left was for Ari Vatanen, who finished second, and the car closest to photographer Maurice Selden's lens is that of third-placed Hannu Mikkola, then also hard at work developing the Audi Quattro for a 1981 World Championship début that changed the face of rallying.

initially to the saloon car racers in the European Championship and German title hunts. Regulations were stricter than the previous Group 2 and the RS 1800 ensured that nearly 2 litres could be obtained under these later regs with a chance of the gearbox staying together.

Zakspeed took the Escort's most prestigious overseas victory of the 1975 season with Hans Heyer and Peter Hennige winning the Kyalami 1000kms. Heyer also won that year's German title, but with the earlier Escort outline. The later shape was used throughout the 1976 season to secure tarmacadam business proprietor Heyer's final Ford Escort win in the series, but these Escorts were now the more radically modified Group 5 models, leading to the turbocharged era and the Zakspeed Capris that followed. In Europe the Group 2 regulations remained until 1981 in saloon car championship events, replaced by Group A in 1982. The rear drive Escort II was handled during 1976 by Alec Poole with a number of other drivers for this British-based machine, including Jody Scheckter, during a season of promise but rarely-realized potential. The best results for the équipe was a third in Czechoslovakia. The problem was mandatory use of wet-sump lubrication; a requirement dropped in 1977.

Back at Boreham they were thinking about tarmac terrain too, building Mk2 specifically for such usage and trying to get the team, plus regular tyre suppliers Dunlop, back into the overseas international swing of things. In 1975 they tackled the *Tour de France* with a yellow RS 1800 built as a compromise between racer and rally car, complete with Panhard rod-located rear axle (which could swiftly be converted to Watts Linkage at this development stage) and 245bhp from its 1977cc to power 2128lbs. Complete with compression strut front suspension and lengthened rear dampers that mounted on what would be the rear parcel shelf area of a standard Mk2, this device showed speed enough on tarmac to put Timo Makinen temporarily into the lead of the Tour, but the final result was

Initial work on developing a tarmac specification for the new Escort resulted in this Manx Rally-winning RS 1800 for Roger Clark/Jim Porter. There were a few embarrassed Porsche pilots on The Island that year...

Recce routine for an old works Escort in virgin white. Ford only got one car to the finish of the 1977 East African Safari, but Bjorn Waldegard's entry was the victorious one, so there were few complaints!

a non-finish, just as it was on October's San Remo World Championship event. However, the problems were not just the mechanical ones of getting onto the seventies World Championship pace with a saloon car against the original purpose-built Stratos supercar of that era ...

Ford at Boreham had effectively been out of the World Championship limelight since the original Escort's heyday before the 1973/74 winter fuel crisis put such a dent in the Ford enthusiasm and budget for competition purposes. Remember, the 1974 'season' started with Monte Carlo being cancelled and a general absence of rallying from the sporting calendar in the opening months of the year. Ford naturally were not 'high profile' during 1974, the last year of the Escort Mk1 and so soon after the crisis. Thus 1975 and the new model gave them a chance to try and put together a susbstantially new World Championship challenge, not just in machinery, but also personnel.

In 1983, I went to the Boreham office that served Billy Barnet and his successor Charles Reynolds to hear from Reynolds how Ford's effective seventies World Championship programme, had had some pretty rocky origins, but which, nevertheless featured some titanic battles with Fiat, who had decided to handicap themselves by using the Abarth-modified 131 in place of brother Lancia's Stratos, for sales and image reasons.

Surrounded by pictures of Vatanen, Waldegard and an evocative pictoral reminder of the organized chaos that is a night rally service area, Reynolds summarized that 1975-79 era.

'That was the best time of all for the Escort; the car was at its best, and we had the best drivers; a whole team that came together. But it didn't start that way!

'I joined FordSport in January 1973, down in South Ockendon. When FAVO closed I came up here with the club and ran it from Boreham. Tony Mason had been doing the rally admin job, but he left during that year and things were just left to drift. It was really on its uppers from a management view: when they went to Morocco in 1976, it was a shambles! Punctures were the problem, but poor old Jeremy Ferguson at Dunlop had to scrabble around getting the right tyres to the right cars, because some of them were on 15inch diameters and others on 13inch!.'

In Britain it was easy to overlook Escort's comparative lack of World Championship form. The year started with Roger Clark battling to fifth on the Monte Carlo, about average for the Ford on past record, beaten for saloon car honours in the class by Walter Rohrl's Opel. At home the year brought the usual Scottish, Welsh, Irish and RAC Rally victories, with Russell Brookes and Billy Coleman underlining that Clark's participation in British home events had raised the standard to the point where the maestro could be regularly beaten at his own game. It was Clark, however, who came home with his second victory in the RAC World Championship round; we are still waiting for another Briton to win once more ...

The 1976 season saw Ford adopt a new Finnish talent, Ari Vatanen, who came to live at the home of Boreham's John Griffiths during his apprenticeship year in the British Home International Championship. Ari's 1975 Escort début on the 1000 Lakes had been typically fast and furious with an immediate scattering of fastest times and chunks of scenery, but his loyalty to Ford outlasted any of his world class contemporaries. Ari had a turbulent début season with Ford, but he came away with that British title, the Tour of Britain (taken in a Group 1 RS 2000 of some 165bhp) and a reputation for a supreme 'win or bust' approach. The 'bust' part referred to an increasing collection of tattered Ford Escort body remnants when things didn't work out ... not to his mechanical sympathy, which remains above average for such a quick driver.

Speaking months before he left Ford for the 1984 delights of running the Rothmans Porsche team in battle, Charles Reynolds confirmed that analysis of Ari's 86 factory

The Ford Rally School was a feature of the late seventies in the UK. Naturally, the Escort was used to provide classic rear drive tuition in slippery surface skills. The three Escort Sports (below) and solitary RAC Rally winning RS 1800 are pictured at one of the School's main bases, the woods around Donington race circuit. The Sports were very easy, and great fun, to drive on mud. When John Taylor led you round at night with the 'proper' RS, the lessons were soon forgotten in the ensuing panic ...

outings had shown 'generally few mechanical problems. We reckoned that if he finished he was a likely winner. Otherwise the car was likely to have been tossed off the road!'

The painfully honest but quietly persistent Reynolds became the full time rally manager in 1977, and it was in February of that season that another key managerial role was filled. Former FAVO engineer and Mexico racing championship winner Allan Wilkinson had been working with Bill Meade on a number of RS product developments at Boreham, before Peter Ashcroft asked him to take on the Rally Engineer's post. This was

Flat-fronted RS 2000s went on winning their Group 1 class in the Castrol Autosport Championship into the eighties. This is the TV Times Challenge example of then Ford at Halewood-employed Terry Pankhurst, contesting the 1981 Gwynedd.

traditionally filled by practical men working flat out with the benefit of experience and minimum of theory. Allan Wilkinson brought draughtsmanship and a systematic approach to the task of taking the Escort's proven specification and ensuring that it was improved in detail durability, whilst drawing up more advanced machinery to succeed the world's most successful all round competition saloon.

In his methodical manner Charles Reynolds retained records of the primary factory Escort rallyists during the period to complete our casting list. The 1976 RAC marked the change in driver loyalties, for Timo Makinen rolled his way out of the Ford contracted lists in the Peugeot-reference registration P00 504R early in the event. That contrasted with the Motorcraft works Escort progress of new recruit Bjorn Waldegard on the same event, finishing third to show what he thought of Fiat Lancia's decision to restrain his progress during the preceding San Remo World Championship round. It was not the first time Waldegard had been restricted by team orders in the Italian ´equipe, where his handling of the Stratos underlined his earlier prowess with difficult cars such as Porsche's 911. Fiat's loss was Ford's direct gain for the 1977-1979 seasons, when Bjorn did more World Championship winning than any other Ford contracted driver, winning the 1979 title for himself in the process.

Hannu Mikkola returned to the Ford fold in 1978 and stayed until the completion of 1980 via his friendship, and a low profile Ford contract, with David Sutton's ´equipe. 'Hannu did not have quite the results of Bjorn with us, but they were super team mates,' recalled Reynolds. 'They would radio each other with stage conditions after one had been through and were generally very honest with each other and superb for us: great professionals.'

Ari Vatanen we have discussed, but it is worth pointing out that he did not leave the Escort for a full season with another make until his 1983 Opel contract, succeeded by 1984 with Peugeot and a restored reputation as a winner.

The winning Boreham-backed Brit whose name and that of Escort interweave

Barred from carrying the word Rothmans, the Escort's livery looks a little strange, but Ari Vatanen and Dave Richards aided the 1979 works effort by finishing second the 1000 Lakes. This picture makes a change from the eternal Finnish yump ...

intimately, was Roger Clark. Even legends have endings in the cruel commercial world and that came for Roger and Ford with a mainly Fiesta Group 2 programme in 1979. Leicestershire's international rally winner went on to a Triumph TR7 in 1980, but he did actually win the Cypriot European Championship round for the second time in an Escort during that Leyland season. Naturally the Cyprus rally winner was a David Sutton/Rothmans machine, the factory pulling their Escort out at the close of 1979.

Two other Brits were retained regularly by Ford at Boreham. Russell Brookes was contracted from 1976 to 1979 and brought along the most loyal sponsor in British motor sport history: Andrews Heat for Hire. Russell, one of life's terriers who persist beyond all reasonable hope, and can turn an early event roll to final victory like no other Brit, contributed home international victories. He was unlucky that the year his Escort won the New Zealand Motorgard Rally it was not a World Championship qualifier (1978). From 1977 to 1979 he scored two thirds and one second overall on Britain's RAC World Championship event, the best record by far of any UK driver in an Escort (or any other marque) except Roger Clark.

Malcolm Wilson was appallingly unlucky. The Cumbrian was a teenage Ford Anglia

Ford were supremely unfortunate not to begin the 1979 season with a win on the Monte Carlo Rally. Here is Bjorn Waldegard, the man who so nearly brought the Escort and Ford their first win in the world's most famous rally. By the end of the year he would be the world's first formally declared World Champion Rally Driver. Note the huge extensions dwarfing the narrower wheels and tyres preferred by Waldegard for ice use, a feature emphasized by the widened arches of the tarmac specification Escort.

Another Boreham built Escort in Rothmans 1979 livery: Ari Vatanen chauffeurs Dave Richards to their 1979 European Championship win in Cyprus.

Hannu Mikkola and Arne Hertz provided the subject for this atmospheric shot on the 1980 Acropolis, but victory – the first ever in the World Championship round for Ari Vatanen – went to the sister Rothmans Escort.

success and had factory machinery by 1977, when he and Graham Elsmore were donated RS 2000 Group 1 Escorts to contest British home international events and the RAC. Wilson came out of that closely fought category with honour and won Group 1 with a fine 10th overall on the RAC in a car with the best part of 100bhp less than the BDA Escort front runners. He proved capable of winning the Castrol Autosport national title twice in an Escort (1978/79), but was severely injured in Scotland during 1980. At the time he was setting times that made both Mikkola and Vatanen comment that Britain really had found somebody capable of Finnish forest pace, but Malcolm's ankles were badly broken in that Highland fling. He drove again that season but there was no doubt this was a crucial career setback. Running with the Rothmans team in 1981 his results included a brace of third overall placings in the Manx and Scottish Rothmans RAC Open Rally Championship rounds. His contribution to the development of the RS 1700T and RS 200 was considerable, but that is a later story ...

Technical topics

Theoretically, the biggest influence on the Escort's international rally progress should have been the switch to the new Group 2, as recorded for the Zakspeed racers. The rallyists, however, were not only able to complete 1975 as a full house Group 4 contender, but actually went all the way until the close of 1981, winning under Group 4 rules! How?

For 1976/77 it was simply a dispensation on behalf of the FIA that existing Group 4 cars, such as the Escort, could keep their radical modifications, rather than revert to the wet sump lubrication, four-speed gearbox and lower engine capacity that the new Group 2 would have dictated, along with many other changes that would have robbed the boxy Ford of a chance to win at World Championship level.

In 1977, however, on an appropriate 1 April date, a new international homologation form for the Escort RS ensured its future as a winner into the eighties, and past the début of

Hannu Mikkola's last Escort RAC and the year in which the Escort monopoly on Britain's World Champion qualifier was terminated. This LAT shot almost squelches of November in Britain; all one needs is a faceful of earth, the crackle of a BDA and the smell of mechanically-disturbed 'clag' to complete the feeling of being there. Mikkola finished second to Henri Toivonen's Sunbeam Talbot Lotus and then went on to win the 1981/82 editions of the RAC for Audi.

its front drive successor. FISA recognition number 650 allowed a fair but theoretical Escort RS to exist! By this stage one needed 400 similar production models to conform to Group 4 and only such cars would be allowed World Championship status with the best chance of outright victory from 1978 onward.

Ford at Boreham in the shape of Peter Ashcroft and ex-Weslake engineer John Griffiths argued successfully that at least 400 Escorts had been built to a specification that handily comprised: dry sump 2-litre, alloy block, BDA; five-speed ZF gearbox; twin-plate Borg & Beck clutch; four wheel disc brakes (vented 10.24in) with adjustable pedal bias for front to rear braking effort; four trailing rod and one transverse location link for the rear axle; modified suspension pick-up points; wheel arch extensions; and a front spoiler. Just like any production Escort you and I would have bought ...!

Actually, it was a breathtaking piece of barefaced sauce that was founded on the fact that the Ford was probably the most popular rally car ever built, in terms of numbers carrying the principal items in an exotic specification. David Sutton used to sell them overseas like the Queens Award for Industry was just around the corner for saturating the Peruvian and Bolivian rally car markets, never mind his European Escort rallying business.

This 1977 Group 4 move ensured the Ford a longer life than any competitive rally car has ever achieved, and even held refinements such as the fact that the wheel arch extension could take another 1.97 inch protrusion for the widest tarmac tyres, whenever required, for the smaller extension was officially part of a limited production car. Incidentally, by 1977 pressure from Ford and Jaguar in Britain had made the Paris-based authorities withdraw the Group 2 ruling requiring wet sump lubrication. It was withdrawn on grounds of engine fragility, as a consequence of having a sump full of oil usually in the wrong place under heavy braking, or tarmac cornering, duress. None of it made any real difference to Group 2 race results, they still contained the usual quota of BMW initials in the premier places ...

Back in the Escort rally world the initial development work on the Mk2 was primarily concerned with the tarmac specification mentioned earlier. Present day Jaguar specialist

1980, but it could be almost any year of Motoring News *Road Rally Championship contention, as Mike Pattison takes the EARS Escort RS through a Cilwendig ford.*

Tom Walkinshaw probably gained his enthusiasm for rallying the Rover products his TWR company also prepared from these lengthy development sessions at venues such as Cadwell Park. I vividly remember Tom's face lighting up with a brilliant Scottish smile when describing times that equalled or bettered Clark's during such sessions, but Roger was always a supreme competitor 'on-the-day' rather than a development driver.

The Makinen car (KHK 982N) I drove in late 1975 for *Motor Sport* was one of a pair produced to further Ford's tarmac speed and was distinguished by Zakspeed racing-style arches to cover up to 11 inch wide Minilites. A compression strut located the front MacPherson strut bottom arms, instead of a roll bar, and the long strut-style dampers at the rear, necessary to clear the bigger wheels and tyres, were moved inboard substantially. On the Tour de France they had used a Watts link, but Panhard rod could be substituted with pre-bracketed speed. I was given a figure of 4½° for castor and 2° negative camber for these quick machines – Clark took one such machine (KHK 983N) to the Isle of Man and beat the speediest Irish-based Porsche 911s – and that had changed little by the time Mick Jones and Roger Clark were sorting out LAR 800P at Chobham in September 1976. A midweek session at the Chobham military circuit, using the tarmacadam twists and crests of the 'Snake' mountain section, left them with 4° 10′ castor and 1° 15′ camber up front on a compression strut front that featured parallel track settings of neither toe-in nor toe-out displacement.

The ⅝inch front roll bar was the same as I experienced on the Makinen car and the principle of softer front than rear spring rate was retained on LAR 800P. To be precise the front springs were rated at 160lb in. and the slipper spring rear leaves (two blades) at 195lb in. For comparison the 1979 forest Escorts from Boreham used 190lb in. fronts and 120lb in. rears; a widely copied combination. For testing the tarmac car was equipped with 7in. rims, Dunlop 418 compound slicks and wheel spacers of ⅜ in. to clear those back dampers, all the shock absorbers being by Bilstein. To fight the twitchiness inherent in an Escort that had a largely forest history, they had lowered the steering rack and aligned it with reset steering arms to combat bump steer.

A familiar sight on British and European Championship events was this David Sutton (Cars) Ltd RS 1800 of 1980-81. It won the Welsh for Vatanen and Richards in 1980 and 1981, and was one of two cars with consecutive registration plates, regularly fielded by Rothmans/Sutton in the British Open Championship.

LAR 800P had a 5:1 final drive in 1976, but the 1975 tarmac car we timed (with John Griffiths clicking the watches) utilized a 5.3 and returned 0-60mph times of some 6.5s, The snag was that, 'speed was limited to little over 100mph at our rpm limit of 9200rpm,' in my January 1976 words.

On loose surfaces reliability and a good torque curve were at a premium, but Brian Hart did develop the 2-litre BDA with fuel injection to 270-275bhp level for 1979. The 1975 tarmac car mentioned offered a very docile 245bhp with 'excellent torque delivery from 4 to 8000rpm,' but forest cars did end up with more than that. The Sutton/Rothmans cars tended to stick with a very conservative Weber 48 DCOE specification, engine builder and 1973 Boreham escapee Terry Hoyle reckoning, 'it's these racer types who go for the last bit of horsepower, I try and make it drivable and reckon the ... thing will last that way, too!' The result? Usually 260bhp at 8500rpm and 168lb ft torque on 7000rpm was reported as average for 1980/81.

Fuel injection was always a mixed blessing in factory minds. True, Roger Clark took a Lucas-injected alloy block to RAC victory in 1972, but that did not predict widespread injection Escorts, even for rallying, until 1978. Then they deployed both Lucas and Kugelfischer systems, with Hoyle later following his own Kugelfischer injection path and still not finding favour over the simply understood and repaired double-choke carburettors. Ford at Boreham did use injection for some of the faster events from 1978 onward, but by the time we saw them back in Britain for the annual RAC massacre of the opposition, carburettors ruled, OK?

Back at our tarmac theme the 1975/76 cars described were succeeded by a 1977/78 specification that was rarely reproduced, but was easy to identify by the 'extensions on an extension' wheel arch, rather than the earlier Zakspeed, or normal, arches. The first time I can recall seeing such an Escort was on November 1977's Tour de Corse, when Jean Pierre Nicolas and Russell Brookes had wide-rimmed Escorts that looked much the same, but which Allan Wilkinson enthusiastically showed us in an Ajaccio garage, were quite different underneath. The Nicolas Ford employed coil springs instead of the slipper leaf

Two Ford drivers take shower after gruelling season.

Nelson Piquet World Formula 1 Champion   *Ari Vatanen World Rally Champion*

1981 was an excellent year for champagne, as long as you had a Ford engine in your car, like these two gentlemen had.

On your left, Nelson Piquet from Brazil.

In only his third full season of Grand Prix racing he drove one of Bernie Ecclestone's Brabhams with a Ford Cosworth engine to the World Formula One Drivers' Championship.

On your right, Ari Vatanen from Finland.

He drove a Rothmans Rally Team Group 4 Ford Escort, prepared by David Sutton Cars Ltd, to the 1981 World Rally Drivers' Championship.

Maybe that's why the Fords in your showroom feel a shade more exciting to drive than other makes. They have racing in their blood.

We wish all our drivers a happy Christmas.

Ford gives you more.

Off with his head! Ari's head was transposed onto Mario Andretti's shoulders to produce this composite World Championship advertisement of Ford success in 1981. This sleight-of-hand was exposed by Michael Greasley, Motoring News.

type described, and I subsequently learned that it was one of a pair built to contest the October 1977 World Championship round, Italy's San Remo. The later tarmac specification was allied successfully with the 270 plus horsepower Kugelfischer mechanical fuel injection layout, hauling just over 1980lb (900kg) along very smartly. This was the lowest weight I could find recorded for the Mk2 in rallying form, where sump guards, accomodation for two people and comprehensive roll cage protection (usually from Safety Devices on works cars) made a mockery of the 1782lb (810kg) minimum sometimes achieved by Zakspeed's racers. For a typical works or Sutton Escort you could reckon anywhere from 2090 – 2156lb (950 – 980kg) rather than the sub-2000lb (908kg) levels achieved by those rare 1977-79 tarmac works Escorts. Cars built for the Safari could be closer to 2420lb (1100kg).

Sometimes Allan Wilkinson had to put weight back into the tarmac specification for durability reasons. Those hardworked and numerically high differential gear sets fairly whizzed round within those strong axle casings and AW devised his solution to the problem in 1978. A boot mounted radiator, electric bilge pump (I suspect the maritime influence of former boss B Meade here: Escort rallycross cars used bilge pumps to clear their mud-splattered screens too!), and fan were set to suck air within the Mk2 Escort's boot, all played their part. Alan Wilkinson pondered which points of the gear sets would be hottest, and adopted the basic principle that transmission oil is used to cool, rather than lubricate. He was smart at Ford and gets smarter still outside, which is probably the reason some former workmates smart at the memory of AW's Boreham tenure.

Charles Reynolds said of Allan Wilkinson's reign, prior to departure for Toyota Cologne in February 1980: 'Allan got the job done. There were no records, no proper spec buildsheets for the cars and no drawings to use when he arrived. Sure, he was clever, but what he did was to bring a solid base of experience to make a super basic car a superior rally car in every respect. Simply, it was a more competitive car for his presence.' Judging by Charles Reynold's progress at the competition helm of the David Richards - inspired Prodrive BMW rally team, the same glowing testament should fairly be applied to CR as well ...

Of the traditional loose surface Escort specification there was little basic change to the

The 1981 World Champion and the Escort's most loyal works driver, Ari Vatanen, with his Rothmans-era co-driver, Dave Richards. David won the prestigious Halda Golden Helmet award in 1981 for his navigational and high speed office administration skills.

The Mk2 could still be seen racing in 1983. Ross Cheever pedals the Ronnie Scott jazz club Escort RS 1800 at the Brands Hatch European GP meeting in a supporting race for Thundersports.

Ari Vatanen drove two Escorts for the Widnes-based MCD preparation concern in 1982 and proved the car could still be competitive. Here is the ex-John Taylor DKP 191T at the opening Rothmans RAC Open Rally Championship of that year, where it finished third with Neil Wilson co-driving. They were seventh on the Circuit of Ireland, after leading and setting eight quickest times. This performance in a new car (FEK 472V) that went very well in Scotland, and the Isle of Man, where Vatanen was partnered by subsequent Peugeot companion, Terry Harryman.

Escort and Hot Rod racing have been synonymous, but this is the unfamiliar combination of George Polley and a Mk2, appearing together for the last time in 1983. The former Anglia star later drove a Toyota-bodied machine with Ford-based running gear.

High preparation standards are a feature of the 1700 pushrod-engined Escorts in hot rod racing from former saloon car racing innovator Norman Abbott and the Brown and Geeson-backed example for Sean Brown.

John Welch shows off the 470bhp ex-Martin Schanche Escort's tricycling abilities at Brands Hatch.

formula outlined in the Group 4 homologation. A carburettor engine was most likely, and it is worth noting that the body preparation was an art in itself. To see one bare, prepared but not paint primed, was to see the art of welding fully extended with myriad little dabs stitching together mass produced seams, or rudely inserted sections for the ZF gearbox, or rear turrets. The roll cage took some of the stress of course, the back legs picking up in the region of the rear damper top mounts and the bars bolted into the steel bodywork for extra rigidity. All the suspension mounting points were stronger and angled from years of experience, but they also had to fabricate the rear floorpan around the intrusion of long axle location links (elongated in the Mk2 initially, but so many suspension layouts were tried it's hard to do more than generalize). The links were normally parallel arms to top and bottom of the sturdy axle with pick up points often provided for both Watts and Panhard rod location for much of the period discussed, the Panhard most likely on the loose.

Multi-leaf rear springs remained the favourite forest medium, along with a front suspension that usually had the roll bar location into the bottom arm, rather than a compression strut. There were simply masses of spring and damper choices to greet Wilkinson on arrival as rally engineer; like the sheer number of halfshafts available in the early seventies this produced some great stories.

(I cannot vouch for the truth of the following popular tale, save to say that it has been repeated to me dozens of times, in and outside the Ford enclave. The gist, for it can be told as a Shaggy Dog story that goes on with different characters puzzling away, was that works Escorts were going out of the door with weirdly assorted components, e.g. Safari rally front coil springs on one side, tarmac low ride height the other! Similarly the dampers would be muddled up and the cars literally thrown together. They survived because they were so well proven, and the drivers simply the best in existence.)

On a similar theme, I can recall panting my way around the miles of corridors and workshops that form the Fiat Abarth factories in Turin. Meeting up with chief development engineer Giorgio Pianta, the gent who sorted out saloons such as the 131 and

The Escort has been ever so slightly modified to stay in touch with the demands of eighties rallysport! Gunnar Kittilson's Zakspeed Turbo Escort finished fifth at the Lydden 1984 international: the best 2-WD result on a day that reflected how 4-WD turbos now rule the rallycross roost.

Lancia 037 with equal practical mileage brio (between racing exploits that are retold with an almost inevitable reference to, 'the time I am beating Ronnie Peterson in Formula 3), I asked Giorgio what he felt the Fiat 131 needed now. At the time it had an independent rear end, flyweights panels and a 16-valve DOHC engine ... He said with an expressive shrug: 'OK, eet is clear. This Carr, she must 'ave the Coswort engine! You know, the Escort is no carr at all without thees engine ...'

That story at least underlines the respect the Italians had developed for the chunky Ford, but when it came to adapting technically their favourite tyre company's rubber to the Escort nobody laughed so much. For the 1980/81 seasons David Sutton was faced with replacing Dunlop, who absented themselves from the Escort cause in the wake of the Escort's 1979 withdrawal, and he decided on Pirelli. There was nothing inherently wrong with the Milanese-manufactured radials, but initially they did not suit the live-axle Escort, having been developed with the steeply inclined negative cambers of the all independent suspension Fiat 131. Eventually it all made sense on 13in. diameter wheels, Sutton being another who could find no advantage in the once fashionable (via Timo Makinen) 15in. wheel diameter.

Aside from the tyres, which did render the Sutton team uncompetitive in some British home internationals of 1980, the Sutton équipe ran a very conservative specification throughout. They relied on the experience of mechanics every bit the equal of Ford at Boreham, supervised by Ron Lumley, to rebuild any of the frequently tattered mounts their second favourite Flying Finn brought back. On one Portuguese occasion No. 1 Finn Mikkola even managed to land on No. 2 favourite Vatanen!

Aaagh, the nostalgia of those slewing, screaming Fords, wastefully streaming traction to the winds of their spinning rear wheels. The car that inspired a scrutineering bay full of 16-valve, rear drive, imitators had entered the era of the turbocharged four-wheel drives, but what of the memories left in their spectacular wake? They tended to fade amongst the 'high tech' realities of the eighties (see Chapter 14).

Chapter 9

Erika's eighties engine

Predicting a contrary future where governments and customers demanded ever-lower exhaust emissions, allied to exceptional fuel economy and improved performance on a fashionably meagre service schedule, Ford set out on a worldwide hunt for these qualities in 1974. That engine, a Compound Valve-angle, Hemispherical chamber (CVH) surfaced in the Erika-coded front drive Escort of 1980. Yet it was partially proved in Fiesta and returned to that model range in 1984. Here is the story of how Ford developed the new four-cylinder in a multi-national programme, 'which cost nearly £500,000,000 to implement...'

TWO years before the development programme for front drive Escorts began under the coding Erika, preliminary work started on an entirely new Ford engine range. Some four months before the new Escort's September European debut in 1980, Ford at Dunton's Ron Mellor was able to guide the technical press around the detailing behind the massive multi-national motor investment. I went along in April to see this significant preview of Escort's new four-cylinder heart, but details were embargoed until 14 May 1980 when Ford told the world the scale of their commitment.

'The new engine, which will have capacities of 1100, 1300 and 1600cc, will be built on a world scale exceeding one million units a year. The total programme, which has cost nearly £500,000,000 to implement, includes the construction of an advanced automated engine plant at Bridgend in South Wales to supply the whole of Europe, and extensive re-equipment of the Rouge plant in Dearborn, Michigan. Engine production is already under way on both sides of the Atlantic and the first examples of cars using this engine will go on sale later this year.' Up to 15 April 1984, some 1.5 million CVH engines had been manufactured annual production equivalent to 458,000 in 1988.

Ford estimated that they had covered 9.9 million miles (16 million kilometres) in the period from January 1974, when the first prototype engine ran, to the 1980 launch. Over 2000 test and development motors were constructed, including those to power 15 Fiestas for further evaluation in 1979 and a further 200 Fiestas received CVH power in 1980, each scheduled for 50,000 mile assessment and which 'went like hell.' in Ron Mellor's introductory words. A colleague who bought one of the original 1.6 Fiestas from the company confirmed this prophesy of the 1984 Fiesta XR2's CVH-aided prowess: 0-60mph was under ten seconds, and top speed comfortably over 110mph, when the 96bhp former XR3 carburettor CVH engine was installed in the facelifted Fiesta XR2. In Europe they built an initial batch of 416 prototype CVH power plants, followed by an experimental run of 792 on Bridgend's production tooling.

The cylinder head was the vital component in trying to combine contradictory characteristics such as high performance, economy and low emissions levels. Ford R&D labs in Dearborn had been looking at head design in 1971, particularly examining the Honda-patented Compound Vortex Combustion Chamber [CVCC]. These emission-conscious principles were used by Honda to 1984 on their home market. Ford found them lacking for their inability to pass strict emission levels without a catalytic converter. That was in 1976, when three basic head designs were assessed: CVCC, wedge (similar to the smaller Kent crossflow pushrod units found in the Fiesta) and the prototype CVH. The latter depended on the classic hemispherical combustion chamber, 'just as the Offenhauser and Riley showed us,' in Mr Mellor's 1980 words.

The classic performance layout, however, typified by the Lotus-Ford Twin Cam of the sixties, was for twin overhead camshafts to serve the valve gear, one shaft for exhaust valves and the other inlet. Ford examined such DOHC powerplants from Alfa Romeo, Lotus,

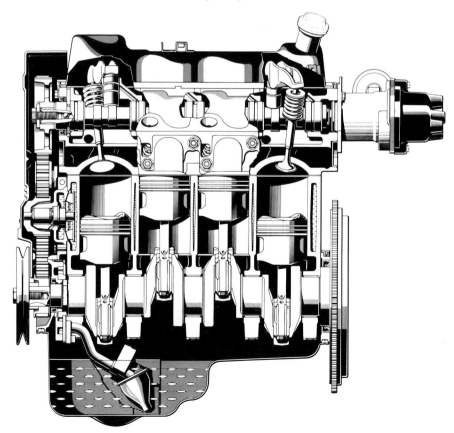

Side view of the CVH reveals most of the key features, including angled cylinder head valves, ridged pistons, belt driven overhead camshafts and stout five-bearing crankshaft.

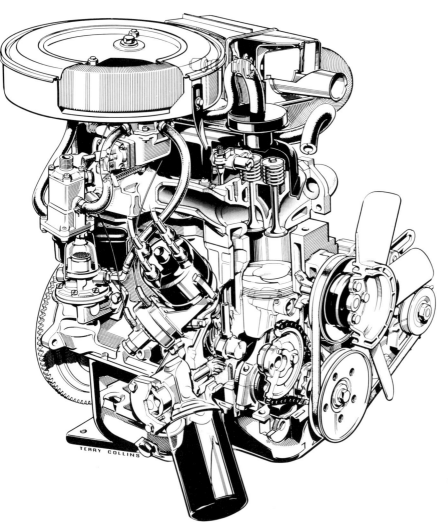

TERRY COLLINS

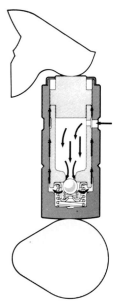

CVH's predecessor was the pushrod crossflow engine of the Kent series with Heron head pistons and upright valves. The same principles are found today in 1.1 Escorts sold in Britain. 9/2

Principles of the hydraulic tappet are shown here with the camshaft beneath and operating arm for the valve gear above.

Toyota and Chevrolet's Cosworth Vega, amongst others, and compared them with high efficiency single-shaft motors from Audi, BMW, Mercedes and the contemporary Japanese. Ford engineers decided that, provided they could get large enough valves into the hemi head, there was no need for the complexity and cost of either DOHC, or the four-valve per cylinder approach – now intensely fashionable and available to Ford via Cosworth's 1969 BDA.

There was the immensely clever Triumph Dolomite Sprint which combined four valves per cylinder with SOHC, but Ford were not convinced they could build this type of unit with the cost and low servicing/durability standards their wide range of customers need. There are still some Ford customers who simply don't service their cars at all, running them until they drop, or running with just an oil and filter change at irregular intervals. The company's reputation for tough power plants was and is based on simpler concepts than four valves per cylinder or DOHC ... And yet, the Japanese seem to be able to hurl large numbers of complex power plants (16-valve, DOHC, electronically-injected Corolla; three-valve, SOHC, injected or carburated Honda, and any number of Turbo terrors) at the consumer, their prices reflecting considerable mass production commitment ...

Ford eschewed such eighties sophistications and applied for nine patents as they

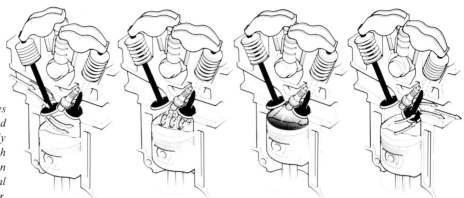

Offset and inclined angles of the valves (emphasized in black) are clearly shown here, along with tilted spark plug location inside a hemispherical combustion chamber.

combined 45° included angle valves with a slight 7° skew angle across that hemi chamber so that the valves could be actuated by the single belt-driven overhead camshaft. Deep breathing was encouraged by large, round, inlet ports (around 1.43in) and rectangular exhaust tracts measuring 1.43 by 1.31in. Inlet valve diameters are listed along with camshaft timing in our Ford-produced CVH chart that can be found on pages 412-13 Suffice it to say that inlet valve diameters were divided into 38mm for 1100s and 42mm for the rest, while the exhausts showed more variety with the 1100 on 32.2mm, 1300 on 34mm and both 1.6 derivatives having a 37mm exhaust valve girth. The twin-choke carburated 1.6 destined for the XR3 (1980-82) and XR2 Fiesta (1984-on) did not have any extra compression or valve size increases, but the longer duration camshaft did provide extra lift in XR-guise, a sporting 10.09mm versus the usual 9.56mm of all other CVH units.

Even the low compression CVH units operated a minimum of 8.5:1 (listed as an option only for 1100 in the launch engine line) whilst the rest ran 9.5:1. Ford Motorcraft single-choke carburettors were specified for all but the XR's 1.6, which had the Weber 32/34 DFT downdraught, twin-choke unit with fixed jets whose size was changed during the opening months of 1981 to provide more progressive throttle opening and reliable idling.

Ron Mellor's pride and joy were the hydraulic tappets, developed in association with Dearborn's experience and that of North American suppliers, but asked to operate without 'pumping up' and losing valve operational efficiency to a considerably higher speed than had been asked for in mass production before: 7000 to 7200rpm. Despite this, the specifications in the workshop manual record that 6300rpm is the maximum recommended rpm for continuous operation on all engines, bar the single carburettor 1.6, which is specified at 6150rpm. Intermittent use of 6700rpm was felt to be safe on all save the single choke 1.6, which was restricted to 6500. Originally, the cam ran in three bearings but many analysis techniques, including high rpm photography, persuaded them to fit five bearings to the camshaft, revise the profile to produce easier valve lift characteristics, and adopt softer valve springs and pressed steel rockers.

Computer-aided block design

The European Ford design operation centres at Merkenich in Cologne and Dunton in Essex were able to make extensive use of the huge computer resources of the parent American concern by taking advantage of the different time zones, effectively using up dead transatlantic time in mammoth number crunching sessions to speed design calculations. As far as the European CVH was concerned – and we have to remember that the American counterpart, like the final USA Escort, was a very different design despite the

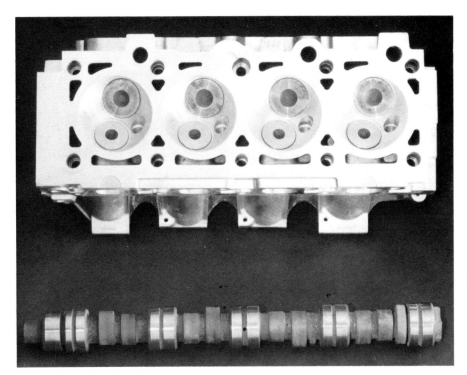

Generous diameters are provided for the valve heads to provide the alloy cylinder head with the effective breathing characteristics that the adjacent camshaft complements.

shared technology – Ford USA contributed extensively to all that head research and combustion chamber shaping; Ford of Germany did the cylinder block, gaskets, pistons and connecting rods. Britain's primary responsibilities included carburation, cooling and water pump design – plus final manufacturing and assembly at Bridgend.

Sand-cast in grey iron with a traditional disdain for siamese block space-saving structure, despite the need for transverse location (a feature of current Honda four-cylinder engines and the legions of BMC to ARG A-series variations), the new CVH cast-iron block sat beneath the deep breathing alloy head. At the time Ford said this was their first aluminium head, ignoring the limited production, sub-contracted BDA, or the Lotus-Ford TC, and there were many who wondered why such a forward-thinking unit had not been equipped with an alloy cylinder block? The answers seemed to centre on cost versus low noise level and adequate strength, although Ron Mellor commented at the time that if Great Britain or West Germany had been blessed with a tradition of alloy mass manufacture, such as that found in France, the story could have been different ...

Computer analysis of the iron block structure, to make sure that its strengthening ribs and sound deadened manners were as precisely calculated as possible, was carried out by Leuven University in Belgium. Mr. Mellor reckoned such computer-aided design (CAD) had saved them about four months trial-and-error work. The five-main bearing crankshaft was of nodular graphite cast-iron, rather than being produced by the forging process. The main reasoning, as ever, was reduced cost but with a safe rpm range stretching toward 7000rpm there was no lack of strength ...

To permutate three different capacities from the initial CVH stock there were two bore sizes and three crankshaft strokes, but the difference between an 1100 crank and that for a 1300 is just 0.014in (0.36mm). The 1.6 litre has almost square bore/stroke dimensions whilst the smaller units are positively short stroke. Testing to ensure constant lubrication with what Ron Mellor described as, 'The cow bell pick-up in the oil pan,' involved subjecting the transverse installation to 0.8 – 0.9g cornering forces and ensuring that the pick up remained

Cast-iron is used for cylinder block and crankshaft, extensive use of computers being made to speed design progress of both.

submerged.

The oil pump, driven directly from the crankshaft nose, worked in association with a carefully baffled sump and an internal system that made sure any high pressure oil was recirculated to the low pressure side of the system in case of leaks. Mellor candidly blamed oil companies not only for the deteriorating quality of their fuel octane ratings in four star grades, but also for the fact that Ford felt unable to pursue the 12,000 mile oil change interval, or even foresee the use of the sealed-for-life lubricant.

Thus the CVH engine has had a 6000 mile service interval in the four years it has been offered, with no need to take the rocker cover off in a routine service, 'because we are not in the business of valve gear adjustment,' asserted Mr Mellor proudly of the hydraulic lifters. Cutting 1.3 and 1.6 engine servicing demands to under 45 minutes at the routine interval also owed a debt to the Lucas or Bosch breakerless ignition systems specified. On the 1.1 CVH or the 1.1 OHV (ex-Fiesta pushrod Kent) that was specified for front drive Escorts in the UK, you will find a distributor which is from Bosch if it has a brown cap, Lucas when in black. These do have contact breakers within and demand an extra 15 minutes service time in Ford's original estimation.

Which engine?

So far as I and the Ford Press garage are aware, by far the vast majority of front drive in Escorts running in the UK have *not* got the CVH overhead camshaft engine in 1.1 litre guise. They, unlike those supplied in Germany and most continental countries (which do have the CVH in its smallest size), use the ex-Fiesta OHV unit of Kent crossflow parentage. This is not an easy point to detect from specification sheets as both CVH and OHV Kent have a capacity of 1117cc with a bore and stroke of 73.96mm x 64.98mm and 55bhp. The pushrod Kent OHV unit, however, has maximum power at 5700 instead of 6000rpm, the OHV unit comes only with 9.15:1CR in Escort guise and has a slight torque bonus over the CVH at 61lb ft instead of 59lb ft, both at 4000rpm.

Visually the CVH can be identified by the toothed belt beneath a plastic cover driving to the overhead camshaft, but just in case you are not sure you will find that the simple ex-Fiesta OHV Kent-descended 1.1 has been coded GLB or GLA (the works manual lists both!) whilst the CVH engines are coded as follows: GMA = low compression [LC] CVH 1.1 with 55bhp; GPA, high compression [HC] CVH 1.1; JPA = HC CVH 1.3; LPA = HC CVH 1.6 of 79bhp single carb spec; and LUA = the XR3 type 1.6 CVH twin-choke of 96bhp. Those codes will be found stamped upon the VIN (Vehicle Identification Number) within box 8. The VIN plate is normally riveted to the front crossmember, the nearest cross-section when you've opened the bonnet.

Cross-checking at Ford showed that the CVH had always been normal basic equipment for 1.1 Escorts in Germany but that the British parts book had only listed CVH as if it were a UK option, so the RHD models normally had the earlier ex-Fiesta 1.1 litre. On the road it makes very little difference either way, but it plays havoc when you are trying to make sense of book data.

Other key CVH original design features included the use of the camshaft drive belt to activate also the water pump, with both fuel pump and distributor camshaft driven. In this context it is relevant to note that the XR3i injection unit is coded LR within the engine section of the VIN plate and that the distributor with its breakerless ignition has a blue cap and is of West German origin. The work involved in converting the Escort engine to injection is described in Part III of our Chapters devoted to 'The Performers'.

Motorcraft were charged with the responsibility of making a 14mm spark plug with copper core to run without fouling at traffic speeds in these power units which produced from 49bhp per litre to the target 60bhp per litre in XR3 twin-choke 1.6 litre trim. Only limited space was available to get a spanner to the plug, so it had to be a ⁵⁄₈in. AF sizing, the complete spark plug protected by a rubber boot of the type we were used to seeing in high performance power plants, such as the Ford Cosworth BDA. The plug leads were new, too. They had cores in glassfibre, impregnated with carbon, sheathed in silicone and insulated with, 'a special plastic known as EPDM,' in Ford's contemporary words. They added, 'An outer sleeve of Hypalon provides stable resistance to oil and engine heat degradation ... For

The high compression piston for the 1.6 shows the unique crown that Ford produced to work with the compound valve angles and hemispherical combustion chambers.

better combustion under all conditions, the voltage output at the coil with the breakerless system is increased by 30 per cent compared with the conventional system. More significantly spark energy is six times greater while the spark duration is doubled.'

Certainly hot and cold starts on the two new Escorts I have owned and all the test cars have given no qualms, although the battery – which can be anything from a 35 amp hr to 52 amp hr – reached a reluctant stage, even in the first winter of XR ownership. It demanded at least the sympathy of a depressed clutch pedal to spin the motor with true grit. The workshop manual I have lists three possible alternator sources: Bosch, Lucas and Motorola with 28 to 55 Amp outputs at 6000rpm according to a choice of four models from Lucas and Bosch, three from Motorola. Incidentally the alternator specification called for a sustained 15,000rpm to be withstood in service.

Original spark plug equipment was of the Motorcraft 12C series, usually AGPR or AGP series in the CVH engines, the 1.6 restricted to AGPR 12C in single-choke/79bhp form.

Performance

Looking at the engines in April 1980 with dry weights between 227lb (103kg) and 246lb (112kg) and power outputs between 55 and 96bhp, it was possible to see that Ford had completed a cost-effective mass production power plant. They revealed, in addition to the test details given earlier, that both European and Federal emission standard engines for America had been developed in Europe: in 1978 they built, 'well over 200 prototype engines

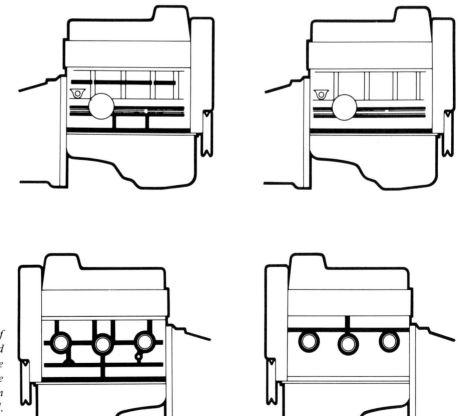

Displaying each side of the cast-iron block. Ford demonstrate how the strengthening ribs were moved during the design and development period, September 1978 to January 1980's solution.

From the exhaust manifold side of the engine, normally the side closest to the front grille of an Escort, within the engine compartment, the CVH packs a belt-driven alternator and cast-iron exhaust manifolding. The Ford-embossed cover hides the cogged belt overhead camshaft drive.

... Some tested on a 600 hour durability cycle which included high speed, full load equivalent to running at maximum speed for over 6500km [40,365 miles]. Development continued in five stages throughout 1979 and 1980, with over 1800 more engines, until the go-ahead was given for mass production.'

Apart from tantalizing glimpses of its potential in the Fiesta we were left rather baffled as to the likely in-car performance of the new Ford motors. Although it was obvious that worthwhile power and reduced servicing gains had been made with a range that would echo Fiesta in the use of thermostatically controlled electic fans for their radiators, rather than the previous mechanical units of rear drive Escorts.

From the carburettor side, normally closest to the front compartment bulkhead in an Escort engine compartment, the CVH shows off Motorcraft-branded oil filter and dipstick. The latter does not straggle through the carburettor inlet manifold's alloy embrace, as it has to when installed in the car, further hampered by the electrical leads for the warning light display!

By Ford's own standards, the CVH set new upper limits for thermal efficiency and showed worthwhile weight gains over the older SOHC engines found in the Cortina. Compared on a weight-for-weight basis against the Kent crossflows the 1.3 litre models in each range were just under 10lb apart, so an alloy cylinder block could have been valid to further improve the CVH's small advantage over the Kent, which was basically a sixties product uprated for front drive use in the Fiesta of the seventies.

Appraising the CVH powerplant four years and 1.5 million European engines later, it is fair to say that Ford's multi-national programme produced a tough, fuel-efficient four-cylinder worthy of a crisp new Escort. In service it has been asked not only to provide 50 horsepower economy but many aftermarket tuners, and Ford themselves, have asked for 125 to 140bhp. This can be delivered with turbocharged docility, provided intercooling is used in association with a reliable turbocharger installation, and the latter figure represents 87.7bhp per litre, about the same as you find in Group A racing Rovers. As far as I know the main reciprocating components of such engines have stayed reliable even when some of the cruder specialists have attacked with an excess of turbo zeal, although those who provided non-intercooled boost and left the standard 9.5:1 compression could persuade the top end of the engine to creak and yield under the strain, eventually!

The engine had been raced extensively in the later RS 1600i injection trim during 1983/84 with success over rivals VW in the first year and class-conquering supremacy in 1984, when it showed greater reliability. In 1983, Richard Longman's West Country concern was extracting over 150bhp; his best figure from mid-season represented 96.9bhp per litre. This, however, was with the aid of some piston-burning high compression ratios in the 13:1 region and there were a lot of engine failures in this trim. By the close of the year and for 1984 the Longman 'equipe's camshaft development work had provided similar power at less risk: this was written after four 1984 Trimoco British Saloon Car Championship qualifying rounds, when Longman himself was leading the series outright in one of the Red Datapost Escort RS 1600s. The Escort went on to win the Manufacturer's title that year, with Richard Longman runner-up to title-winner Andy Rouse.

In August 1983, just 28 years after he had joined the company, Dunton Engineering chief Ron Mellor reviewed the story of CVH in service. Reliability ? Mr Mellor laughed, almost with relief that we were not starting off on the dreaded new Escort suspension controversy (see subsequent Chapter!) and happily recited, 'the CVH was actually better in launch year reliability than the run out old engines!'. He confirmed that there had been two suppliers of the hydraulic tappets which had contributed to the service durability and low noise levels: Stanadyne and Eaton, and that 6500rpm had been selected as the rpm limiter cut-out point on the injection engines because of the tolerances of production which could 'allow up to 6700 to be reached. Theres's no point in using these sort of revs anyway, all you get are diminishing power returns,' he said.

Asked if there had been any notable service problems for CVH in the opening years of what is expected to be an exceptionally long production life, Ron Mellor recalled: 'We had to put a sticker on the oil filler cap to make sure they pushed it down tight after use! Externally there were some cosmetic changes to seal the engine bay and prevent the ingress of road dirt that earlier models experienced. Then there was that business with some of the journalists who insisted on filling the fuel tank right up. You really shouldn't trickle fill it to the brim, we did all that tank work to make sure it didn't percolate cold fuel drawn from underground tanks, when filled within a hot car left to stand immediately after fill up beside a hot autobahn.' In other words the expansion chamber at the top of the Escort's fuel tank was there to accommodate the phenomenon GP racing teams have exploited in 1984: that cold fuel can be squeezed into a smaller space than petrol kept at normal in-car temperatures.

A cross-check amongst Ford dealers such as Thomas Motors at Blackpool, Stormont at Tonbridge in Kent, and my local agent in Henley revealed that Ron Mellor's confidence in the CVH – and indeed, the Escort in general – was not misplaced. There were isolated problems with water pumps and some of the harder RS 1600i conductors had reportedly experienced trouble with the overhead camshaft belt drive.

Ford's claims to have thoroughly tested the power unit before production seem justified to this author. My personal experience of the power unit extends across at least 30 test examples and 43,000 XR3/3i miles in my own examples. I have neven been let down by a major failure, although my original XR3 did take to coughing up all its water on occasion and was much improved by a jetting and emulsion tube change in the Weber carburettor. Perhaps the most convincing examples came from early pre-production prototypes at Lommel, Ford's Belgian test track, where I once spent five days with three passengers aboard travelling at speeds between 80 and 95mph with an extremely low mileage example that gave no trouble at all. They hadn't even finished all the trim details on that car, but mechanically it was A1. The engine is harsh, or noisy, in harder use, but it does seem efficient and durable provided that the overhead camshaft belt is regularly changed.

Chapter 10

Engineering an eighties Escort

'Simple is efficient', was the slogan chosen by Ford's British advertising agents at Ogilvy & Mather. Creating a product that looked so simply correct was a complex multi-national business that created some controversial characteristics

'THAT'S a damn nice car', growled Henry Ford II when he first rode in a reasonably accurate prediction of the new front drive Escort early in 1978. Now Henry Ford and urbane diplomacy were not natural soulmates and he hardly needed to be effusive in praise of anyone, least of all employees creating an expensive new concept to carry the legendary family four letter surname. So that forthright opinion was valued by the engineers and creators of that body style, sheet steel which went a step beyond the hatchback.

After the sale of literally millions of rear drive Escorts, cars that epitomized conventional thinking and styling for the generation before VW's Summer 1974-launched Golf hatchback, Ford were faced with their most important European design challenge. For the replacement Escort would have to incorporate front drive technology, and with it a standard of product features that would simply not have occurred to the product planners of the sixties. Consider a small Ford with a brand new engine, an accent on aerodynamics and independent rear suspension. A car to compete not only with the obviously successful Golf hatchback formula of 1974, but capable of adaptation to American needs, production anywhere in the world, and preferably capable of competing on those markets for at least five years without major styling change. There was the assistance of Ford's first successful front drive car, Fiesta, which was in the pipeline for production in 1976. The Fiesta, famous for its pioneering role amongst multi-nationals in using a purpose built Spanish production plant but *not* Ford's first European front driver (Taunus 12M), would provide a starting point for Ford front drive Escort transmission development. Ford's smallest seventies

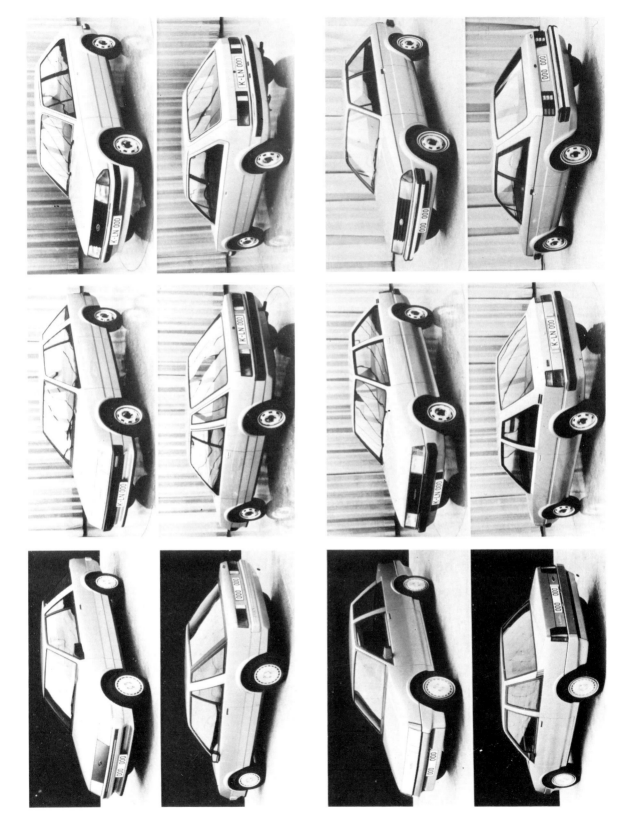

(opposite page)
Decisions, all my life,
such decisions! These are
some of the 1976 and
1977 full-size glassfibre
models that Ford
examined and finally
rejected on the way to
the production front drive
Escort shape. The main
styling themes, and where
they originated can be
clearly observed,
particularly the Cologne
study's extra rear, side,
window. They had this on
a two-door, but it
actually only made
production with five-door
coachwork. The model to
the lower right has the
grille and lamps about
right, and a similar
shape, without the rear
boot extension of the
production Escort; it
completed many wind
tunnel hours.

Neat wagon dreams
showing some affinity to
the old Astra Kadett
estates and highlighting
the 'body kit look' under
the back bumper.

European also provided a later convenient engineering base on which to try out the independent rear suspension on three stretched Fiestas.

Development responsibilities are often difficult to ascribe accurately in a sprawling multi-national mammoth such as Ford, but broad areas which took on the main aspects of Escort were, Ford at Dunton, Essex: interior style, suspension design, steering and brakes,

Tough estate styling is complemented by a wide wheel design and the correct side window, tail light theme. Such side rear windows were needed only for the 5-door estate.

engine development, performance and emissions, and engine electrics; and Ford at Merkenich, Cologne: engine main structures, external body style and body electrics; proving ground trials, including responsibility for suspension ride and handling, plus all transmission work.

As you can see, an item like the all new independent rear suspension (IRS) layout would be drawn and designed in the UK and then handed to the German engineers, for practical development to the production stage. Ford of Germany would make wide use of the Belgian Lommel test track under their control, and of testing mileage in such diverse circumstances as Finland in February (down to-30°C and below), contrasting with 50°C plus found in proving trial for Escort in Arizona during Summer 1979.

Even when one thinks one has tidily disposed of a responsibility such as styling or engines engineering, one may find that the overall head of department is based in a different country! Supreme examples for Escort were Ron Mellor's position at the summit of the engineering labyrinth and Uwe Bahnsen's position, Vice President-Design. Both operate from Dunton to control key functions in Germany, too; it really *is* a multi-national.

Back in 1977 this study for the projected Escort replacement showed drawing board promise.

The Escort XR was originally in the programme as an S-derivative, but gradually gained equipment and extra engine power, plus the new designation, when it was seen that an increasing number of customers wanted more features than the rather hackneyed S-models had traditionally offered. It had been hoped that the XR3 would perform absolutely on par with the VW Golf GTI, even with the carburated engine. Finally, both production aerodynamics and weight conspired against defeating VW's fuel injected 110bhp with a carburated 96bhp. Thus the XR3i was a necessity

Quite a few people thought the original XR3 tail spoiler was 'over-the-top', but these 1977 studies show Ford had rather more aggression on some designers' minds!

Uwe Bahnsen was a particularly fine example of Ford's European breed and he recalls how different Escort design was, commencing with drawings in 1975, to his earlier career in styling. 'I started 25 years ago in Germany with a good saying to follow: never ask a designer to design a bridge, but ask him to make a way of crossing a river. That way there is no limit placed on creativity...'

In a spacious and comfortable office at Dunton, Uwe Bahnsen explained the contrast of sixties design work and working on the same subject – but with responsibility for aerodynamics included – in the eighties. 'Originally we would be responsible for the shape aesthetically. Aerodynamics were not a major element, but I must say we did not do too badly at all. The first car in which I was active was the Taunus 17M. For this car we made some small scale-models only to check the aerodynamics, which were not bad at 0.40 Cd. Now it is more professional in every respect. We define much more closely, the package we will offer based on what market research has told us the public will demand. There would be a full feasibility study over 100 days to define, with the help of models, exactly what we wanted, *before* we got locked into a complete programme. No, I don't think aerodynamics are a restriction on a designer. Now, it is true, we cannot think of a shape without that aero background, but it is not constraint. Look at the Mercedes 190, Audi 100, Citroen BX and Sierra. All are born in the search for aerodynamic efficiency, but they have a *wider* spread of looks than many earlier mass production cars. They are *not* all the same.'

Making the Escort look different was not a problem, but its features were born in the answer to a problem. The Escort's rear driver predecessor was rated at 0.448 Cd, slightly inferior to the original. The conventional Golf hatch, and the shapes Ford drew as competitors hovered around 0.43. The target was under 0.40; Dunton and Merkenich-based Geoffrey W. Howard (not the well known former *Autocar* journalist who worked for Ford at the time, though little of this current Escort knowledge would have come to light without his incisive guidance) was assigned the design team task by Bahnsen. Working in five wind tunnels outside Ford – a second full size tunnel adjacent to the Cologne styling studios was still under construction in 1983, for the original Ford tunnel is not suitable for full scale car aerodynamic studies – they were able to tackle the problem with the aid of full-size glassfibre models by Autumn 1977. Such models came complete with engine and body gaps so that they could be fine-tuned, the first time Ford had been able to tackle aerodynamics in this manner, which is a lot more realistic than using scale models.

However, all the fine tuning didn't disguise that 0.40 was impossible to beat with the original outline. 'Comparatively late in the programme we did some significant body modifications,' revealed Bahnsen. In the studios, which always seemed to have a Golf lurking somewhere in the background for constant comparison, the Escort finally took on the sheet metalwork that would win it so many friends. As well as final approval on 18 March 1978 for the aerodynamics in a clay rendition.

Bahnsen explained: 'First we extend the back end "bustle" by 1.28in. (38mm). Then, instead of having just a flat rear deck, we make a lip of 0.20in (5mm). So then we freeze the back end design again and we go forward. At the front the hood surface is extended 50mm, so that it goes over the headlamps.' At the time there were plenty of arguments against such moves: increased weight, cost and subjective views about appearance, because the Escort now looked unlike any rival and Ford were not noted for styling bravery in Europe. The Sierra changed all that, of course, and reminders of Bahnsen's affection for that model decorated his office.

The aerodynamic figures had dropped sharply with the extended body. Ford put the normal saloon at 0.385, estate at 0.390 and the later Escort XR3 on 0.375. The latter was quite an achievment in itself as that model was specified with 185 section tyres and two wing mirrors from the start. XR3 modifications to the basic shape, which lasted into XR3i,

Variations on coupé possibilities and a sporting small estate. A coupé version of the Escort was provided in the American market, but sales volumes were small compared with Ford pacesetters such as the Mustang and Capri, both of which were also based on other mass production running gear.

but were modified on the RS 1600i, comprised a large deformable plastic 'tea tray' rear spoiler, *à la* Porsche; plastic extension to standard steel front spoiler. The latter is split into two injection moulded sections that sweep into spats to shroud those fat front wheels. Look ahead of the rear wheels and one finds similar spatted protection in plastic. As originally developed the XR3 was credited with a 0.385 factor, as for the ordinary saloon, but in the final 12 months run-in to public announcement the factor dropped, for no material reason that I could see, the bodywork remaining the same during that period.

Some time after the Escort's launch there would be a German media controversy over the new small Ford's aero efficiency, so it is worth emphasizing that Ford used five well-known wind tunnels – including Mercedes' Stuttgart facility, Fiat, and VW at Wolfsburg, plus MIRA for some correlation and to ensure that a corrected figure, reflecting the variations between tunnels, could be issued.

Uwe Bahnsen had some fascinating observations of the hard-won Ford experience in practical aerodynamics.

'We found the Mercedes tunnel gave us the best on-the-road figures, and we should make the point that we measure vehicles with the load distributed as for our fuel economy

After the small scale 'clays' comes the full-size rendition in a mixture of clay and wood. This outline dates from 1977.

tests, so it can be unrealistic to compare our figures. For example VW load their cars a different way for their aerodynamic tests, and this makes a big difference to the final figures.

'But all of this is not so important to the customer as the discoveries we made *after* the new Escort was in production. Then we test again at Daimler Benz and find just how critical the production body tolerances are. If the maximum tolerances on fit for the various body panels – say the relationship between roof and tailgate frame, bonnet to wings and door frame fit to A-pillar – *if* these are on the original top tolerance, then the drag factor for a new Escort goes from 0.397 to 4.07!'

Mr Bahnsen chuckled a little at the memory, but that controversy did the public an enormous favour in tightening up all body fits, and ensured that all sealing, particularly around the front doors, was also doing a good job. A chart was issued to manufacturing to provide set figures, 'with no tolerance allowance,' in Uwe Bahnsen's words.

Also from 1977 is this prophecy of the fascia which has details such as the rocker switches and vertical heater controls correctly anticipated, but the major dials never made production in this clean and unfussed form, more's the pity!

Body talk, Mk2

Aerodynamics may be the mass manufacturer's buzz word of the eighties, but people still have to be accommodated within and, much more important, motivated by the appearance to buy...or at least not deflected by body style from purchasing Mr Ford's pride and joy...

Uwe Bahnsen: 'We continuously monitor our customers in this C-class, so we had over 10 years experience when it came to designing the new Escort. Market research input is continuous because we need to know what the customer does with our cars after purchase. Originally this class of car was fairly basic transport. Because of changes in many fields – more performance from less engine capacity; more sophisticated suspension and tyres; a new realism after the first oil crisis – customers ask for many of the qualities we used to offer only in larger cars – smoothness, quietness and very complete equipment with items like electric windows and so on – but they want them in this smaller class. Our response in the Escort was to make a car like the 1.6 Ghia to try and provide the comfort, equipment and finish of the larger D-class cars of 10-15 years past. A small Granada, if you like...'

'Our research tells us of retired people who are prepared to spend to get good features, who are more critical of day-to-day abilities. They buy at high cost, but expect cheap running costs. For them, maybe the 1.3 Ghia Escort with electric windows and a sunroof is the right answer,' said Bahnsen of one population group that clearly demonstrates the breadth of market a company such as Ford have to cater for with the same basic product. From XR3 to 1.3 Ghia, or from 1.1 Pop two-door to 1.6 Ghia five-door, Ford reckon the dimensions will, 'accommodate about 95 per cent of the population: the cut-off point on maximum height for our averaging purposes is about 6ft 6in.,' reported the lanky, but not 6ft 6in. tall, Ford styling chief.

Naturally, Ford do not promote the success of VW's Golf in establishing new standards for this class, but I have prepared a chart which shows the principal dimensions of the 1980 Escort compared with the original 1974 Golf range; and the larger replacement Golf II of 1983, of which Ford and GM probably played a significant part in influencing the VW stretch via their eighties success of Escort and Astra/née Kadett. You can see by the changes in Golf dimensions just how competitively close this business is and the longer term development path Escort may follow...

	Ford Escort	1974 VW Golf	1983 VW Golf II
Length	156.3in. (3970mm)	150.2in. (3815mm)	156.9in. (3985mm)
Width	62.5in. (1588mm)	63.4in. (1610mm)	65.6in. (1665 mm)
Height	52.6in. (1336mm)	55.5in. (1410mm)	55.7in. (1415mm)
Wheelbase	94.4in. (2398mm)	94.5in. (2400mm)	97.4in. (2475mm)
Front track	54.5in. (1385mm)	54.7in. (1390mm)	55.6in. (1413mm)
Rear track	56.3in. (1430mm)	53.5in. (1360mm)	55.4in. (1408mm)
Kerb weight			
(3-dr, 5-dr,	1683lb (765kg) to	1694lb (770kg) to	1859lb (845kg) to
min/max)	1837lb (835kg)	1848lb (840kg)	2068lb (940kg)

Thus it can be seen that Ford provided a front drive Escort with about six inches extra length over the first Golf, but the Ford-VW duo were otherwise extremely similar, save for Ford's near 3 inch advantage in rear track, something VW attended to – along with a similar overall length to Escort – in Golf II.

Battling that extra Escort length through the Ford product committee meetings and the cost accountants was a tough task.

Wind tunnel testing at Aachen university was followed by a lot more work with full-size models. The basic shape of the car changed in the tunnel development, this model being one without the extended tail section that became a new Escort hallmark.

It is also worth noting that coupés were thought worthwhile in the USA, using an Escort base, whilst Ford of Europe never felt the need to create the kind of Scirocco coupé partner to the Golf within the Escort range. Uwe Bahnsen felt, talking in 1983: 'We still have Capri to do the coupé job for us in Europe. The potential of the sector is limited. OK, now we had a tremendous impact with the Capri and only Fiat were really in that game with us. Since then we've had Scirocco, Opel, Mantas, Renault 17/Fuego. The max share you can have is a six percent of total market, which has to be split with everyone now making coupés.

'It's all about priorities. Nice to have a coupé Escort, but we're talking about 50-60,000 units a year and the company likes 100,000 to 150,000, because we are talking about a unique body – not like the Cabriolet, Estate-wagon or van variants of Escort. They've done it with the Lynx in the US, but you must really change all the components for a good coupé or you don't get the real thing. I think we're better off with XRs...'

Unlike the van and estate Escort-derivatives the XR's potential as a separate model was not originally recognized. Bahnsen recalled, 'We looked at the coupé concept, but not seriously. With the idea of a sports Escort, we got serious. It was not part of the programme, but it was not difficult to sell. Everyone recognized the potential in management. I don't really know where the XR part came from, but I do remember there was a feeling against using 'S' anymore; just too many were using that badge. More important to me was that high power CVH engine. It could not have been better for our purpose, but you know it could have just ended up as an option on Ghia...'

'We developed XR in a full scale glassfibre model for the original design concept – and it was basically the way it looks today. However, we did some modifications in the wind tunnel; things like the air deflectors around the tyres because those big fat covers and wide wheels were getting us up over 0.39 Cd again.' The author has spent a lot of time idly speculating the origins of that XR label, knowing that the Porsche style rear wing and Lamborghini/Porsche 928 wheel style were in the system for the majority of the Escort's 1977-1980 gestation, but uncertain which bright marketing spark came up with the XR badge.

The XR-7 tag was applied to the American Ford Mercury division's 1967 Cougar, a

A 1977 Customer clinic assessed Escort styling appeal to potential purchasers in Manchester, just one of many marketing investigations.

large luxury sports saloon in the Thunderbird or Jaguar XJ-S sector. That XR badge has had a long production life, but in Europe the Escort was the first to use XR nameplates. It was followed by the Fiesta XR2 and Sierra XR4i, the XR4Ti badge exported from Germany to America upon a 2.3-litre turbocharged Sierra 'Merkur'.

Weighty solution

'Some people just see a £ sign and weight together. So when we made the proposals to lengthen the Escort about 3½ inches for the aerodynamics there was some reaction against this,' felt Bahnsen. There was, however, the benefit of some extra luggage space to boast about, and potential customer reaction in clinics as far apart as Manchester, Cologne and the USA had already been so positive toward the Escort that the model's impetus, particularly with a parallel American development schedule, could not be denied. Incidentally the American Escort shared not a single body panel, but the USA did initiate the engine programme.

Also a couple of months behind the main three- and five-door Escort design, development and engineering programme were the estate and van versions. Mr Bahnsen commented, 'With the van, it was the first all new Escort van for a long time, because that second rear drive Escort picked up so much of the first Escort's panelwork, so it was very important to make it the best possible combination of car and load carrier in that class.'

'In fact we made a design study of an XR-type van, a leisure vehicle for weekends that could be a camper and sport fun car, a bit like they have in the USA. I think we showed this Escort once, but there is not the volume in Europe to support this kind of sports van, so it was never made.'

One of the Manchester 1977 options open to Ford was this smooth five-door of recognizable Escort lineage.

The Escort van that did go into production was not to appear until early 1981 because there was substantial engineering change, as well as panelwork, to complete. The steel back half is obvious enough, but note the neat incorporation of vestigial side glass behind the front doors and the extended 98.4in. wheelbase for a vast 94cu ft load area behind the two front seats. Mechanically it used the same engines as the launch 1.1, 1.3 and 1.6 non-XR Escorts, with similar front end running gear, but the single-leaf spring dead axle was completely unique to the van, for the Estate car – which was available by the closing months of 1980 – used the usual independent rear end layout of the saloons and was built on the same 94.4 inch wheelbase.

From a Ford studio point of view the van needed completely new rear sheet metal and it also used an 11 gallon (50 litre) fuel tank in steel, as well as those twin rear doors. The estate was built, 'as low as possible for the floor, which we made in double skin metal to sandwich the fuel tank and hold the spare wheel beneath the load compartment with

In 1978 Ford judged potential customer reaction to a very fair prediction of how the estate model would eventually appear.

maximum strength,' reported Mr Bahnsen. The estate used the usual saloon capacity of an 8.8 gallon (40 litre) fuel capacity, but naturally had its own sill-level tailgate. With one large fixed sidewindow per side and a load capacity of 57.6cu ft with its back seats folded, the new Escort estate measured 158.8in. long in place of saloon's 156.3in.

So Ford had created a pretty and effective body for a new Escort, but what of the running gear that would be asked to co-operate with those new CVH engines (discussed in detail during Chapter 9) and the Fiesta 1.1 crossflow?

Timing

A Ford 'Firm Timing Plan' blueprint shows clearly how the design team work, and necessary managerial approvals between customer clinics, occupied the bulk of early Escort front drive development resources. During 1976/77 one can pinpoint progress via curt notations that remind you just what a complex series of commands are needed to create a current car. It's not just a question of drawing a body, modelling it and then asking engineering to turn it into moving sheet metal...

For the Erika-coded Escort five main activities were headlined as: Program (yes they do spell it that way!); Preparation; Design; then Electrical, body, transmission, chassis; engine installation & Vehicle Engineering (the last six items treated together as one separate activity); Prototype Test & Development; Certification and Homologation.

Ranged against these headings was a monthly calendar stretching from October 1976 to the same month in 1980 with a detailed – to the day – plan of action. From this we can see that Program Preparation and Design were really *the* pre-occupations during 1976-77 with detail Design work primarily finalized through 1978: instrument panels, steel wheel patterns; grilles, front and rear lamp style frozen during 1978. The XR alloy wheel was approved, with the grilles, on 14 August 1978. Seat trims were given the OK early in December, the last date for detail approvals stretching to 28 February 1979. From a design viewpoint 31 August 1979 was 'Product Planning cut-off for actions requiring new or changed parts'. In other words, about a year before public launch in September 1980 was the last chance to do anything really significant, but modifications of existing components could, and would, be made up to 31 January 1980.

The building and testing of prototypes for mechanical evaluation went on in parallel with much of the design period, with specifications for the earliest prototypes issued in April 1977. Turning the designer's ideas into just the right amount of correctly stressed metal was aided firstly by CAD (Computer Aided Design) techniques, a process similar to that used on the Escort's new cylinder block to predict accurately where stress will occur and what structure will be needed to combat such duress, without adding excess weight. To speed these computer analyses an extremely important multi-national link was established in November 1978 between Ford at Dearborn's Cyber 176 computer and the less powerful computer banks at Dunton and Merkenich.

Still more structural laboratory work was required before 14 mechanical prototypes were built, 'modifying Fiesta bodyshells to take the new advanced Escort running gear and to incorporate as much of the Escort sheet metal as possible. These were mostly used for durability testing and development of component parts, although some ended their days against the barrier in early crash performance investigations,' said a Ford technical document issued in 1980. From January to November, 1978 was set aside for intensive testing with mechanical prototypes, a process continued from February 1979 to the final engineering sign-off OK that harked back to original Escort and beyond. For the new Escort that final engineering OK was predicted to be 21 January 1980. That reflected a constant stream of prototypes that gradually assumed 100 per cent of the production

Uwe Bahnsen and his team were so proud of this XR Escort van that it was displayed publicly, as well as within Ford for appraisal. The inside continued a sporting pleasure theme, but the European sports van market was adjudged to be too small by comparison with that of the USA to make the project worth continuing.

After managerial approval the clay models are measured via this gantry of probes in a bridge over the finalized shape; the probes record a 3-D image of the body proposal.

Escort specification via a further 28 prototypes, at least 26 of those constructed in 1979.

Sheer long life strength, or plain durability testing, was a big part of engineering's job and here Ford employed Lommel in Belgium primarily, with the specific hot and cold weather climates of Finland, and Kingman, the Ford Proving Ground, Arizona, to complement their findings. Ford reckoned there would be over ten million prototype and pre-production miles on the CVH engines at launch time, with experience from over 2000 such engines being fed into a programme that also included 2500 separate wind tunnel evaluations. Not quite so glamorous, but vital to the longer term private owner and resale values was the continual fight to improve corrosion protection. I was privileged to work at Lommel for a short period prior to the Escort's public announcement, and saw the tortures of deliberate salt application applied to a large number of vehicles to provide premature rusting. Even the most prestigious names in the automotive business wilted under such assaults and I can believe they found 255 new Escort body locations for specific anti-rust measures as a result of such experience.

Mechanical labour

'Fiesta was the key to Escort and front drive, no question,' said Ron Mellor briskly briefing the writer as to the practical engineering work that produced the first front drive Escorts. 'Once we had done Fiesta the Escort was out-performed on every front: as night follows day, so we would have to tackle Escort in the same way. In fact, we'd already planned the floorpan and the front end layout. From an engineering viewpoint you could say we started at the bottom and worked up.'

'We had the major new mainstream engine in the CVH, which we've discussed (Chapter 9), so we knew a package had to be engineered around that East-West power pack...'

Thus the transaxle containing the original four-speed forward ratios and front final drive differential gears, was mounted 'end-on' to the transverse engine. Drive is passed on from the engine crankshaft via the clutch – a single dry plate increased from 6.5in. (165mm) to 7.9in. (200mm) for the 1.6-litre – to a gearbox input shaft. A parallel output shaft is part of the constant-mesh design and the output shaft takes the power on to the differential, which had final drive ratios from 4.06:1 to 3.84:1 on original Escorts, with the numerically lowest 3.58:1 reserved for the non-XR 1600 saloons.

The smaller 1100 and 1300 Escorts actually had the same gear ratios as Fiesta with an overdrive fourth of 0.95:1. For the 1600 the transaxles were extended by 0.35in. (9mm) to accommodate broader gear sets and reinforced bearings. The steel specification for the differential pinions and throughout the final drive was of increased strength on the larger capacity 1.6-litre Escorts, too.

The transaxle's aluminium casting was in two sections and originated from Fiesta. Unequal length driveshafts were installed on all models, the larger capacity utilizing a 0.96in. (24.5mm) short left-hand shaft whilst the smaller engines demanded only a 0.88in. (22.5mm) circumference. The short shaft was of solid construction, the longer right-hand unit was considerably enlarged – 1.69in. (43mm) total – but hollow. Tubular construction of the longer shaft was necessary to beat the low speed resonances that Ford had encountered during development. Both shafts had constant velocity joints at each end, the inboard ends integral with the stub shafts of the differential, designed for quick release to speed transmission overhaul times. It is important to remember that the Fiesta had established that Ford could build a front drive car with exceptionally low running costs. One of the traditional reasons for buying the rear drive Escort models – particularly for the fleet use that accounted for so many Ford sales during the design period – was ease and low cost of servicing.

Gear ratios from Fiesta on the 1.1/1.3 Escorts meant: first, 3.58; second, 2.05; third, 1.35 and that 0.95 fourth. The 1.6 saloon and XR Escorts started all over again in the first three ratios, but shared that top gear: first, 3.15; second, 1.91; third, 1.27. There were three final drive ratios juggled to suit power outputs from 55bhp/1.1 litres to 96bhp/1.6 litres, spreading from 4.06 to 3.58.

Gearchange quality was vital to Ford since they had won such wide praise and plenty of driving school business with front drive Fiesta and the previous Escort generation. Basically, they took elements from both generations and produced an extemely good four-speed shift. However, at the risk of boring those who know, can I reiterate for the benefit of those who have read some sources crediting Escort (particularly XR3) with a *five*-speed gearbox throughout its life that original front drive Escorts had a quartet of gears only. Optional and standard availability of five-speed Escort transaxles came in March 1982 and involved some fundamental engine bay engineering that is discussed in detail during the next Chapter. At this point it is merely relevant to note that Ford's use of

The Granada estate's 'umbilical cord' to the disguised Escort prototype is recording suspension data 'in-flight' during 1979 trials of the new Escort layout.

the rear drive remote control gearchange mechanism for a transaxle worked brilliantly for the four-speeders, but shift quality on the five-gear models is not so precise, almost poor by Ford's previous standards. Fiesta's remote change plastic housing was used with stabilizer bar and positive adjustment register, but they halved shift rod movement and restricted compliance of the rubber mounting bushes to improve gearchange quality 'across the gate.'

Suspension

Although the Fiesta was used as a starting point for suspension development in 1977, when they built three stretched Fiestas to test proposed layouts including the independent rear end, the end result was entirely different – and caused a major media controversy in the UK.

The front end was closest to what had gone before, particularly that of the 1.1 Escort which used the usual Ford MacPherson strut system with stamped steel track control arms and separate forged tie bars extending forward from the outer ends of those TCAs. As on the transmission and engine, a 1.1 Escort owed a lot to Fiesta in this department.

On the CVH-powered models the front end continued to use MacPherson struts again, but with a roll bar doing its transverse anti-sway job, and picking up on forged track control arms, to provide also the longitudinal location that the 1.1's tie bars provided. All models had struts with coil spring encirclement, offset from the side axis to provide some reduction in side loadings and 'stiction' forces that upset ride quality. Rubber insulation was inserted between spring and seating at each end of the coils to fight harshness and noise.

The dampers themselves came in for a lot of swift changes after launch in the UK. The original specification was a twin-tube hydraulic unit with a progressive rubber bump stop on the piston rod having an extension to guard against road dirt damaging the finely machined piston rod. For the XR3, Bilstein gas dampers were utilized, these being of monotube design with the bump stop housed within the gas filled compartment and a separate shroud for the piston rod. Again there would be alternative damper settings swiftly available post-launch, but aimed at the rear end specifically on XR3 where the springing was of different, progressive, principles to the rest of the range.

More testing, but this time in Arizona, where the Escort is asked to enact a little role reversal with a sturdy pick-up truck!

Fiesta experience with negative scrub steering geometry influenced a move to zero scrub radius front end geometry to further reduce steering effort and steering wheel twitches over road ridges. Such systems are usually promoted on the basis of increased safety when a tyre deflates, or for more manageable braking under panic or varied surface conditions.

The back end was also designed in Britain by a team under Egon Goegel (Chief Engineer, Vehicle Engineering) and Gunther Hargen (Principle Engineer, Vehicle Engineering) with all development and proving mileage a German responsibility, making intensive use of Lommel test track's varied circuits. The British market, even though the cars may have come from either Saarlouis or Halewood originally, was serviced by shock absorbers from Woodhead or Armstrong.

The back end layout spoke of an honest attempt to provide a superior ride to Fiesta's beam axle with Panhard rod and location links, for the Escort had independent lower arms that carried in their pressed steel embrace separate mountings for the inboard coil springs and long strut-style dampers. At the lower leading edge of these arms, location rods led their kinked (to avoid the inner edges of wheel and tyre) path forward to mounting points that align less than an inch behind the rearward edge of the front doors. Again a rubber insulator was used between the top of the coil spring and its body seating.

The XR3 had progressive rate rear springs to co-operate with its gas damping. At their softest rating they were 128lb in., the same as for the rear of the Estate, and at their hardest they went beyond the specification of some production racing saloons to 220lb in.! By comparison the 1.1 used a 101lb in. rating at the rear, half that of XR3 and a figure your bottom would certainly confirm!

At the front the XR3 was far from the stiffest sprung Escort in the range; that distinction belonged to the 1.1 without an anti-roll bar at 124lb in. Escorts 1.3, 1.6 and XR shared a rate of 98lb in. with the Estate carrying the biggest front roll bar (24mm) and 107lb in. springs. Again XR shared its bar (22mm) with its less generously powered CVH cousins.

Naturally, we will return to the suspension question in the next Chapter, which deals with the final product and its development in public. I should add at this point that even three years after Escort's launch there was a strong feeling from the UK-based Ford

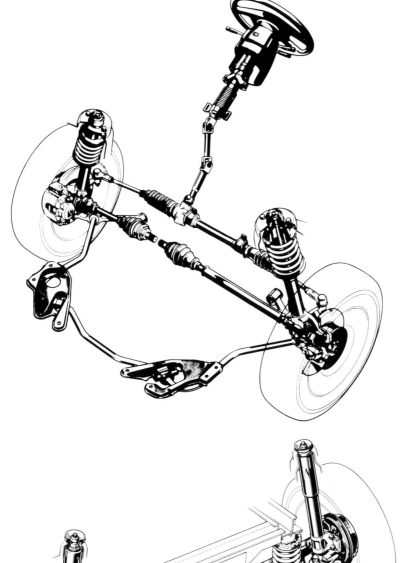

The safety-conscious rack and pinion steering is common to all Escorts, but this suspension system with the anti-roll bar incorporated in the lower suspension arms was not used on the lowest-powered 1100 Escort, or the first RS 1600/Turbo models.

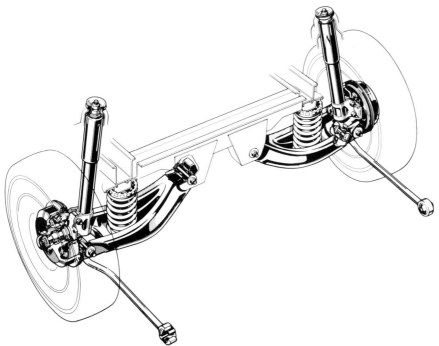

The original IRS with its transverse arms, separated spring and damper units, plus location arms. Mounting points for both the inner arm attachments and the leading ends of the tie bars were modified from May 1983 onwards in production, at which point the front struts were also given Sierra-style top mounts. At both ends the extremes of positive and negative camber, allowing the Escort a rather 'knock-kneed' look in 1980-83, were eliminated.

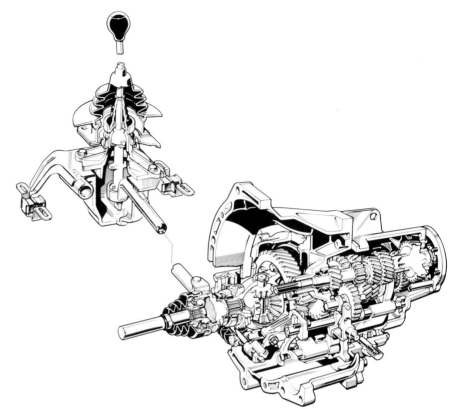

The four-speed transaxle was developed from that of the 1300 Fiesta and had a notably good gearchange, via an improved linkage. Five-speed gearboxes were not made generally available until February 1982.

engineers, particularly the management who had to defend the Escort against adverse UK comment during its first 12 months, that the suspension gripe was all a lot of media fuss that had little relevance to the customers, who bought the new Escort in record numbers.

Specifically, Ron Mellor opined in 1983: 'Ford of Germany were totally satisfied with this aspect of Escort's behaviour. The British press led the issue and it was the media rather than the customers who didn't like our suspension. There was no customer fuss, in fact our feedback was of plenty who were really pleased with this aspect of the Escort compared with the previous rear drive models.' Nevertheless Ford did offer a number of post launch changes, that are subsequently detailed, before finally tackling the fundamentals of the problem with suspension angles all revised from the rather odd front positive camber, i.e. 'knock-knee' stance (with the inner edge of the wheel and tyre closer to the centre of the car than the top outer line of the tyre), and similarly the rear end was modified to rule out the rather 'splayed-wheel' negative camber angle contrast of the original Escort. The basic alterations, which really did tackle the problem, with multi-million pound tooling production alterations to the body mounting points, came in progressively from May 1983, the actual start date depending on the factory. Note that *all* Orions were equipped with such mounting points from the start – and I have yet to read a serious criticism of that car's riding abilities over the kind of bumpy British B-roads that the Ford track at Lommel could not simulate.

The XR3 story on suspension development was slightly different. Bilstein at Ennepetal, North of Cologne, were called in to help find some sort of ride quality rather late in the programme. Given the fact of those tremendously powerful rear spring rates with progression, allied to a type of suspension Ford had not experienced before, and the use of 14 inch diameter wheels with then very daring (for mass production) 185/60 series rubber

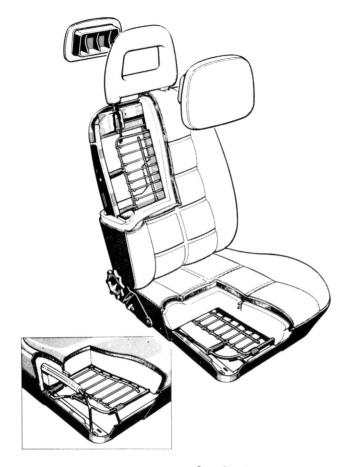

Inside the Escort seat, some technology from the earlier Taunus/Cortina experience was incorporated. The seating has a pressed-steel frame with a flexible wire mesh platform and small coil springs to fine tune the support provided. There's also a lot of foam within ...

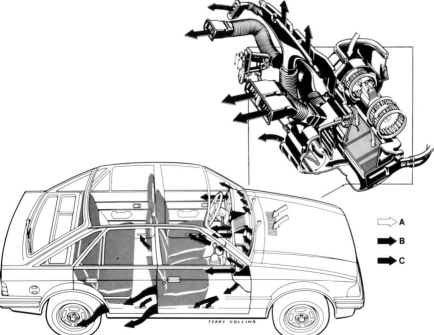

TERRY COLLINS

A
B
C

Ford ventilation systems have traditionally been effective, and the new Escort reflected a considerable amount of wind tunnel work to make sure that the outlet areas, mounted in the outer edge of the door frames, provided a frequent change of atmosphere within. The heater has three speeds and is notably quiet on the lowest setting.

Terry Collins completes the technical picture with one of his illuminating cutaways of the Escort, eighties style.

on broader alloy wheels, it was no surprise that even gas-damping's best known exponent failed to come up with a convincing answer. There were optional high quality RS Ford Bilsteins that helped, but for the mainstream engineering department at Ford that was no answer.

Finally the XR3 was re-engineered on the suspension side *before* the mainstream Orion/revised Escort breed of Summer 1983. Again the suspension's extreme angles were tackled, but by far cheaper stop-gap methods, the back progressive springs were deleted and the Bilsteins went in favour of uniquely machined Girling shock absorbers. Those modifications, and others, are detailed in Chapter 12.

Stop!

In common with the suspension system, there was evidence that Ford engineers had specified the best technical braking features the accountants would allow. Thus there were ventilated front discs on both 79 and 96bhp Escort 1.6 models, the 1300 and 1100 Escort sharing the 9.45in. disc diameter but lacking the 29 ventilation ribs and nearly a third thinner than the width of the vented units on the more powerful Escorts. All cars used a 7.9in. diameter servo (optional on the 1.1 base) with hydraulics split diagonally into twin circuits via a tandem master cylinder. In line with the European Economic Community regulations that find rear wheel brake locking illegal in an emergency, there were twin 'g-sensing' valves to control pressures within the braking system to the rear wheels. Pad and lining wear can be checked without removing the wheels, but the Ghia and XR models also had a warning light amongst the new instrument display that lit via sensors within the front disc pads. Incidentally, if you fitted non-standard pads without such sensors, as I did, the brake pad warning light would drive you to distraction with false warnings...

Rack and pinion steering was a natural as the Escort originally pioneered its use within the Ford line, and there is some sharing of components with Fiesta revealed in the workshop manuals for both models. The Escort, however, was developed with a 19.55:1 rack ratio and 3.69 turns lock to lock, whereas Fiesta operated on 18.62:1 and a slightly nimbler 3.4 turns. In both cases the rack was mounted well away from crash impacts, behind and above the front axle line.

We had the basics of a very appealing and efficient front drive Escort to take the badge into the eighties. How did it progress in the public's palms?

Chapter 11

Worldwide winner

From its Autumn 1980 launch in Europe and America, the Escort quickly established its commercial success on both sides of the Atlantic, co-operation with Mazda via Ford USA taking the basic front drive package into the Far East and Australasian markets, too. Not only did the Escort hatchback design evolve with features such as five-speed gearboxes and fuel injection, but a number of bodies marked Escort's versatility too. Estate, van, two-door coupé (USA only), Cabriolet and the consciously separated three-box saloon called Orion. All came of Escort stock ...

FOR Ford in Europe and America the Escort was a dramatic success, a key product in leading the American end of the company back to profits after some staggering losses in the early eighties. In Britain the press were allowed to talk about the car from 3 September 1980, with sales and the heavyweight TV commercial campaign from Ogilvy & Mather gathering momentum from 25 September onward, using the 'Simple is Efficient' theme and a five-door 1.6 Ghia streaking around the Lommel test track.

Ford of Germany listed 23 Erika-coded Escorts in their 1979 production records, but the mass production tap was not turned fully on until August 1980. By the end of that introductory year Saarlouis had made 91,639, Halewood some 36,726 and 740 had been made in Knock Down (KD) kits.

In its first full month on the UK market, October 1980, the new Escort beat the Cortina by over 1000 units and continued to hold a sales lead over Ford UK's epitome of rear drive commercial success until February 1981. The Escort finished 1981 nearly 20,000 units behind Cortina, comfortably ahead of Fiesta, the car that broke the front drive ice for Ford of Britain. From 1982 to the time of editing this section, January 1990, the Escort continued to hold the overall yearly sales lead in Britain, interrupted only in the early days of the Sierra-Cavalier wars, or by occasional monthly exceptions to the rule of Ford leadership. When this was written the best UK Escort sales year was 1983, when were shifted 174,190 Escorts to 159,119 Sierras, 137,303 Austin/MG Metros and 127,509 GM Vauxhall Cavaliers, with the fifth-placed Fiesta as only other car on the British market over 100,000 sales.

In America, Ford vice president Lou Lataif was able to boast, 'Escort – America's best selling car – is a prime example of Ford's dramatic quality gains'. Speaking in 1982 he added, 'during 1981 it outsold each of more than 70 imported car lines available to American buyers. So far in 1982 it has been the nation's best selling car line – foreign or domestic – and nine out of ten Escort owners say they would buy another'. The authoritative *Road & Track* put the car neatly into context as the first American Ford with front drive saying: 'The Ford Escort/Mercury Lynx certainly seems to be right on target. Ford admits that getting the person who has spent his life driving Lincolns and LTDs to accept smaller cars is difficult, and so even though this new FWD design is a very compact package, Ford engineers and stylists went to some lengths to give the car an illusion of bigness. You won't get any strong complaints from us on that point as it hasn't resulted in any real design compromises. Economical, space-and fuel-efficient and entertaining-to-drive are labels that we are ready to apply to Ford's first domestic FWD offering,' wrote John Dinkel in the October 1980 issue.

In Germany and other LHD markets the Escort immediately did well, too, but the counter attack of VW's Golf II pushed the Ford challenger backward. By April 1984, for example, the Golf had sold 104,383 to lead the opening months of that year, compared to 32,662 for ninth placed Escort and over 70,000 for the old model Opel Kadett, which was rebodied later in 1984.

By 1982 Ford were able to claim that worldwide production of the Escort, at 823,000 units in the first full year of production (1981), had outstripped the VW Golf (759,000) and Toyota Corolla (702,000). Also in 1982, the Escort reached a million faster than any Ford of Europe product had managed, the millionth front drive Escort coming from Halewood's lines on 13 October 1982. In 1982 the worldwide production figure for the small Ford continued upward with 847,000 made, and again Ford, with the authority of Detroit's *Automotive News* who supplied the statistics, could claim to have beaten VW and Toyota.

Also setting records on the other side of the world was the Mazda 323, sold in Australia under the Laser and Meteor badges. The Escort and Mazda 323 are not the same in detail, but Ford's American engineers and those of Mazda, in which Ford has over 20 per cent shareholding, did sit down at the planning stage together and produced similarly clean front drive designs, which share principles rather than interchangeability as a general rule. One well known exception that proves this rule partially is the five-speed and four-speed transaxles, plus the American and Japanese automatic gearboxes. Mazda got the contract to build the original four-speeders for US Fiestas and the idea carried over onto Escort, but even here Mazda build both in separate factories and actual parts interchangeability is said to be minimal on the manual boxes. So as far as the author is aware the American Escort utilized an American -built ATX automatic of which over a quarter million had been sold when the European Escort was offered with the same 'lock-up' auto in 1982.

By May 1988, when Ford was introducing its '1988-1/2' models to the American home market, the parent company could state ... 'In the United States, the Escort was the best selling car in 1987 with sales of 392,360. Since the car's introduction 2,549,895 Escorts have been sold in the United States, making it the best selling car of the 1980s'. Ford in the USA added that the Escort now sold in 'more than 60 countries'. Quoted 1987 sales of the Escort had reached about 460,000 in Western Europe and 52,000 in Brazil, where it is both manufactured at Sao Bernado and exported.

J. Walter Thompson went
for the World car angle
when they launched the
Escort to the American
public on behalf of their
multi-national client, the
Ford Motor Company.
Although the name's the
same, the car is totally
different to that found in
Europe.

BUILT TO TAKE ON THE WORLD

Escort Liftgate... 4 doors and
wagon room when you need it.

Now there's a high-mileage American
car that can take on the imports... in
big things like front-wheel drive, and
a new patented fuel-efficient automatic transmission... in features like
front bucket seats scientifically contoured for comfort... cathodic elec-
trocoating to fight rust... Lifeguard
Design Safety Features like a safety-
designed roof structure, safety-de-
signed front end structure, split-ser-

vice hydraulic brake system, steel
guard rails in the side doors... and in
touches like Halogen headlights that
give you whiter, brighter light than
conventional headlights... and

Escort offers a s
cooling air-conditic
Recommended s
nance—as specifie
manual—averages

Escort's interior is so roomy it is officially classified as a com

NEW FORD ESCORT

Escort puts a world of better ideas at your fingertips.

Escort 3-door Hatchback. High mileage, room, and a long list of standard features.

ast-
nte-
er's
one

hour for each year of driving (10,000 miles), based on Ford current labor time standards. And ask about Ford's Extended Service Plan.

Come drive a world car. Whether you buy or lease, see your Ford Dealer now to order your Escort... 3-door Hatchback, 4-door Liftgate or even a Squire wagon option.

EVERY ESCORT HAS ALL THESE FEATURES *STANDARD*

- Front-wheel drive for traction.
- Fully independent four-wheel suspension for smooth road-holding.
- New-design compound valve hemispherical head (CVH) engine.
- Fully synchronized manual transmission with fuel-efficient overdrive 4th gear (automatic available).
- Rack-and-pinion steering.
- Front stabilizer bar.

- Bucket seats...scientifically contoured for comfort.
- All-season steel-belted radials.
- Lifeguard Design Safety Features.
- AM radio.
  (May be deleted for credit)
- Electro-drive cooling fan.
- Diagonally split-service brakes.
- Pin-slider disc brakes.
- Self-adjusting clutch.
- Front wheel bearings need no periodic adjustment.
- Hideaway luggage compartment.
- Fold-down rear seat for extra cargo.
- Rectangular Halogen headlights.
- Flash-to-pass headlight control for freeway passing.
- Handy European-style wiper-washer fingertip control lever. And more.

FORD ESCORT

FORD DIVISION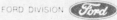

INTRODUCING THE NEW WORLD CAR

ENGINEERING TEAMS FROM AMERICA AND OVERSEAS JOIN FORCES TO CREATE A NEW CAR WITH BETTER IDEAS FROM AROUND THE WORLD

Top engineers drawn from the worldwide resources of Ford Motor Company teamed up to create Escort.

They pooled their expertise ... compared, tested, evaluated, experimented—to come up with better ideas. The result: a high-mileage car built in America to take on the world. Escort will be made in America for American drivers ... with other models built and sold overseas.

HIGH MILEAGE THROUGH ADVANCED TECHNOLOGY

Escort's fuel efficiency comes from highly efficient new power teams, the use of special weight-efficient steel, refined aerodynamics and other new and better ideas, not less car. In fact, Escort has the room of a compact (based on EPA Volume Index)

ESCORT	30	44
	EPA EST MPG*	EST HWY*

EVEN HIGHER GAS MILEAGE THAN THESE LESS ROOMY SUBCOMPACTS.

VW RABBIT (GAS)	28	42
TOYOTA COROLLA H/B	28	39
HONDA ACCORD	27	36

*Applicable only to sedans without power steering or air conditioning. For comparison. Your mileage may differ depending on speed, distance, weather. Actual hwy mileage and Calif. ratings lower. Excludes diesels.

ONE OF THE MOST POWER-EFFICIENT ENGINES AVAILABLE IN AMERICA

Escort's advanced-design compound valve hemispherical head (CVH) engine focuses the incoming

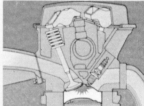

combustion charge for power ... ciency. Result: high mileage p... power for freeway driving.

And Escort has a new man... transmission with fuel-effici... fourth gear overdrive standard.

FRONT-WHEEL DRIVE AND FOUR-WHEEL INDEPENDENT SUSPENS...

Escort has front-wheel drive ... f... wheel fully independent suspens... ... rack-and-pinion steering ... st... lizer bar and new all-season st... belted radials. And Escort ma... use of a special steel—high-stren... steel—along with other weight-... cient materials, for high milea... Plus Escort offers a special all-r... fast-cooling air-conditioning syst...

Simple is efficient.

The new Ford Escort.

Put another successful way by Ford USA: 'about one in four Ford cars built worldwide is an Escort.'

The new Escort in Britain

After intensive marketing research all over Europe – there were 33 separate surveys in Britain, Germany, France and Italy between February 1977 and November 1979 – the latest Escort arrived in the United Kingdom as a three-engine range of three/five-door hatchbacks with a choice of equipment from basic to L, GL and Ghia, priced from £3374 in late September 1980. The Estates – 1100, 1300 and 1600 – arrived along with the original carburated XR3 (the latter detailed in Chapter 13) at prices from £3757, which compared

Inside the most luxurious Ghia Escort, the basic disposition of controls was as for all models, but the seat and door trim was restricted to the most expensive models outside the XR performance line.

with £3525 for the cheapest Fiesta 1.1-engined five-door hatchback, as from November 1980.

The 1117cc ex-Fiesta engine and four-speed gearbox was offered in all three bodies with a choice of plain or L trim. Basic equipment included the rack and pinion steering and disc front brakes, but servo assistance and adjustable seat backs were an option, along with many other items on this model. Useful everyday items such as a heated rear window and cloth seat trim were options, too. Ford did not intend that one had too much for one's £3374 start to the Escort ladder, generally pricing above slightly better equipped opposition at this stage and relying on new model novelty and a new styling approach to shift showroom metal.

The L trim brought that seat back adjuster, plus Sandford fabric trim, 'improved rear seat contours,' two-speed wipers, lidded glovebox, three-speed heater fan, and a heated rear window – its elements extending downward to ensure a rear wiper would free off on frosty mornings, too. Unfortunately the L-owner did not get that back wiper as standard, finding it on the option list for just short of £73. A brake servo was £47.32. In general the L-designation transformed the interior from rep's monastic punishment cell to acceptable family accomodation with the items we now take for granted as basics.

As discussed in the engineering chapter the 1100 Escorts were fundamentally different to the CVH-powered 1300 and 1600 in the use of front suspension without an anti-roll bar. The company immediately inserted the roll bar layout, along with vented versions of the 9.45in. front discs and 155/80 SR radials for the 1600. The 1.3 litre CVH L Escort did without the vented discs, but did have the roll bar front suspension and 155 section tyres to replace the basic 145/80 SRs, both mounted on 4.5 x 13in. steel wheels.

Internally both cheaper Escort trims were characterized by two-spoke steering wheels and the single pane viewing panel for twin-dial instrumentation, one for speedometer and the other containing water temperature and fuel gauges. Even in the cheapest models the plastics were carefully toned and it was obvious Ford had looked long and hard at Japanese trim qualities. Folding rear seats applied right from the cheapest model (though only on L and above was a push button lock suppled for tailgate access: it was just a turnkey job on the basic) and the official load figures were 20.3cu ft as a four/five seater, or more than double that (48.7 cu ft) when the rear seat was dropped forward; split rear seat folding, à la Metro or Capri, was not offered, until Autumn 1984.

According to *Autocar* figures the 55bhp 1.1 Escort was no sluggard. Their September 1980 test revealed a best one-way check of 97mph! The average was still over 90mph, 92 to be pedantic, and they managed a sparkling 15.5s from rest to 60mph. Sparkling? Well, the Mini Cooper 997 of the mid-sixties used to take over 17s to complete that task and *Autocar's* figures showed the Ford to be about three seconds faster than a Toyota Starlet. Let's not get too carried away, however. There were plenty of other small cars in 1980 that could match that 0-60 figure. At this end of the range most observers were far more interested in the 36.9mpg the Escort recorded, a little behind said Toyota and in a different class to Renault's 40mpg plus Renault 5 supermini. Generally the Escort has the most thrifty performance/mpg balance in 1.3 litre CVH trim ...

Talking of trim, let's remember what you got in GL badgework. Not the 1.1 engine, for a start! The choice was between the 69bhp 1.3 or the 79bhp, 1.6, both of new CVH stock of course with the 1.6 also offering a useful bonus of over 25% extra torque from its extra 301cc. A GL brought a four-spoke steering wheel (settle down, and remember the ad slogan: *'Ford Gives You More!')* plus the simple microprocessor activated warning lights for: brake pad wear, low levels of washer, and oil, plus a shortage of engine water or fuel – all covered by five orange warning lights. I found there were no special prizes for illuminating the quintet simultaneously on one particularly tired example!

The GL specification concentrated on extra equipment internally with a Ford P21 push button radio and a large clock counterbalancing the usual solo speedometer, the instrumentation layout just as for the Ghia/XR3 with a separate fuel and water temperature section between speedo and clock. One still had to pay extra for the rear wash/wipe, and a mirror for the passenger door was not included in the GL price either. One did, however, get 155/80 radials on 5 inch wide rims in this model, which also attracted custom with the halogen headlamps and worthwhile extra soundproofing.

As the 1.3 and 1.6 could be had also in Ghia trim the following performance orientated remarks also apply to those models. The 1.3 returned a 99mph absolute maximum for *Autocar* in Ghia trim, accelerated from standstill to 60mph in 14 seconds and smashed my consumption theory to bits with a rather unattractive 28.7mpg in original four-speed form, when 70mph demanded 3950rpm (17.9mph per 1000rpm). Regarding the petrol consumption of the 1.3, I can only say that it was always the best of Escort engine options in my hands and record the fact that *Motor* managed 30.9mpg from their four-speed test example and 31.2mpg from a five-speed. From memory I recall *Autocar* retesting some of

Outside the near-£4900 1.6 Ghia there was plenty of brightwork to tell everyone this was the more expensive version, but the basic clean line was unspoiled. Note the three side-stripes beneath the useful rubber strip: an almost military regimentation of status!

The new Escort earned a Design Council award as well as a Car of the Year accolade in its début year.

the Escorts, particularly the 1.3, because of the extreme difficulty of accurately brimming the fuel tank. That second test produced 31.8mpg for *Autocar*. Brimming the tank is an mpg checking method we journalists continually use to the despair of engineers such as Ron Mellor, who dismisses such techniques as 'crude'.

Performance for 1.6 GL/Ghia? I only have figures from *Autocar* for the five-speed, which retained the same horsepower; these were 11.1 seconds, 0-60mph, and 101mph. *Motor's* original four-speed GL 1.6 was fleeter at 10.7s for 0-60mph and 103mph. In both cases the mpg figure was slightly better than the 1.3, at around 32mpg. In general, this 1.6 of 1980 was extremely competitive on performance and economy compared with the similar capacity Golf or Vauxhall Astra, its main advantage being on the economy front. Altogether it was quite a shock to see how all of this trio would see off a respected sporting name such as Lancia with their 1500 Delta of 85bhp (97mph/0-60mph in 11.5 seconds); the mass producers really have made enormous progress in this respect. I find it hard to believe that, editing this in 1990, I have just returned from trying a new Astra capable of 132mph: where will it all end?

Back with our favourite Escort, an investigation of the Ghia optional trim level, as applied to Escort, showed that only the 1.3 and 1.6 engines could be specified, but in the Escort line Ford have not combined Ghia trim and XR3i power – that was reserved for Orion at press time. In September 1980 Ghia brought the Escort the usual interior upgrading with wood capping veneers and 'crushed velour' seat trim. Most useful Ghia items were the tilting and sliding glass sunroof, the first we had seen on a production Ford, complete with its own louvred blind; you could not specify this on Estates and the extra cost on all other Escorts of the period was over £215.

Ghias could be identified by their extra chrome, unique hubcaps and 'triple body side stripe', but many owners, as with XR3, specified over £1000 of extras amongst the 43 optional items available. It is easy to look back with (optional) tinted spectacles and think that all Ghias came with electric windows, tinted glass and metallic paint. In fact, the neat rocker switch–actuated electric front windows were £134.12p; tinted glass was £35.40; and a two coat metallic was offered for another £73.49. Then one could specify central locking at another £113.30, a headlamp wash layout for £70.67, opening rear quarter windows at £30.60. There was in-car entertainment which went up to £280.57 for the Ford-branded SRT 32P stereo cassette player and MW/LW/VHF radio unit, although if it were specified on a Ghia or GL/XR3 the price was £217 with an allowance for the standard P21, which featured no stereo cassette. A plain radio with push button MW/LW selection, delivered all the puny wattage which Ford accountants can inflict when exercising their buying power.

The Ghia and XR got a passenger door mirror as standard, but only the XR3 and

Estate managed a standard rear wiper; otherwise it was £74.91, even for Ghia! You may find a Ghia with 175 tyres resting on its five inch steel rims – no alloy option was offered during 1980-84 – and these were an optional replacement of the standard 155 that could also be specified along with the 5 inch wheels on all models for £43. Only the XR3 came with alloys in 1980 and these were standard until the advent of the XR3i when a steel wheel with aerodynamic hubcap was offered at a saving of several hundred pounds over then optional XR alloys.

Press & public reaction

'I've just been driving Ford's all new Escort and, to be quite honest, I can't believe how good it is.' That was the scoop reaction *Car* magazine elicited from a Car of the Year judge who betrayed the trust invested in him when he was given an early Sardinian test of the car before the rest of the media and public could get at the machine. Headed 'Super Ford', the generous spread was extremely warm in general tone and included the opinion 'The ride isn't up to the most absorbent French standards, but it is probably a very clever, and certainly comfortable, pan-European balance; and none of the French cars that manage to better Escort's ride handles as well as it does. Thus Ford have achieved a suspension mixture that should keep French and Germans happy, appeal to Italians and be a positive revelation for a mass market car made in Britain – especially a British Ford!'

Of course it is really easy to snigger at such quotes now, in the light of the controversy that blew up in Britain over a ride that caused the *Motor/Autocar* testers to blanch. For example here is *Autocar*, '... it is all the more distressing to have to say that ride quality is disappointing, and this after a last minute damper change on all press cars (and hopefully production models). The car's springing feels well chosen, but not as if the damping rates have been properly matched to it. At all speeds over anything but truly flat surfaces (rare) one is aware of a constant busyness about the ride. The characteristic is plainly felt at moderate speeds, where it can translate into a bouncy ride over smaller bumps and knobbly surfaces, pitching or rear dipping over wave formations or a floating feeling over long undulations. Long bumps met in mid-corner can also be more than usually upsetting, causing a momentary rocking motion.' The quote is taken from their September 27 report of the 1.3 Ghia conducted by the conscientious former-Lotus GP driver, John Miles.

I was inclined to the *Car* view of an astonishing advance in small car handling, which I believe they put on a par with the Alfasud after a session at Lommel test track. After Lommel use of a car normally laden with three other adults (which did wonders for the ride and was the basic parameter to which Ford developed the ride and handling compromise) I switched to its use in Britain. I started off with a basic 1.1 and wondered where the hell all that choppiness had come from? It certainly was not present, quite the reverse, in Lommel use, which shows the dangers of test track development and differing market road conditions ...

Motor, like many other elements in the British press, followed up the introductory fracas with an attempt to get to the bottom of the problem entitled, 'A ride on the wild side,' published in the 15 August 1981 issue and guaranteed with that headline to send a shudder down any self-respecting PR's spine! They really went at the task properly with five rivals, including the tremendously competent Alfa and the sweet-riding Citroen GS, and a Ford engineering management team including Egon Goegel and Gunther Hargen. They laid on a 15-mile test route and got the Ford executives to judge their own car's suspension performance against that of their opponents with, 'A commendable and courageous degree of honest objectivity,' in *Motor*'s summary. This was an exercise that left them feeling that, 'The difference between winners and losers is not a vast chasm between

The American big sellers of the 1982 model year were the two-door; five-door, and five-door estate (right). Some of the styling features were dictated by American legislation as much as differing transatlantic mass market tastes.

Yeah, Escort's two-tone for real in the USA! Specifications for five-door and later coupé models will be found in the Appendices.

excellent cars and atrocious ones, but a narrow dividing line between good ones and very good ones. And the more gently you drive, the narrower the distinction.

'Neither should Ford feel disheartened or damned by the Escort's mediocre ranking in this exercise. Even on its ride and handling which are our concern here, it is a vastly superior machine to the Escorts we tested last Autumn.' What had Ford done to the car since its September 1980 début? Egon Goegel told *Motor* of a number of changes made with speed and minimal alteration to the basic concept, concentrating on damper suppliers. Goegel revealed. 'The third set you then got [for test] was a set which we had developed together with Armstrong, and that was very close to the settings which we now have in production: it was a kind of first development step to get better control of the vehicle, to take the floating characteristics out, but at the same time as getting better control we also unfortunately took some of the ride comfort out ... What you will see today is a vehicle which had almost the same settings as you saw in your third test car ... It is the car that every customer would get if he bought a 1600 Ghia; Armstrongs front, Woodheads rear

In September 1980's launch range the 1.3 GL was just over £4350 and became a very popular business choice for aspiring reps.

with settings released off production as we built it for the British market. Some are built at Halewood, some at Saarlouis, but the shock absorber sets we use for the British market are always the same: Armstrong front/Woodhead rear or Armstrong/Armstrong.' In that first 11 months Goegel admitted that Ford has also changed the 'hardness but not the dimensions of the front and rear track control bushes,' leaving the spring rates well alone.

It would not be the last we heard about Escort suspension, but as noted in the introduction to this book the commercial success was already assured by this stage, and Britain proved one of the strongest markets for the Escort right from the start. The Society of Motor Manufacturers and Traders (SMM&T) had statistics for October 1980 to 1 April 1981, roughly the first five months in Escort's UK life, that showed that 40,225 of the new model were sold in this period, finishing second only to the Cortina, prices now covering £3528 to £5576 for a Ghia 1.6 five-door, or £5692 for the XR3. Even then, there were about 1,200 old rear drive Escorts about the place and the obsolete model had sold so strongly that it finished in sixth place during that post-front drive Escort launch!

Aside from the alternative damper settings through 1980-81 in Britain, particularly aimed at damping out the rear end restlessness, the first official Escort additions came with the announcement on 5 February 1981 of the Halewood built Escort 35 (1117cc/55bhp) and Escort 55 light vans, the latter being available with either 1296 or 1597cc CVH power rated at the same 69 and 79bhp as that of saloons. As discussed in the previous Chapter, it was the rear end of the van that was really different to other front drive Escorts, not only in its capacious panelwork, but also the ultilization of racy single leaf spring dead-axle layout. There were company insiders who wanted to put it on the ill-sorted original XR3!

Priced from £3166 exclusive of 15 per cent VAT, the new Escort vans soon carved out a category-leading 30 per cent plus share of the market. For Ford of Britain there was the May 1981 Design Council Award for 'elegance of engineering, detail design and low maintenance requirements,' to add to Escort's 1981 Car of the Year Award (the other judges were as impressed as that *Car* correspondent!) and awards gained in five othcr European countries emphasized the new Escort had made a significant impact in its launch months. Even in April 1981, when a strike had interrupted the supply, a quarter million Escorts had been made in the first five months and Britons were picking a very high proportion of GL and Ghia models to gladden corporate dollar counters.

Also in Spring 1981, Ford displayed a 2+2 sports coupé based on the Escort, but unlike the September 1981 début for a prototype Escort Cabriolet to test public reaction, there was no intention to make the Ghia *Avant Garde*. It used the 94 inch wheelbase of the Escort and was not dissimilar in length, but the reported Cd was 0.30 thanks to a smooth top body shape and the influence of GP racing inspiring a full length undertray.

September 2 1981 saw the first formal running changes to the Escort with the annoying Econolight incorporated into the speedometer. Its red or yellow bulbs illuminated in reaction to differing manifold pressures to warn of heavy-footed driving technique, trying to do the same job as VW *et al* were implementing with their mpg/litre per 100km monitors and yellow arrows for optimum economy gearchanging. There were also minor trim changes to the headrests at this point, L and GL getting these A-frame devices, whilst the GL also gained a passenger door mirror as a standard item.

The convertible Escort at Frankfurt in September predicted the production model – which did not reach Britain until the close of 1983 – in most respects. This despite Uwe Bahnsen underlining its prototype status with the comment, 'It is at present only a design study.' Key features included a hood folding mechanism that allowed an elegant line with the rag top down, particularly important as the Golf lost most of its boot space and overall good proportions, to say nothing of being rather difficult to park with the lumpy folded hoodline intruding on the driver's natural field of vision when reversing. The Escort had a neat fabric bag to stow the foldaway hood and a rigid rollbar that also served as the mounting point for fixed rear quarter windows and the forward seat belts. Reinforcements, particularly to the low sills (rocker panels) were needed to compensate for the loss of structural toughness without a sheet steel roof, but this weight boosting move was one of the few negative aspects of a careful design that retained much of the back seat and boot space that many predecessors in this newly reborn fashionable convertible style had ignored in the rush to the market place.

Five-speeds arrive

February 26 1982 was the release date for Ford's 'new transmission; the first to give five

The CVH engine was installed within Escort to allow plenty of accessible space for the inline transmission. Such overall simplicity in layout would endear it to the business community, as well as the private owner. This is the 69bhp 1.3-litre unit.

forward gears on a European Ford car'. They meant production car, of course, for Escort and Capri had been chasing busily through five gears on the circuits and over rally stages with the aid of five-speed transmissions since the late sixties. If one were really fussy, one could have pointed to the ZF five-speed *Ford* GT40. After all it was a Ford Advanced Vehicles Production car, complete with a list price of some £6500 in 1965!

For the front drive Escort, Ford developed the five-speeder strictly from the original four-speed; indeed, the first four ratios were identical with an 0.76:1 final drive added. That does not mean they all provided the same ratios, for the 1300 stacked up as: first, 3.58; second, 2.05; third, 1.35; fourth, 0.95 and fifth further overdriven at 0.76. For the 1.6 litres of both XR and L/GL/Ghia specification, the intermediate ratios differed in that first was 3.15; second, 1.90; third, 1.27 but fourth and fifth were the same. Not so the final drives; the 1.3 litre was mated with a 3.84 (22.5mph per 1000rpm) and the low profile tyre, 14 inch wheeled XR achieved the same mph per 1000 revs figure, using a 3.58 as well, whilst the 1.6 L/GL/Ghia used their 3.58 and 24.2mph for every thousand rpm. Ford reported that, 'At a road speed of 75mph the overdrive fifth gear reduces engine speed by 20 per cent to 3100rpm'.

Naturally, the company also spoke in glowing terms of fuel economy bonuses for the extra gear, varying from 10 per cent on the ordinary 1.6 litres to 11 per cent for 1.3s and, 'as much as 14 per cent on the then twin-choke carburated XR3.' Overall neither *Motor* nor *Autocar* figures relevant to the 1.3 models relate this benefit in overall figures; *Motor* managing 30.9mpg overall in a 1.3L and 31.2mpg in the five-gear GL. Their calculated figures did, however, show a bigger touring bonus from 35.9 to 38.4mpg, fractionally under 7.5 per cent.

Personal Imports

Originally the Ford press service spoke of an £85 charge for the 5-speed on all 1.6s, save the XR3, but by March it was included in the standard catalogue price. For the 1.3 my 1 April 1982 catalogue reports only a five-speed option price for a 1300 L/GL or Ghia at £125. By that Spring date the Escort range in Britain started at £3905.53 for an 1100 Economy three-door and escalated to £5750 for either five-door Ghia 1.6, or XR3. This reflected a Ford of Britain reaction to a home price war and the growth of Personal Imports to the UK, a facet of the Common Market that particularly affected Escort Ghia and XR3, which could be bought for significantly less in continental Europe than they could in the UK. In May 1983 Ford marketing manager S.F. Cholaj informed me that overall, Ford Personal Imports had gone from 203 in 1980 to 5503 in 1982. There were 3183 Escorts in that 1982 total, and something had to be done. Ford reduced Escort prices in the UK an average 4 per cent, and improved the product on all series. Also, they cut the cost of the XR3 by 7.3 per cent and the Ghias by 7.9 per cent.

Specifically those product changes involved the five-speeder for the 1.6 litre models, locking petrol caps throughout the range and an upgrading for the L, which took on the passenger door mirror, quartz clock and trip mileage recorder. The GL gained remote control operation for the driver's door side mirror only; Ford certainly know the way to the price-comparison browser's heart! The Ghia's plusher walls reverberated to the sounds of a combined radio and stereo cassette player, and it was embellished further by an electrically retracted and raised aerial, *and* tinted glass for the sensitive souls amongst the clientel.

In a May announcement wrapping all these moves up in one package, Ford also gave me official fuel consumption figures to back their assertions of five-speed savings. The best figure returned was 52.3mpg for a 1.3 five-speed versus 47.1 for the same model with a quartet of ratios. The biggest percentage saving? As predicted it was for XR3, 21 per cent

The five-door estate reflects accurately that earlier styling drawing side rear window. This LHD version from Switzerland's market is known as the Kombi.

The three-door estate model was available in basic trim from over £3700 in November 1980.

for the constant 56mph drone leaving the five-speed carburettor model (on the UK market officially only until October the same year, when XR3i was announced) on a return of 49.5mpg. The worst 'urban' figures were those of XR3, but here again the 28.5mpg of the five-speed XR3 was an improvement over four-gears, albeit a smaller 2.9 per cent. *Autocar's* tests revealed constant-speed savings that varied from 47.4mpg versus 48.6 at a constant 30mph in the 1.6GL to 30.3mpg versus 32.8 at 70mph, in both cases the higher figure belonging to the use of fifth as compared to the original fourth at a steady speed.

Within the engine bay of a five-speed Escort it should be noted that Ford had not only to change the transmission internally, but also to remount the engine no more than 0.67in (17mm) to the offside. Obviously, the driveshaft lengths were altered, one shorter, one longer, to compensate for the five-speed layout. Today Ford use the revised driveshaft lengths on four- and five-speed Escorts.

The opening day of the 1982 Geneva Show, which was settling into its eighties home adjacent to that tidy city's international airport, was 4 March. Ford picked that day to highlight a new Escort to bear the RS badge; the RS 1600i. This German development of the carburated XR3 offered 115bhp from an engine equipped with mechanical valve lifters in place of the vaunted hydraulic system. It was distinctively finished and was modified in most sporting respects: suspension, spoilers, unique alloy RS wheels, 50-series tyres, plus competition inspired seating and four-spoke steering wheel. The model is examined in

A hatch with more back.

Same efficiency.

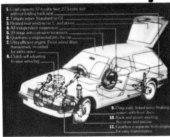

The Ford Escort is already winning praise for its high performance and low fuel consumption – so much so that it's just been voted Car of the Year 1981.

The new estate is engineered just as efficiently. Thanks to its streamlined shape, its light weight and its advanced engines, even the smallest version, the 1.1 litre, will reach 89 mph.* And the biggest, the 1.6 will do 45.6 mpg at a constant 56 mph.**

Not only that, but it's designed to be one of the cheapest cars to service. It goes 12,000 miles between standard services with only a minor service at 6,000 miles.

And features like the self-adjusting clutch and brakes that can be checked without removing the wheels mean that even the 12,000 mile service is quite straightforward. 1.3 and 1.6 litre engines have breakerless ignition and self-adjusting tappets as well.

As for rust proofing, the body is protected by a 20-stage treatment that includes total immersion in anti-corrosive paint, wax injections into doors and box sections and a tough coating of chip resistant PVC inside the wheel arches. It's built to last.

Extra space.

The new Escort's estate back gives you a whopping 27.5 cu ft boot without folding the rear seat, something your passengers will no doubt appreciate! (You can take even more luggage than the hatchback without leaving anyone behind).

When you do fold the seats the estate turns into a removal van. 61.8" long, 39.3" wide (between the wheel arches) and 33.5" high. That makes 57.6 cu ft. Perhaps still more important, with its flat floor, low sill, and big door it's very easy to load and unload.

The Escort owes its package efficiency, as the engineers call it, partly to plain common sense and partly to advanced computer technology.

The engine is mounted sideways so it occupies the least possible space. And it drives the front wheels so there's no need for a transmission tunnel.

On the road the estate handles as crisply as the hatchback. A stabiliser bar is fitted to the all independent suspension to compensate for heavy loads.

The Escort estate is also available in L or GL trim (as illustrated) and it's at your Ford dealers now.

So if you're looking for a car that's engineered as efficiently as the Escort, but even more spacious, just ask to see our hatch with more back.

FORD ESCORT ESTATE CAR

The British ads for the estate concentrated on the facts, and carried a small logo (bottom left) to remind readers that this estate was based on the 1981 Car of the Year.

detail during the following Chapter, along with the October announced Escort XR3i, the 'i' once again denoting injection, the latter a product of the Special Vehicle Engineering Group (SVE) at Dunton. The SVE comprised a team of largely ex-FAVO Ford engineers who had also been responsible for the commercially extremely successful Ford Capri 2.8i and the Fiesta XR2.

In this general Escort development Chapter it is relevant to note the strong commercial appeal of the sporting Fords. The RS1600i was still commanding prices

In February 1981, they released the three-engine, two-weight payload Escort van range to the British public. The ingenious extra side window was instantly identifiable, and has become a very familiar sight on UK roads.

beyond £7000, i.e. beyond the original £6700 list cost Ford demanded at the commencement of UK availability in October 1982, some two *years* later, when it had been obsolete for more than a year! The XR3i's October launch gave Ford the chance to reveal; 'As a percentage of total UK Escort sales, those for the outgoing XR3 have been increasing steadily and currently stand at 9 per cent. For the freak month of August they were 22 per cent! Comparing similar 10 month periods in 1981/82 – so as to get a valid basis for comparison owing to the model change from XR3 to XR3i – we see that Ford sold 10,169 Escort XRs in 1981 (8.82% of total Escort) and 12,959 (8.9%) during 1982. So the XR sporting hatchback trend was far from the limited production pattern of the seventies FAVO RS models ...

Using that same 10 month period in 1982 and the statistics of Ford's marketing wizards I discovered that the general Escort sales pattern was for the 1.3 model to be the most popular derivative, selling double the total of 1.6 which was over 12,000 units up on the 1.1. By this stage the van had increased its predominant stake in the class to 41.54% of all sales.

The next important mainstream Escort addition was the November 1982-released, £371, automatic option for all 1.6 models, Estate or saloon, but not the XRs. This was the unit used for the ATX American Escort discussed earlier, complete with 2.79:1 first, 1.61:1 second and the direct 1:1 top. Even the final drive ratio of 3.31:1 was the same as Ford USA specify for both injected and HO, carburated, 1.6 emission controlled versions of CVH. These were rated at 85 and 80bhp respectively in 1983 model year specification, close to the 79bhp of the single carburettor European CVH – then in production.

Ford constructed 14 prototype automatic Escorts to develop the transmission in detail for European use, backing this up with a further 20 Escorts in fleet use with the three-speed auto. Called a Split Torque transmission, this patented automatic unit deviates from normal auto torque convertor use in that the wastage of mechanical effort caused by the hydraulic coupling of the converter is locked out by use of a mechanical bypass'. In other words, this automatic uses direct gearing to provide more efficient power transmission, but in varying proportions, according to the gear selected. For example in top, motorway consumption at steady speeds is particularly enhanced, compared to a conventional torque converter auto, because 93 per cent of the power reaching the gearbox is handled mechanically. In second the mechanical side of the transmission receives 62 per cent of the output, 38 per cent being taken to the torque converter which can provide a maximum of 2.35 mutiplication of overall gear ratio. In first, which can be selected manually, the drive is all handled by the torque converter to a maximum of 44mph at 6000rpm. Second will yield

The Escort's two-door coupé shell for the USA (seen here in the 1983 model year) was billed as the lowest drag factor-body in American production when it made its debut at 0.34Cd. This is the Ford EXP version, the Mercury counterpart being known as LN7. The frontal view is of the 1982 EXP, but the 'bug-eyed' look remained a constant theme. Underneath the cars were mechanically as for all North American Escorts, cheaper versions featuring all-drum braking. All models are strict two-seaters.

77mph at the same time (max power on the 1.6 CVH is at 5800 revs) whilst Ford report that 101mph would be available at 4900rpm under favourable conditions. For ordinary road use this simply means that 75mph in the auto actually demands a more restful 3590rpm, rather than the five-speed's 3885rpm, that top gear selected very much with American highway conditions and maximum fuel economy in mind, so there is absolutely no reponse to sudden acceleration demands in top!

I drove a 1.6 GL so auto-equipped in 1983 and found there were some lurches in engagement from second to third with a distinct thump as top went home, and some vibration despite the damper that has been installed within the gearbox to defeat the CVH's lusty power delivery. This was in May 1983, by which time factory moves were beginning finally to sort out the suspension, but these RHD cars preceded those moves and I have to say the Estate was particularly bad over B-roads in an unladen state. Then I actually compared it back-to-back with the similarly rough riding original XR3, albeit one that had a second set of rear dampers from Ford, and the Estate exhibited many of the sporting Escort's Bronco-busting characteristics.

Ford's automatic-equipped vehicle's efficiency in fuel consumption and performance was more impressive. They used official figures from 27.9mpg 'urban' to 43.4mpg at 56mph, versus 30.7mpg and 49.6mpg for an equivalent five-speed, with comfortably over 30mpg at 75mph in both cases, to back up their auto's claim to increased mpg efficiency. They rated 0-62mph at 13.9s for the 1.6 auto, 2.9s longer than the manual. *Autocar* only got 25.6mpg overall, including their usual performance session at MIRA, but 0-60mph was a very respectable 12 seconds and they managed just over 100mph as a maximum. Including the town convenience of the automatic and the price asked, the Ford automatic option for the Escort struck me as a thoroughly worthwhile option, the vented brakes of a 1.6 being perfectly adequate to cope with the extra braking load that is inevitable.

In February 1982 the general availability of five-speed transaxles for the Escort was made public, although which models had the feature as standard was swiftly altered by UK marketing decisions in an increasingly cost conscious UK market. Mechanically, a thorough engineering brief Ford at Dunton passed on to us recalled that mainshaft and layshaft had required extra length; the selector components were changed to suit new gear positions; a new fifth gear synchronizer was needed, and the engine mountings had to be changed, because the increased width of the transaxle demanded both motor and transmission be positioned a further 0.67in (17mm) to the right (O/S) of the Escort five-speed. Naturally, four-speed models also followed suit to ease production cost, a remark that also applies to the new gear lever and gear change components that were developed to suit five forward gears.

For just over £370 in November 1982, most Escorts other than the least and most powerful could be specified with a Ford automatic transmission. It had three ratios, and a lock-up mechanism to allow better fuel economy than is usually the case with automatics under main road cruising conditions.

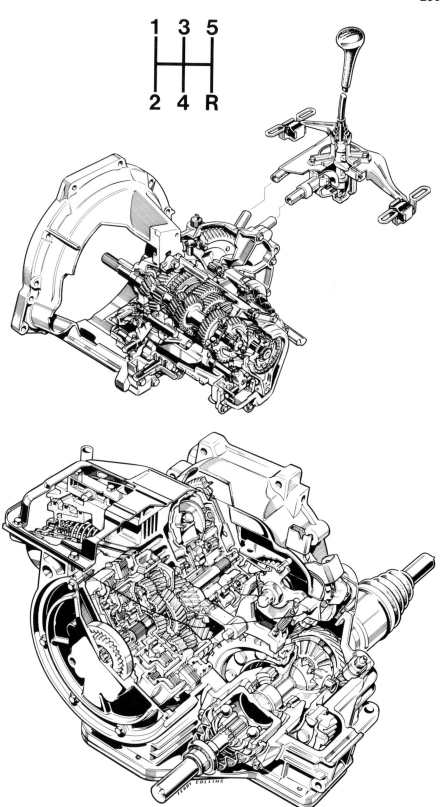

To commemorate the
1,000,000th new Escort
FORD MOTOR COMPANY LIMITED

Even freelance authors got to hear all about the millionth Escort ... 13 October, 1982.

In the closing months of 1982 Ford could boast in the UK, 'More Escorts have been sold in Britain in the first ten months of 1982 than in the whole of 1981,' adding that the Escort now had an 'uncatchable 22,300 units,' in hand over the second place Cortina for an overall sales lead. More important for Britain and the pride of the oft-abused Merseyside workforce was the statement: 'Halewood plant currently supplies 75 per cent of all Escorts for the British market, but this will rise early next year when RHD production of the high performance Escort XR3i, currently imported from Germany, is transferred to the Merseyside complex.' My February 1983 XR3i was German-built, but generally the Spring 1983 onward XRs should have been sourced from the UK, delayed by a separate transport workers stoppage that made it impossible to get Escorts in any numbers because they were all locked within Halewood's gates!

During the winter of 1982/83 there were a number of Escort sporting announcements that have some relevance to general Escort development outside our detailed sporting chapters. Most significant long term was the 3 December 1982 announcement of a Ford Escort Turbo Rally Championship. The 1983 series was not particularly well supported, but Ford at Boreham's engineering of an intercooled and turbocharged CVH 1.6 for sale to competitors as part of a rally preparation kit emphasized the interest Ford had in developing a turbocharged derivative. Just as for five-speed gearboxes and fuel injection, Ford were lagging behind their opposition in technical innovation, but they do take thorough steps to ensure that technical advances are fully investigated and tested before asking customers to pay the price. I have never felt I was a paying development guinea pig when driving a production Ford, and two roadside stoppages in 18 years frequently Ford-biased motoring speaks for itself ...

So the 130bhp Escort Turbos for British national rallies were a little more significant than just pure competition cars, but the January 1983 announcement that, 'Production of the new Escort RS 1700T is scheduled to begin at Saarlouis, West Germany, in March,' referring to the front engine turbo with rear drive and gearbox, proved premature. Stuart Turner was forced to axe that project and the C100 sports car when he took over the European Motorsport job again in 1983, a subject we explore in a subsequent sporting chapter. What was relevant in the sporting announcements from the once all conquering Ford Motorsport department was the use of RS 1600i in the prestigious, controversial, British Touring Car Championship, for the Escort dominated the smallest class in 1983-85 as the VW Golf escalated to 1.8 litres and a new class, leaving behind a natural rivalry that had speeded Escort's front drive racing development.

The Orion is a splendidly comfortable, classically styled little saloon. But with front wheel drive, a five-speed gearbox and all Ford's latest electronic technology, its engineering is strictly contemporary.

The Orion is a brand new addition to the Ford line-up. A compact five-seater with four doors, and a conventional boot; its styling is traditional.

But that's where tradition ends, and 20th Century technology takes over.

For as you're about to discover, the Orion is to throw back to the past, but a thoroughly modern car, one which introduces new standards of comfort and refinement to its class.

The Orion is available as a GL or Ghia, with fuel injection. The latter is designed for the driver who likes this luxury, combined with speed (it will reach 116 mph and accelerate to 60 mph from rest in only 8.6 seconds).

But let's look round the model that's most typical of the range, the Ghia.

Like much classical design it has a certain economy of line.

There is no unnecessary decoration. It doesn't need any. Its beauty is that everything is strictly functional. The bumpers, for instance, are made of light weight polycarbonate which springs back into shape after minor knocks.

When you open the door, the first thing you notice is that air of calm that comes from cut pile carpet and tasteful cloth upholstery. You're back in civilisation.

The driver's seat, a new design, is generously padded and holds you firmly. It even has an adjustable support for the small of your back.

You'll find the latest equipment at your fingertips.

Power adjusted, heated mirrors, variable speed intermittent wipers, and a multi-function digital clock are among the many standard features.

The dashboard bristles with switches and warning lights for everything from low windscreen washer fluid and oil levels to worn disc brake pads. So you seldom need to open the bonnet.

Then there's the ventilation system. This doesn't just keep you warm, it keeps you fresh too. Because it supplies cooler air to your face than your feet.

And such is the attention to sound deadening that even the holes that carry wiring from the engine compartment into the car are sealed against noise.

Here's another nice feature. The radio

aerial's built into the back window, so attached to twist for aerials because there's nothing for them to break off. Signals are actually received by the heating elements in the glass.

A stereo radio cassette with four speakers and a joystick balance control is standard. So are central locking (a sure roof which tilts or slides), electric front windows and tinted glass.

As for your passengers, we don't treat them like second class citizens. The front passenger's seat has an adjustable lumbar support just like the driver's. And one of the best features of the Orion is the way you can stretch out in the back. There's more leg room, knee room and head

in the back seat fold down. (They're split 60/40.) So if you have to carry something large and awkward, a double-bass for instance, you can push it through. It's the next best thing to having a hatchback.

Now let's look under the bonnet.

You've a choice of engines. 1.3 or 1.6 litres or the GL and 1.6 with fuel injection in the Ghia.

These are the proven CVH engines, over a million of which are already on the road.

The engines are, of course, mounted transversely and drive the front wheels, which partly explains why there's so much space inside the Orion in spite of its compact dimensions. It's the ideal layout for a car this size.

Among other engineering landmarks are tappets which adjust themselves and need no routine maintenance; electronic ignition that stays in tune for life, and a unique alloy cylinder head design featuring hemispherical combustion chambers.

The figures in the table speak for its efficiency.

Standard service intervals are 12,000 miles with only a minor service needed at 6,000.

You've also a choice of gearboxes. A 5-speed manual is optional with the 1.3 litre engine and standard with the 1.6 and 1.6i. While the automatic is an option with the 1.6 it's another engineering breakthrough, in that it features a mechanical by-pass which gradually takes over from the hydraulic drive as your speed rises.

This accounts for the remarkable fuel efficiency of even the automatic Orion.

Suspension? Predictably it's all independent. As befits the character of the car we've tuned it for comfort. But although this means it's quite soft there's very little body roll.

The 1.6i Ghia is set up rather more firmly, with a rear anti roll bar and gas filled shock absorbers. So it handles more like the latest Escort XR3i.

You can see the new Ford Orion at your local Ford dealer now. We think you'll agree it's a modern classic.

FORD ORION

**The new Ford Orion.
A modern variation on
a classical theme.**

*The Orion was
announced for the UK
market in July, but was
not sold in volume until
September 1983. Only in
the penultimate
paragraph is Escort
mentioned, reflecting
Ford of Britain's initial
determination to distance
the car from its
hatchback origins.*

Five-door Estate

By 25 March 1983 and an announcement of the five-door body option to boost the Estates beyond their 15,000 record sales in 1982, the most expensive Escort was the £6834 RS 1600i. A Ghia five-door amounted to £5980 and the range-starting 1.1 E Escort three-door was now over the £4000 barrier at £4062. The five-door Estate derivative was simply the addition of rear doors in that lengthened body: the cheapest was a 1.1 at £4802.05 instead of the three-door Estate's £4624.75, but the 1.6GL, plushest five-door Estate option, nudged close to £6000 and Ghia-land.

An Escort to cater for registered disabled people at considerable financial saving came in April 1983. It combined a previously unavailable combination with the auto three-speed mated to the three-door saloon or Estate. It had some useful basic equipment ready for conversion to handicapped needs and the prices showed a saving well over £1000 in both cases, as compared with costs to the general public.

Star influence

The next official Ford of Britain Escort change came on 25 August with the two-model Cabriolet line, but Dunton Engineering Chief Ron Mellor confirmed, 'In the plants that now build Escort, which is to say Halewood and Saarlouis, plus Valencia in Spain which has been on stream with Escort as well as Fiesta since 1982, there has been a gradual change to new suspension mounting points for the Escort floorpan. It started as of May 1983 and you can take it that all Orions supplied in the UK have the later suspension, too. Basically we had to re-engineer the front end of the Escort for the diesel engine installation and while we were at it there was the opportunity to install the Sierra type upper mountings for the front struts and bring the front wheels to a vertical position. There were also some steering system changes and we modified the rear suspension geometry as well. In the latter case we changed mounting points and also brought the wheels toward a vertical stance, when the vehicle is static.'

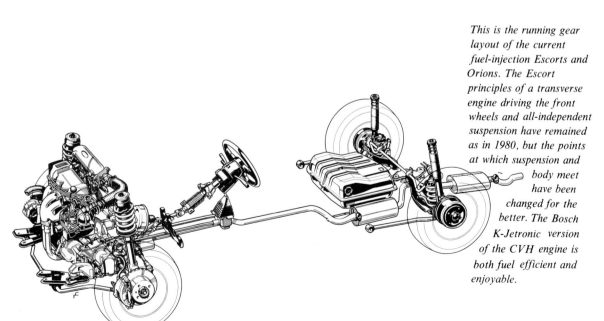

This is the running gear layout of the current fuel-injection Escorts and Orions. The Escort principles of a transverse engine driving the front wheels and all-independent suspension have remained as in 1980, but the points at which suspension and body meet have been changed for the better. The Bosch K-Jetronic version of the CVH engine is both fuel efficient and enjoyable.

The point of the Orion was to provide a booted alternative to the Escort, but the model also marked some important mechanical improvements including the use, from the start, of the revised suspension.

This is the American Mercury Lynx RS with wheels that speak of the European XR3. Like the Ford-branded GT counterpart, US customers are offered an electronic fuel injection set-up, but less than 90bhp was the result in emission controlled form.

Orion Saloon arrives

The Orion neatly mucks up our Escort chronology, for it was announced in July 1983, but was not available until September the same year. Ford insisted on regarding it as a totally separate sixth product line in their car range, but its mechanical and centre pillar-onward alliance with Escort is obvious enough. We have to regard it as primarily outside the scope of this book, for reasons of title and space – *not* inherent worth – but its technical interest in previewing the diesel engine and providing a very effective base for that multi-million dollar modified suspension cannot be ignored. It is worth reiterating that its 0.375 drag factor and re-sited split seat provided definite pluses over its aeroback cousin.

Yet Ford have affirmed that they intend to stick by the hatchback style for the majority of their big sellers. The Orion had a specific task to do, fighting VW's Golf-based Jetta from a slightly upmarket stance that was subsequently slightly lowered in UK aspiration with the 1984 introduction of an Orion L to complement the initial Ford Orion launch line of 1.3, 1.6 and 1.6 injection models. The latter cars were offered only in GL and upward trim levels, prices reaching beyond £7000. By 1984 the Orion was a regular top ten stablemate of the Escort, but at the lower end of the sales chart. Many cynics felt the Orion's primary job was to reassure shocked former Cortina owners that they did not have to buy the Sierra, which was regarded as quite radical in Britain!

In detail these Escort rear suspension changes amounted to dropping both the location link and centre mounting point body attachment holes. Specialists such as Richard Longman in Poole soon featured the new inner transverse arm and forward location link mounting points, incorporated in their competition cars with no bother. The front is more complex, for the top mount features a new attachment point to provide a home for transplanted Sierra strut top mount technology. The Orion has an overall length of nearly 10 inches extra, 165in. total.

It bettered the Escort Cd owing to that extra length. The revised wheel/strut angle, accommodating ball thrust bearings instead of a conventional plain bearing removes some 'stiction' in the system and apparently transforms wide-wheeled machines like the XR at parking speeds, providing a lighter steering action. On the general subject of Orion and Escort 'commonality' it should be noted that the Orion injection featured softer rear spring rates in alliance with the usual XR gas-damping, because Orion has a rear anti-roll bar for the injection model. It's worth noting that Ford had not gone to 60 series tyres on even the 105bhp injection Orion either, thus preserving ride quality of earlier Orions.

Billed as, 'The first European open-top production Ford for 20 years,' the Escort Cabriolet was announced in Britain for 25 August 1983 and went into production during September, finally arriving in RHD during December of that year. They were the most expensive Escorts in the range; A four-speed 1.3 starting proceedings beyond £7000 (£7346) with a 1.6/79bhp Cabriolet based on GL trim (though with 'XR3i-type door armrests and stowage bins, front seat lumbar adjustment and black door sills,' in Ford's British office words) at £7513. Then there was the XR3i-based injection model with the usual 105bhp engine (also found in Orion), with pure XR trim, including the now three-spoke small steering wheel and the later seats.

Ford claimed the boot still held more than 8cu ft and that, 'No fewer than 80 per cent of the body panels are new or modified.' Most were strength retention moves, such as beefier side rails, and both front and rear crossmembers were stronger too. The windscreen surrounds, their pillars and top rail were obviously also unique to the Cabriolet, which was built by Karmann at Osnabrück in Germany, just as the old style Golf Convertible continues to be constructed at the same premises.

The fabric hood of the Cabriolet was sensibly constructed and stylish, but left a big

Closest to the European Escort in overall looks was the four-door station wagon; this is the four-door GL of 1983 model year.

The 1988-89 Escort 1.9 GT from Ford in the USA showed that they had studied very closely what was happening in European performance fashions. The car reportedly drove a lot better than its predecessors.

three-quarter rear blind spot. This is particularly noticeable when joining a motorway, but once on such carriageways, the view directly behind is extremely good, owing to the use of glass for the heated rear window. The convertible aspect has been properly executed with a scissors-construction hood frame with two handles and safety catches, all that need releasing, before folding the hood down. When furled it is located by two more safety catches and can be protected within the vinyl cover. The remaining boot area is more accessible than usual, owing to the low lip above bumper height compared to the Escort hatchback, and it has been finished with a carpet on all models. For additional load space one can still fold the back seat forward, but one does not have to tilt the rear seat backrests to tuck the hood away, which is the case for the Golf rival. In a straight side-by-side comparison one can also see that Karmann were able to tuck the Ford's soft top out of sight, easing reversing problems when compared with the Golf Cabriolet.

Straight line performance of the injection Escort Cabriolet was a little down on the equivalent 105bhp XR3i. *Autocar* had not tried one when this was written, but *Motor* recorded 114.1mph and 0-60 in 9.2s versus the tin top's 116mph and 8.6s, perhaps because of the Cabriolet's kerb weight of 2140lb (973kg). Fuel consumption seemed unaffected with figures in the 31-33mpg band from a number of independent testers.

What Car?, the biggest selling motoring magazine in Britain by 1984, continued the feud between injection Escort and Golf with a Cabriolet comparison and said this of the

Cabriolet models are expensive but fun. Here we see the Escort convertible in carburettor trim with hood raised and lowered. The tonneau cover neatly restrains the hood but, as with the top raised, visibility for parking is not as good as the standard car.

Ford in summary: 'So good to look at, so strong on raw excitement, could easily have come first if not for its over-harsh engine, snatchy gearchange (a five-speed) and tendency to body flex over poor road surfaces.

'On the bonus side, the 1.6i has exceptional handling, superb steering and scintillating performance. Its higher top speed is another attraction. And, coming down to earth, it is significantly cheaper to buy and run than the GTi; it has a bigger boot, better hood and, at the moment a stronger chance of drawing a crowd.' Why did it lose to the now old fashioned original Golf? Basically because of the VW's refinement and the merits of the 1.8 VW engine versus the 1.6 CVH, which seemed worth the extra £404, even if the VW was by then of the old model shape in Cabriolet form ... and likely to stay that way for some considerable period.

Whilst the Escort Cabriolet was proceeding into West German production in September 1983, that month was also used to release details of basic and important improvements to the Escort range. They could make a formal announcement of the Sierra style front suspension, confident that all three factories were now making Escorts of this

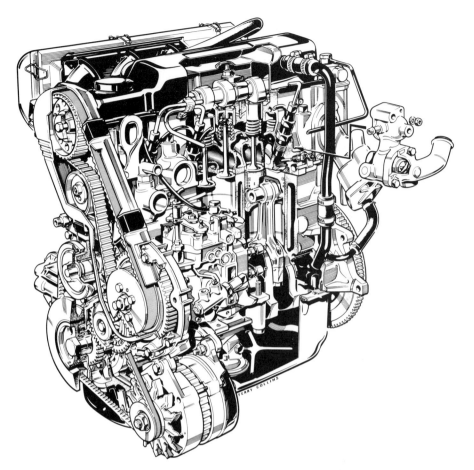

Ford developed this brand new overhead cam diesel 1.6-litre of Dagenham manufacture. It was offered to UK motorists, together with the hope of 70mpg at 56mph, from Autumn 1983 onward at prices from £5854 for the three-door Escort. Initial reports rated it above the pace-setting VW Golf diesel, particularly in respect of quiet operation on idle and smoother performance.

This English-registered limited edition (750) all-white Cabriolet was pictured during the Ford international launch of the 4x4 Scorpio and RS 200 road car in Sardinia. It cost £9990 in November 1985.

Now with a much refined ride, the Escort marched into the mid-eighties with poise and best-selling confidence. A 1.6 Ghia such as this cost £6807 by the end of 1984 whilst the Cabriolets culminated in an £8902 binge for the fuel injection model with the also 105bhp ex-XR3i-powered Orion costing £7520. Although many different styles and engines had been offered since the front drive Escort's launch, its primary appeal remained that of clean looks, equally crisp performance and straightforward service from a large dealer network.

specification. By this stage the Escort was also available across the range with a 10.5 gallon fuel tank, an item previewed by Special Vehicle Engineering at Dunton for the October 1982 XR3i.

September 1983 also saw the basic models gain halogen headlamps, heated rear screen and passenger door mirrors, with reclining front seat backs, head restraints, upgraded trim and intermittent action for the wipers. So, in three years the base customer began to gain the L and GL original features, but at a cost we will discuss later! The L was provided with a centre console at this stage, and a radio with a built-in stereo cassette player. GL was offered with the rear screen wiper/wash arrangement, standard at last! On Escort, the theory is that the aerodynamics do at least relieve you of the motorway chore of needing a wiper all the time to clear the scummy particles from the back screen, so the rear wiper is not so important. That is true, but it is a vital feature in city rainfall use, where the air cannot carry away droplets that obscure the rear pane.

From the Ghias in September 1982, the in car entertainment (ICE) went all stereo (both radio and cassette player), and central locking came away from the optional cost list and into standard equipment, along with a lumbar adjustment for the front seats, centre console and a redesigned two-spoke steering wheel. One can distinguish such Ghias by their revised hubcap design with smooth centres and slotted outer edges.

The 50mpg Escort

The price of progress, which included a heavily revised 1.1 engine (new camshaft, revised inlet porting, dual outlet exhaust manifold), started at £4187.74 in November 1983. The 1.1 continued to be the OHV Escort design, rather than the small CVH originally expected and it retained mechanical contact breaker points as opposed to the lower maintenance precision of the contactless electronic Ford systems found in all 1.3/1.6 CVH Escorts. The attraction of the 1.1 on paper was its 53.3mpg at 56mph and 42.8mpg 'urban' in the official figures: only the 1.3 CVH exceeded 50mpg in the rest of the range (52.3mpg) at 56mph, but none of the rest could get near that 'urban' 1.1 figure, all of them around 30mpg in town simulated street use, save the 1.6 injection which recorded 26.6.

As of November 1983 the revised Escorts reached a maximum of £6308.98 for the 1.6 Ghia; £6654.89 for the XR3i and £6157.83 for the best equipped estate, the 1.6GL. By this stage another power plant was being readied for the 1984 Escorts ...

Announced in August 1983, Ford's 1608cc diesel was an all new design with cast-iron head and cylinder block using Ricardo Comet pre-combustion chamber inserts. It went

The 1985 American models, including the 5-door Escort, concentrated on improved sound deadening and gearchange quality. A turbo version of the EXP coupé was also listed before the Europeans could buy RS 1600 Turbo but it did not reach the showrooms.

into production at Dagenham during the Autumn of 1983 and was gradually made available in the Orion, Fiesta and Escort front drive designs. Inherent strengthening features of the 80 x 80mm diesel included fillet rolling the crankshaft and equipping it with eight counterbalance weights. The Bosch rotary injection pump was driven via a crankshaft connected gear train to reduce overall length for front drive installations.

Now...a 70mpg Escort!

In all three Ford front drive designs the 1.6 litre diesel was rated at 54bhp on 4800rpm and 70lb ft torque at 3000rpm. The 4800rpm mark was also the maximum permitted for crankshaft revs, so driving the car to full economical advantage involved a rather different technique to the 6000rpm plus possible on the CVH Escort. Economy was the key attraction. Ford could now advertise an Escort capable of 70.6mpg at 56mph, 48.7mpg at 75mph and 51.4 urban mpg, over 10mpg bonus on even the most parsimonious petrol power plant around town.

The 21.5:1 compression diesel was offered in three/five-door hatchbacks and for estate with a choice of L or GL trim. Prices started at £5853.95 for the three-door saloon and escalated to £6719.50 for a 1.6 GL estate of five-door specification, these quoted in May 1984.

The diesel impressed connoisseurs of the sparkless motor, and Ford held a number of economy demonstrations that returned beyond 70mpg when journalists were being tempted by prizes! Far more important to the high mileage public or business user was that Ford had sat down and thought through the diesel application from re-engineered front end to a purpose-built engine, built on a line designed specifically to produce such power plants. It was not a dieselization of an existing power plant, although there was Kent crossflow ancestry in the iron cylinder block.

The Escort sailed into 1984 as a front runner in an enormous variety of mechanical and trim options, leading both UK and USA markets. In Britain one could have three- or five-door bodies in convertible, saloon or estate style; diesel or petrol power from 50 to 105bhp; and four- or five-speed gearboxes. In the USA they were not offering the Cabriolet and the styling was significantly different to that of Europe, particularly front and rear, but the choice of door apertures on estate and saloon was common with a three door 'sporty coupé a feature of the line from 1981 to 1984, though looking likely to be dropped when this was written. The coupé was billed as having, 'the best aerodynamic efficiency rating – an 0.34 Cd – of any standard equipped American-built car,' when it was introduced in 1982.

The basic Escort coupé format was that of a two seater 'bubbleback' available either as the Ford EXP or Mercury LN7. The wheelbase remained at 94.2in. but length was 170.3in. instead of the US hatchback's 163.9in. or 165in. for the wagon (estate). The Coupé gained most on the drag factor front from a 50.5in. height, rather than the normal American Escort roofline 53.3in. above earth. Width was the same 65.9in. Specifications of selected American Escorts and coupé cousins are given in Appendix III for comparison with European models.

Ford were naturally non-committal over Escort's future developments beyond 1984, but there is no doubt that the original styling represented the company well for four years without significant European alteration. With a 1983 Golf 2 and a 1984 revision of the GM-owned Opel-Vauxhall Kadett/Astra range, its chief European competitors, there was naturally new bodywork ready for 1985/1986, formally débuting in the opening month of 1986. Bringing anti-lock brakes within reach of a far larger number of customers, the 1986 European Escorts also put availability of a turbo model beyond the constrictions of a motorsport homologation number. Read all about it in our shiny new following chapter and our updated look at The Performers, which completes our coverage of the later front drive Escorts.

The way ahead? Ford-owned Ghia have shown many variations on the Escort theme, this Brezza being displayed at Turin in 1982, when some of the journalists were able to drive it. Snags included a high body-weight in the show time rush, but the idea of a sleek coupé body for the Escort in Europe ought to have some attraction post-Capri.

Shape and powerplant principles of the 1992 Escort? Ford displayed this Eltec concept car at the September 1985 Frankfurt Show. Aside from wide-spread electronic management of engine, variable-ratio automatic and ABS anti-lock braking, the Eltec also had this electronic fuel injection 12-valve version of the 1.3 CVH developing 80 bhp.

Chapter 12

The 1986 breed

A fresh look, along softer lines, advertised the presence of significant engineering changes, including the availability of anti-lock brakes. An enormous variety of bodies and engines (50 to 132bhp) emphasised Escort versatility.

Press-previewed via numerous winter 1985/86 outings on slippery surfaces to show off the Lucas Girling anti-lock braking, the latest Escort and Orion thinking for Europe became available from late February 1986. Using the slogan 'You Don't Get Ahead by Standing Still', Ford of Britain débuted six engine choices at prices from £4921.27 for the Fiesta-derived 1.1 OHV three-door to £9816.55 for the fuel-injected Cabriolet. From the start a revised (but no more powerful) XR3i was available, but its story and that of the July 1986 Escort RS turbo is found in the following chapter, *The performers, part 3*.

Recalling that the Escort had been the number 1 seller in Britain since 1982 – when it first demoted Cortina to second slot – and that Ford call it 'The World's best selling car', startling changes were unlikely in 1986. The commercial wisdom of such an evolutionary approach could be seen at the close of the year, when a record number of multi-national Escorts had been made (963,000) in 12 months to eclipse VW's Golf and Toyota's Corolla. In 1987 the Escort sales boost was not quite maintained, at a World production figure of 949,000, but it was still enough to hold off the Golf and Corolla. Total production of front drive Escorts 'now exceeds 7.0 million' said Ford early in 1988. That figure is still some three million down on total Golf production between 1974 and 1988, the Golf obviously selling at a far superior rate whilst enjoying front drive six years earlier than the Escort.

By 1988 the Escort was being manufactured in the United States, Canada, Great Britain, West Germany, Spain, Brazil, Venezuela and Argentina. In January 1988 Ford

The facelifted Escort of 1986 contributed to a record sales year. Its smoother face covered many mechanical revisions, including more power for the 1.6 CVH and a 1.4-litre version of that engine.

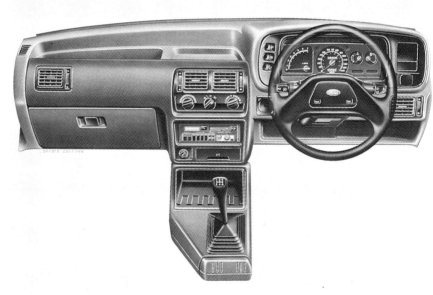

The fascia and trim changes were all aimed at giving the Escort the kind of interior previously seen on larger Fords, particularly that of Granada and Scorpio. Large central speedo and wider availability of tachometer were instrumentally most obvious.

estimated that more than four million front drive Escorts had been sold worldwide.

In Britain the Escort continued to be the number 1 after the restyling, selling 178,000 in 1987 to head the all Ford 1-2-3 result of Escort, Fiesta and Sierra. That near-180,000 sales result was the best front drive Escort year to date in Britain, eclipsing a 1983 high of 174,190.

Incidentally, the four-door Orion cousin to the Escort took on the relevant mechanical and styling changes detailed herewith for the Escort. Orion production had exceeded 300,000 when the facelift cars arrived. In Britain the Orion had finished eighth in the bestseller lists in its own right for 1985/86, improving to seventh in 1987 with a record 69,262 sold in the United Kingdom.

Analysed by model name, the later generation Escorts paraded in 29 different models.

The Popular was cheapest and customers could choose between three-door saloons or estates. Engine and transmission alternatives were restricted to four-speed manual gearboxes alongside the older Overhead Valve (OHV) petrol engines, five-speed for the 1.6 diesel.

Traditionally the top-selling Escort in Britain, accounting for more than 40 per cent of all UK Escort sales in 1988, the L-badge has become synonymous with company car fleets. A quartet of bodies was proffered in 1986: three-door in saloon and estate, or five-door in the same alternative outlines. Similarly four power units were listed in 1986: 1.3 OHV; 1.4 CVH; 1.6 CVH and the 1608cc diesel. Four-speed manual transaxles were usual with the 1.3 and 1.4 motors, but five speeds came in the five doors of 1.6 litres, petrol or diesel. A three-speed auto was offered in company with the 90bhp petrol engine only in five-door saloons.

The GLs featured six saloon or estate five-door Escorts. They were energised by CVH engines (1.4 and 1.6), or the diesel; all had five-speed gearboxes and the auto appeared again for 1.6 CVH only.

Further up the trim scale – marked by a standard tilting and sliding sunroof, plus electrical operation of front windows and central locking – the Ghias continued. Mechanically, Ghias featured only 1.4/1.6 CVH petrol power, five-speed gearboxes or an automatic for the 1.6. Initially they were the absolute summit of luxury features. A competitive British market gradually forced Ford to adopt more of their features on lesser models, and to introduce new designations, notably the LX, to package such features together. In the Orion line the 1988 Motor Show answer was to unearth the 1600E Cortina badge and use that to put in a very passable Ghia + impersonation.

The Cabriolets were billed as 'the best-selling convertibles in Europe' and came either with a carburated 90bhp or the XR3i power unit and badge for 105bhp. Both had five speeds, of course, and 1.6 litres.

Specifically in Britain, the engines lined up with 1.1 litres and 50bhp pushrod engine of Fiesta fame as a starter unit. It had done Escort duty previously in the sub-£5000 category to start the range. The presence of a 1.3-litre, five-bearing version of the OHV engine in 60bhp trim to supersede the UK market 1.3 CVH engined Escort, in company with the 1.4, showed that the old Kent engine principles still had plenty of UK sales life left.

Details of engine dimensions and power outputs are in our appendices, but it is worth noting a new CVH in the 1.4-litre, and a modest extra ration of power offered in twin-choke carburettor versions of the CVH, both designed to please the business market's taxation break point at 1.4 litres and the consumers' ever-increasing expectations.

The new CVH's 1392cc was born of a 77.24mm bore and 74.3mm stroke, instead of a 1.3 CVH's 80x64.5mm. As for all 1986-onward CVH engines, a 9.5:1 compression was specified, highish on four star fuel but relying on the revised combustion chambers for effective detonation. Instead of the earlier 69bhp from 1.3 litres, the twin choke 1.4 provided 75bhp.

A 1.6, now in twin-choke form and yielding 90bhp in the facelifted Escorts, could be compared with 79bhp from the previous single, variable venturi, 1.6 unit. The same engine capacity continued to be available in fuel injection and turbo forms for the XR and RS models that are discussed in the next chapter, but it is worth noting at this point that neither deviated from their official and original outputs of 105 and 132bhp. Significantly the XR3i was now engineered by mainstream company engineers rather than SVE. The turbocharged RS had no upper limit fixed to its production, which was no longer geared to Ford sport requirements.

Dealing with the engine changes first, the most significant change on all CVHs was a move to leaner air/fuel mixtures. Instead of the 14 or 151 that was common Ford practice,

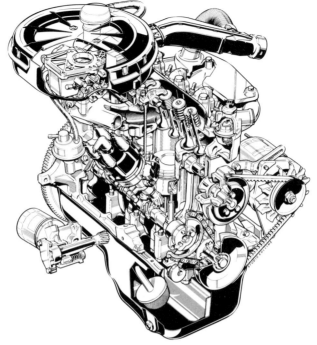

Overhead valves without an accompanying overhead camshaft distinguish the redeveloped 1297cc/60bhp Escort 1.3 engine that has much in common with the 1.1. Note the chain drive from crank to side camshaft.

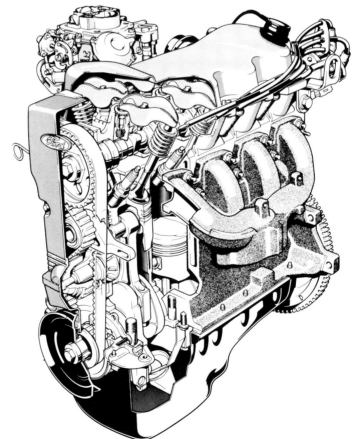

Belt-driven overhead camshaft for the later 1.4 CVH motor, father of a lusty 75bhp, is shared with the uprated (to 90bhp) 1.6, as is a Weber twin-choke carburettor.

the company had developed the replacement Escort units to 'operate under light load in a regime up to 18:1' air/fuel mixtures. Visually the change was most obvious in looking at combustion chamber shapes, now more like a squashed heart outline whilst the XR3i version of the CVH remained rounded. The 1.6 and 1.4 CVH chambers looked pretty similar, but inlet port sizes differed to accommodate different mixture flow rates.

At this stage the company made the necessary changes to accommodate unleaded fuel running, hardening valve seats and advising that the distributor should be reset to retard timing 4 degrees. Power and fuel economy losses were said to be 1–2 per cent in 1986.

Ford further claimed, in a press notice embargoed until January 29 1986, 'at these air fuel ratios engine efficiency is significantly improved (leading to exceptional fuel economy, particularly in light load, mid-range running) and exhaust emissions targets can be met with minimal effect on engine performance'. All true, but in my 31,000 mile experience of the 90bhp 1.6 in an estate body, heavier throttle applications (such as climbing routine Thames Valley gradients) led to pronounced and persistent pinking. We did get it sorted out by the local dealer, but it took three visits and the disappearance of Formula Shell from the UK petrol market finally to banish this worrying problem.

Other important changes within the tough four-cylinder OHV motors covered the fitment of electronic breakerless ignition on the 1.1 unit to cut service times, and 'swirl inducing inlet ports, optimised camshaft timing and fuel outlet exhaust manifolds combined with low friction pistons'. The 1.3 amounted to a longer stroke version of the 1.1 'Valencia'-originated four. Low friction pistons, dual exhaust manifolding and five main bearings were part of the revised OHV 1.3 recipe, which used a twin-choke carburettor instead of the 1.1's variable venturi Ford-patented carburettor.

From 34 to 70 mpg

Fuel consumption was the leading asset of the OHV 1.3; Ford asserted that it used less at 90 km/h (56 mph) than some class diesel rivals! The figure given was equivalent to 57.6mpg and was repeated for the 1.4 CVH. Even the carburated 1.6s were credited with more than 50mpg at 56mph. Indeed, all the carburated Escorts were credited with more than 34mpg in the worst of Urban returns. The OHV 1.3 was the best town bet at 38.2mpg – unless you fell for diesel charms at 48.7 Urban mpg, or an incredible 70.6mpg in 56mph cruising mode.

The 13 per cent power gain of the 1.6 CVH (up 11bhp over its predecessor) was attributed mostly to the redesigned cylinder heads (high-swirl lean burn, in FordSpeak) but there was no doubt the company did also work hard on reducing internal friction. That was typified by the adoption of a new low friction oil pump also fitted to the other CVH engines and by the research and development completed on piston and piston ring design in the 1.1/1.3 families, as for the CVH.

Outside the engine bay, styling and braking stories vied for attention. Styling is the simplest to tell, for much the same process as had been applied to the second-generation of Fiesta was repeated on the Escort, particularly the extended bonnet line. Ford claimed the 'modern style' reduced aerodynamic drag by up to 8 per cent which meant dropping from 0.397 to 0.365 in the skinniest-wheeled hatchbacks.

In detail, the drooping bonnet line and blended headlamps co-operated with a lowered water radiator air intake to improve the aero-factor most obviously. However, the rear was also subtly altered and an Orion-style lip creased into the tailgate to complement rear light lenses that were now smooth, rather than the previous Mercedes/Granada inspired 'wrinklies'. Moulded polycarbonate bumpers were said to give low-speed damage resistance if those behind were overcome by awe and wonder, and forgot to brake ...

Anti-lock braking to the people

Anti-lock braking became an optional feature that was listed at £315 from March 1986 for all five-speed, CVH-engined Escorts. The system was not the sophisticated electronic wonder of Robert Bosch/Alfred Teves fame, but it was a sincere attempt to improve safety at an affordable cost. Unfortunately, when I checked in October 1988, the public reaction had been predictably apathetic. 'About 3 per cent of customers opt for the system,' reported Ford Press Information manager Martyn Watkins. He also pointed out that it had by then achieved standard status on the RS Turbo.

Developed by Lucas and Girling, the Ford rendering of ABS anti-lock braking was dubbed SCS (Stop Control System) and had also been extensively evaluated by Austin Rover. It relied on the comparatively minor contribution made by rear brakes in a front drive car facing an emergency, and the normal X-pattern split of such braking systems.

British press introduction came in a wintry Finland to highlight the advantages of optional anti-lock braking. Customer reaction to anti-lock was lukewarm and Ford had still to offer the system as standard on anything less than the RS Turbo by 1989.

Kevlar drive belts from the driveshafts are driven at nearly 3 times the road wheel speed at the pulley of the modulator. The latter acts on both brake circuits individually, sensing speed and controlling brake line effort. When the over-run sensor detects a deceleration of more than 1.2G, inertia causes a dump valve to open and release pressure in the braking line. As the brake releases, steering and skid control can be maintained by the driver under all but the direst circumstances. Once the input speed of the relevant front wheel is back to that of the decelerated flywheel, a sensor notes that synchronisation and shuts the activated valve. This action can take place up to six times a second, but the brake pedal should remain firm as the master cylinder is at that point isolated from the system.

Ford, Lucas and Girling contributed to an extensive development programme that completed a reported three million miles. Certainly, when I went North of the Arctic Circle with Mercedes there were Escorts out in the snow and ice that was also being scarred by the passage of 400 horsepower Porsche 959s. More relevantly the police co-operated in such pre-production mileage and many of the pre-production SCS vehicles exceeded 50,000 miles in daily use.

In practice the quality of action supplied at the brake pedal could vary markedly. I was not over-impressed on sheet ice at the Finnish introduction, but a subsequent British winter week with the system left me with nothing but admiration for its pioneering introduction. Just remember that it does not shorten stopping distances, but it does allow the driver to retain control far longer than would normally be the case. SCS offers the chance of steering an alternative path around the hazard to the 99 per cent who would otherwise lock the brakes and slide straight into an impact.

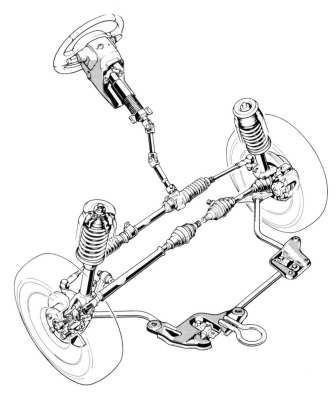

'Front and rear suspension followed the principles established in 1980 and revamped in May 1983. Inevitably spring and damper changes were instituted. 'Front springs rates are now 20 per cent stiffer,' said the company who also replaced track control rubber bushes by low friction ball joints and 'revised' the position of the front anti-roll bar.

Disc/Drum brakes continued for all models, vented front discs of 9.4x0.9 inch on all CVH models (1.4 to 1.6i) and 7.1 inch rear drums were common on all but injection CVHs, which had an 8 inch drum.

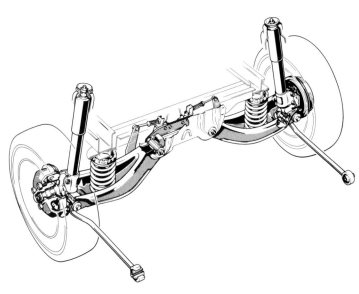

Another worthy move was to fit the Chubb-style locks of Granada/Scorpio to the doors, hatchback and steering column, plus a similar locking action for the petrol cap, the lock a standard item throughout the range. No sill buttons were featured on the doors and it was hoped the models would be considerably harder to steal. They were certainly a fiddle for the average owner to operate via new keys. Lacking the deadlock feature of some current Vauxhalls, BMWs and Volkswagens the new locking system was far from the ultimate deterrent.

As ever, the suspension was attacked, Ford being incapable of leaving this area alone during any era of the Escort's evolution. Front spring rates went up on the non-sporting models from 83lb in to 100 lb in and the front anti-roll bar (still plugging into the TCA, Track Control Arm) had a modified path, its axis pivot down 10mm/0.4in. The inner joints

The workhorse five-door in L-trim displays the 1986 snout and polycarbonate bumper/spoiler with six side window style.

At the rear the ridged lamps had gone and the bootlid gained a small crease of Orion inspiration that contributed to improved ('5-8 per cent' said Ford), but not sensational, aerodynamics. This is the Ghia model, sold as five door only, with a choice of 1.4 or 1.6 CVH motivation.

of the TCAs were jointed in hard plastic rather than the rubber joints used in previous mainstream models.

The smallest wheel rim size was 4.5x13 inch, but you had to buy a Cabriolet or an XR3i before anything larger was standard equipment, the Ghia Cabrio unique on a standard 5x13 fitment. Tyre sizings, begun at 145 SR on the Popular, escalated to 155 SR for the L and the remainder of the range, including Ghias.

The interior trim and fascia were completely overhauled, the resultant clean layout picking up inspiration from its bigger Ford brothers and retaining a 'user-friendliness' that always earns Ford high marks in comparative tests. Instrumentation put the accent on a central speedometer, one flanked by a clock and water temperature gauge in Popular and L-trim models. From GL upwards a digital clock took over and a 0-7000rpm rev-counter was provided.

New options in the cabin area included a heated front screen for just £100, central locking priced at £234.07 on GLs (less on XR3i) and – new to the Escort – a fuel computer. The latter would supply average or instant figures, but was listed only on Cabriolet and XR3i, at £113.01, when the revised Escort was announced.

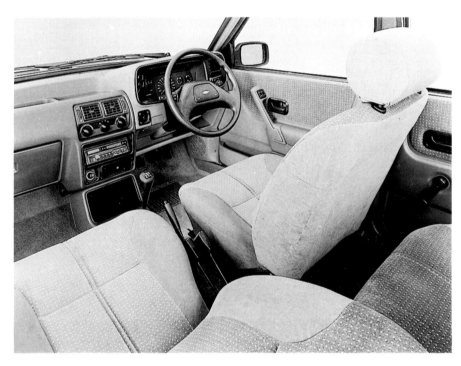

Inside the Ghia we see the Escort interior at its plushest. The buttons for the electric windows (front only) can be seen in the door armrest moulding, but this picture also demonstrates the post-1986 rotary heater controls and two-stalk steering column beneath a two-spoke steering wheel.

Standard equipment listings became fuller in the normal eighties style. For example, *all* 1986 onward Escorts received a heated rear window (operating an effective time delay automatic switch-off), remote control twin-door mirrors and the rear wash wipe system was part of the package for all but the basic Popular. The '60/40' split and folding rear seat, reclining fronts, were also allowed throughout the newer Escort line, along with a rear parcel tray to hide the hatchback's load. Of safety import were two-speed wipers with intermittent wipe, halogen headlamps, rear foglamps, repeat side flashers and reversing lamps, which had also become standard items.

Performance & progress

Available in Britain by March 1986, the revamped Escorts were generally well received as logical developments of their predecessors. Nobody was fainting at the sheer excitement of the latest Ford débutant, but *Motor's* closing comment on their 1.4GL in that first month of new Escort sales summarises prevailing press comment. They said, 'Ford's restyling of the Escort has resulted in a stronger family resemblance to the Granada, which some people will like for its upmarket aspirations. But the new nose is not to everyone's taste after the clean cut squareness of the previous car, and the look of its interior may not appeal to fans of its predecessor.

'The new Escort is an improvement over its predecessor in most departments, even if it still has faults in its poor road ride and handling. The car also has an impressive list of options, including the Granada-pioneered heated front screen and the cheapest ABS on the market. But many of these extras ought to be standard on a GL, and some of them even cost extra on the top-of-the-range Ghia and XR3i models,' concluded *Motor* in their March 29 1986 issue.

Performance was a strong attribute even of Escorts that were not sold on their statistics. All but the OHV 1.1 and 1.3 models exceeded 100mph, and the 1.3's 94mph in independent trials was backed by a best flying quarter mile of 96mph. The fastest Escorts were naturally

On the road the 1986 Ghia Escort packaged all the later improvements as standard, plus a glass sunroof, central locking, tinted glass and four-speaker stereo. Either 75 or 90 carburated horsepower was available but no equivalent to the fuel injection Orion Ghia.

those with the performance badges, but the 1.6 returned an average close to 10 seconds for 0-60mph, was timed at 108.3mph, and still averaged nearly 33mpg for *Motor*.

In fact it took as RS Turbo to drop below 30mpg in the new Escort range, and that was for a week or more of the hardest possible use. The best overall mpg figure I have filed for the new Escorts is 34.6 from *Autocar's* 1.4 CVH – a remarkable performance in such testing circumstances, one that was only exceeded by the 1.1 (36.9mpg) and the diesels in the first front drive outline.

As in the previous Escort, one of the earliest British market moves was to make a low cost variant available for the disabled. Ford used a 1.6L three-door in automatic transmission trim as the basis for a vehicle which could be adapted to meet special needs at an ex-factory cost of £5560 in April 1986.

A new version of the cabriolet was offered immediately, a contrast to the Golf which stayed in 'Mk1' shape. This Ghia trim option was dropped, leaving only XR3i specification from August 1987 in Britain.

Five door estate emphasises the bodywork versatility that the Escort offers. This is an L-trimmed variant with 60:40 split folding rear seat action of all Escort Estates beyond 1989 Popular specification.

June 1986 was the British début month for both the RS Escort and Cosworth Sierra, but in this chapter our next concerns came in February 1987. By then the cheapest Popular 1.1 was £5312.61 and both Ghia and XR3i were over £10,000 in Cabriolet bodywork. At this point Ford looked to clear away some extra L-specification models under the Special Edition tag 'Bravo'. All were in five-door hatchback bodies and came with a five-speed transmission hitched to the 1.4 or 1.6 CVH power units. In the opinion of trade sources, standard equipment at £6990 for the 1.4 Bravo or £7206 for the 1.6 was extended enough for these models to be worth a 'slightly higher' price than the equivalent 1.4 or 1.6L.

Noses, old and new. The English-registered wears the 1986 look of all models beneath Cabriolet/XR3i and Turbo, whilst the German factory Escort displays a look that was announced to Britain, with many specification updates and the 1.3 HCS engine option, in October 1988.

In August 1987 the company declared that they were dropping the 1.1 version of the Escort, leaving the 1.3 to act as the starter model for the range; by Autumn it was over £5600. When this edition was composed, in the Autumn of 1988, the cheapest Ford Escort exceeded £6100. The most expensive Cabriolet and RS Turbo models had accelerated toward the £12,000 barrier, priced at £11,874 and £11,838 respectively.

Also in August 1987, Ford said that the Ghia version of the Cabriolet would be axed in British favour of the XR3i badged model only. The Cabriolet was actually in something of UK state of flux that year, travelling through a £11,234 two-tone special edition and gaining a £500 power hood option that continued in 1990.

Other items covered in the 1987 special edition included an RS parts rear spoiler and colour matched to the upper body paint. Such cars are easily identified by their choice of only two twin tones: Strato Silver/Mercury Grey or Crystal Blue/Strato Silver. All had blue soft top hoods. Standard equipment extended to central locking, alloy wheels, long range driving lamps; stereo radio/cassette player and electrically operated aerial.

The power top was engineered by the co-operative efforts of the SVE department in Britain and the Cabriolet production constructors, Karmann of Osnabruck. The top, with its glass rear screen, looked as before, but an unobtrusive cabin button activated hydraulic operating arms and an electric motor. Once the twin safety catches were released and the engine turned off, returning the ignition to its first click position, the power top was ready to strut its stuff. Based in the luggage compartment, the power unit could fold away the roof in just 15 seconds. Raising the roof was just as simple, and Ford had put in a failsafe to prevent electricity reaching the hood motor, should you have left the tonneau cover clipped over the folded roof. If there was any other electro-mechanical failure, the hood could be raised and lowered manually via a T-shaped tap on the hydraulic pump.

A very important longer term step in the marketing of the Escort in Britain was the September 1987 advent of the 1.4 and 1.6 LX. Only sold in hatchback and 5-doors such LX designations found a permanent place in the model range, snugged in between L and GL. Standard features in 1987 extended to: tinted glass, glass sunroof; rev-counter; and stereo radio/cassette player.

Also in the Autumn of 1987 was the announcement that the Popular would gain the rear wash/wipe it had lacked from the beginning of the later generation Escort's sales. The

State of the art. XR3i became the only Cabriolet option in Britain, whilst in LHD markets (as the number plate hints) you could have a catalytic converter fuel-injection engine that developed over 100bhp. Late in 1988 the model became available with a Cosworth Sapphire wheel style, but remained on 14 inch, rather than 15 inch, wheel diameters.

Escort L was awarded a standard five-speed gearbox and improved in-car entertainment, whilst the GL attained central locking and sunroof as routine production equipment. There was not a lot they could do about the Ghia, so they heated the door mirrors and upgraded the stereos.

July 1988 marked a general price increase of 2.5 per cent across the Ford range, and it was at that point that the 1.3 Popular reached beyond the £6000 barrier as the lowest cost model, now priced at £6121. As noted some Escort variants now cost double that (more with extras), but in a business car/user-chooser market that tolerated the new tag of £23,750 for a 4x4 Granada 2.9i Scorpio, it drew little comment.

Criticism of current Ford prices is now only seen safely contained in the private buyer's conversational exchanges with a dealership. Mainly along the lines of 'How . . . much? You must be joking!' The dealers are not joking, of course, and the Ford of the late eighties was one of the most profitable companies on earth, Britain an essential ingredient in maintaining those margins. Whatever happened to Ford motor company's traditional role as a provider of basic and low cost transport?

Also in the Summer of 1988 Ford went for some further special edition models. In Escort terms these covered an £8040 Cosmopolitan, which was based on the 1.3L and finished throughout its five-door framework in white. The treatment engulfed the wheel trim, wing mirror mouldings and is also identified by red inserts to the bumper and body side contours. The package provided a tilt-and-slide glass sunroof, electrically powered front side glass; central locking and stereo radio/cassette player.

Also a July addition to the Escort choice were the GL Plus designations. They applied to the 1.4/1.6 CVHs and brought the tilting glass sunroof, central locking, quad speaker stereo radio/cassette player and the aerial incorporated in the rear screen heater element layout. Prices started at £8205 for the smaller engine derivative and went to £8432 on the 1.6, more for the equivalent Orions. The latter four-doors were apparently nicknamed O'Briens inside Ford, so they must have restarted Irish production again, without telling anyone!

The Autumn 1988 Motor Show season brought a flurry of further Escort modifications. For the customers an extra dose of equipment for the L (tilt and slide sunroof), LX (central locking) and GL (power mirrors and front side glass) was a lure under the advertising banner 'Escort standards raised again'. No further increases in price were levied for the extra equipment.

The Autumn 1988 estates picked up on the generally improved levels of equipment to offer a glass sunroof above L-trim, the first time a sunroof had been offered at all on an Escort Estate. Central locking was also available, but without including the tailgate. The radio aerial was moved into the rear screen heater element area.

Escort in 1989 motion showed greater poise and the higher levels of equipment needed to face the increasingly sophisticated opposition. 'Bitty' details such as rain gutters and side door mouldings were cleaned away in the early nineties replacement, along the lines of this eighties Eltec show car, but don't expect the Eltec's multi slat automatic sunroof ... yet.

Power top became available on the XR3i Cabriolet as a £500 option. It is restricted to use at rest!

Technically, Ford preferred us to concentrate on 'new high technology petrol and diesel engines' and 'a variable-ratio rack and pinion steering system'. The 'new' HCS (High Compression Swirl) motor turned out to be a reincarnation of the iron OHV 'Kent' unit. This was a rebirth that the company claimed had demanded £60 million in development 'but [the engine] has been so radically redesigned that virtually no common parts remain.'

Principal benefits were gains in homologated fuel consumption figures (+ 11 to 18 per cent) and power gains: up 3bhp to 63 total PS on 5000rpm and an official 101Nm of torque at 3000rpm replacing the same peak rpm and 100Nm. Hardly radical, but they had official recognition to quote 62.7mpg at 56mph rather than 57.6mpg; 45.6mpg at 75mph rather than 43.5 previously and a fine 44.1 Urban mpg on the ECE 15 cycle in place of the 1986 quote of 38.2 Urban mpg. No independent tests had been completed at press time; Ford claimed a maximum of 98mph for the HCS Escort and 0-60mph in 13.1 seconds.

Internal changes for the HCS embraced a further exploration of Ford self-styled Lean Burn operation (air fuel ratio moved to 19:1) and a compression equal to that of the CVH petrol units, 9.5:1. Listed new items were named as: redesigned cylinder block; cylinder head; ignition system (no distributor, twin coils); Weber TLD twin-choke to replace the Ford carburettor; and all reciprocating components, especially the crankshafts, connecting rods, gudgeon pins, pistons and rings. Bore and stroke of the lighter internal components was fixed at 74x75.5mm, yielding a familiar Ford Escort capacity of 1297cc. Familiar capacity yes, but a far cry from those short stroke Escort crossflows of the seventies.

Statistics for the revamped diesel were more radical at a lower (£50 million) reported investment. Listed amongst the changes were the 'introduction of a thermoset plastic manifold', which Ford believed was 'a technical first for a manifold of this type in volume production'. They also expected it to predict the use of a lot more under-bonnet plastics, despite a hostile environment.

Instead of 1608cc the Ford-at-Dagenham sparkless motor grew to 1752cc on an 82.5mm bore. That substituted for the previous 80mm; stroke is near all-square at 82mm.

Power gains were reported at + 17 per cent for torque (now 110Nm) and 60bhp at 4800 revs replaced 54bhp at the same peak. Ford quoted a near two second reduction in 0-60mph (now 14.8 seconds) and a 3mph gain in speed to a quoted 94mph. More relevant to most

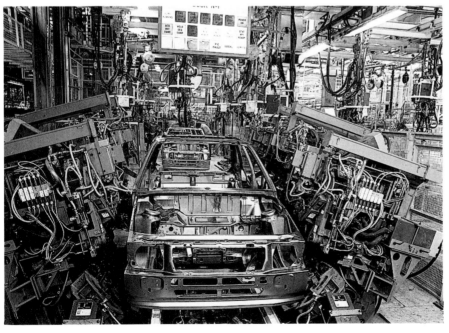

Twenty years of Escort production – over four million Escort-badged Fords – at Halewood, Merseyside, are distilled in these three pictures. The Mk4 robotic line makes a stark contrast with the three men at work on the 1968 line. People, not robots are still to the fore in the later assembly stages. In March 1988 Halewood employed 'around 10,000' split into Body, Assembly and Transmission plants. Output has risen fantastically since the 'Bad Old Days' and daily capacity is now set at 1,200 cars a day, plus '3000 gearboxes and transaxles'.

business diesel customers was the economy, but the switch to 1.8 litres lost them that 70 + mpg on 56mph eye-catcher, now homologated at 67.3mpg. However, in the real Urban world of mpg Ford had improved their diesel's consumption returns up to 44.8mpg from the previous 43.7, so owners could expect a slight overall gain in daily town use.

Now for something completely different, let's see how the performance versions of the front drive Escort developed...

Chapter 13

The performers, part 3

Front drive was no deterrent to Ford returning to their RS roots for a special Ford of Germany Motorsport Escort injection model – and many of the seventies Ford Advanced Vehicle Operation engineers resurfaced for the vastly improved XR3i. Here is the story of their development and capabilities.

TREKKING across the acres Ford hired at the 1982 British Motor Show in Birmingham, one could be forgiven for thinking that the company were suffering a peculiarly British form of Escort marketing schizophrenia. Within a display naturally overlooked by the debutant Sierra, the latest hot Escorts stood side by side and within the same £6000 to £7000 bracket that encompassed the doyen of the hot hatchbacks, VW's 1800 Golf GTI. In the ensuing months I lost count of the number of people who asked whether the Escort RS 1600i or XR3i was the better buy? The magazines and those that drove the cars (myself included) generally seemed to plump for the officially less powerful XR3i – only to then find potential customers bombarding us with further queries on how that particular Ford faced up to the rapidly multiplying opposition! By the Spring of 1983 Renault, Fiat, MG, Mitsubishi Colt, GM Vauxhall-Opel all had 105 to 115mph hatchbacks in this higher performance price bracket.

Yet Ford were not attempting to counter the GTI with two simultaneous Escort options. Each Escort had a specific purpose – arriving on the Continent at distinctly separate periods. The RS 1600i was the first to appear and its specification reflected its early start in the performance race, initially failing to include some later mainstream developments such as the larger fuel tank and bigger rear brakes that were part of the XR3i.

Although the RS 1600i cost British customers slightly over £7000 on the road in the opening months of 1983, and had a specification biased toward sports use at the expense of

Full-scale wind tunnel work all over Europe was a time consuming part of the front drive Escort's development, utilizing five major facilities (including that of Mercedes-Benz) in over 2500 separate tests. The XR3 was part of that massive workload and sported unique front and rear spoilers, plus shrouds to deflect air around wider wheels. The result was a claimed 0.375 Cd. This was a good figure for the period, but by 1984 major rivals were hovering around 0.35 Cd. GM Vauxhall-Opel established a new low in small car sporting aerodynamics with 0.30 Cd recorded for Kadett GSE/Astra GTE.

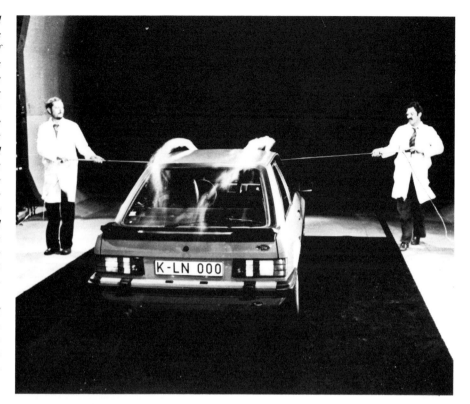

The original RHD XR3 interior with the small two-spoke steering wheel and clear 7000 rpm/140mph main instrumentation, striped seats (Laser) and an extra-cost cassette player/radio. A push button MW/LW radio was the standard snap crackle and pop Ford fitment!

Efficient engineering plus adrenalin.

What leaps from 0-60 mph in just 8.6 seconds, rushes on up to 113 mph, and clings to the road like a competition car, yet returns an almost unbelievable 40.9 mpg at a steady 56 mph* and requires less maintenance than most family saloons?

Answer: Ford's astonishing new XR3.

Tuned for the eighties.

The XR3 story began four years ago, just when the fuel crisis had really begun to bite.

That's when Ford went to work on a new front wheel drive Escort.

The target they set themselves was to design a car that would cost even less to run than its predecessor. But perform as well or even better.

The sports derivative of this new Escort, designated the XR3, was to become

the purest expression of that ideal – the epitome of the fast, high-efficiency hatchback.

High power. Low service costs.

The heart of the XR3's exhilarating performance is its brand new high-efficiency engine, a triumph of elegantly simple design.

With an aluminium cylinder head, hemi-spherical combustion chambers, high-lift overhead camshaft, twin choke carburettor and breakerless ignition, it produces no less than 96 bhp from only 1.6 litres.

Efficient shape. Light weight.

It's the XR3's strikingly efficient shape that releases the engine's full potential.

Thanks to a deep front air dam, the fairings round the wheels and that big dished rear spoiler, it has a drag coefficient of only 0.375.

Equally vital to acceleration and fuel economy, computer technology has kept the car's weight to a minimum without sacrificing strength.

Limpet-like roadholding. Businesslike cockpit.

The pleasure of driving this refined little machine is sharpened by its phenomenal roadholding.

Suspension is independent all round with pressurised gas filled shock absorbers and supple coil springs, ventilated disc brakes and rack and pinion steering. And the car squats low and wide on those beautiful alloy wheels with

their advanced ultra low profile tyres.

Deeply contoured bucket seats provide a businesslike driving position. The steering wheel is small, the pedals broad and firm, and the gear change short and crisp.

A nice touch, the rev counter is positioned in its housing so that the red line is at the top.

And here's another example of the technology that's gone into the car, a new electronic module activates an array of warning lights which allow you to check oil level, brake pad wear, radiator and screen wash levels with-out leaving your seat.

Best of all, this red blooded sports car can carry four people comfortably and has a load capacity of 48.7 cu ft with the back seat folded.

So at £5123† it's totally practical, not just a rich man's toy.

If you'd like something to stir the adrenalin, ask your dealer to arrange an XR3 demo.

*Government fuel consumption figures...

†Price correct at time of going to press...

FORD ESCORT XR3

ESCORT

During the 1980-81 winter, Ford of Britain's advertising agents, Ogilvy & Mather, ran this campaign for the £5123 original XR3. The ads were nicely detailed with plenty of information but Ford supplied figures that were a lot more optimistic than those of the German counterpart (see Chapter 11), including a 0-60mph time of 8.6s.

Alloy wheels reminded onlookers of the Porsche 928, and rude things were said about the tail spoiler being 'over the top'. Later the XR3's visually-similar descendant (XR3i) was judged in terms such as, 'The Escort gets it about right: it's smart and striking without being in anyway flash or overbearing. Build and finish are fine'. That was Motor *commenting in a group comparison that included the Golf GTI 2 and Vauxhall's new Astra GTE ... 8 December 1984.*

road manners, there was no shortage of UK customers. A few did manage to jump the gun, however, by purchasing LHD examples with a rather firmer brake pedal action (for reasons which will become apparent) at the equivalent of £5426 in its native Germany.

Differing origins

The Escort RS 1600i was conceived by Ford Motorsport in Germany and inspired onward by then Ford of Germany chairman, Bob Lutz. It had the single-minded purpose of providing Ford with the best possible specification to race and rally within the 1982-introduced International Group A regulations. The Escort XR3i was a skilfully upgraded XR3 destined to provide an enthusiastic Ford buyer with an improved specification for normal road use – and the opportunity to look VW Golf GTI owners in the eye with pride at their choice. For fuel injection, effective suspension and many other detail improvements were included in this German and British-manufactured (January 1983) Escort derivative.

The XR3i was engineered in Britain for both LHD and RHD; LHD production, commencing at Saarlouis on the Franco-German border from October 1982. The car, which amounted to a completely modified XR3 within a much smaller and more restrictively financed group than the mainstream group, which originated the front drive Escorts, was the work of the 1 April 1980-founded Special Vehicle Engineering (SVE) group. Drawing on the experience of ex-FAVO engineers as a nucleus, these Dunton Research & Engineering Centre employees had previously produced the engineering behind 75,000 performance Fords, including Fiesta XR2 (Autumn 1981 UK début) and both LHD and RHD Capri 2.8 injection. The latter went on sale for nine months in LHD form before blossoming for British buyers in July 1981. At one stage the 2.8-litre Capri was gobbling over half of all UK Capri sales, so that the original target of 2500 a year was surpassed with such ease (over 11,000 had been sold in Britain alone by Spring 1983; 7000 across Europe by June 1982) that SVE were offered XR3i by a grateful and somewhat surprised management!

By October 1982 the 115bhp RS 1600i had been converted to RHD and immediately sold well-beyond Ford's expectations, despite a price premium over the similar performance of the XR3i. Senior Ford management attribute the car's success as much to its visual recognition points – particularly the seven spoke RS wheels – as to the vehicle dynamics. Front and rear spoilers were unique to this model but provided no detectable wind tunnel benefits, the deeper front spoiler possibly offsetting the effect of yet larger wheels and tyres.

Although Bosch K-Jetronic injected, as for the XR3i, the RHD layout for the RS 1600i was totally different in the engine bay. Note the Ford Motorsport ID for the finned rocker cover over mechanical (as opposed to the usual hydraulic) valve lifters and twin-circuit system for AFT ignition, placed to the right of the rocker cover-mounted oil filler cap.

External instant recognition points on the 115mph RS 1600i were the use of quadruple auxiliary lamps in the UK, the RS wheels, comprehensive striping, enlarged front spoiler and the deletion of XR3's rear wheel spats.

RS 1600i progress

Competition was the *raison d'être* behind RS 1600i, just as it had been behind the 1970 RS 1600, but the fuel injection, front drive, Escort was spawned in a far more demanding automotive world than the environment which governed its predecessor by a dozen years. The RS 1600 was produced at a small plant in small numbers by people who knew exactly what they wanted for the job ahead. In 1970, Group 2, for which the RS 1600 was built, demanded that 1000 similar cars be made before recognition was granted. Then, inspection of numbers was unknown by those outside the country's sporting body, and the company making the proposed base for a competition car.

By the eighties we had all suffered both the oil crisis and a worldwide recession, with motor manufacturers in Europe under ever more intense scrutiny for their competitiveness against the Japanese, compliance with an awesome bunch of Euro and local vehicle regulations, and a pattern toward increasing production line automation. Add the fact that Group A regulations demanded production of not 1000 but 5000 of a particular model before it could be recognized for international motor sport and you might begin to grasp why there were some limitations facing German marketing executive Fritz Böettinger and Motorsport's long-suffering engineer, Otto Stulle, in the conception and execution of RS 1600i. Indeed, one British engineer listening to a disparaging comparison of the XR3i and RS 1600i, favouring the British development said bluntly, 'The RS 1600i was a man and boy job – they did a damn good job of making the car available at all...'

To Motorsport in Germany, especially Lothar Pinske, the department's eagerly persuasive successor to Michael Kranefuss, must go the credit of instantly seizing on the new Escort's need for fuel injection. Ford's massive main engineering centres had concentrated on creating the carburated CVH engine and I could find no evidence of any factory department experimenting upon fuel injection for the new four prior to Motorsport. This was something of a surprise, given the prevalence of such an induction type today and the example of the Golf GTI. It really does appear that Ford in Europe considered injection a six-cylinder Granada, Capri and Sierra feature, although that for Sierra was originally to be on the 2.3 V6, rather than the proven 2.8i.

It is unofficially said that Ford Motorsport began their injection experiments in late 1979 with pre-production front drive Escorts and the complete Bosch K-Jetronic layout as applied to the Golf GTI. By 1980, Stulle was talking of 150bhp in Group A competition guise and the RS Escort was designed to be competitive around that figure. Former European Motorsport overall boss Karl Ludvigsen (who was replaced by Stuart Turner in March 1983) was behind the scheme enthusiastically, but there was a distinct struggle before the main company engineers would agree to the disruptions of making first an agreed 3000, then 5000, such fuel injection engines. As of January 1983 it was expected that at least 8000 would be made, for demand in Britain and France really was quite extraordinary – a distinct contrast to the sluggish greeting that awaited the RS 1600, 1800 and 3100 in the seventies. Some 8659 of the RS 1600i Escort were made; 2608 sold in Britain.

By April 1981, Motorsport had completed their RS 1600i production development programme and their total knowledge was handed over to SVE at Dunton to give them a basis on which to work for the full mass production XR3i. In fact very little cross-fertilization occurred 'and we went our own ways', as SVE manager Rod Mansfield recalled in 1983.

The engine Motorsport developed featured alterations in all key areas besides the obvious adoption of the mechanical K (for Kontinuous) Bosch injection. The cylinder head carried a 9.9:1 CR instead of XR3's 9.5:1 with enlarged 40mm bore tubular exhaust manifolding. Such pipework served as the exit for valves that were allowed an unshrouded operation by the head porting and compression modifications, plus the use of solid lifter tappets, rather than the hydraulic units of all other CVH-engined Escorts. The camshaft profile was unique to the vehicle with as much lift as possible whilst complying with European emission requirements. The extra lift was needed for the car's sporting aspirations – Group A regulations control any modification in this area strictly.

Production XR3 pistons were retained, but the engine electronics were much admired. AFT (Atlas Fahrzeug Technik GmbH) in Germany provided the computerized electronic ignition which literally counted every tooth on the ring gear in order to provide flywheel actuation of the triggering mechanism. No distributor was needed, with advance/retard and twin ignition coils incorporated in a system that could literally sense every engine impulse. A crankshaft rpm-limiter that reduced revs gently, instead of the abrupt ignition cut-out found on seventies and sixties Lotus/BDA engines, was another useful electronic

'Those magic magic RS wheels,' was the enthusiastic description of the seven spoke alloys voiced by one Ford director when speaking about the RS 1600's rapidly increasing status as the collectable Mk 3 Escort.

feature, along with the K-Jetronic over-run fuel cut-off. The latter was hitched up to the standard Escort Econolites within the speedometer, ensuring maximum glare every time the device operated, and total night driving distraction!

Incidentally, the rpm-limiter played a vital role in German marketing, for it was deliberately set at under 6500rpm to inhibit the RS 1600i's 0-100km/h (62mph) sprinting abilities. Why? Because insurance rates escalate so sharply in Germany in line with preset performance parameters. This partially explained why the RS 1600i's test track acceleration abilities were either slower or only equal to those of the XR3i. If Ford had allowed the solid lifter 1600i engine its head then its high rpm ability, i.e. that beyond 6000rpm, should have underlined that it really did have more power (115bhp versus 105bhp) and torque (109lb ft versus XR3i's 101lb ft) than the XR3i.

The Appendices give a fully factual account of engine and other specification differences between the original XR3, XR3i and RS 1600i, but it is worth pointing out some subtle differences in power delivery and Ford figures that colour-in some of those back page statistics. In Britain, all three models were credited with the same maximum power point, at 6000rpm. The French publication *auto hebdo* published their road test of RS 1600i Number 12 on the Ford Cologne pre-production press fleet, and commented on the official 5750rpm peak proving that there was no reason why a modified production engine should be any less flexible than an ordinary mass production unit. The French were also told of maximum torque at 4500rpm, the German publication *auto motor und sport* agreed with the figure quoted but reported a 5250rpm peak; *Autocar* went for 5250rpm, too.

For the customer what mattered was that power and torque increased in a predictable manner amongst the three sporting Escorts. Thus the XR3 provided a 96bhp starting point for the XR3i to progress to 105bhp, and the RS 1600i to an official 115bhp. In torque terms, or the pulling power that largely determines how easy a car is to drive on the road (and is often more important than sheer bhp in rallying and some forms of touring car racing), the XR3 offered 98lb ft at only 4000rpm, while the XR3i provided just another 3lb ft some 800rpm up the rpm scale (101lb ft at 4800 revs) with RS 1600i attributed with 109lb ft, some 1250rpm beyond that of the XR3 it was based upon.

Chassis changes

Equally important to the driver were the chassis and transmission changes included in the RS 1600i. The Motorsport Escort stuck with the XR3's 3.84:1 final drive but specified an 0.88 fifth gear in place of the 0.76 used on late-run carburated XR3s, or any Escort with the optionally available European five-speed gearbox. Ally this strange fifth gear with 15 inch wheels, two inches larger in diameter than ordinary Escorts (one inch more than for the XR3), and Dunlop 195/50 VR radials, the lowest profile covers ever fitted to a production Ford by 1982, and you end up with 20.7mph per thousand rpm. Thus you could wind the RS 1600i to 6000rpm, fractionally over 124mph, on an autobahn downgrade and still preserve the engine, but the point of this was largely lost on the British press who saw a machine as being little, if any, faster than the simultaneously-available XR3i.

In Europe the RS 1600's September 1981 début at the Frankfurt show and subsequent low volume availability alongside the less sophisticated XR3 ensured that comparisons were generally more favourable: *auto motor und sport* recorded a top speed of 191.5km/h (118.9mph) for RS 1600i versus 181.8km/h (112.9mph) for XR3. It has to be said, however, that both the French and German press seemed to agree on 0-100km/h in 9.6 to 9.8s, mere fractions faster than the carburated car. The British fifth wheel exponents recorded below 9s for 0-60mph but were generally not so impressed owing to the availability of XR3i and its similar, sometimes superior, performance on an official 10bhp less!

Back with the RS 1600i specification we find that the British adaptation of the car – performed by a small team of Ford RS technicians under the management of Bill Meade at Boreham from June 1982 and resulting in British Market Type Approval from November that year – immediately plumped for the 195/50 D4 Dunlops rather than the Continental-specified 190/50 HR Phoenix. The French market, expected to absorb up to 1000 of the 1600i model, had a unique problem with the Phoenix not recognized for distribution and a 60 series cover had to be alternately offered for that market. In all cases the attractive 15 x 6in. wheel of seven-spoke design and Ford-branding was used, that wheel destined to become the RS offering on many other eighties Ford products.

Hard work successfully aimed at increasing front wheel drive traction under duress was centred upon the use of a separate 26mm front roll bar with aluminium chassis attachment, and separate links from the lower arm of the MacPherson strut running forward to a body mounting. Normally, Escorts have a combined roll bar and lower arm link, so the RS 1600i arrangement is usually called a 'remote' bar, leaving the wheel location links to get on with their job separately from the function of an anti-body roll bar.

At the rear an anti-roll bar of 18mm diameter was specified, unique to this Escort as even the XR3/3i lacked a rear anti-roll bar. However, *Hot Car* of May 1983 commented vigorously on the lack of any rear bar on their test car, which was one of the vehicles also used by *Autocar* (GJN 704Y), so we can assume that this item was originally ordered by Motorsport and reflected by Ford in their press material, failing to make the journey through the car's limited production span!

One could, however, see and feel the evidence of all the other RS 1600i suspension work. Bilstein dampers got the push in favour of Konis and the front springs mounted onto platforms that enabled a one inch lower ride height. The springs, front and rear, remained those of the XR3, but the damper, roll bar and ride height changes at the front resulted in a totally different feel to the car. A cynic would say it got harder in ride and twitchier than ever, but it certainly put a grin on most faces and provided an extremely effective competition base, which was its role in life after all.

It is worth emphasizing, because contemporary magazine reports were once again all at odds, that the RS 1600i did not benefit from the XR3i suspension geometry changes;

such a statement is easily supported by merely looking at the positive camber front wheel and negative camber rear wheel attitudes of the RS 1600i. Now look at XR3i, and you see that the front and rear wheels are not set at any noticeable angles, whereas all the original front drive Escorts shared the 'knock kneed' positive camber front (where the top of the wheel is further out than the bottom) with the opposite splayed out arrangement of the rear wheels. The additional changes that were made to the XR3i front and rear suspension legs are detailed later, along with the running changes made for RS 1600i. Ford Motorsport engineers had put together an 18mm rear anti-roll bar that assisted the handling enormously and you may find, like the larger rear brakes mentioned below, that a keen owner has installed such an item. The rear anti-roll bar was still listed by Ford Motorsport parts operation at Boreham Airfield under order code 909.4599. You should note that this bar will not fit cars made after May 1983 and that 1989 saw the move of the Motorsport parts operation back to its sixties home at Boreham. However, Motorsport parts is berthed to a different (and smarter) office block to that which saw the sixties birth of what has become a multi-million pound-a-year business.

This brings us to some important changes in the RS 1600i's production specification that were brought to my notice during preparation of another book concerning the RS Fords. A small owner-survey brought comments from Scottish-based Steven Reid, a keen concours competitor and were mostly echoed, or amplified, by Jeff Mann of KT Dartford, a useful source of Ford, particularly RS, parts in South Eastern Kent. I have extracted the outline of what was done, but a full account will be found in the March/April 1987 Ford RS Owners Club magazine *Rallye News*.

As we have said RS 1600i suspension was based on reworking the 1981 XR3 carburated Escort, but that is not the complete story. For Ford did include the RS 1600i in the important running changes that were made for the Escort and Orion in 1983.

In May 1983 Ford brought the RS 1600i closer to the production specification of other Escorts, ten bodyshell changes accompanied by important suspension moves and fitment of a 47-litre fuel tank in association with a repositioned fuel pump. It is because of the enlarged tank and associated changes that the Ford anti-roll bar kit mentioned earlier is not recommended as an instant fitment. However, the post-May 1983 suspension was altered, as Steve Reid identified in his comments: 'apparent with the bonnet up because a disc held by a nut replaces the large rubber and two nuts of earlier cars.' Steve Reid also pointed out that trim went from the 'crushed finish' of earlier cars to a smoother and more conventional cloth finish on post-May 1983 RS 1600i Escorts.

The switch brought RS 1600i – like other Escorts and Orions of the period – into line with Sierra-type front struts and top mounts. The RS model maintained its individuality with Koni damping. The front struts mounted in revised strut towers; the noticeable rear wheel negative camber of original Escorts and 1600i was eliminated.

I had the opportunity of trying the later suspension in Jeff Mann's shining RS 1600i during a session with a number of RS Fords at Boreham Airfield; part of a fabulous day for an early 1988 issue of what subsequently became *Autocar & Motor*. On smooth surfaces, and with the proud owner alongside, there was little I could do to check the effectiveness of the later suspension over the kind of bumpy country lanes that had made me feel the original was 'twitchy'.

What I could do was marvel once again at the standards to which these performance Fords are preserved today, this one better in every short run aspect (particularly presentation) than could be achieved with a busy 1982-83 press car, one which had its diary full of new drivers each week.

Back in 1982 we find that the RS 1600i retained the usual 1.6/XR3 ventilated front disc brakes and seven inch diameter drum rears, but Ford in Britain did offer an eight inch diameter rear drum conversion kit as an aftermarket fitting. Considerable criticism, in and outside Ford, was devoted to the brake pedal action of the RHD RS 1600s. Bill Meade was moved to comment that quality 'varied' on the braking action, some suffering the dreaded 'soggy pedal' disease and sinking toward the plush carpet with unnerving rapidity.

The braking quality suffered, compared with the perfectly adequate XR3 with the same layout, because Ford had no original plan to make the RS 1600i in RHD and so a complicated conversion seemed the right answer at Boreham when they were faced with an injection unit with the brake servo in the way. If you look underbonnet of an XR3i you will see the RHD model simply loops its injection ducts all the way round the usual RHD servo. On the RS 1600i they used a cross-shaft with linkages and a rocker that avoided the need to move the LHD servo, and demanded no complicated further Euro paperwork. Unfortunately, the inevitable variations in quality control and lost motion from brake pedal via linkage to the servo gave the RS 1600i the sort of varied braking response that is a feature of some RHD VWs. Once you get the brakes on the retardation is as prompt as ever.

Bells & whistles, buttons & bows...

In the passenger department and outside one found many of the reasons that 700 RS 1600s were sold so rapidly in the first four months of British availability. The interior was excellent, with the usual clear instrumentation augmented by comfortable and supporting ASS front seats, trimmed in heavyweight fabrics that matched those at the rear and echoed Ghia levels of interior quality.

One could have fairly criticized the lack of any extra instrumentation in a sporting derivative – an oil pressure gauge would have been nice at least – but the four-spoke RS steering wheel of 14 inch diameter, instead of the XR3's 13.5 inch, was universally admired.

Externally the RS 1600i had 'all the business', in apt slang description. The badgework and stripes were obvious enough, but one did wonder why the XR3's rear wheel spats had been deleted from the front of the back wheel arches. Perhaps the theory was that the new spoilers front and rear (stamped Escort Motorsport 9057708 rear and Escort 81, 9057705 for the deeper front air dam) were more efficient, needing no assistance despite the wider wheels and tyres? An engineer told us that the company had checked out the replacement front and rear RS spoilers to see if they made any perceptible difference to the aerodynamics and the research showed nothing worth talking about. It may well be that front end down loading is increased thanks to the lowered ride height and deeper spoiler, but the fashionable aerodynamic drag factor is probably slightly worse than a standard XR, owing to the extra below-bumper front lamps fitted in LHD and RHD, plus those fatter wheels and tyres. It is relevant to note that when Ford in Germany tackled the Sierra XR4i, in the wake of Audi's well-received 100 with its 0.30 Cd trumpeted far and wide versus Sierra's 0.34, they did not augment tyre and wheel width significantly. Ford Germany contented themselves with a 5½J rim and *adding* a complete set of lower body panels, plus that double-decker rear spoiler set, before claiming a reduction in Cd to 0.32. We have yet to see a twin back spoiler XR3... Maybe you will soon be seeing it on the streets, if it's as good an idea as Ford claim for Sierra, RS 500 or the earlier XR4i.

On the RHD RS 1600i I tried the headlamps were just H4 units marked 'made in UK', the auxiliary driving lights before the usual Ford aerofoil grille were by Carello and the under-bumper rectangular units were constructed by Hella. Variety is the source of light?

For the record, the engineering and approval procedures that the RS 1600i's small UK team had to perform included: radio suppression; UK mpg ratification; a new glovebox

The October 1982 LHD version of the XR3i slightly preceded British production (January 1983) and Continentals showed a stronger preference for the wider steel wheel fitment of the standard car than did Britons.

design for the interior, the original having been filled in by part of the electrical system during the RHD conversion; the new steering wheel (in Germany it was a three-spoke model) and replacement of the aluminium crossmember; a safety standard 'sled test' for the seats; plus an installation check for the UK seat belts. Then they had to gain official recognition for the UK tyre choice, never mind all that work surrounding the brake linkage, although strictly speaking the responsibility for that and the RHD would be that of Ford Germany.

Incidentally, the official UK mpg figures obtained were: 28.5mpg in the 'urban' cycle, a fine 46.3mpg at a constant 56mph and 35.8mpg cruising at 75mph. *Autocar* got very close to the 'urban' figure overall, recording 28.3mpg over 513 miles; *auto motor und sport* produced 27.7mpg; *auto hebdo* in France went testing around the Nürburgring and its environs to manage 24.6mpg.

Overall the RS 1600i was an excellent recipient of the RS tradition. Just like the RS 1600 it went out to do battle in competition effectively, although the change in international regulations since the seventies ensured that any chance of outright victories being repeated by this RS Escort were slim indeed. On the road it was appropriately rorty – one youth magazine described it as making you 'feel like a world champ as you zip through the gears with that fabulous growl from the engine room.'

XR3i: just a little i above a transformation...

The Special Vehicle Engineering team within the engineering lab building at Ford's Dunton R&D establishment is a comparatively recent introduction to the company's production engineering, but its roots go back to February 1960. That is the date SVE manager Rod Mansfield joined Ford on the general engineering side; ten years later, virtually to the day, he was a prime mover in the first Ford production car in Europe to feature fuel injection (the Capri RS 2600) and ten years after that classic Capri's memory had faded he found himself – 'at nine o'clock on the morning of 1 February 1980' – appointed manager of the embryonic SVE. Ironically, their first project was a fuel injection Capri, the 2.8 injection...

The SVE team was created within the main Ford engineering system via the enthusiastic influence of Walter Hayes (who has also put in 20 years of enthusiasm for sporting Fords) and Bob Lutz. The latter is a keen and exceptionally competent driver, who

The fuel-injected XR3i became available in Britain around the same October 1982 period as the first RS 1600i derivatives and cost considerably less; from £6030 when this O&M campaign spread was conceived. Ford had now become a little more realistic over the acceleration claims and spoke of 8.8s from 0-60mph, a time slightly slower than they originally asserted was the case for the XR3! In fact 90 per cent of UK tests show this later 0-60mph time more than justified, along with a 116mph maximum and 30mpg economy under duress.

worked for Opel and BMW before joining Ford. Mr Lutz retains his enthusiasm for fast cars of proven engineering and handling ability, an enthusiasm he developed in just the same way as he flew fighter jets and mastered motorcycles, as asides to becoming one of the most influential Ford of Germany chiefs. Lutz later joined Chrysler USA.

That SVE had to be born at all served only to remind one of the Ford Advanced Vehicle Operations closure in the mid-seventies. Whilst that Aveley line was mothballed, the engineering spirit lived on eventually to become part of mainstream engineering once more. Unlike the famous TV cops and robbers statement preceding each episode of yet more unlikely mayhem, one could truly say, 'none of the names have been changed to protect the innocent!' Perusing the list of those who worked on the XR3i Escort transformation you will find many whose expertise energized the previous generation of high performance, rear drive, Escorts.

SVE exists to produce performance derivatives of production Fords, but it does so within strictly limited resources. This demands ingenuity rather than cash, and the XR3i demonstrates what a little practical development engineering can produce perfectly. A good example of the fundamental difference in approach lies in the front strut modification of the XR3i. SVE knew that they wanted the front wheels to present all the available tread width to the road with the wheels in an upright position, rather than the original positive camber attitude. They were also made swiftly aware that any fundamental alteration, such as a new upright drilling to relocate the front strut and thus produce the desired front wheel attitudes, would cost 'in excess of one and a half million dollars!' That may sound a lot, but bear in mind that Ford are tooling for a car produced in the largest possible numbers, and any change should ideally be incorporated across the range.

Faced with this impasse, and a similarly huge sum demanded if they moved the top mounting location of the strut (as mainstream Ford engineering were planning at the time of writing), SVE sat and went through the Sherlock Holmes process where all the possible solutions were impossible – so they selected one of the impossibles and made it work!

The XR3i did not immediately adopt the three-spoke steering wheel of slightly greater diameter, but you will find it on most Spring 1983 onward examples, coupled with the change in seat and door trim, which was included from the production start. Most, not all, XR3is with three-spoke steering wheels have the later suspension set-up, incorporating the mainstream changes of May 1983. The latter changes improve the car almost as much as SVE's rethink for XR3i suspension did over the original carburated XR3. Strongly recommended ...

Engine bay for the XR3i shows layout contrasting with the similarly fuel injected RS 1600i. The brake servo on RHD cars is linked to the foot pedal via a transverse shaft. The 105bhp injection CVH is also used in Orion and Escort Cabriolet.

Basically they 'bent' the angle at which the lower end of the strut fitted into the hub, taking out 2° of positive camber, by a process that is detailed in due course. But first the cast list...

Rod Mansfield recalls that it took all of the ten engineers then employed within SVE to provide the finished XR3i after utilizing ten prototypes through most of the 12 month development period. Overall responsibility for the project, reporting to Mansfield, went to the experienced Harry Worrall. Aside from his fabulous memory Harry also employed his suspension systems knowledge particularly on the XR3i.

Another former FAVO employee, Mick Kelly, undertook responsibility for the steering system, the test fleet and administrating the test mileage at Ford's Belgian test track, Lommel. Former FAVO engineer with a racing background, Mike Smith worked with ex-truck and van engineer John Hitchins on the ride quality and other practical development engineering on the suspension; but both of them ensure one appreciates the work Girling put in to adapt their gas-filled struts to the Ford, 'They burnt a lot of midnight oil on our project,' was the team's verdict on the South Wales arm of Girling.

Geoff Fox was charged with responsibility for the body and the interior trim within the department. A chance meeting, however, brought me into contact with a self-mocking young man from the mainstream Ford drawing office responsible for interiors ('We're the pencil-pushing poofs,' he said gaily!), and he pointed out with some justification that the new Escort's interior was one that had set standards within the European industry. But 'the others were catching up with that Laser fabric trim. I know imitation is the sincerest form of flattery, but for the XR3i – and the later Capri five-speed injection, incidentally – we decided to go for this Monza man-made fabric'. As with the upgrading of interiors for other 1983-4 model year Escorts, the thinking behind the switch is that the Monza trim, often used with a velour outer section to each side of the seat squab, hints at greater quality. In most cases this seems successfully to remind potential customers of previous Ford Ghia passenger area trim. Incidentally, a new three-spoke steering wheel of 14 inch diameter was specified and incorporated in all but the very earliest production XR3i examples, which retained the previous 'dinky boy racer' two-spoke design that most of the press derided.

John Mitchell was the sixth SVE engineer on the project, looking after the increased demands placed on the electrical system by the adoption of fuel injection, and the brain-battering task of completing homologation paperwork for the LHD and RHD models that SVE crafted.

Gavin Dixon was the engine man on the project. At Dunton there are 80 cell-based dynos, most of which seemed to be occupied during my visit, literally from morning to night – and doubtless right through the dark hours, when a major programme is under way like the CVH's original development. The limitations on what could be done to the engine by SVE were severe, extending even to the retention of the XR3's 9.5:1 CR at a time when ever-higher compressions were sweeping through the motor business in the quest for increased mpg...then came the proposals to ban lead in fuel! Perhaps the enforced retention of the production compression turned out to be a blessing after all...

Gordon Prout was responsible for the cooling and ancillary systems, such as intake and exhaust manifolding. Tony Batchelor did what is generally agreed to have been 'a brilliant job' on getting the balance and specification of the brakes just right. Indeed *Autocar* reported in their tests, 'The U-tube decelerometer fluid plunged almost out of sight to record a conservatively estimated 1.2g – a quite outstanding performance that we cannot recall having seen on any recently tested road car'. Mr Mansfield merely comments that, '*all* the SVE staff do a brilliant job'!

Ray Diggins had a wide brief with the development of some new 14 x 6in. (as opposed to the normal XR 14 x 5½in. alloy) steel wheels with nylon-filled slotted covers and the development of the far more sophisticated fuel delivery and return high pressure lines.

The wheels were fashioned along Ford Design lines but had to overcome both practical problems and top level Ford of Britain management prejudice before production. Even then British Ford boss Sam Toy was not enamoured of their looks and, after six months XR3i sales, the cheaper steel wheel XR option was noted by its absence both on the streets and in the official Ford catalogue. Yet, as the engineers pointed out, we were being offered extra rim width at less cost.

The XR3i changes

'We have not missed a production (Job 1 in Fordese) date yet at SVE,' said Mansfield proudly, in 1983; that record was maintained for the XR3i. The job was commissioned in October 1981 and LHD output began at Saarlouis on 4 October 1982. In Britain, there had been a plan to introduce to Halewood production the carburated five-speed XR3 in the Spring of 1982, instead of manufacture under Ford of Germany's wing only, but low

The 1984 model year XR3i. The XR3i offered badge and mechanical changes over the XR3 rather than notable exterior styling mods. Internally a three-spoke steering wheel gradually replaced the original two-spoke, along with a Monza fabric in place of the original Laser striping.

output and the well-publicized labour problems prevented the prestige sporting Escort making its British RHD manufacturing appearance before January 1983. From that date on you *could* buy a UK-manufactured high performance Escort for the first time since the FAVO days – although Mk2 Escort Sport owners might argue about that statement! Most UK-made XR3i production came after Spring 1983.

The two major concerns that Wolfgang Beesor of Product Planning outlined in his comprehensive SVE briefing for the injection Escort were that it should adopt fuel injection – only logical in view of the RS 1600i/Golf GTI – and that the suspension be improved in bumpy road and other everyday usage. Needless to say, SVE had been involved in every step of that product brief, for they had to advise what was practicable at this stage in the front drive Escort's life.

Given that the mechanical principles and wide use of Bosch K-Jetronic were widely known in 1981 one could have been forgiven for thinking that the Escort adoption of injection was a very simple process. Think again and consider that the following items needed attention: a new fuel tank incorporating a high pressure (70psi) electric fuel pump as near as possible the lowest practicable fuel pick up point; strengthened fuel lines to withstand pressurized fuel delivery, and return fuel line to ensure that any surplus was syphoned back from the engine bay to the rear tank. There was a 10.6 gallon (48 litre) item instead of the previous 9.0 gallon (41 litre) one, because of an inspired negotiation session that allowed SVE to 'pull forward' availability of a tank destined for other future Escorts.

Still on the fuel injection front, they needed to plumb in an accumulator pump so that, when one switched off even overnight, there remained a reservoir of 70psi pressure ready for the next engine start. One engineer observed dryly that one could describe the Bosch K-Jetronic system as more 'of a continuous spray than fuel *injection,'* because it just keeps squirting mixture through. The electronic fuel pump referred to earlier, however, is only operational when a sensor tells it that the engine is cranking over at 60rpm or more; this ensures that, should one crash or stall, the fuel supply is cut off until one consciously demands it again via the ignition switch and starter motor.

To power the increased electrical demands, (the fuel pump demanded 11-15 amperes alone), a 55 amp/hr battery was installed in place of the XR3's usual 43 A/h item. Another feature of the K-Jetronic by the time that Ford adopted it for the Escort was the air valve and electro-mechanical fuel switch that cut off fuel supply on the over-run. Familiar in BMWs and similar German products, Ford chose a switch-off point at 1400rpm and below, which operated a little more smoothly than the penny/Dm saving 1000rpm and less cut-off points selected by some of the prestige marques. It may be worth noting that there was some anonymous background comment to the effect that Bosch were not particularly co-operative and that the use of the more sophisticated and complex L-Jetronic was outside the design brief from the start on grounds of cost. On the road the improvement over the previous carburated CVH engines is so startling that no reservations need be expressed in warmly commending the adoption of fuel injection for this mass production Escort.

New inlet and exhaust manifolding was specified, the intakes being pressure die-cast with an intermediate sandwich plate. The exhaust manifolding amounted to a productionized cast-iron derivative of the Motorsport RS 1600i tubular exhaust layout. Rod Mansfield remembers one small injection tweak that 'we had to try just before establishing the homologated top speed for the German TUV authority. We reckoned it should do closer to 190km/h (118mph) than 180 (112) and had geared it so that fifth gear was a usable fifth that should be right for top speed, rather than as an overdrive.

'When we came to try the car for its maximum speed run the result was 182km/h (113mph)! Eventually we had to incorporate a little cold air ducting, which went into production of course, feeding the general fuel injection induction area.' Those last-minute

Body kits such as these, the top view snapped by the author in Munich and the side view by Norman Hodson at Cars & Car Conversions, told Ford that there was a need to make any further performance Escort look different, as well as travel faster ...

Ford's version of the body kit-look drew on as many existing parts as possible, including the XR3/3i back spoiler and an Orion injection front unit. All looks different in white ...

ducts provided 186km/h (115.5mph) and honour was satisfied!

Incidentally, fuel injection was originally going to be an option on the XR Escort, with the carburated model carrying along beneath the XR3i, but that idea went out of the window, possibly because of the company's increasing interest in carburated XR2 performance versions of the CVH Fiesta, harking back to the original Escort engine development programme.

The suspension work centred upon a fundamental rethink of the problems facing the front drive Escort. As Mike Smith put it, 'The progressive rate springs on the rear of an XR3 had to work in association with single-rated dampers. So, while it may well be possible in future to provide a damper that thinks along with dual rate springing, we felt that our interests would be best-served with single-rated (linear) coil springs and new dampers.'

The fundamental changes on XR suspension comprised new Girling front and rear gas-filled dampers with mountings that made it possible for SVE to eliminate rear wheel negative camber and front wheel positive camber. At the front this was done by taking the bottom of the tube and machining a very slightly angled bottom section to the casing, providing a new mounting to the lower upright casting without the need for an expensive re-positioning of the hole bored in that casting. To the eye the 'bend' of the casting is imperceptible, but the angle of the front wheel is evident for anyone to see.

At the back the top two holes of the mounting bracket on the long telescopic leg (also referred to as a 'strut' at Girling) were obvious targets to modify the rear wheel angles inexpensively. In fact, just the lower of the two bracket holes had to be re-positioned; some 2mm outward on the lower orifice proved adequate.

Detail suspension changes included lowering the front ride height by 1.18in. (30mm) and the back by 0.79in. (20mm), the front end yielding both aerodynamic and driveline angle benefits as well. No rear roll bar was adopted – or needed, in my experience – but the front bar went up a little from 0.87in. (22mm) to 0.94in. (24mm). 'We also adopted generally softer bushes throughout the suspension system,' I was told.

At the front the usual 98lb in. stiffness of the XR3 coil spring was retained, but at the back the usual XR3 jogging kit of dual rate progressive coils building from 128lb in. to 220lb in. was softened appreciably to a single 102lb in. The handling results were widely praised in Britain and included the *Autocar* comment, 'Try as we might we could not provoke any quirky behaviour.'

The braking modifications – aside from the use of the RHD servo as detailed in the RS 1600i account – sounded simple in that they adapted the eight inch diameter drum back brakes of the Escort van, instead of the inch less offered at the rear by the original Escorts. In fact, detail work included new hubs and wheel cylinders in the search for elusive balance, and compliance with Common Market regulations that insist the front wheels must lock *before* the rears; something FAVO had encountered when the rear diameters of the RS 2000 were altered without consultation. As we have seen XR3i also attracted strong praise for its braking performance, and at this point we should remember that the tyre specification was not altered at all. Released, or approved covers in English markets, were Goodyear NCT, Pirelli P6 and Dunlop D3, as for the original car. By the time you read this it's possible that Uniroyal and Firestone will have joined that select band; witness the wide use of Uniroyal for the XR4i.

At first sight the transmission work looked simple, too, with a van-type 4.29 substituted for the usual XR 3.84:1, giving 20.29mph per 1000rpm instead of the original XR's frenetic 17.89mph (meaning a motorway 70mph was 3450rpm in fifth in place of XR3's four-speed 3913rpm). In fact Mr Mansfield grinned amiably once more as he detailed SVE's work which had included, 'recognizing that the van final drive was designed for van-type torque! Naturally we had to specify the manufacture of thicker final drive gears to cope with a fuel injection 1.6 rather than an economy-carburated CVH...'

SVE aimed to provide a useful *five* forward ratios and *Autocar* found that 6500rpm realised 31mph in first, 52 in second, some 77mph in third and 104mph in fourth. By comparison the original XR3 provided 34,56 and 84mph in the lower ratios at 6300rpm, the limit then indicated on the tachometer. In top the XR3i proved capable of 118mph at 5800rpm; the RS 1600i revved at 100 revs less for the same speed and the original XR

Where it all began on the factory Turbo Escort front. Bill Meade's team at Boreham created this carburated turbo road car for senior managerial assessment in 1981.

Ford contracted works driver from 1985, Mark Lovell, made his name winning the 1983 Ford Escort Turbo rally Championship in a car prepared by MCD (now RED) at Widnes.

managed 114mph at a screaming 6350rpm.

'I can't remember anything other than a good reception for one of our cars,' reported Mansfield of the twice yearly top management approval sessions that take place at Lommel, 'and the XR3i was no exception.' The progress of the car was evaluated by such luminaries as Sam Toy on 7 May and 23 July at Lommel with the final engineering sign-off taking place at the traditional SVE Nürburgring venue ('Because its fun,' they say unabashedly!) on July 26-28 with the same cars as were used at Lommel.

It perhaps says a lot about the logical development path followed, and the warm reception generally given to the transformed XR, that one of their biggest problems concerned keeping those slotted style wheel covers in place around the Nürburgring ...Mansfield retains the Klaus Ludwig-autographed successful cover in one corner of his airy Dunton office as a reminder that even the simplest ideas can cause problems in practice...

Enter the Turbo

When it became time for the alliance of turbocharged CVH technology and RS Escort

John Taylor displays the 1983 carburated Escort Turbo rally car. The following year the series allowed Ferguson's Viscous Control limited slip differential and the cars were 'a lot easier to handle', in Lovell's words. The feedback from the 1983-84 series improved the transaxle strength and traction of the Escort Turbo RS road car considerably as well.

allure, the Special Vehicle Engineering section within Ford at Dunton had changed considerably. Expansion was the key theme, and by the time I called in to complete these notes on the Parisian show débutant Escort RS Turbo (October 1984) around a half dozen SVE regulars had been boosted to 53 personnel. They were working in some odd corners of the newer 'Dyno building' of the Dunton complex. In fact, Mike Smith and his RS Escort team were actually operating from within a walled-off section of the canteen! The engineering did not seem to suffer for its strange gestation environment...

The multiplication in personnel, many of them well known faces from Ford at Boreham 'on loan', was the direct result of SVE's earlier projects; sales of SVE-engineered Fords exceeded 500,000 in the Autumn of 1988 and the Escort XR3i was exceeding an annual sales rate of 45,000 a year across Western Europe. The Escort RS Turbo was actually the sixth SVE car. Its predecessors were: Capri 2.8 injection; Fiesta XR2 with crossflow, pushrod, Kent engine; Escort XR3i; Escort Cabriolet (mainly liaising with Karmann, and detail engineering, but they were responsible for a softer ride); the later Fiesta XR2 with CVH engine of carburettor XR3 origin; and then the RS Turbo itself.

The origins of the turbocharged Escort went back to the competitions department at Boreham and the period following the September 1980 launch of the front drive Escort. Almost immediately Bill Meade and his assistant, Terry Bradley, started work on various prototype Escort Turbos. Not just competition embryos but Escorts that could be assessed by management for their sales appeal to the public as well.

From those early efforts grew the Escort Turbo Rally Championship of 1983-84, in which 1.6-litre cars were equipped with the Garret AiResearch T3 and generally offered power outputs from 125bhp upward. Boost was restricted with a wastegate, but some Boreham prototypes showed that it was possible to reach 140bhp, even with the single Weber 32/34 DMTL twin-choke carburettor.

By 1983 there was an £1000 turbo kit aimed at Turbo Championship competitors (Ford RS code number 9096000) that provided an 8.5:1 CR CVH with a standard 1.3/1.6 cam profile giving a reported 125bhp at 5800rpm. Maximum torque was 130lb ft and competitors were recommended to keep to 6500rpm or less. I drove a road car thus equipped (JNO 20Y) for a week in 1983 and it showed what a suitable subject the CVH would be for a civilized turbo road car, capable of rather better performance than a 2.8i Capri with 20-25mpg available, according to the driver's mood.

Exciting though these prototypes were, all concerned knew they could be a lot better.

All the engineers I spoke to reported that fuel injection had seemed vital for a sophisticated road car in the eighties, a car that had a lot more potential than that of a 5000-off homologation special. Another key technical item that formed part of the recipe from the start was the 'VC' or Ferguson Developments Viscous Control unit, a sophisticated limited slip device that is usually known as a Viscous Coupling amongst Ford engineers. The VC operates with attractive smoothness and efficiency, compared to the mechanical types of limited slip device, owing to an internal construction of slotted vanes and silicone fluids as sensitive recipients of varying transmission loads and traction demands. The viscosity of silicone fluid used, and thus the degree of 'bite' that the limiting action will provide in apportioning power, is measured in centistokes.

Ford Boreham had used the Viscous Control as part of their late seventies and early eighties development programme for the Fiesta, admiring its beneficial effect not only on front drive traction, but also the snatch-free handling characteristics. When I drove Keith Ripp's multiple championship-winning Fiesta BDA of over 220bhp, at Lydden Hill rallycross circuit, I could see exactly why Ford had followed this path. Ripp's powerful front drive Fiesta could be pointed accurately over a variety of surfaces, without a trace of the steering wheel tug and consequent weaving that usually afflicted the quicker front drive machines.

SVE had to do a lot of development for the road on the VC unit, progressively backing off from rally silicone fluid specification of 60,000 centistokes to a final 12,500 centistokes, but there was never any doubt of the VC's desirability for the new Escort RS Turbo. Direct feedback from competition to road development is rare amongst major manufacturers, but whilst Ford SVE were working on the RS Turbo from Spring 1983 onward, steps were taken to introduce the VC for Escort Turbo Rally Championship competitors in 1984. Bill Meade, like Terry Bradley and engines expert John Griffiths, was loaned by Boreham to Dunton for the duration of the RS Turbo programme. Mr Meade ensured that he continued to attend Escort Championship rounds to obtain direct competitor comment.

I was guided through the turbocharged Escort's development by SVE manager Rod Mansfield with courteous patience and humour, but the official structure had changed so that Sierra engineering chief Hans Gaffke took final responsibility for SVE from 1 November 1984. By that time the 15 month development programme for this Escort was over, but the teams also had two Sierra developments, including XR4x4 and 16-valve RS Cosworth to complete. Gaffke operated from a Merkenich base in Germany but the staff we discuss here all worked from the Essex R&D centre at Dunton.

Rod Mansfield explained the background to SVE's involvement in the sporting RS: 'In January 1983, John Hitchins from our regular engineering team oversaw the introduction of XR3i into British production at Halewood, and it was obvious we were going to be asked to do more. Especially when Stuart Turner took over from Karl Ludvigsen in the Motorsport job, shortly after the XR3i came on stream in Britain'. Incidentally it should be noted at this point that, as of May 1983, the XR3i changed over to the later Escort suspension mountings and the need for the special SVE strut modifications was at an end. The same damping and spring rates were retained, but the new top mounts and the effectiveness of the original SVE conversion have provided a car that rides appreciably better and is easier to park. I can only say it is worth owning a post May 1983 XR3i, as my original West German manufactured counterpart, sold in Britain during February 1983, was not a patch on one of the later staff cars that Ford kindly provided for me to try as this book was going to press in 1984. Grrr!

The brief for the RS Turbo came from Ford Motorsport but was later refined by the product planners to appeal to the public a little more. It should be noted that Ford's mainstream engineers had worked on a mass production turbo Escort, but this was ditched as the RS programme gathered pace. There was a larger-production turbo Escort RS, but under revised sheet metal from the summer of 1986.

Working on the RS Turbo programme under Mike Smith's overall leadership was the Boreham trio mentioned (Messrs Meade, Bradley and Griffiths) plus John Hitchins and Gordon Prout, Colin Dixon and Terry Ferrari, the last two both engineering agency men who had also worked at Boreham. Also originally from an agency source was John Harris. Ford admin expert Stan Thompson looked after parts procurement procedure for the eight RS Turbo prototypes built.

Basic Motorsport demands for this Escort in Group A future trim included 'suspension to accept 180 to 200bhp,' recalled Rod Mansfield. 'That meant tie bar front suspension and the limited slip differential were musts. So far as the turbo engine was concerned it is our policy, and Ron Mellor at mainstream Ford engineering confirms, that we do not turbocharge engines without intercooling. It has been done by Ford in the States, but our conditions are very different.' Here it is relevant to note that Ford talked about the RS Turbo as their first European production car with turbocharging, but some of the specialist magazines felt it was the second such car, counting in the Zakspeed-manufactured carburettor Capri Turbo that was sold through German Ford RS dealers in 1982/83. Just 200 were made of those Capris; personally I feel Ford were correct to make the statement about RS Escort Turbo being their first *production* turbo model. The European qualification was needed because there had been a 2.3 Turbo engine in Ford's American Mustang for some years; orginally a notably nasty installation.

Outlining the body changes Mr Mansfield demonstrated that it was not just cosmetics and the burgeoning body kit industry that led to this Escort's extended appearance. 'The body package of wheel arch extensions had to accommodate tyres with up to a ten inch width – around an 8½ inch wide rim. The Mike Smith team identified the need for 15 inch diameters, in order to provide the maximum choice in motorsport rubber. We also knew that a 4.27 final drive was a Motorsport departmental requirement, as one of only two choices then allowed in Group A.'

The Bosch KE-Jetronic system was specified to fuel inject the engine, because the E letter denotes an electronic control of the vital warm up period. Also, it was felt, such injection the only way of getting efficient performance with good emission characteristics, and docility for a wide cross-section of the public. The Garrett AiResearch TO3 turbocharger of larger dimensions than the TO2 was specified by Ford Motorsport for pure power reasons and initially bothered SVE because, 'We thought it would be too big for road use, with a lot of lowdown lag and a big shove at the top end. In fact, on the road you wouldn't know it was turbocharged, it's just so flexible. John Griffiths did a marvellous job here – it really could be an Orion 1.6 L, but quicker!'

Through the courtesy of an SVE engineer I was able to try an early prototype to judge the validity of this statement, and it is absolutely true. The RS Turbo drives away from a cold start with better manners than any carburated Escort and provides a solid stream of power that is an example to any rival of how an eighties turbocharger layout should perform. Couple these genteel manners with a very genuine 125mph capability, and acceleration that is far better than the official 8 second plus figure would suggest (owing to a sub-60mph second gear). Writing before production examples were available I could only come to the conclusion that Ford had created a very worthy RS Escort indeed, particularly as the company log spoke of 30mpg averages.

A full specification of the RS Turbo is supplied in the Appendices, so I will not reiterate every detail of the 132bhp/133lb ft Escort's specification here, but a few more development memories are called for.

Obtaining power and surplus torque was no problem, but transmitting it to the road

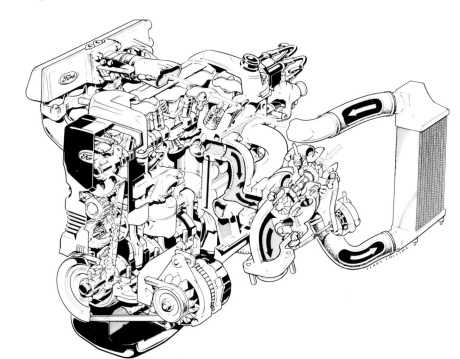

Cutaways show upright small intercooler location for the road car and emphasize new front suspension layout with individual corner brackets for lower arm location rods. The engine provides over 130bhp, but its attraction is the supreme flexibility with which power is delivered, hot or cold.

did present snags. Much of the development work was devoted to beefing up the Escort transaxle. Rod Mansfield remembered: 'The official torque peak is at 3000rpm, but you would find near enough that 133lb ft spread across a very wide power band indeed. Given that we have a Ford test that involves a start stop procedure, with a cruel tearaway up through the gears, plus constant on-off throttle changes, it was obvious we would have to make changes in the transaxle. These tied in exactly with the feedback we were getting from the rally championship.

'Basically we went from XR3i's final drive of 4.29 to a 4.27 by using bigger, stronger, transmission teeth, rather than the finer teeth that are usually specified for mass production

New Recaros are installed for the road Turbo, but the XR3i's three-spoke steering wheel and interior trim remain unaltered.

use. I don't think we have encountered any noise problem on that score – and I challenge anyone to detect the difference between it and the XR3i.

'We also found that the championship cars were cracking gearbox casings and suffering bearing failures. So the casings were stiffened up with bracing webs and the squash-fit Belville washer was replaced with carefully sized shims...but I think it was the stiffer casing that doubled transmission life in Ford's test procedure,' concluded our guide.

Interwoven with the transmission behaviour was the practical ride and handling programme as they endeavoured to get the best out of the Viscous Control in a public road sense. As related they settled on a figure of 12,500 centistokes for the fluid, but the car was still pulling from side to side under heavy acceleration and fine-tuning the suspension was not the answer.

Due to the persistence of the Michelin representative, Ford SVE engineers finally assessed a unique 195/50 VR 15 in the MXV low profile series that were first generally used in the 1984 Renault 25 front drive saloon. Dunlop, Pirelli, Goodyear; these were the familiar tyre brands on SVE products, tried and proved company relationships that took a lot of breaking. Yet Michelin actually did have an answer to much of that unplanned snaking and weaving, for the 'footprint' was of a totally different shape to that exhibited by its rivals. Mike Smith outlined it in sketch form for me and I could see that Michelin were effectively doubling the contact path through an elongated tread, whereas the usual low profile footwear from Michelin's rivals was short and fat, by comparison. Peugeot 205 GTI owners will know that their choice also wears Michelins (185/60 sizing). The front end stability and grip of that model further emphasises the technical qualities offered by the French radials, further enhanced in 1988 via the MXV2.

Suspension development was along a combination of RS and XR lines, but benefited from the start with the post-1983 suspension basics that had to be incorporated early in the XR3i's production life. The XR Escort supplied its spring rates; 'damper settings that provide a front-end rate approximately half that of the rears,' in Mike Smith's illuminating

External decoration was modest by RS 1600i standards, but it attracted a lot of favourable comment when the RS Turbo made its début at the Autumn Paris-Birmingham-Turin show rounds of 1984. Production began in December 1984 with a British list price beginning at £9,250.

Seven-spoke RS alloy wheels, limited spoiler and body changes are clearly defined. All gave the all-white (with very few factory exceptions) production run a distinct character.

The face of the turbocharged Escort with colour coded grille, driving lamps and the extra width of wheelarch extensions clearly shown.

chassis description. Mike added that the Girling monotube dampers were from the same source as XR3i, but they are set softer and everyone seems to like the result. In fact, the mainstream engineers in Germany have asked about incorporating this setup on XR3i itself. Front and rear anti-roll bars ensure that the resulting comfortable ride – astounding along well known Essex lanes in a back-to-back comparison with my own 3i – is not allowed to develop excessive roll angles in hard cornering. Add the superior limited slip differential action and you have the recipe for fast cornering without the front-end wheel hop that many XR owners experience.

In principle, the front-end layout, with the roll bar separated from any lower wishbone location duties, is the same as for RS 1600i. In fact, these deleted the aluminium crossmember and went for separate front corner mounting brackets to the front suspension tie bars, the original ball joint for these being replaced by a bolted mounting point at the forward end of the tie bars.

When it came to crash testing time for the RS Turbo, the car failed first time through and heavy cast-iron mounting brackets for those tie bars were substituted. Far from an engineer's dream, but it was the only safe route to be sure of passing a second test and thus stay within the limited budget allowed. Incidentally the sheer volume of paperwork generated by Bob Brown's homologation activities for this and other SVE products underlines that this car was a product of 1984, rather than cheerfully crammed together over a Boreham weekend in classic Escort Twin Cam mould!

The 1.6 litre CVH engine was 'basically that of XR3i between the obvious intake and exhaust manifolding changes,' explained Rod Mansfield. He added, 'We retard the timing on 3i camshafts by using a 1.3 cam sprocket; there's the obvious drain feed to take the turbocharger's oil supply, and the rocker cover needs extra studs to hold the intake turbo tubing.

'To validate a new engine for Ford production, the basic tests include cycles for $5\frac{3}{4}$ hours at maximum torque, as well as the same period at maximum power, around 6000 revs in our case for 300 hours. The high speed durability was no problem, but when we applied maximum torque consistently – an unrealistic condition for a turbo since it always accelerates out of that band, given its head – we ran into corrosion and cracking problems in the nimonic exhaust valves. These eventually bent and dropped into the engine with predictably damaging results,' reported Rod Mansfield.

Ford SVE switched to a sodium-cooled exhaust valve and these successfully concluded 180 and 300 hour cycles, in which the $5\frac{3}{4}$ hour tortures applying full torque were also included.

Sources from other production models were naturally raided wherever possible. Thus you find the front grille is of Orion injection origin and the back tailplane is simply a colour-coded standard XR3 component. The vented front discs and production back drums were as used in Escorts from 1.6 litres upward, and there were genuine regrets on the development team that they had not been able to uprate this aspect of the car. They did not feel this on safety grounds, the car always seemed to stop adequately, but simply because – in British market terms at least – the sub £8000 VW Golf GTI has four-wheel disc brakes, whilst the £9300 upward Escort RS featured a mixed system. In this connection overall weight was forecast to be slightly up on XR3i. Writing before a production example had been made I could only record the predicted 2090lb (950kg), split 1243lb (565kg) front and 847lb (385kg) rear, using homologation data as the source.

Performance progress

The first generation of XR3 and RS European Escorts were successful at their allotted tasks, the XR frequently exceeding 10 per cent of all Escort sales with profitable panache in Britain. In fact, for the first half of 1988 the XR3i accounted for 9.57 per cent of all British Escort sales, a figure which excludes the XR3i badged Cabriolet (2.68 per cent in its own right) and the second generation RS Turbo (2.89 per cent).

According to SVE figures a tidy December 1984 to December 20 1985 saw the start and finish of the predominantly white Escort RS Turbo originals and 8604 were made. Subsequent enquiries lead me to believe that the majority were sold in Britain, 5576 to be precise. For comparison, Ford of Britain gave me a production figure of 8659 for the earlier RS 1600i, and later research revealed 2608 registered in the UK between 1982 and 1986, over 2500 of them in the 1983 sales season.

Before considering the second generation of XR3i and RS Turbo, I want to have a look at the career of the American performance alternatives. A European may snigger and sniff 'what performance?' yet the Americans are the ones currently operating 1.9 CVH motors whilst we wheeze along on the original 1.6 in petrol performance form (1.8 for European diesels in 1988, but that is hardly our subject matter here...)

The GT series grew from a model originally listed as the SS. As for the rest of the line at the time (and today) it was built on a 94.2 inch wheelbase and weighed just over 2000lb. Power came from a twin-choke 1.6-litre CVH and varied according to state and emission requirements, but you could reckon it corresponded to about 70 SAE bhp, only enough for 100mph with four gears. There were lots of external appearance items, badges and stripes, but it amounted to a pretty ordinary Escort sporting a lot of blacked out areas, the inevitable front air dam and 'handling suspension'.

For 1983 the SS went in favour of the GT and multiple-point fuel injection for the 1.6. During the model year an 'HO' (High Output) designated motor was also available, but not on the GT. It was a Holley-carburated unit and allowed about 80bhp. All GTs had Michelin TRX wheels and tyres (165/70 R 365) and reworked suspension to go with a spoilered, telephone dial alloy wheel appearance that Ford USA linked to the 'highly acclaimed high performance XR3 that has been the image car for the European line'.

Clean 1989 model year American 1.9 Escort GT picks up an earlier RS wheel style and the 'bodykit look'. Performance is now a match for appearance and wide-tyred chassis.

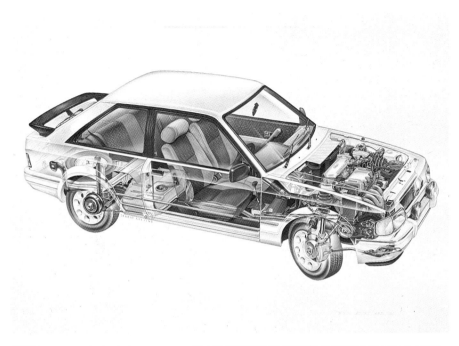

Cutaway XR3i displays basics of all Escorts, plus fuel injected 105bhp CVH (scheduled for another 10bhp in 1989) and uprated suspension. One that shares 24mm front anti-roll bar with the RS Turbo, but lacks the rear 16mm bar of the RST.

Gear ratios and 8.7 inch diameter clutch plates were shared by all 1.6-litre Escorts, but final drives varied from 3.58 (1.6) to 4.27 (XR3i), or 3.82 for the Turbo.

Front 9.4 inch vented discs are shared with all non-turbo CVH Escorts, as is the 7.9 inch vacuum servo, but the 8 inch rear drum brakes belong to XR3i alone.

The 1986 Escort XR3i in the studios of Ford during late 1985 exhibits the replacement and optional (£250 in 1989) alloy wheels (6x14) and hoop rear spoiler that accompanies new bodywork.

The multiple-point injection (an electronic Bosch system, made under licence) engine, also sold on other American Escorts, was said to give 83 SAE bhp at 5200rpm. This was enough to provide '0-60mph capability of about 11 seconds with minimal effect on fuel economy,' said Ford USA. Standard features included a five-speed gearbox and front and rear spoilers.

In 1984 the American equivalent of SVE (Special Vehicle Operations, SVO, headed by Michael Kranefuss) had prepared a fuel-injected and turbocharged 1.6 CVH of 117bhp and 8:1 cr instead of the usual injection GT's 9.5:1. Unfortunately this unit, and its attendant

Koni suspension, destined also to put some life in the two-seater Escort based Coupés (LN7/EXP), never made it into production. They were listed in the press material OK, but an insider told me, 'durability was suspect and an intercooler was not part of the plan,' this despite an 8psi anticipated maximum boost pressure.

Through '1985½' and into the 1986 model year, the parent Ford company developed the 1.9 petrol engine option. At first it appeared as a twin-choke carburated unit to replace the usual 1.6 CVH. That meant the GT Escort was 'temporarily discontinued' and that turned out to be true. The GT badge, plus the XR3 designation for the equivalent Mercury Lynx, returned in the 1986 line, but with Bosch-licensed, multi-point, electronic fuel injection. The same power unit train was also available in the two-seater EXP Coupé, the Escort-based two-door returning to the Ford range midway through 1986.

The 1986 injection CVH was an overall stretch over the 1.6-litre, its 1859cc supported by a bore and stroke of 82x88mm whereas the European 1598cc is provided by an effectively square 79.96x79.52mm. The American unit naturally operated on lead-free fuels, the 9:1 cr motor generating a respectable 117bhp at 5200rpm. Torque was also superior to any European normally aspirated performer (but not the Escort RS Turbo) at the equivalent of 120lb ft, but that peak figure arrived at 4400rpm. That was the highest torque peak I have on record for any performance Escort, save the XR3i's 101lb ft at 4800rpm.

The American GT or XR3 counterparts could reach up to 118mph now and the chassis became a lot more entertaining to drive with a big grip bonus from 195/60 HR 15 rubber on production aluminium 6x15 rims. The front anti-roll bar of the Escort was the best part of an inch thick on all models, but for the GT, XR3 and EXP Coupé a rear bar of 0.47 inch complemented that 0.94 inch front fitment.

The brakes remained the disc (9.25 inch diameter) front and drums (7.1 inch) rear mixture, but power-assisted steering was standard on these American performers. This was relevant to how the car felt ('pretty good' seemed the average American press comment) because the power option allowed just 3.04 turns lock-to-lock rather than the usual 3.5 twirls.

The performers stayed on through 1987 in much the same trim, but the Mazda-made

German XR3i demonstrates the standard 6 inch x 14 steel wheel and covers that are less frequently seen in Britain.

diesels were really killed by tightening emissions requirements in their weakest areas. For example, there was a 2-litre diesel offered from 1984, but it died late in 1987 model year. In 1988 it was time for the slow selling EXP two-seater to face the axe and Ford's traditional half-yearly ploy brought us 'moderate upgrading to the hatchback and wagon models, including plastic bumpers, new fenders, tail lamps, body side moldings, quarter panels and liftgate'.

More functionally, all Escorts gained 14 inch diameter wheels, whilst the GT sported a new grill and rear spoiler. All continued on the 94.2 inch wheel-base. Drag coefficients were now quoted as 0.38 for the GT shape, which measured 169 inches length instead of the usual 169.4 inches and weighed 2452lb. That meant the American GT carried 205lb more than a European Escort RS Turbo. The company had now also officially noted that the GT carried a 1.1 inch diameter front roll bar rather than the standard 0.94 inch stabiliser.

XR3i development

For the 1986 edition of the fuel-injected XR3i, development responsibility passed from Special Vehicle Engineering to the mainstream engineering groups that had developed the rest of the range, excluding RS Turbo. Stuart Black, supervisor of the Escort and Orion ranges within the British-based Programme Office (that used to be Product Planning), guided me through much of the change-over detail. This was a process that would help make the subsequent passage of XR4x4 Sierra from SVE to mainstream a lot easier than the nitty gritty of the XR3i proved.

The XR3i picked up on all the changes that were made for the 1986 Escorts, including the raised steering rack (adopted to try and control bump steer), and combined those

The second edition of the RS Turbo blows in for July 1986. Note the side sills and bonnet vents amongst few visual distinguishing points over the equivalent XR3i.

Rear view of the Summer 1986 Escort RS Turbo shows logo and XR3i shared (but colour coded) rear spoiler.

elements with its own bodywork alterations and the fuel injected engine. It is also worth noting that the XR3i badge became increasingly important to the Cabriolet's UK sales life, finally becoming the only specification offered in the soft top.

Unique XR3i external body changes were confined to the front and rear spoilers; 'forget the wheel shrouds this time around, John'. Naturally there were wider wheels and tyres, a 6 inch rim width now adopted in either steel or alloy, but a 185/60 tyre sizing remained. The extended body line and mild rear end changes of the later Escort were part of the XR3i as well and helped justify the 0.36 Cd claim.

Internally the new instrumentation with central speedometer was adopted before the dull two-spoke steering wheel. A pair of more sporting front seats inhabited a Daytona-trimmed cabin that lasted until the 1989 model year. Then the 'Zolda' (yes, that *is* how Ford spell the Belgian circuit name of Zolder...) trim pattern appeared.

Although there were no engine or transmission changes, the later XR3i felt rather different to its predecessors: more predictable, plusher, plumper (106lb in independent tests), slower and more expensive. The March 1986 price was £7853.95, or £8168.93 including the Lucas Girling SCS anti-lock braking.

New alloy wheels remained on the resented, but profitably massive, option list (£222.85). Also extra cost items were the £325.97 sunroof, electric operation of the front side glass (£203.14), as were central locking (£171.62); electrically operated and heated driving mirrors (£96.88); longer auxiliary driving lamps (£102.57) and black paint – may the ghost of Henry Ford stalk every £101.55 thus extracted!

A heated windscreen (£96.88); fuel computer (only on XR3i badged saloon and cabriolet at £113.01) and a selection of Ford-badged stereos were also options. Gradually some of the more popular options crept back into the standard specification. Notably, Spring 1988 saw the sunroof released from its optional status, as was central locking that model year. Power windows and mirrors also became standard, but not until the 1989 season.

The '3i' motor remained rated at 105bhp on 6000rpm, delivered through the previous 4.27:1 final drive and 185/60-HR 14 rubber, but like the second RS turbo acceleration was sapped by extra weight; obesity caused by higher levels of equipment and the 'Granada feeling' to the interior.

Autocar returned 0-60mph in over 9 seconds (9.6 secs, down a second on their previous best), but the compensations were a best of 118mph (116mph mean) and a very slight improvement in petrol consumption, 30.8mpg instead of 30.5mpg to include all test work. That means owners would be unlikely to drop much below the 33-35mpg band and tells you one of the reasons (high resale, simple servicing at low cost, an appearance that appeals to a great cross-section of the British public are others) that the XR3i continues to sell in simply enormous numbers. By October 1988, over 200,000 Escort injection XR3s had been sold across Europe.

Very few running changes, outside the incorporation of extra standard equipment to mollify some public disapproval of the options, was made in the 1986-89 life of the European XR3i. There was the 1989 trim change noted earlier, but most significant to the driver was an Escort and Fiesta alteration. This concerned a replacement external operating mechanism for the 5-speed transaxle that was introduced as a September 1987 modification to ease the gear change quality back toward the standards of older 4-speeds. On a five-speed layout the Reverse slot is simply engaged by depressing the lever to obtain the detent position opposite fifth.

For 1989 the Escort range gradually took on a variable-ratio steering, engineered by varying the tooth spacings on the rack and pinion. It reduced the effort of parking, yet did not detract from the accurate steering that has always been an Escort plus point. Unlike the American Escorts, no power-assistance was offered, nor any consequent reduction in steering lock-to-lock. For the 1990 year (ie, after the August Summer holiday break in 1989), the XR3i would reach 108 bhp in the engine department, an improvement resulting primarily from the adoption of an EEC IV management and replacement injection systems. That was accompanied by the fancier alloy wheels of Cosworth inspiration and a new tailpane.

Incidentally LHD markets have been increasingly offered an adaptation of the 1983 American standard fuel injection XR3i motor. Complete with catalyst and lead free fuel operation through Bosch KE-Jetronic injection, it delivers 90bhp and started its European life in Switzerland.

Ford personnel at the February launch of the 1986 Escort commented of later XR3i suspension, 'The effect has been to lengthen the anti-roll bar, and the steering arms have been dropped. In general, front spring-rates have increased and every effort has been made to improve traction as well as high speed stability with slight geometry changes, raised ride height ['SVE originally dropped it 18mm, now it's been raised 10mm!' said one pilot plant engineer wryly] and a solid, plastic type of joint, has been introduced at the inner end of the Track Control Arms.

'Another suspension change is that Fichtel & Sachs dampers, gas-filled twin-tube units, are now used,' concluded our Ford informants. These important alterations to the basic product were lumped together in the March 1986 Ford brochure, as 'subtle but significant changes to the fully independent suspension'...!

Second generation RST

After rumours that Ford mainstream engineers would take over the design and production development of the Escort Turbo in order to countermand big volume rivals such as the Renault 5 GTT, the second edition Escort RS Turbo was a more thoroughly revised machine than we might have expected. The company never did go into the wholesale mass manufacture of a cheaper turbo, but no upper production limit was set on the sale of the later Escort RST and many fundamental changes were made by SVE.

It is only fair to report that many British RS purists did not like the new character, and there were many accusations that it was simply 'an XR3i with a turbo on it'. I hope that what I have written allows readers to judge the issue less emotionally than that.

Alongside the Sierra RS Cosworth, July 15 1986 saw the official Ford announcement that the Saarlouis-built Escort RS Turbo was back to head the February 1986 Escort range. Production of the first RST finished on December 20 1985 at 8604 examples. There was only a short intermission in the British Ford showrooms because most dealers had original RST models to sell off. Only then could you get a sniff of a discount deal on the first Escort RST, a model which now seems to have attained classic status through its motorsport origins.

'Engineered to quicken the pulses of people who really enjoy driving,' in brochure-talk, the RST followed the style of the 1986 Escort in all but details. It was visually connected to the XR3i bodywork, rather foolishly in my view. Harry Worrall at SVE was the project engineer in charge of redeveloping the second generation Escort turbo. A survivor of FAVO and SVE, the quietly courteous Harry Worrall reminded me that, without a need to support a separate motorsport homologation schedule, key features could be deleted from the later turbo.

Significant sacrifices were the 4.29 final drive of competition-biased acceleration characteristics, the aggressive extensions upon standard Escort wheel arches and the need for tie bar front suspension.

The primary visual clues to distinguish it and the XR3i now is the use of an extension sill between front and rear wheel arches, which are modestly extended. There are the Sierra RS-style bonnet vents on each side of that 1986 extended 'smooth snout'. Colour-coding extends to the rear XR3i spoiler, plus the mirrors of catalogue illustrations.

The new look demanded a hefty premium. Basic price was £10,028 and the inevitable Custom Pack – based on the usual sunroof, electric front glass operation and central locking – extracted another £572. However standard equipment did include the £300 plus Lucas-Ford mechanical anti-lock braking system that was optional on all other five-speed/1.6-litre Escorts. Also part of the standard equipment list in 1986 was tinted glass, radio/stereo cassette player, rear seat belts and those auxiliary driving lamps.

By late 1988 one was only offered the choice of buying the Custom equipment, a decision implemented from the Summer of 1987. Including the July 1988 price rises, the cost of a Custom-inclusive Turbo had risen to £11,838.

RS turbo cutaway emphasises turbo intercooler alongside the water radiator, comparatively large (ex-Sierra XR4Ti) front disc brakes with standard anti-lock SCS, plus 16mm rear anti-roll bar. Recaro sports seat cheered an interior that retained a padded two spoke steering wheel because of German legislation.

The 1986-88 XR3i and 1986-90 RST shared the same five-spoke alloy wheel theme, when the 3i was optionally equipped with alloy wheels. Yet the wheels were totally different designs dimensionally and in spoke detail. The 3i continues on 185/60 HRs mounted upon a 6Jx14 inch version of the new wheel. Meanwhile, the later RST retains 15 inch wheel diameters and 195/50 VR tyres upon 6 inch ledges, usually from Dunlop or Goodyear on early examples.

Today you will find that the second generation RST was factory-approved on Uniroyal, Dunlop D40 or Goodyear Eagle NCT, the latter back on the car after a short spell away in road noise disgrace. It may also help to note on the tyre choice question that the production racers used buffed Yokohamas for their 10-lappers, or BF Goodrich TA2 and that cover's racing R1 option. TV presenter Mike Smith and co-driver Lionel Abbott consumed only Dunlop D4s of German origin to win the 1986 Snetterton 24-hours in the Ilford Escort RST.

Drag factor for the new RST is an improved 0.36 Cd, most of that drawn from an overall 8 per cent drag reduction claimed by Ford for the later shape Escort. Principally the advantages have come from removing the front grille and smoothing the nose contours, but there is also a vestigial Orion-style lip in the tailgate and the XR3i/RST share a raised rear wing design modified in 1989, as seen on page 384.

The RS did not adopt the later XRSi alloy wheel patterns, but the turbo did accept a change to a pronounced 45 degree lip for the rear wing one that altered both XR3i and RS Turbo, the latter retaining colour-coded distinction from XR3i. Kerb weight was expected to rise slightly, and the car, tested at nearly 2250lb for *Autocar*, had the heaviest figure I have for a performance production Escort outside America.

At last the Turbo did gain uprated braking. The mixed disc/drum system was new to Escort. At the front they were based on those of Sierra XR4x4: 260mm/10.2inch diameter ventilated to a thickness of 24mm/.94in. The rear were up an inch in diameter, but still drum operation: 229mm/9in by 44mm/1.75in.

The CVH turbocharged engine looked as before, but hid away as many changes as could also be found in suspension. Most importantly the Bosch-Motorola management system received those part throttle calibrations, taking ignition advance into more secure zones and releasing the optimum fuel economy under lighter loads.

As this German example shows, the Turbo now has no production limit and was available in many LHD countries. Wheels look similar to an XR3i, but are 15 inch instead of 14 inch, totally different rim offsets and provided a unique spoke design.

To recap, there are three distinct stages in standard engine management programmes for the Escort RST. The first-generation car's equipment with its strictly enforced 0.55 bar maximum, an overboost cutout cutting the engine completely in my test track experience. Then there was the recalibrated computer spoken of above with its part-throttle mapping for the 1986-87 Turbos.

During 1988 the long-anticipated (Harry Worrall spoke of it at the 1986 introduction for September début) anti-knock sensor was incorporated. This was a vital addition because it retards the ignition when detonation is detected and will thus give the hard-driven example, or those with the boost raised, much improved durability prospects. The additional knock sensor should cope with any grade of fuel, including lead free, for it is a so-called 'active' system that modifies the ignition curve in relation to fuel octane within the revised Lean Burn chambers.

'Lean Burn' reminds me that Ford had utilised much of the 1.6-litre CVH's 1986 model year changes in the turbo unit, but Lean Burn itself was not an objective for either the XR3i or RS Escort. An 'improved efficiency' oil pump was adopted, but how it was improved was not revealed. I suspect it had a lower pressure output because Ford mainstream engineers had fought friction to uprate the basic 1600 from 79bhp to 90bhp. Slight changes in cylinder head porting and combustion chamber shape and oil pump came as part of the package, but the Turbo retained its 8.2:1 cr and Bosch KE-Jetronic injection.

Specific SVE alterations for 1986 included a one piece inlet manifold, plus 'detail design changes to the air-to-air intercooler for greater efficiency'. More importantly Garrett had started to ensure that the World's mass producers could follow the Japanese, plus Audi and Porsche in West Germany, who were served by a new KKK water-cooled turbo unit in 1984 (Audi 200/Porsche 944T). A water-cooled centre bearing housing on the T3 Garrett turbo should ensure longer bearing life, particularly in the heat-soak situations in which the proud operator switches the motor straight off after a hard session belabouring the wastegate dump valve.

Suspension was far more like that of the XR3i than before, picking up the 1986 changes. These included 'moving the front stabiliser bar's mounting points forward, thereby reducing the nose's inclination to lift under hard acceleration and dip when the brakes are applied,' according to Ford.

SVE's approach on the RS Turbo was to take this new XR3i base and counter some of the criticisms made by press and public of the original RS Turbo handling. More stability, less twitchiness was the philosophy behind the changes implemented.

Harry Worrall's team tackled the new RST by first substituting XR3i's 19 kilogramme

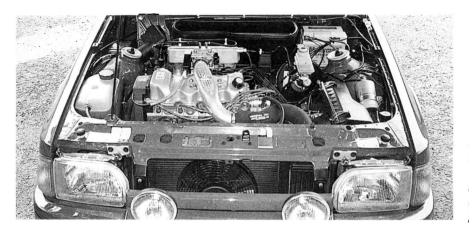

The turbocharged CVH, Ford's European pioneer in the field continued at 132bhp, but engine management changes continued throughout its production life.

per newton metre front springs and 46.5kNm rears with 24kNm fronts and 52kNm rears. There is not an enormous disparity in spring rate front to rear, for the Escort's unique independent rear suspension produces such leverage distortions on the apparent spring rate at the back. I am assured that the figures given represent an 'honest attempt to try and equalise out the front to rear rates'.

Harry Worrall added, 'The original turbo was very hard at the front and very soft at the back in springing and damping: we have gone for a softening of the front and hardening of the rear and hope to hve achieved a better overall balance.'

Note that the Fichtel and Sachs gas dampers remained from XR3i. I understand the 24mm roll bar was of the same girth, if not the same outline and mounting points, as has been present since the advent of XR3i. The rear anti-roll bar of Orion extraction was continued at the rear of the Escort RST, but this time the diameter was given as 16mm.

Also relevant to the handling was 'a general tightening up in manufacturing tolerances for the front VC differential. We did not alter the plates of the specified fluid viscosity, but we did find a change in tolerances assisted us in the fight to avoid any fierceness in the differential's action,' reported Harry Worrall.

Performance claims were for a slightly higher maximum speed (128mph) than previously, but the same 8.2 seconds 0-60mph sprint. The top speed increase was based on using that reduced drag factor and 3.82:1 final drive fitment as relevant factors.

In practice many of the magazines and owners were disappointed with the performance, at least two journals returning over 9 seconds from rest to 60mph, including *Autocar*. None of them noticed a significant improvement in velocity either, a typical quote being around 125mph. Bearing in mind the increased weight, the taller final drive and the fact that so many Escort Turbos are not delivered with the maximum boost permitted (I am told the factory tolerance extends from 0.4 bar to 0.55 bar), we should not be surprised at the independent performance figures. However, the *Autocar* machine was handicapped particularly badly by its slow gearchange under pressure, a fault that has now been tackled in the USA and Europe.

That elongated final drive also helped fuel consumption. Fuel figures released by Ford were 25.9 Urban mpg; a frugal 42.8mpg at 56mph and a reasonable 34mpg at a constant 75mph. The transaxle changes majored on a stronger eight-bolt differential unit with shot peening process. It was engineered by mainstream in place of the six-bolt differential to suit their 1600s. Further detailed Escort Turbo features from 1986 are given in Appendix II.

In the next Chapter we step back in time to the RS1700T: one Escort performer that did not make it, but which set new standards in two-wheel drive development of a saloon car theme. There is also comment on later-eighties Escort competition activity.

Chapter 14

Follow that!

New regulations and the increasing high technology content of rally cars from Renault, Audi and Lancia faced Ford in the eighties. Following the amazing and consistent seventies success of the rear drive Escort, Ford Motorsport plumped for a rear gearbox and drive turbocharged successor [RS 1700T]. Ironically, despite Boreham's long and arduous hours on the project, the 1700T did not make it to the international motor sport arena whilst the front drive RS 1600i for the mass production Group A category did. Not a tale for those appalled by big company buck-passing ...

WRITING this chapter less than a fortnight before Ford's British-based top brass were due to say 'yea' or 'nay' to the final 1984/85 financial hurdles in front of the 4-WD RS200 mid-engined turbo (the RS 1700T's successor as the company's Group B rally challenger for international rally laurels), it was difficult not to feel we had seen it all before ...

For the mid-engined two-seater drew on much of the 15 March 1983-cancelled Escort RS project's turbo Ford-Cosworth BDA equipment and had been the subject of just as much speculative writing, despite a complete blanket on comment that contrasted with RS 1700T's public presentation on a Ford Granada update launch in Belgium in August 1981.

When Stuart Turner cancelled the RS 1700T he had been back at the reins of the motor sport division as Director of European motorsports for less than a fortnight. Why did he do it?

You can simply ask the former rallying managerial and co-driving legend, and he will be as frank as he thinks you deserve. Yet, on the record, the post-RS 1700T cancellation and pre-formal rallying Group B announcement period was covered by that journalistic fire-fighter: 'No comment.'

Try and follow that ...
Escort RS 1700
prototype (WVW 101W)
in the midst of endurance
trials at Boreham in
1982.

We are, however, talking about a major Escort development that covered 18 Boreham-built prototypes – including three new road cars handed to Dunton's Special Vehicle Engineering aces in a late attempt to 'productionize' a 170 vehicle run at Saarlouis. We are talking about, also, a potential winner in international rallying that had been assessed by Bjorn Waldegard, Markku Alen, Pentti Airikkala, Ari Vatanen and Malcolm Wilson. Lancia-Star Alen's 1983 Welsh session produced favourable comments versus even the 1983 World Championship-winning supercharged Lancia 037. In short we are talking 'major money' in Fordspeak, the loss of $2.2 *million* dollars at January 1983 exchange rates (approx £1.43 million), just in preparations to produce a new Escort.

Obviously there had to be painful problems for Stuart Turner to face a loss like that with managerial equanamity, and there were. The car was simply not fit for the Ford production system. Nobody would take the financial responsibility of producing anything up to 200 roadgoing RS 1700Ts of unproven durability. [The generous documentation loaned to me over the past two years covers production of 170, 180, 186 and 200 cars at various project stages.] The Ford of Germany Saarlouis plant were as helpful as ever – these people had made the original RS 2600 Capris and many other performance Fords – but Ford management, for the RS 1700T, or agin it, simply never recognized the manpower and finance needed to make such a car. And with no 200 production run to inspect, there was no way of gaining homologation and the recognition needed to join an international rallying game where squads of engineers back at mainstream R&D get involved with routine exotica such as 4-WD, turbocharging, mid-engined machinery, exotic lightweight body materials and all the other paraphernalia needed to win events from Monte Carlo to New Zealand in eighties World Championship rallies.

Ford would not commit the resources needed today, but Boreham tried to do it anyway, with little more manpower or finance than they had in Escort II's heyday ...

The path to obscurity

Well before a traditional RAC Rally victory in November 1979, Ford at Boreham management were considering, in detail, how they were going to face the sport in the eighties. The team were Peter Ashcroft managing Charles Reynolds (Competitions Co-ordinator), homologation specialist John Griffiths, and practical engineer Mick Jones. Allan Wilkinson was there, but was destined to depart to Toyota for the early eighties; he

A 1979 two car assault on the Monte Carlo rally with Group 2 Fiestas gave the factory hope that front drive might work, for Ari Vatanen, pictured here, adapted to front drive with stunning ease and finished tenth overall in a 160 horsepower machine. Roger Clark also finished. In later Monte years privateers also repeated the top ten feat with Ford's Fiesta.

was replaced by former Porsche Weissach engineer John Wheeler, who bore the brunt of RS 1700T and RS200 development thereafter.

Peter Ashcroft and Michael Kranefuss (Ford Cologne-based European Competitions director until 18 November 1980, when he left for what effectively became the premier motor sport job inside Ford: Director Special Vehicle Operations, Ford at Dearborn) continued discussions, in which the usual British preference for rallying and the usual German one for racing could be seen. Ford, as elsewhere, depends on human beings, and Michael Kranefuss has demonstrated his racing commitment consistently since his days at the Ford Cologne-based Capri team.

Touring the 1983 Frankfurt Show with Michael Kranefuss, his amiable accessibility a stark contrast to British-based Ford personnel's necessarily pursed lips of that period, the racing message shone throughout, from Formula 1 to every derivative of touring car racing, whether on ovals, circuits or straightline quarter miles. Particularly as the Audi Sport (300bhp/4-WD and over £50,000/155 road mph) and 186mph Porsche Grüppe B (4-WD with 400bhp and twin turbos) caught his eye. 'What can you do against such cars?' he wondered aloud. By comparison the RS 1700T was a backyard concoction. It might have won rallies, like Toyota's simple Turbo, but Ford wanted better odds.

One can pinpoint the beginning of the abortive Escort programme with the 14 June 1979 documentation in Mick Jones' extensive job listings of a Fiesta with North-South front engine and rear drive, built amidst the 1000 Lakes Mk2-shelled works cars of the period. A month previously they had mocked up such a machine, but it all led to nothing, the company deciding they could not publicly abandon front drive for a car sold on that basis: work ceased on 8 August 1979. According to a perceptive interview published by *Cars & Car Conversions* in January 1983 with Allan Wilkinson, 'The Ford Motor Company's continuing and somewhat public struggle to make its RS 1700T Group B contender competitive has its origins back in those early months of 1977. At that time the

specialized Fiesta was intended to be a direct replacement of the Escort in Group 4, a car that would carry through until 1983, when it was to be replaced by a V6-engined Sierra.

'But the idea was scrapped after a scant four months work ...' There followed details of how Michael Kranefuss had resurrected the idea for that brief flurry in 1979, adding: 'By August a chassis had been completed. The new machine was between four and six weeks away from being a runner when, without warning, orders were given to stop work on the project again.' Eventually it was taken out of the box a third time, but this was to supply mechanical heart to Escort Prototypes P3 (2.9.80) and P2, which was started 20 days beforehand in a fit of Irish logic.

Whilst the practicalities were enacted at Boreham, a new factor in the management and image within the company of any new competition car came from the establishment of a Performance Strategy Group, headed by Stuart Turner's Motorsport predecessor, Karl E. Ludvigsen, whose name may be more familiar as a respected motoring author.

This strategy group, and subsequent other paperwork generated by the vain effort to keep British and overseas based Ford executives enthusiastically behind a project, one that was bound to disrupt the production lines, took on ever more desperate tones as the ramifications of manufacturing a Kevlar-bodied Escort special through the Ford system became unpleasantly clear.

Boreham took prosaic practicality as its route ahead and assessed the possibilities 'in field', or actually at the popular Welsh forest testing venue of Nant yr Hwch. Between 7 and 8 January six drivers – including Malcolm Wilson and outstanding female rallyist Louise Aitken – were given tuition in front drive technique by the world's best in that speciality, Stig Blomqvist. They had on hand three Fiesta specifications, but such sessions and Blomqvist's expertise could not hide the eventual conclusion that front drive, in the recommended Fiesta shell (for size and weight considerations), gave no blind forest stage time advantage over the old rear drive Escort. This was true, even if the Fiesta was BDA powered and possessed the magic of the Ferguson Viscous Coupling limited slip differential ... A further test in July with Blomqvist, and a BDA Fiesta with superior power to weight ratio to Ari Vatanen in an Escort, showed the old faithful rear driver to be an average of nearly 2½ seconds per mile faster. So they needed a new rear drive development!

Whilst P1 could be referred to as 'FiEscort' in Mick Jones' irreverent notes, P2 and P3 primarily investigated the German-penned exterior body style and the practicalities of wedging a North-South BDA into an engine bay design for front drive. It is only fair to say that this aspect may have been underestimated at Boreham, for the Mk2 had a very slight rearward weight bias – 46 per cent to 54 per cent in final 1979 rally trim -- and the early RS 1700T prototypes with their attendant turbo plumbing and cooling up front placed up to 53 per cent of an increased weight (compared to old Escort II) in the nose. Another aspect of converting a front drive car to rear-end power delivery was that the front passenger compartment bulkhead was in entirely the wrong place. The basic new Escort design was biased to provide maximum interior space, taking advantage of a transverse engine. Also the pick-up points for ideal front drive roadgoing suspension, and a potential rally winner with rear drive are at different ends of the design spectrum.

Boreham plugged on and by 9 December 1980 had started to build the important P4 Escort prototype; a non-turbo BDA North-South conversion of a silver RHD XR3, the first Escort BDA runner in the new shell. For the record the remaining P-designated prototypes, some of which appear later in the chapter and all of which had the inspired Columbia coding to tie in with work inauguration and the launch of that first Space Shuttle (in which Ford's American electronics division had been involved), are listed as follows, together with the date the Boreham workshop began their construction.

10.2.81	P5	Delivered in green, ended up as white Show car for July 1982 onward usage with Merkenich style.
9.4.81	P6	White shell designated for Monte Carlo originally.
9.4.81	P7	Better known photographically as WVW 101W, with a 2.4 litre Hart 420R engine. Tested, to bodily destruction, against the Portuguese scenery by Ari Vatanen.
15.7.81	P8	Silver road car, possibly based on P4, that became a white road car and was 'closed' after an Essex accident dented the roof, amongst other damage, in staff hands. Became a red car for SVE by 25.10.82.
26.3.82	P9	Finished on 26.7.82 and handed onto SVE as road car prototype for durability trials.
19.10.81	P10	Priorities other than date order existed when this well known 1700T rally machine (WVW 100W) in LHD débuted. Eventually a very successful machine ...
29.1.82	P11	Finished by 30 February and used in torsion tests with and without front wings. Became a LHD emission test road car by 1.8.82.
19.10.81	P12	LHD road car that had a sunshine roof. Originally used for seat belt tests; passed to SVE.
27.2.82	P13	Went straight to SVE as new when completed, 1.11.82.
	P14*	

*No reference to P14, but a show car was inserted between P12 & 13: this could simply have been P5 revived.

–.8.82	P15	New blue RHD for SVE, finished 8.11.82.
20.10.82	P16	LHD rally car.
5.11.82	P17	LHD rally car.
No date	P18	Also a rally car, finished 6.11.82, to Safety Devices.

It is a fascinating list, and reflects some hard labour by a Boreham team, half of whom had never seen a rally by the close of the project. It does not cover all the cars manufactured, for several, according to a senior executive, were passed along the lines at Saarlouis to make sure they fitted the jigs in production anticipation. One such car was 'wrapped up in a plastic bag and preserved,' according to my source.

To my mind the sportiest looking Escort of all, and it still looked low and mean when I saw the prototype a few weeks before the axe fell.

Back at the bloodbath that was RS1700T development, we must also recognize the role of Hannu Mikkola's 1979 RAC Rally winner, WTW 569S. This was used for most of the comparison testing between old and new, covering venues in Portugal, Wales and Boreham itself. The new Escort also went durability testing at Bagshot and had two favourite Welsh haunts; Nant yr Hwch and Clynsaer. As ever the old Escort proved hard to beat, but they ended up with a very handsome 4-second 'conservative' forest mile advantage, and some near-ecstatic comments were rife as to how old fashioned the RS 1800 had begun to feel by February 1983.

Yes, it did take them an inordinate amount of time to get that P10 prototype rally flying on forest mileage, but then they were trying to sort out the road car as well!

In retrospect the road car was *the* crucial aspect of the constantly slipping, and finally axed, RS1700T programme. We can imagine the powerful Performance Strategy Group (PSG), with Ford of Europe boss Bob Lutz usually in the chair, and a variety of equally potent management names, frequently bewildered by motorsport's inherent death wish for obscure regulations and breath-taking costs, struggling to make sense of the high-minded performance image sentiments. These were seductive visions that dragged them into an arena suddenly peopled by real opponents; corporations like Renault, VW-Audi and Fiat-Lancia with ingredients such as 4-WD, turbocharging and mid-engines were not going to roll over with fright at the spectacle of a converted Escort. This was a total contrast to the technical lead the Escort had enjoyed in the seventies, courtesy of the engine, proven components, and the world's most experienced and able 'cross-country tinkers'.

Officially, 24 November 1980 was the date on which PSG sanctioned the development programme that would produce a car senior Warley management at Ford bragged of as their Group B rally winner. Important in ensuring funds were available and that their American counterparts or seniors stayed interested, but embarrassing to those who realised how the competition world had changed since the days when a £100,000 contract with Cosworth almost guaranteed a decade and more of engine dominance in premier league rallying and racing ...

Plodding through those increasingly desperate days, months and years of PSG meetings and mounds of paperwork, the group observed costs going through the roof. In

February 1981, the car's hoped-for cost was below £10,000. By June of that year, a more accurate analysis revealed £11,700 + as more likely. Similarly PSG watched tooling estimates accelerate as fast as the car was reputed to. The first tooling estimates were to provide for just under £170,000; by June 1981 that was £212,400; but January 1983 and the last minute scurry around alternative assemblers outside the Ford system (Aston Martin Tickford; Reliant; Lotus with some FF Developments 4-WD contingency planning) they had set aside the dollar equivalent of more than £271,000!

These escalating costs had little to do with inflation and a lot more with increasing sophistication and a weight reducing diet for the RS 1700T. During 1981 it had been established that 36 production modifications to the basic body would be needed, including rear turrets for the dampers, a rear bulkhead and a crossmember to pick up on the transaxle gearbox. The latter item started off as a Porsche 924/944 series transaxle and became a specially commissioned Hewland unit. Other key suppliers were involved, too; Kevlar panel technology, for instance, was to come from Segar & Hoffman. By January 1983 the dollar equivalent of more than £105,000 was needed, just for this aspect.

Similarly, the final price of the cars that might have been sold through the Ford RS outlets of Ford in Britain and Germany, with limited Type Approval confined to those countries (that process would cost about £13,000 in Britain alone), rocketed ahead. By July 1982, the estimates were around £23,000 with no dealer margin, and losses made on the German market, where prices could not be pitched so high. No, Ford management were not being greedy; in fact it amazes me that they contemplated such contradictions of the Ford creed as would have been necessary to make the RS 1700T a reality. In the end the talk was of making the legitimate 200 and scrapping over 130!

Ford Motorsport personnel during 1982 were allowed to talk more freely about the car in public after that Summer showing of the RS 1700T, and it emerged that their fidelity to the original B-regulations, of providing the public 200 run with all the key competition elements, was going to result in a steel-crank Cosworth BDT of 200 road horsepower. The standard specification would result in a 135 to 140mph maximum, with 0-60mph visualized around 6.5s for a road RS weighing about 2420lb (1100kg). Other standard components, in a car that would have retailed beyond £30,000 at normal Ford profit levels – and a minimum of £25,000 by 1983 – included: Bosch engine management; Hewland five-speed transaxle; Recardo front seats; trimmed and shaped rear seats; and a wide use of electronic aids such as power windows, electric radio aerial and so on to help justify the price. They even contemplated some extra trim, in the form of a centre console and wood panels, to help the showroom traffic beyond that boggling price tag, with a kind of Custom Pack seventies approach!

Another of the 1981 Ken Shipton/Ford Photographic shots of the car we saw badged as the RS 1700T in August 1981. In the later stages of the development programme the wheelbase was lengthened to assist a slight rearward weight bias and a serious weight reduction programme was proposed.

Durability testing at Boreham in the 1982 winter we see they also tried doing without bonnet louvres altogether and concentrated on letting air in all over the front valance. Note also the removal of one inner headlamp for extra cooling purposes. Ponder on the simple bodywork and wonder if that registration number really belonged on this car? The information I have, and the tree line, suggest it is December 1982, long after WVW 101W was offically written off ...

The road car was an intriguing prospect, but there were technical problems with the rally car outside the burning problem of how to make the fabled 200 ... The primary concern, which I had not heard voiced before I started this book, was that of weight. There had been early 1981 talk of 2068lb (940kg) for the 200 run 1700Ts and down to the class minimum 1958lb (890kg) for the evolution 20, bearing on which we should add that it was not until Lancia and Opel successfully fielded lightweight cars of more power through the evolution process that Ford were aware they would be able to follow suit. Thus, the fundamental principle of building a very expensive and honestly competition-engineered basic car for the 200 run was partially negated by rival development during RS 1700T's gestation.

Back with the weight we find that the P7 prototype RS actually weighed 2560lb (1140kg). P10 was 2396lb (1089kg) and Boreham produced a 25-point dietary plan for 1983 that would have taken it down to 2198lb (996kg) and then 2054lb (934kg) on evolution, but such a process needed yet more finance. Incidentally, Ford of Germany had offered to race the car in Group B to help establish the image for a proposal to sell around 80 road 1700Ts in Germany, and that inevitably brought Zakspeed's name into the picture too. Naturally they considered Zak's operation for contracted-out assembly, too, but then there were very few alternatives they had not explored to get the albatross road cars out of the Saarlouis plant, which had a deadline production 'window' so that Columbia could make her entry of 6 April 1983. Any later and Orions and 1984 Fiestas would be bounding joyfully over all corners of the establishment and only basic bodywork, rather than a more complete in-house assembly, could be contemplated ...

Meanwhile, how was the RS 1700T performing in the test programme for the rally car? On 5 October 1981 Nant yr Hwch was the mid-Wales venue for P7's Hart 420R to roar into action for the forest premier of a new generation in Ford Escorts – but it was not an auspicious occasion. My information is that Bjorn Waldegard was the driver and that a proprietary wheel broke after 11 laps. Over 2.6 miles the new RS returned 2m 59.0s for Bjorn, compared to Ari's 2m 56.7s. in 1980 with the old model and a 2m 58.4s for Stig Blomqvist's Turbo 99 of 1979. Not a bad start ...

The same venue and a modified P7 (actually weighing nearly 2288lb (1040kg), with a

The combination that might have ruled the early eighties? April 1982 and Ari Vatanen poses with P10, the turbocharged prototype that did the majority of development work, particularly on this session as Ari modified P7, the Hart 420R-engined Escort, against the Portuguese scenery!

slight rear bias) was to put to work with its installed 260bhp in Pentti Airikkala's hands during February 1982. WTW 569S was also on hand to give a Mk2 comparison. The results were extremely good and it was to Boreham's credit that back-to-back advantages for the new car without the turbo were not greeted with, 'Now we'll flatten them all,' but with a sombre analysis of work needed, particularly to shift some more weight rearward. Over a 5 mile lap the advantage had been as much as 14.8 seconds!

The next major test date, 20-30 April 1982 in Portugal, took an inordinate time to set up with suppliers such as Pirelli and Bosch actively involved along with an uninvited press presence (yet the car was decalled in approved photographic manner ...!)

In ten days, all but two testing, or in the workshops, P7 and P10 were pitted against old faithful WTW 569S and the results were widely, though unofficially publicized. The best comparisons came at Candosa with six complete runs over dirt and 4.03miles (6.5km). Ari Vatanen produced 5m 9s upward and 5. 4s down in WTW, versus 5m 10s for the P7 with another day producing 5m 6s and 5m dead downhill for the turbocharged P10 RS 1700T, also courtesy of Mr Vatanen. The engineering conclusion was that the car averaged a 2s per stage kilometre advantage over the old Escort and was even quicker than the fabled Stratos. Even in a very much prototype form it was felt it would be competitive against all but Audi on the slippier stages.

BUT: reliability was not good; Boreham were obviously not yet ready to tackle championship events with a team much altered since the November 1979 withdrawal, and without in-field experience for many members. It was also not a particularly easy car to work on, and the front end goemetry/weight distribution needed fundamental work to bring gravel road competitivness above the rather meagre advantage it then enjoyed in turbo form over the Group 4 1979 Escort. Incidentally, it was P7 that got written off here, and that was a slight blessing, since the under-staffed personnel for mechanical work could tackle the awesome workload in something less than the total exhaustion that was previously threatened ...

The Portuguese session of 1 April 1982 with Ari at work in typical Escort style. It was felt that the car would be competitive against even Audi on all but the slipperiest surfaces, even at this stage. However, further fundamental engineering and team work was obviously needed if Ford were to return effectively to World Championship events.

Night running was part of the April 1982 Portuguese schedule, too, and all concerned found the work load heavy. Although Pirelli were concerned in the project right from the start, and continue to be in involved with the 1984-85 RS 200 prototype 4-WD car with success, it was found that Michelin fronts and Pirelli rears produced good times at this stage in development!

During December, some intensive durability work was tackled at Boreham with a number of drivers and over several days, using a mixture of tarmac and mild dirt over a laid out lap of just over 1½ miles. They covered nearly 220 miles (below target) but still found they could get a very sensible handling compromise using Michelin fronts (as they had experimented in Portugal) with Pirelli rears! A new factor was the incorporation of the FF Viscous Control differential, and this was so good that it became a feature of RS 1700T.

The rough roads of the military establishment at Bagshot, traditional rally-durability torture ground of Ford and many other British-based teams in the past, received several visits from the embryonic RS 1700T. Poor old P10, appropriately re-prepared, faced the music, with Malcolm Wilson the most frequent driver.

Listening to accounts of those 1982 sessions is not a task for the mechanically sympathetic and, as on previous occasions from earlier sessions, I noted that the team were not satisfied with the legendary Bilstein gas dampers. There were internal recommendations around this period that Bilstein be dropped, just as had happened in the move from XR3 to XR3i in production. An outsider, even with the benefit of two years' research and earlier experience of Ford, cannot judge what was going wrong, but the previous cosy relationship was certainly notable by its absence.

Perhaps the most significant session in terms of encouraging RS 1700T's creators, was that held in Clynsaer and Nant yr Hwch during the first two weeks of December 1982. Present was the man who had given Audi No. 1, Hannu Mikkola, such a fright on the November 1982 RAC Rally; Lancia's Markku Alen (a former Escort pilot before establishing such a loyal record in Italy over a decade) and Malcolm Wilson. Ari Vatanen had really been forced to leave his beloved Ford for Opel in order to continue an active competition career when the RS 1700T continued to suffer setbacks, but his first full season with Opel/Rothmans was not until 1983. Then he switched, with apparently effortless competitive ease, to Peugeot's 205 Turbo 16 4-WD in 1984 and racked up that company's debut World Championship victory (his home 1000 Lakes event) on the car's third championship outing and a succession of World-class rally wins.

The results of that December testing with Alen/Wilson were extremely encouraging.

The Germans race XR tidily, the Brits go their own way! Hans Stuck leads Rolf Stommelen, Manfred Winkelhock and Alan Jones ('Fly Saudia') in a special 26 July 1981 race for production XR3s at Diepholz aerodrome. The race was backed by Bilstein and lasted 49 laps with Audi star Stuck leading the rest home. The British XR3i event has typical 'celebrity' mayhem going on, Barry Robinson abusing the Pirelli P6s on this occasion at Paddock.

P10 now weighed 2396lb (1089kg) in dry homologation trim, distributed 47 per cent front/52.4 per cent rear, which compared with a 52.7/47.3 per cent front-bias for the same prototype number in Portugal, and 44.1/55.9 per cent tail-heavy distribution in the last of the winning Mk2s. Such figures underlined how difficult it had been for Ford Boreham to approach the favoured rearward mass distibution of the rear drive Escort. Particularly with a new car intended to have front drive and over 60 per cent of its mass in the nose.

From figures culled over the years I was slightly surprised how effectively the Mk2 had been made tail-heavy and can only add the unofficial comment that I believe Allan Wilkinson motivated a fundamental shift in engine location during his tenure at Boreham, principles that he effectively developed on Toyota's behalf, along with a strict slimming diet, resulting in a World Championship 1-2 win in New Zealand in 1982, for restyled Celicas on their début ...

When P10 appeared for those December 1982 Welsh tests it was a much altered car, with what amounted to a front-end redesign of the engine bay and front suspension/

Mark Lovell tackles a Manx ford on his 1983 run to Escort Turbo Championship victory.

steering geometry providing not only the noted weight bias shift, but also a wider front track, based on Sierra-length track control arms, with 3° negative camber beating much of the old understeer. Front and rear anti-roll bars, plus a substantial (50 per cent) increase in wheel travel, allied to softer springs, had combined with the viscous coupling differential to bring warm comment from the drivers and super stage times.

Markku Alen was especially complimentary about the Escort in comparison with both the old Fiat 131 and the car that was then frightening Audi in World Championship events (winning the following year's manufacturer's title), Lancia's 037. In times, Markku proved that little over 2 miles of Clynsaer forest would provide the new Escort with a 5s advantage over the Mk2. And they had a job finding a layout clear enough of snow to provide realistic results! Malcolm Wilson underlined the potential even more dramatically with times that averaged 2.65s a mile and 5.05s per mile faster than the obsolete Escort.

Now there was talk about the work to be done before the first event, for the car had been encouragingly durable. The Pirellis had a possible puncture problem, but wear rates bore no relationship to the original carcass-shredding performances. This Ford was obviously capable of winning at World Championship level against allcomers – save Audi on a specialized ice event, or wherever the going was consistently abnormally slippery.

Engineering in a quietly effective and practical manner the Boreham team – under the overall influence of John Wheeler – had turned the new Escort into a potential winner, with a lot of help from Bosch (particularly Dr Zucker) and Pirelli. Certainly, here was a car that could have taken the laurels wherever Toyota/Opel actually won with their rear drive machines, and probably was in with an evens chance against Lancia and Audi, depending on the going. *If* they could field the car immediately in 1983, there was little doubt it would now at least show honourable speed.

The plot, however, was not going so well back at the Ford mother ship on star-base Warley, Essex. Despite pleas from Boreham management that were formally expressed in Spring 1982, asking that they be allowed to shed production-associated development tasks in favour of concentration on providing a competitive motor car, together with a basic specification for the road car, little was actually completed to speed this obvious priority. Ford politics played a part, in that Bob Lutz departed for the upper climes of Ford USA (he returned to the Warley base and European management by 1984) and Karl Ludvigsen swiftly departed in his wake, effectively removed from controlling the Ford Motorsport programme in Europe from February 1983.

Whilst Boreham and SVE at Dunton pressed their minimal manpower resources to the limit – and unspecified Ford managerial men went seeking quotes from Aston Martin, Reliant and Lotus to leap the production obstacle – Stuart Turner returned to European control of Motorsport. I am told that it was Rod Mansfield of SVE who actually had the unpleasant task of first conveying to Boreham that their project was 'not on' from the production road car angle. The road car's potential unreliability from a lack of proving time, not a lack of soundness in the engineering principles, was just too risky in warranty terms and the likely damage that could be done to Ford's eighties aspiration toward greater engineering status. With so many prominent Ford personalities and associated egos 'on the line' for the Escort project, there are any number of smokescreens laid to obscure the methods adopted to achieve the delay that finally ensured RS 1700T missed its Saarlouis dates and any chance of international glory.

A brace of pictures from the 1983 Lombard RAC Rally show Ford stalwart Malcolm Wilson with Phil Short taking the MCD Services Group A RS 1600i to a top-twenty placing (13th) and a class victory. A sister RS 1600i for Louise Aitken Walker retired after 37 stages.

Back in Britain by 1988, the South African specification of the Escort RS 1700T (said to be car 7, nee WVW 101 W) can be seen on a car privately owned by Cumbrian Simon Nutter. This hardworked and much altered machine won the South African Nissan international in 1986 and had also been endurance raced in 1987! Doesn't look so good, does it? Were all those extra bonnet and roof vents really vital? Picture from Cars & Car Conversions/*Tony North.*

As to the RS 1700T itself, technical details are shown in the Appendices, for it had proceeded to the point of having a completed, but not stamped, homologation form for the road car, and the rally version is also well documented. When Mr Turner inevitably cancelled RS 1700T and the embarrassment that was the C100 Group C racer, 21 RS 1700 BDT engines had been built at JQF outside Towcester, and 55 transaxles were complete, along with 60 sets of Kevlar panels from Segar & Hoffman. It was known that 775 unique (sometimes just modified) parts would be required in each road car and, by 11 February 1983, Saarlouis had also made two bodies in white to prove this limited production could work. Over a million pounds in direct resources had been irretrievably lost, but unofficial

In 1983 and 1984, Richard Longman's West Country enterprise represented Ford in Group A racing with the Datapost-backed Escort RS 1600i for himself and Alan Curnow. Our picture is from Donington 1984 and recalls a year in which the former Mini ace once again won the smallest class, and came close to winning the overall title for the second year in succession.

The most successful Mk3 Escort in international terms was that of 1984 European Rallycross Champion Martin Schanche. Working with loyal support from Gartrac in Godalming, Surrey, the travelling Norwegian mated his 1.8-litre ex-Zakspeed Turbo of a minimum 470bhp with ex-Hewland employee Mike Endean's transmission technology to provide a 4-wheel drive, Sachs-sponsored, Escort that beat even the best in Audi Quattros during 1983-84. A second such car, with independent rear suspension, was constructed for John Welch late in 1984. Incidentally Gartrac is owned and operated by two former Alan Mann Racing employees; Endean's 4-WD system is known as Xtrac.

estimates, covering all overheads, put the loss at well over £4 million.

Under a press embargo of 12 noon 15 March 1983 and the heading 'Ford Motor Sport Cancellations', the final public blows were dealt in the following words.

'Ford today announced the cancellation of plans for participation in international motor sport events with its C100 sports car and Escort RS 1700T rally car.

'Making the announcement Stuart Turner, who was appointed Director of European Motor Sports two weeks ago, said: "Having spent some time looking hard at our existing plans, I have become convinced that we are not moving in the best direction if we are going to resume our former position in international motor sport. This does not mean that we are giving up; we still believe firmly in the importance of motor racing and rallying both as a shop window for our products and as a vital link in the technical development of future cars. Make no mistake – we shall be back, although not with the cars we have under development at the moment.

"Our motor sport engineers have been very busy over the past three years and we have learned a great deal from the work they have done. But motor sport has always been an area in which technology has changed very rapidly and we have a number of new approaches we want to develop further before we take on the competition – which has current battle experience to draw on".'

The statement went on to draw attention to the previous Escort's success and confirmation of continuing 'local motor sport programmes run by Ford in Britain and Continental Europe'. For the Escort RS 1700T, and the immediate morale of all who had given their collective physical, mental and competitive talent to the fat-wheeled Ford, it truly was the end.

Some of those key people are now outside Ford of Britain – scattered as far as South Africa (along with some of the RS 1700 rally Escorts) in the case of Michael Jones, master mechanic. Yet the vision of the Escort that would have once again defeated the finest in international competition fades only slowly within minds that spent so many years trying to convince a sleeping giant not to slumber on past silverware and victory laurels.

Of course it was not all in vain, there is plenty of RS 1700T technology that lingers in the Essex air for release beneath other bodies. Yet, to any Escort enthusiast, it was a low blow, comparable to the closure of FAVO ...

When the cars left over from the Boreham project were shipped to South Africa to compete locally, quite a few modifications, both mechanical and to external bodywork, were carried out. The programme was under the control of Bernie Marriner at Port Elizabeth in the summer of 1983, but former Boreham legend Mick Jones arrived to take over the following Summer. South African sources say the 1983 RST won its first event, (Pineapple Rally, East London) and that it weighed only (2134lb) 970kg with most of the aerodynamic appendages removed, its 1.7 litres yielding 330-360bhp. In Britain, factory competitions personnel said it went better, the closer the South Africans ran it to original specification! Mr Jones ensured both sides communicated, for the car was winning again by 1985, but RS Sierras were more important to Jones in his 1988 South African managerial role.

The front drive competitor

In retrospect it is ironic that Ford competition personnel took every rear drive or 4-WD avenue so seriously for the Escort, yet the cars that have been racking up points and class trophies in such diverse occupations as World Championship rallies and Group A saloon car racing, have been closer to production base than any Escort winners since the initial Group 1 cars of the seventies.

Even Stuart Turner was somewhat surprised to find that he was required to pick up a World Championship trophy for the Escort at the close of 1983 at the annual FIA presentations in Paris. He grins widely at the recollection of picking up recognition at such a prestigious level as the result of privateers' efforts (mainly Italian-based) with the Escort in Group N!

The most successful Mk3 Escort in international terms has been the Group A RS 1600i, but even with wide continental use in 1983 and 1982 it could only be described as a class car, not a successor to the RS1600/1800 outright winners that preceded it. In the premier British-based championship and at lower levels the RS1600i has been a regular competitor, most emphasis put behind the efforts by Widness-based MCD Services to run a regular class winner for Louise Aitken and, less frequently, Malcolm Wilson. Such cars appeared on the 1983 RAC Rally and Wilson in particular showed top twenty pace in the blue and white 1600i with 'about 20 horsepower less than the Golf GTI'. At that time, and on into Golf II guise, if you hadn't got a Group A Golf 1.8 you were probably wasting your time, unless it was snowy Monte/Swedish in which case you went down VAG's Audi 80 quattro route, if you wanted a win in Group A.

Initially, the 1600i was extremely unreliable, particularly in the transmission department, for rough rally use, but Wilson proved that it could go the 1983 RAC Rally distance with a fine 13th overall and a class win. The trouble was, that Grundel's works VW was eighth overall for first Group A car home in an event won at a canter by Stig Blomqvist's Quattro. Basically the 1600i did not have the power to stay in touch with the pacemakers, and if one were able legally to produce the power, the transmission could be back in trouble again ...

MCD, now renamed RED (Rally Engineering Development), were as badly affected by the Ford rally programme delays on RS 1700T as anyone. They ran both Roger Clark and Ari Vatanen at various stages in Mk2s with competitive speed from Ari on home international rounds with their car, even in isolated 1983 appearances, but it had been the 1700T that was the forthcoming attraction to keep MCD interested in comparative chores such as running the 1600i on Boreham's behalf. When it became obvious that the 1700T was not going to materialise, MCD manager Dave Campion and owner/driver Geoff Fielding renamed the company and produced a turbocharged 2-WD Sierra (R-E-D 4T) that led the British national series through much of 1984 in Louise Aitken's hands.

As for the front drive rallying Escort, the limelight shifted gradually to the turbocharged models that Bill Meade and company had engineered at Boreham in the eighties, providing a basis for the 1984 Escort RS Turbo road car (further developed by SVE at Dunton: see Chapter 13) and for the 1983 Escort Turbo Rally Championship, a series won by the very promising Mark Lovell in 1983. Obviously the RS Turbo road car should have provided Ford with a new Group A challenger for the mid-eighties onward. It is interesting to note that the Viscous-Control differential, first seen on works Fords when the Group 2 Fiesta was seriously campaigned (Vatanen was tenth on the 1980 Monte in such a front drive Ford), making another effective appearance. The difference in overall placings for Escort Turbos on national British rallies between 1983 and 1984 was largely in the 1984 fitment of the VC differential, which made such 125/130bhp Escorts a lot easier to drive, as well as faster through the stages. Incidentally Mark Lovell was entrusted with the job of driving the prototype Group A Escort RS in several British events of 1984 in the Shell RAC National series, but the car was initially rather uncompetitive and unreliable. Later, Ford Motorsport made some progress with a reported 185bhp being fed through the front wheels, but the Group B prototype RS200 was obviously occupying more of Boreham's development schedule than the Group A RS. Despite the development of many new transmission components, including a far stronger five-speed gearbox, the Boreham-backed

RS Turbo never was able to extend the Escort's rallying reputation and the front drive Fords remained effective race, rather than rally mounts. Mark Lovell did go on to greater things, winning the British Open Rally Championship for Ford in the 1986 Group B RS 200. So the factory were right, in terms of results, to forget the RS turbo for rallying.

By a quirk of fate, and the contribution of continental privateers, Stuart Turner was able to pick up a substantial trophy at the 1983 FISA awards. Ford documentation credits this to the XR3i, but I could find no evidence of Ford being credited with any World Championship marque points at all in 1983, whatever the type of car. *The* moment of World Rally Championship glory could be attributed to an RS 1600i Escort for speedy Mauro Pregliasco who led the Group A squad on the 1983 San Remo, but Alfa Romeo ultimately triumphed on home ground. That season's RAC Rally also saw Malcolm Wilson's Group A RS 1600i finish thirteenth overall, outgunned by Kalle Grundel's VW Golf GTI and an Opel Ascona that both made the top ten.

In racing terms the RS1600i made an extremely effective mount in the smallest class of the Trimoco RAC British Saloon Car Championship. The Richard Longman Datapost team turned out immaculate red examples of the RS 1600i in 160 plus horsepower Group A trim to collect the 1983 class title and run in the top three point scorers overall for 1984, with a chance of winning the title right up to the last, October round. Drivers were the traditional combination of proprietor Longman and Alan Curnow and some driving impressions of their 1983 car can be found in Chapter 15. Incidentally they finished 1984 winning Ford that UK class title and Longman was runner-up in the RAC Trimoco section for championship drivers.

The RS Turbo proved a more effective car in terms of overall results and was always a contender for the outright British title because it dominated its class until the 1987 arrival of the BMW M3. The RS Turbo debuted at Silverstone on June 9 1985 in the traditional hands of Richard Longman and managed sixth overall, a convincing class win and a new lap record close to 103mph average. Although the Longman package was quick straight out of the box, the turbocharged Escort's greatest racing 1985 feat in Britain was scored by Stuart McCrudden Associates and their Ilford-backed Group N production racer.

Despite the late homologation of the vehicle (June 1 1985) and consequent mucking about with an uncompetitive XR3i, the McCrudden team swiftly got their Terry Hoyle-engined RS Turbo to flamboyant pace. Managed by Ed Abbott at the Willhire Snetterton 24-hour race, brother Lionel Abbott and media personality Mike Smith finished sixth in 1985. By 1986 the entire équipe had their act superbly sorted to win Britain's only 24-hour race outright. They also showed class-winning capability regularly, upgrading to a Sierra RS Cosworth for 1987.

The RS turbo proved an adept production racer in many hands. Most successfully after the Abbott/Smith victory at Snetterton was the capture of the 1987 outright Uniroyal title by the BF Goodrich and Duckhams-backed Welshman Franklyn 'Karl' Jones. All year Karl showed frightening speed, enough to defeat all but the Sierra RS types outright in the Richard Asquith Motorsports-prepared RS.

When Jones was paired with Patrick Watts for the 24 hours a repeat win looked on. However the 1987 season Sierras showed unexpected reliability to complement their speed and Jones himself moved up to an RS500 for the British Group A series of 1988.

Escort production class racing dominance was finally only eclipsed in 1988 events. Then the professional JQF Fina-BMW team demolished the class. The exception were those within the Monroe Group N series, David Shead taking 1988 class victory with a Bristol Street Group turbo, but not the overall title, which went to Sean Brown's Sierra RS. I have driven both the Jones and Ilford RS turbos (Jones actually acquired one of two Ilford RS types) and impressions of the cars are in the last chapter.

One of a pair: Mike Smith's Ilford-backed Group N Escort RS Turbo awaits the start of a Uniroyal production racing practice session at Castle Combe. Besides class wins, the Smith celebrity driver/Stuart McCrudden team alliance also wrested outright victory for the Escort in Britain's only 24-hour race, Snetterton's Willhire annual. 14/3

The flying display was routine from former Formula Ford Champion Karl Jones. His Asquith Motorsport Escort RST remained a winner throughout 1987. Victor of the Uniroyal series, the talented Welshman raced the Sierra RS 500 in 1988-89 British Group A events. 14/4

For 1986 the Longman/Datapost équipe made a serious outright Championship challenge with two Escort RS Turbos developing over 260bhp. They were driven by Longman himself (an outright Champion in the late seventies with the Mini 1275 GT) and Alan Curnow, also a talented Mini exponent and a vital link in the Longman-Datapost sponsorship package.

Right up to the penultimate British Championship round it looked as though Longman could take the outright title against former Brooklyn RS 1600i pilot Chris Hodgetts. Unfortunately it was at that vital race that a turbocharger let go under the high boost pressure of a competitive Group A title runner, and Toyota/Hodgetts were champions.

During the season, Richard Longman conquered the class on six out of nine rounds and set fastest lap on four occasions. Longman finished a class champion, again; Curnow

The class-winning run of the Escort RS Turbo in the Group A British Championship was completed in 1987 by Mark Hales. the Terry Drury Racing (TDR) Escort was phenomenally powerful on occasion (over 300bhp on the dyno) but lacked money for development outside the engine bay.

was third in the class. Richard was runner-up to Hodgetts in the overall 1986 RAC British Saloon car Championship.

During 1986 a new Group A British Championship contender emerged to challenge Richard Longman. Also using an RS turbo, the colourful Terry Drury prepared a demon quick (in a straight line) Escort for *Fast Lane* deputy editor Mark Hales. They had Duckhams backing, but like Karl Jones and Richard Asquith's Escort and Sierra eras this effort was a triumph of bravery and ingenuity over frugal finance.

In its first season Mark Hales showed that the Drury Escort could be quicker than the Longman version. Donington in 1986 yielded Mark's first class win and the car went on to score seven further class results in 1987, capturing the class title, but finishing third overall in the British series. When I spoke to Mark Hales about that season he was almost embarrassed that 'there was so little opposition until later in the year. There was a couple of Alfas and the occasional Nissan, but when Frank Sytner came with the Prodrive BMW M3 he was up to *eight* seconds a lap faster!'

In fact Messrs Hales and Drury had made the best of their low-cost position. Phenomenal power was cheaply available – up to 308bhp was seen on the dyno – and the engine proved reasonably reliable in view of its + 20psi boost levels. In fact a regular 18psi was adopted versus Richard Longman's slightly lower regular figures, but the point was that the Drury machine had a relatively undeveloped rally chassis rather than Richard Longman's carefully detailed running gear.

Mark Hales recalled: 'It was a wild, wild racer. Even Alan and Richard used to tape up their wrists to cope with the steering, but ours was worse. The engine was safe to 7500rpm, but there was no power progression, so you were stuffed if you tried to accelerate suddenly in the 4500 to 6500rpm band. That meant it was really best at Thruxton, where so much of it can be run flat out.

'We also had the close-ratio rally box where Richard had the wide-ratio road gears and we never seemed to have the right ratios. But with a Viscous Coupling front differential, carry-over Group II Fiesta style suspension at the front and Terry's Leda-damped rear end it simply seemed to plough straight on, but everywhere! There was none of the lift-off oversteer that you'd expect to use in a front drive car and it was frankly as good as it was going to be on its first outing; all because we simply didn't have the time or money to further develop it by going testing...' concluded the bearded scribe, who was talking about the RS turbo season during a 1988 in which he proved he could win outright in Group N with a Firestone-backed Sierra RS.

The Mark Hales/Terry Drury Escort saga is a tale of what might have been, but remember it was enough to ensure that the RS 1600i/RS Turbo run of RAC Class victories was continuous from 1983-87.

The tremendous loyalty that Ford earned for the Escort, particularly in Britain, resulted in a number of rear drive conversions of the Mk3 body appearing in national events, for which homologation was not required. These varied from fragile and fast to regular national round winners, usually based on the Gartrac conversion, which is also further described in that last Chapter. One such car even found its way to the States for use as a Mercury Lynx rally car! Only fair really, for Boreham engineers were puzzling over a US Escort GT when I called to catch up on their eighties progress, just before the axe fell on the RS 1700T.

Overall it is fair to say that the Escort's previous competition reputation was a considerable factor in the commercial success of the front drive design. At the time of writing the 1990 prototype 7-speed Escort RS Cosworth 4x4 had won its first event, in Spain. Let us hope that the World Rally Championship version (due in 1992/93) will be as successful.

Yes, this RS 1800 shot does belong in 1988, not 1978. Young James Renwick took NRA 500W to third overall in the 1988 Cellnet/Autosport series in a remarkable display of Championship consistency and private preparation expertise. Will the Escort RS Cosworth be capable of the same feat in 1998?

Chapter 15

The golden roadies

From 1968 to 1989, from V8 to inline four, the Escorts kept coming in ever wilder varieties and more sophisticated derivatives than Britain's previous speed industry darling, the Mini.

'ESCORT, what sort of name is that for a modern saloon? Most people will think of that van Ford used to have – why couldn't they think of something new?' That was the kind of reaction to be heard in the West London Offices of the sixties that I inhabited during the period of Escort's introduction, but once we had laid hands on one, the name seemed totally irrelevant, for by then it was obvious that it was going to be a huge success.

By February 1968 the hotter Escorts were racing onto the *Cars & Car Conversions* car park with a variety that surpassed even the ubiquitous Mini at its prime. The production range was assessed in England, following the January, 1968 Morocco introduction, and gave us a good starting point to evaluate the 'wild ones' that followed so fast.

An 1100 – with front disc brakes and radials, as per the usual press car practice of fitting maximum options – was joined by a 1300 Super and a 1300 GT for those first appraisals. I remember the car as particularly 'driver friendly' with such slick four-speed changes that the clutch was only really needed to get away from rest.

Compared with previous older Fords, particularly the Anglia, I suppose the most immediate bonus was in refinement: the seats were more logical in rearward adjustment, doing without that strange Anglia tilt and adjust mechanism, and the plastic three-spoke wheel felt positively dinky, by previous standards, at under 15 inches diameter. A Mini of the period had a huge two-spoke black plastic flying saucer that doubled up as a steering wheel.

The standard equipment was not impressive by eighties Japanese-elevated standards. However, with good forward visibility over the precisely defined bonnet line, and good –

Dave Gray, better known for his BBC camera work, was a regular contributor to Cars & Car Conversions *in the sixties and he caught this May 1968 outing for me in the Player's No. 6 Escort 1600GT. The meeting was one of a series held by the Thames Estuary Automobile Club (TEAC) and the venue was also later used to sort out aspiring rallycrossers for the Lydden Hill TV events.*

though not the greatest – Ford ventilation, the Escort cabin was a desirable place for front seat passengers.

Back seat accommodation and vision out of those deliberately restricted rear 'portholes' was not particularly appealing, but plenty of young families today and then seem happy to enjoy their joint outings from the rear of the smallest Ford in the 1968-74 range. The back seat could be used for amorous activities of the most lingering and intimate nature – but the estate was in a totally superior category for such entertaining and enjoyable pastimes.

The boot was hardly capacious with the intrusions of the vertical spare wheel, and 9 gallon petrol tank to accommodate. Again one could get in enough baggage for a family foursome without serious discussions arising about the date of divorce, should mother's baggage load exceed the usual 7.5 tonnes.

Underneath the chrome FORD-embossed bonnet, the crossflow engines looked lost! It was entirely fair for Ford to claim excellent engine access. The simplicity of parts then used meant one could drift into a Belgian Ford dealership with a dead engine and find a mechanic of retarded appearance to help fix with little delay a problem like a severed throttle/clutch cable, or even an electrical component. Roadside repairs today, even of carburated Escorts, are necessarily not easy with the emission and sophisticated electronics that we now carry. However, the chance of a breakdown is a lot less today.

Like the gearboxes, all the engines were smoothies, both by yesterday's standards and those of today. The four-cylinder Kent units seemed capable of absorbing almost any rpm and the five-bearing bottom end ran trouble free even when abused on service intervals, or by the kind of rev-happy enthusiast who enjoyed exploiting those sweetly-exchanged four ratios.

Straightline performance was just on a par with the chief contemporary opposition in 1968-71, and the uprated power units of 1971 were a worthwhile investment for 1100/1300 owners, as the unit didn't seem to demand perceptibly more petrol.

The 1300 GT was originally tried mainly with the 4:1 diff ratio, but I did drive both 1968 modified cars on the 3.9 or 3.7 and the post-1971, more powerful, 1300 GT on a 3.9. In my opinion, the high rpm needed to sustain even the legal limit on motorways was unacceptably disturbing – and the Escort's crosswind stability was not reassuring under such circumstances, either! The 3.9 is a more peaceful solution, with the later engine ensuring one loses little perceived acceleration (compared with 4:1), but enjoys quieter, faster motorway manners and even more weaving... The GT's acceleration was nearly always fully-used, because making maximum use of that engine and box was such a pleasure, but fuel consumption did tend to stay around 25-27mpg under such regular duress, rather poor by eighties 1300 Escort standards.

I did drive a drum-braked 1100 once, but I didn't enjoy it very much. Fords of that era (and some today!) can follow road cambers and broken edges with distressing familiarity when the brakes are on, usually pulling leftward, towards the kerb. The drum braked 1100, and some subsequent MK2 drum braked derivatives could compound this problem by pulling either left or right, just grabbing untidily, when wet.

No sooner had the first flush of enthusiasm for these obviously rugged, yet mechanically refined, original Escorts been generated than the performance specialists perceived salvation in it, saving them on a receding wave of 'Mini-mania!'; a uniquely British disease that allowed purveyors of anything from an initialled key fob, or wooden gear knob, to a full-house racing engine, unlimited access to the wallets of the temporarily deranged Mini-maniac.

Thus in 1968/69 *Cars & Car Conversions,* and its beseiged staff were plied with every Escort conversion west of Dagenham. Supercharged, enlarged, transplanted, all seemed to arrive for a thrashing. This in the days before Ford filled such obvious gaps as a higher performance level than 1300 GT could offer, without the expense of a full-blooded Twin Cam; the latter arrived with us by May 1968.

Initially there were tuned 1300 GTs from companies such as Broadspeed, Allard and Mark Ridout, the latter a cheerful rally driver of some repute. Allard's supercharged 1300 came complete with his effective 'Allardette Tramp Bar' well-proven on Anglia axles, and was sensational. It really felt as though a 3-litre engine had been dropped within, whenever one planted one's foot on the throttle at low to medium (say 5500) rpm. The acceleration times to 60mph, 9.2 seconds, were close to those of the Press Escort TC, but there was considerable pre-ignition and ruinous combustion chamber detonation at any attempt to top 100 to 105mph in fourth. Fuel consumption was also uninspired at 22.5mpg.

Of the conventionally tuned GTs, Broadspeed's boost was by far the best. Widely available for some years, in three stages, these Broadspeed Fords were proved with test mileage such as reconnaissance laps of the Nürburgring for Roger Clark and company, when Broad successfully campaigned two of his 1300 GTs in the 1968 Six Hours event at the classic German track.

My chief memory of Broadspeed's white Stage II demonstrator was not of the 10 second 0-60mph capability, or the easy 7000rpm gait of an engine continually exploited to produce 26mpg, but of Ralph Broad driving this scribe out of Birmingham and on to the A45 Coventry dual carriageway. Overawed by this maestro of the UK saloon car racing scene, I perched dumbly as the birdlike profile behind the specs pecked its way through a somewhat disjointed conversation; one conducted at around 14,000wpm, to cope with Ralph's rapid brain and low threshold of boredom.

I tried to placate, with platitudes of the 'what-a-fantastic-conversion-Ralph' idiom, the ravening beast within this normally mild-mannered and courteous Brummie. Yet we plunged further downhill, toward the largest roundabout I have even seen... The little white Escort, not even a sporty steering wheel or a widened wheel to its name, plummeted toward certain doom at some 6600rpm in top. Ralph swearing on his mother's grave that 'it'll pull 7 in top any time,' and occasionally flicking a passing glance at the collection of kerbs and greenery now approaching the toughened screen at over 95mph. 'I believe, I *believe,* Ralph,' I blubbered in shameless cowardice as motorized doom lurched toward an Escort, one now twitching in response to an awakened Mr Broadspeed.

I survived to drive a lot more Escorts, and even to share a far more frightening drive with RB in a paralysingly impressive Capri 3-litre. I swear that the Broadspeed Escort aviated two wheels over that roundabout, and that Ralph never did so much as caress the brakes throughout the whole episode. I think the police appeared on the horizon at one point during this 1968 Escort demo – but their natty white and red-striped Jam Sandwich was no match for a now thoroughly aroused Mr Broad...

After the tuned 1.3, the trend switched to 1.6-litre crossflows of Cortina/Capri parentage, anticipating the 1970 Escort Mexico. None of them was as good as the production Mexico, in my view. Some were smarter; I remember Lumo of Luton building a particularly well-finished metallic green Escort 1600 GT 'Piranha', and Peter Gammon (former club racer who used to give Colin Chapman such a competitive racing time in the fifties), had an Escort 1600 GT conversion that returned 26mpg and 0-60mph in 10.1 seconds for *CCC's* June 1968 edition. Usually these conversions retained the GT's 12 inch wheel diameter and compact four-speed gear box, which could barely cope with 1.6-litre torque in place of 1.3 GT output.

Of course, people did tune 1.3 GTs into the seventies, although the emphasis switched to FAVO Escorts of the RS 1600/RS 2000/Mexico breed. I can recall Janspeed lending *Motoring News* an ordinary 1300 tuned beyond GT levels in 1971, a vehicle that seemed to attract the worst kind of passenger. It was returned to the formidable figure of the drily humorous Janos Odor, but only after it had been parked backwards upon the portals of the RAC in Belgrave Square. A passenger decided it would be fun to see what happened to a tuned Escort in a downpour cornering situation, if you applied the handbrake *now!*

One can still buy the conventional Janspeed tuning equipment like the famous fabricated steel exhaust systems for all Escorts, of course. Some of it developed around that 1971 flyer, but many of the others who played with the Ford in the sixties and seventies are extinct, including Broadspeed.

The next Escort conversion trend was the major surgery transplant. You might have thought the Mexico had finished all that off, but specialists like SuperSpeed at Ilford (John Young, the sixties Anglia name along with racing brother Mick) would provide a 2-litre SOHC Cortina-engined Escort – previewing the 1973 RS 2000 – and many concerns such as Crayford (Eliminator) and Jeff Uren would pop the Ford Essex V6 3-litre of 138bhp rating into the Escort! As FAVO's production trio from Ford established themselves, along with a visually similar Escort Sport based on the 1300 GT, these hybrids faded away. I even drove one Escort mongrel with an alleged 200bhp, the Richard Martin Hurst Escort-Rover V8, which was so quick it hurtled the *Motor Sport* fifth wheel into the empty grandstand accommodation at Silverstone. It was great, but best for drag racing for fivers on the Great West Road rather than displaying cornering finesse.

The V6 Escorts were all surprisingly good in the handling stakes – usually based on Escort TC wide wheels and running gear – considering the extra nose weight. There were few that didn't run 0-60 in the 7 second bracket, but stopping them consistently over a hard B-road run was a major driver preoccupation. As a cheap introduction to drag racing, or sprinting, with 200-250bhp easily obtainable from the V6 as a by-product of Capri's racing record, the V6 Escort Mk1 must still make hairy-chested sense. The Rover V8 is ever more tempting, but most of the V6 Escorts I tried used a Ford Cortina 1600 GT or Corsair 2000 E gearbox. This required no major transmission tunnel attack to accommodate a bulk that's a lot less than that of the ZF five-speed of works rally cars or the RM Hurst Escort V8, or that of the Rover SD1 77mm five-speeder.

Back with production excitement, the May 1968 outing with an Escort Twin Cam and a 1969 week with a test car left such a strong impression of awestruck admiration that the TC remained my favourite production Escort until the advent of the RS 2000. I cannot recall the RS 1600 loaned to *Motor Sport* showed any *measured* performance advantage over the Escort TC, which seemed to have more mid-range response than the Cosworth BDA in street form. Today it is still comparatively easy to buy Twin Cam engine parts from the Lotus specialist, whereas BDA parts are from a limited production run, a small part of a *racing* company's output, usually at racing prices.

In action the TC still had that chain cam drive rattle and gargling throatiness from dual, twin-choke, carburettors, whilst the RS 1600 had a distinctive whistling engine note that caused traffic neighbours to glance again at the innocuous white Ford alongside. Both were rapid by the standards of the day, particularly at 1.6 litres: BMW and Alfa Romeo waited until their 2-litre models to offer the 9 second 0-60mph and 112-115mph top speeds that both these fast Fords could provide.

Today we take similar acceleration, and slightly higher top speeds, for granted in the 105bhp Escort 1.6 XR3i, its improved aerodynamics making the slight top end difference and contributing (together with a standard five-speed gearbox) to *enormously* improved petrol economy; 20-23mpg was my norm in the TC/RS Escorts, whereas my current XR3i provides 31-33mpg. Of course, there is no comparison between my quiet and (optionally) well-equipped XR3i and the TC/RS 1600's of a decade ago and more for everyday use with a spice of sporting flair. *But,* give me an original Escort TC and the by-roads of Oxfordshire, Berkshire, Hampshire and Wiltshire. Then the grin of pleasure from conducting a car where the front wheels are for steering only, not also pulling in apparent contradiction of one's enjoyable cornering desires, and the XR can stay at home for the day! When the nostalgia is over, it's front drive Escort time again for frugal fun.

As all-rounders in their era, particularly for UK use, I believe the 1970-1974 Escort Mexico and 1973 to 74 (LHD & RHD) RS 2000 were unmatched. I was privileged to drive in a Boreham airfield comparison between the Triumph Dolomite Sprint and its FAVO Ford rivals – particularly the RS 2000 – and I could see and feel what a cleverly engineered car the Triumph was. *Potentially* this was a far better bet than the Fords, but the reliability was suspect and the body notably dated, even against an Escort due for replacement. There was the Firenza 'Droopsnoot' with its 2300 SOHC engine and a floppy five-speed gearbox, but commercially the Fords established a wider taste for high performance at an affordable price; one that provided a foundation for future sporting Escorts to sell in daunting numbers, despite the absence of an effective Escort motor sports programme during 1980-89.

The competition Mk1's are dealt with separately, but even so it is hard to do justice to all the Escorts driven, particularly when working for the company between September 1972 and January 1975. Perhaps the most useful way of selection is by accumulated mileage. That means the 34,268 miles in an Escort 1300 GT Estate, shared by myself and my wife from March 1974 to 1978, takes 'pole position'. This willing machine covered over 40,000 miles in all, having spent the first 5000 miles of its life serving Stuart Turner's family on the management lease scheme, and it really demanded only the occasional exhaust manifold or clutch cable throughout its family life, though when I used it as a rally service vehicle the springs sagged permanently when asked to take an RS 2000 engine and spares! The major fault was the metallic silver paint, which eventually flaked off the roof in embarrassing motorway showers. I prepared it with a friend, and two fried Black & Decker rotary power tools, for the Ford-standard respray in blue. It was very, very smart but bubbles of rust appeared 3 months later, and it had to go...We all missed its capacious carrying capabilities a great deal, particularly the low sill to load the tailgate. It would cruise at 85mph very happily, but was strongly affected by motorway side winds on those long flat panels.

At first we seriously thought about building an RS 2000 estate as a replacement. I had tried such a combination at Ford, courtesy of then Ford Sport supremo Charles Reynolds, and the company had built at least three Mexico/RS 2000 Estates at FAVO for further

Early RS days. Rod Mansfield (left) became the man to talk to regarding performance Escorts, and here the author is seen trying to absorb Mexico lore not long after Rod had become one of the founding members of Ford Advanced Vehicle Operations. The Mexico GNO 463H was nicknamed 'Purple Passion' and was loaned by RM for the author's second race. It ate Lotus Cortinas, but the tyres could not cope indefinitely with this kind of cornering approach ...

Looking at the results sheets, the Lotus Cortina was driven by Danny Sullivan of the USA. It seems that this could have been the 1985 Indianapolis 500 winner during his British track education ...

sales potential analysis. Personally I always thought FAVO was an under-used facility in terms of accomplishing such small run tasks, and that it stuck too rigidly to an all-Escort Saloon output.

Next to the absolutely reliable estate GT, my biggest mileage must have been accrued in PEV 805K, a former show car with big wings, seven-inch prototype four-spoke wheels and 185/70 Goodyears propelled by a standard Mexico power plant. That covered 20,000 miles with impressive reserves of sheer grip. One could throw this car at a hairpin bend in second gear and it would slither so gently sideways that one could have attended one of the unrelenting Ford business meetings, and still have time to ease on gentle opposite lock.

I used the metallic bronze PEV 805K until the milometer read 29,800 and we had been together for 11 months. In the 20,000 miles that I contributed to its total, this curvacious Escort was not as reliable as the other Fords I have used. A lot of this was traced to using a local garage who fitted non-standard plugs and other electrical equipment that produced a misfire on several occasions. That it was a show car could be felt by the number of times the plug leads became detached, or other gleaming components slipped adrift. Later on it did run reliably, though somewhat slower than standard in a straight line, and it was thirsty enough to hover around 25mpg, rather than the 27-29mpg I was used to in most Mexicos. It also consumed those fat tyres at a UK Allcomers Record pace for punctures – only the efforts of Bill Meade kept it on the road as the prototype wheels were occasionally replaced, too.

Another bronze Mexico, but this time with the extra ancillary lamps and vestigial sumpguard of the Clubman Pack, was my first regular company car at Ford – before that I borrowed whatever ingenuity could produce. Unhappily, I decided to investigate the rally properties of this pristine ex-press demonstrator on our semi-detached's drive, and a mild respray was necessary before the car was 24 hours old. Thereafter we covered about 6000 miles together, but far less adventurously than in the original Mexico, which had spluttered to the Paris show and the Belgian 1973 Spa 24-Hours. The Clubman Mexico stayed from October 1973 to May 1974 and went back to the Company with 12,000 miles recorded, many of them rather skittish in crosswinds on a higher ride height than normal.

The replacement was NHK 272M, a yellow 1800-miler with wood trim inside and the excellent Comfort Pack seating. Complete with the black vinyl roof this machine went off on a tour of Wales almost immediately and distinguished itself in memory by once popping open the driver's door under cornering duress. It is possible that this freak occurrence saved me the major embarrassment of rolling the car within a mile of Ford's Warley HQ, because the lower door edge dragged along the tarmac and stopped the horizon tilting any further across the screen top... We did 9200 miles together in totally reliable and pleasurable harmony. As far as I know the Mexico then went to Tony Dron, the racer/journalist, but he sold it pretty rapidly to support his brave move into full time racing.

As the next 'firm's car' was an RS 2000, I should summarize my Mexico feelings of the 35,200 miles in three economical (27mpg average), reasonably rapid (105 honest mph mostly), Ford Escorts with the safest handling and braking standards; Mexicos that never strayed toward motoring melancholia. The Mexico was a proper Ford: strong, affordable, fun and easy to service. It was spoilt by a vibration about 4000rpm, just above the legal 70mph limit, but just a flick through that still unmatched four-speed gate was enough to forget any blemishes on one of the most honest cars Ford Motor Co. ever manufactured.

There were plenty of other Mexicos – one with an alloy-block Brian Hart 140bhp BDA for evaluation, and sheer excitement – and I can remember half a dozen more without thinking for long, but nothing alters the foregoing opinion.

Racing the first Escort

Just as Ford themselves sprung the first Escorts upon us in competition, together with retail availability, so the chance to drive the smallest European Ford in motor sport trim was equally swiftly presented. Even my first drive in a pre-production Twin Cam was accompanied by short sections of a loose surface session with the 160bhp TC used in rallycross, and for the Acropolis World Championship round of that debut 1968 season.

Compared with the similarly powerful, but Tecalemit Jackson fuel-injected, Cortina

In 1969 Lumo Cars – a Tricentrol Division – let me out in this immaculate 1600GT conversion for Motor Sport.

TC of 1967 (my first full road test car), the works rally Escort felt nervously agile with stunning acceleration. Where the Cortina would arc out lazily into any powerslide angle the novice selected, the Escort demanded prompt counter-steer movements at the Spingalex wheel's deeply dished rim to 'keep it on the black bits' of soaked Essex lanes.

Today the hottest of the hatchbacks would scrabble toward the acceleration rates of this works car from 16 years ago. Audi have sold a perfectly docile turbo road car with 40 horsepower more, plus 4-WD, since 1980; but still the memory of that black and white 'Twink' is coloured powerfully with exciting emotion. Memories composed of speed and gargling, rattly, twin overhead camshaft sound. An editor friend has a rude expression: 'How many squirts per mile?', to assess the erogenous excitement quota of any machine. For me the thrill of the 'ordinary' TC's slithering standing-start getaways – always flattering the driver's ability – plus that first works TC's stunning aural and fingertip-tingling impacts, were enough to win that rude editorial award for speed in the sixties.

Player's No. 6 were big in autocross sponsorship in 1968, and they allowed me some exciting miles battling around ½ mile courses in Essex and Middlesex in one of several hybrid Escort 1600 GT pushrods, which anticipated much of what the Mexico would provide in 1970. These Willment-prepared Escorts were capable of taking on quite experienced clubmen in the favourite Ford prior to Escort, the redoubtable 1650 Anglia. Traction was never a strong point chez Ford, but when the 1600 GTs were kicking up mud and the leather rim wheel had used all the opposite lock, there was no doubt of an instant Roger Clark status to the apprentice within.

When Ford decided to race the Escort with Broadspeed in the 1.3-litre Group 2 class, they let us have rides around Brands Hatch with the drivers. I got Chris Craft. The living legend of saloon car speed (he was a later European 2-litre sports car champion for Chevron) grasped the injected 1300 GT by the bit of its 140 odd horsepower and demonstrated the difference between professional style and amateur dream. Chris literally went for top gear in places where the most optimistic outsider would have demanded a downchange, interspersed with heavy braking. The downdraught 1.3 litres sang to over 8000rpm readily enough, but the cars were not fully reliable in 1968.

The 1971 Mexico Challenge produced a surprise winner in the ample form of Vauxhall-contracted Gerry Marshall, his golden Esso Uniflo Escort defeating a class field that frequently included Jody Scheckter, Ferrari's 1979 World Champion. I drove that Marshall Mexico, and the later Avon-shod machine of Andy Rouse, resplendent in regal purple Broadspeed house-colours. Both drew on some 100/105 flywheel bhp from their Formula Ford-line single-carburettor crossflow engines.

Even in the early seventies Andrew Rouse had the knack of fine tuning a production car to suit his neat driving style. One could see that quality in the 1988 Kaliber Sierras he prepared, and the 1972 Mexico exhibited all the usual Rouse flair for extra front end grip and tidy, consistent braking. Marshall's race Mexico was just as quick in a straight line, but tended to slide into helpless wheelspin on slower corners, such as at Brands Hatch at Druids, whereas the Silverstone trial of Rouse's car showed no such weakness around the equally low-speed Becketts. Both were champions' cars, and they shared the mechanical basics, but the results showed how even a tight set of what we would now term 'Production Saloon' regulations, could result in cars that might not have shared the same production lines, so far as their driving characteristics were concerned.

The blue printed 1600 GT engines were naturally similar, and equally desirable, for the bigger crossflow responds well to a thorough rebuild. Offering far sweeter attainment of 6500rpm, and a solid power delivery throughout the useful 3000 to 6500rpm spread, the performance in blueprint guise reminds one of the worthwhile difference between handbuilt pedigree and mass production mongrel.

I raced two Mexicos myself, in 1971, part of the novice licence procedure that qualified me for a full season during 1972 with the visually similar 1300 GT Sport. One of those 1971 Mexicos was nickname 'Purple Passion' owing to its uniquely fruity paint shade. Rod Mansfield, then at FAVO, lent the car, complete with some then very low profile road tyre Dunlops, modelled on the Denovo and a cover offered to Lotus. I ran the car in my second race as a novice at Brands Hatch Handicap for road cars. Then lap times were around 65 to 68s: today an XR3i from the fleet operated for celebrities will turn about 61s on average...

That FAVO Mexico was so good that it was up to third in the overall order very quickly, but it oversteered enough to earn an *Autosport* picture of its spectacular sideways stance on its way to Cooper Straight! Yes, I spun it through the infield, clear almost to Clearways; but it still gave us a top ten finish in a 15 car field.

The 1972 Sport was backed by Castrol, prepared by Janos Odor's Janspeed concern in Salisbury by Norman Clancy (who is still with the world famous exhaust manufacturers). I was most fortunate in obtaining some superb racing Dunlops, for this initial year of Production/Group 1 saloon car championship racing permitted full racing tyres. Today the two national club series feature the latest in low profile road tyres from Uniroyal (who sponsor one race series), BF Goodrich, Pirelli and so on. Then a set of ex-Roger Williamson F3 slicks spread themselves incongruously over our 5J x 13in. steel wheels, with the result that the Escort had so much adhesion, compared to top-heavy height, that three- and two-wheeling moments marked normal progress, even with the less radical wet weather covers.

Complete with an old BMC Special Tuning bucket seat and a colour scheme that changed every time I crashed it (twice in 40 races) this Sport had a very honest 80-85bhp.

Gerry Marshall's Tiran Auto Centre Mexico, winner of the 1971 Championship, gets the MN *track test treatment at Druids.*

The 7000rpm 'Mickey Mouse' tacho spent most of its working life at the end of the scale, where it was exhilaratingly smooth and amazingly durable. Ford were then kings of the homologation game and even this national club racer came with a limited slip differential, a final drive option over 4:1 and a new exhaust manifold in fabricated steel that gave us a 3-5 bhp lift a few races into the season.

There was not much class opposition – they moved a rear engine NSU 1200 TT out of the price-fixed class only after I had managed to flip the Escort over it – but there were plenty of other good Escort Sports to fight for class honours. We were never going to win the overall title, firmly the property of the unbeaten Comrade Tony Lanfranchi in the lowest-cost Moskovich 412, but even Ivan Dutton and John Lyon's fierce class tussles with our Janspeed screamer would not prevent us taking the Castrol Group 1 Production Championship: class £600-£900, and runner up position on points overall to Lanfranchi. In the parallel Britax Production title hunt Lanfranchi won again, but I lost the class title to Ivan Dutton, who started racing the Sport later than we did, but won more races. My tally at the end of the year was seven class wins and the same number of record laps, but whenever the car finished – and it only ever failed to make it because I crashed it! – it was in the top three of the class, which usually had half a dozen competitors. It finished second to Dutton most of the time, and this included some overall race results, where there were enough runners.

I have every reason to be thankful to the Sport. It developed a mechanical problem just once; the gearbox jammed in third at Mallory Park, but still earning Championship points. The little 1300, which we timed at 0-60mph in some 11 seconds, handled so well that very little effort was needed to turn it into a corner from any unlikely track-battling position. The tail would only slide out in the wet, the conditions under which the car scored most victories.

Memories? Mostly of other cars at crazy angles, followed swiftly by similar two-wheel aviation as I encountered the problem they had just survived! Sometimes the racing was close enough to read the rev counter of the Sport in front and almost hear the panting from the lunatic behind...

The *best* racing Escort I ever tried was the Broadspeed RS 1700 of 1971. Normally its 250 BDA-based horsepower were conducted by John Fitzpatrick in a series of giant killing Group 2 Championship events. As for 'my' Sport, we tried the car on the *Motoring News* fifth wheel gear, but the results – Mr Fitzpatrick at the wheel – were sensational. From rest to 60mph occupied under 5 seconds, and the figures generally displayed that this 9000rpm wonder was not losing too much to the V8s it chased – and sometimes beat – on the straight. It had a vestigial front spoiler and token leaf springs, running the Len Bailey torsion bar rear axle layout.

This RS racing Escort was an overwhelming pleasure to drive, whether clattering on the timing straight at 2500rpm, ready for another immaculate getaway from Fitzpatrick, or rushing along the sunlit Hangar Straight at Silverstone's GP layout at some 9000rpm and 140mph. Even in my tentative hands it ran laps in the 100mph/1m 46s region. I saw why Group 2 Escort drivers of the seventies – such as Andy Rouse, Dave Brodie and Vince Woodman – all nominated the BDA Escorts as their favourite racing saloon, even after a decade of widely different subsequent experience.

Rally Escorts: factory fare

The original Escort outline was at a peak of British supremacy during my Ford employment, and I was lucky enough to drive hundreds of miles in Roger Clark's most successful RS 1600, LVX 942J. This was the car that began its career winning the 1972 RAC Rally for Clark, and it just went on winning thereafter. It seemed a shame Ford did not retain this classic Escort, but it was sold for Adrian Boyd to rally from an Ulster base and ended its original bodyshell days with the sound of breaking glass... and crumpling metalwork!

My main mileage in LVX came after the Escort epic that was the 1973 Scottish Rally, when the Fords captured a complete top ten results sweep! The Esso backed car for Clark was heavily scarred around the wheel arches and floorpan, but only from the pounding of Scottish stones, not accidents. One can judge the stage quality and the consequent battering on the Ford flotilla by that fact that the works Escort débutant Tony Pond had to have the axle of his car wired and shackled into place, all conventional mountings long since distorted beyond use.

After a night of celebration that extended to dawn, prize-giving was a shattering blare of skirls from the pipers, followed by the long trek south in Roger's winner. The

A sunlit session with John Fitzpatrick's 1.7-litre Broadspeed RS 1600 of 1971. From continual drag racing starts for the Motoring News/Motor Sport *fifth wheel (0-60 in 4.8s; 0-100mph in 12.0s; 0-120mph in 17.7s) to the exhilaration of 138mph at 9000rpm, the factory-backed Ford behaved with faultless forgiveness for the stranger at the wheel. The crash hat came from present day TV commentator and former colleague, Andrew Marriott (A.R.M.)*

Bitter struggle: Richard Longman was a former Janspeed employee, and I was expected to beat him when we met at Mallory Park in 1972 in our 1300GT Escort Sports. We finished more or less like this, Richard ahead of course ...

acceleration for ordinary road use with the low ratio differential and a good 230bhp was akin to Polaris in full flight. Careful tuition from Pond, in his works Escort ahead, shrivelled the A9 South to one of those flickering ribbons of unwinding tarmac that persuade you somebody has speeded the film remorselessly. There was a speeding fine on the Cumbrian section of the M6 – the interior mirror was notable by its fractured absence – and a hilarious episode on the North Circular. The exhaust system aft of the engine manifold had also fractured and the result within London's confines can be noisily imagined. Whilst I tried to wire the departing pipework into place, a drunk staggered into view and slumped beneath a car tilted for access across a pavement, gutter and slow lane. Considering the heat of the medium artillery bore piping, it was a wonder that he did not immolate both of us with a single alcoholic exhalation, but we survived long enough for the constabulary to kneel into investigative snoop position.

Other alloy block RS 1600s from the factory came my way for filming sessions at functions such as the Beaulieu-based test day of 1973, where I was allowed to make my own autocross test track for the factory machine (000 96M) with 2-litre BDA power, and the twin-downdraught Solex-carburated original RS 2000 (PVX 446M) that had served Roger Clark to win that year's Tour of Britain. The 000 96M registration was well known at the time, its achievements including second on 1973's RAC Rally.

The RS 2000 had less than 140bhp and was typical Ford fun to fling into long sideways slides around the ¼ mile figure of eight that I had contrived. The pukka BDA was harder work because Roger Clark was absent, test driving a Rolls Royce and winning a cunning side show in which Rootes had connected the steering up back-to-front! Of course, we Ford men simply commented that it was hard to tell the difference between the resulting errant Hillman Hunter and the production offering... Back at the works Escorts, some TV people needed their pix *now*, if the Factory Escorts were to go 'on air' that evening. So I waddled the works car round my improvised circuit with gusto in Roger's helmet. This was one of the best days of my time at Ford. I was almost embarrassed to take the pay cheque that month...

There was another factory RS 2000 specification for the MkI that involved appealing to clubmen in the aftermath of the fuel crisis. This had big sidedraught dual Webers and a 10.5:1 compression in a carefully assembled Pinto package that produced over 160bhp, a figure not approached by the Group 1 RS 2000 until the dual Weber downdraughts were substituted along with a new exhaust. The 1974 result was a pretty rorty car in the sense of rough, tough power, a mainly impressive torque, rather than the thrust of a BDA, or the later solid power curve of the Group 1 RS 2000. The handling was able to cope with 160bhp

*'Dead boring these Group
1 cars', said all the
Group 2 competitors
when I deserted writing
for racing in 1972. As
you can see, keeping it on
four wheels was not my
forte: here the Sport is
seen at the old long
circuit Snetterton (45);
and upside down at
Brands Hatch after a
squabble with present day
Jaguar connoisseur Graig
Hinton's NSU 1200TT.
Despite my attacks on its
smartly presented body,
the Escort finished all but
three of some 40 races
entered in two national
championships and was
runner-up for the overall
title in the 1972 Castrol
Group 1 series.*

easily, since a lot of the BDA chassis mods had been carried out, including four-link location of the axle. The idea did not really take off in Ford package form, whereas literally thousands of the Group 1 engine parts must have been sold – but one often finds club Escorts built to this kind of specification, although its just as likely that they will have crossflow power.

Finally, on the factory RS 1600 front there were a glorious few days spent with Timo Makinen's 1974 RAC winner (GVX 883N). In Colibri Brown with maybe 10-15bhp more than Clark's 1972 RS 1600, it proved much easier to drive on the road, for Brian Hart's men did a remarkable job in assembling what they always simply reported as Cosworth

PR in motion. Ford held a test day for journalists after the 1974 RAC Rally. Here I check out Sue Baker's driving position, ensuring that she made it from her Evening News *job a decade ago to eighties televised eminence ... The works RS 1600s in my tentative hands were the winner of that year's event (GVX 883N) and the seventh placed Clark/Mason machine, 000 96 M. Unforgettable Escort excellence ...*

No it wasn't as fast as that Broadspeed Group 2 RS, but the Norman Clancy-tended Sport was also a treat to drive ...

The well publicized PEV 805K became my own road car soon after I joined Ford Motor Company.

parts with more power and docility, a *very* rare competition occurrence! The reason I was able to drive the car, however, and return to it again for ecstatic squirts around the highways and byways of Essex, was simply that a journalist had asked, 'Why do you only put a four-speed box in such fast cars?' This was after a week's urban testing, and I first thought he had never needed fifth. A telephone call, however, revealed that he had simply been engaging second to start off, subsequently using the box as an H-pattern four-speed, composed of second to fifth, leaving first (over on the left) neglected in the usual competition isolation. That is how flexible Brian Hart-assembled Cosworth BDAs of 123bhp per litre were by 1974.

There were many other sporting Mk1s, including very fleet Fords from the late Peter Warren (inside the 1971 RAC top ten with an iron block 1.8 RS) and George Hill, but the Mk2 must get its fair share of mentions too...

On the road with Brenda...

As it was for the Capri II, my road mileage in the later Escort body was initially limited by leaving Ford immediately after the Dorchester Hotel launch of the Mk2 Escort in January 1975. My love affair with Lancia's Beta Coupé distracted attention from the British trip to

Portugal that Ford laid on for journalists to drive the range outside the RS products.

I covered a few miles in a four-door Ghia 1.6 in 1975 and also experienced the 1.1 and 1.3-litre newcomers subsequently. First impressions were of a thoroughly improved Escort on the creature comfort front. The still unmatched Cortina/Capri 'eyeball' swivelling ventilation sockets and superbly arranged instrumentation were certainly worthwhile. Not only were the instruments clearly visible beneath that single pane, but they were large and notable for black and white clarity.

Passenger space was claimed to be superior, but occupants commented more warmly on the absence of that claustrophobic feeling when using the rear seats, the presence of the original Escort's 'portholes' producing many complaints of unloved rear accommodation that the later car's glazing bonus overcame. I think it was on the Scottish Rally of 1975 that winner Roger Clark neatly encapsulated most Escort driver's thoughts of the restyled model: 'It feels much the same, but the view is different.'

On the road it was noticeable that the suspension had been softened with a view to trading off a little original Escort sharpness for a more civilized ride, but the rack and pinion steering still provided first class ability to point the Ford in the required direction with speedy accuracy.

Along with a more supple ride – albeit one that was still unlikely to worry even other live axle engineering rivals for a moment on the score of its behaviour over bumps – came slightly lower noise levels. Since the Escort was now available in plusher (Ghia) trim levels than had previously been offered, this was little surprise, but the general standard of long distance comfort was of particular value to Escort's motorway manners.

Some variants did show petrol economy gains. The general weight gain and a slight loss of aerodynamic penetration, however, meant that the private owner was likely to find that the equivalent power unit within the Mk1 and Mk2 showed slight performance *and* economy gains in daily use in favour of the original car. In sporting terms this could be contradicted by the Mk2 RS 2000's clear superiority over the first 2-litre RS, and by the rare RS 1800's bonus in straightline speed and overall single-carburettor parsimony compared with the RS 1600. But it would be a brave Ford product man who insisted that the 1600 Sport had any speed/consumption merit over the 1600 GT Mexico...

The RS versions of the later Escorts arrived at *Motor Sport's* offices during the reign of a comparatively liberal regime, one that allowed one of those new fangled group tests to adorn their hallowed pages. Thus, we were the only people (that either Graham Robson or myself have discovered) to test the 1.6 SOHC Mexico with a fifth wheel, a process repeated in the same feature for the beak-nosed RS 2000 and RS 1800. All appeared in the February 1976 issue. Their times appear on page 162 of this book.

The results were very much in line with the respective torque and horsepower claims. The RS 2000 was quickest off the mark to 30mph at 3 seconds dead to the 3.2s of the Mexico and RS 1800. The RS 1800 then drew gradually away, returning 8.6s versus 9.8s for the RS 2000 and 11.1s (Mexico) for the much quoted 0-60mph sprint. By 80mph the RS 1800 was stomping away from the RS 2000, 15.4s versus 19.2s, and this was borne out by the side-by-side performance: the poor Mexico returned 23 seconds for 0-80mph. As to maximum speed I commented, 'Where the RS 2000 is trying to elbow its way past 105mph, the RS 1800 is bellowing grimly past 110, intent on recording its eventual maximum of 115mph. Under the same conditions the Mexico is very hard put to exceed 100mph.' Full figures from *Autocar* should be sought in the Appendices for historical comparison purposes, but I thought the back-to-back approach returned interesting results at the time, and I see that article has now been reprinted outside *Motor Sport,* including an appearance in the handy Brooklands Books series.

The RS 1800 may have been slightly quicker, but there was never any doubting the longer term sales winner, the RS 2000. The Mexico was just not quick enough beyond the capabilities of the cheaper, pushrod, Escort Sport 1600. There was a lot of charm in the later Mexico, its handling so well-balanced with comparatively little torque to push a chassis attuned to the needs of restraining and entertaining with over 100bhp in the bigger-engined brethren. I thought the Mexico was worth the extra at the time – and a later encounter with a second such car in and around Donington Park underlined that preference over the 1600 Sport – but the public bought the cheaper alternative, of course.

I drove the RS 1800 through two separate test periods; the second occasion was after a crash repair, required after another magazine's attentions. Initially I thought this was a classic combination of exciting engine and capable chassis. I was happy to put up with power unit growls because of acceleration that was brilliantly matched to country lane exploitation via a unique (on the Escort product line; it had German Granada/Capri parentage) four-speed gearbox.

Balanced on the throttle and steering into a second or third gear power slide, there was little that was more exhilarating than cabbing an RS 1800 flat out. The trouble was that cars also have to be used in more mundane circumstances and be produced in mass production quantities to make economic sense. Even slightly better economy than the RS 1600 in my hands – 21 to 24mpg – failed to offset the impressions of that second encounter. The RS 1800, JJN 981N (yes it was another Boreham-built press car!) returned out of sorts, and I could concentrate on the less desirable aspect of the British homologation special syndrome: rorty and basically unrefined to live with, although a huge improvement over the RS 1600 in cabin equipment. Terrific for a fleeting affair, but forget daily married life!

In 1975, Ford of Britain possessed the technical elements and the experienced manpower to make a credible and efficient 16-valve saloon a *decade* before such devices became fashionable for public sale at high profit ratios in the eighties. The RS 1800 did the traditional Ford homologation job on numbers that are not discussed even today, but it could have been so much more with Ghia trim and a small engineering refinement budget...

RS 2000s seemed to self-duplicate at Standard House, and I have the advantage of being able to draw on the experiences of *Motor Sport/Motoring News* photographer Maurice Selden who drove 211,000 miles in three examples (one a Mk1)! For me there were two original road test RS 2000s – one had a 'singing' differential after a lot of hard work on slow corners had led to excessive differential oil surge – and the second became my Group 1 rally car of 1976. There was also Bill Gwynne's twin-carburettor Oselli Clubman engine in an RS2 that proved capable of winning the *Motoring News* road rally championship, a car I drove several times.

Maurice Selden's experience of the white original RS 2000 he had (KUW 69P) extended over 85,000 miles, from an August 1975 purchase at £1400 to an August 1977 part exchange for £1000 against the later RS 2000. That first car had the wood fascia centre console but steel wheels, and was so reliable that Selden had his first note of trouble at 45,000 miles! Then new dampers, springs and struts were installed, but shortly after its return the RS 2000 was fitted with a new propshaft to overcome workshop damage.

The next problem was at 50,000 miles when overheating was traced to the electric radiator fan going on strike. The sensor had come out of the radiator and was rewired into place. The alternator was replaced at 60,000 miles. So after £1400, two years and 85,000 miles Maurice Selden had nothing but respect for the rugged Ford and instantly bought a black Mk2, reg. no. VPK 217S.

This machine cost £4400 and was sold for exactly half that after 80,000 miles. It was the most attractive car our photographic ace bought, shining in black with a Custom Pack and alloy wheels, but it was not the most reliable... 'After 2000 miles the clutch cable was

My comeback to racing in the Mk2 1600 Sport was assisted by the mockery of my fellow scribes and the number 13. Here Ian Phillips, then editing Autosport (subsequently Leyton House March Grand Prix team manager), finds that a rampant J.W. is dangerous, even contesting a top five position. To the 1600 Sport's eternal circuit, it finished the event, still in the top six.

Front or back, the yellow KHK 982N Boreham-prepared Escort RS 1800 for Timo Makinen was an imposing mid-Seventies Escort experience. This LHD RS was designed for tarmac use and had 245bhp in 2128lb/967kg, but was exceptionally easy to drive (albeit not at Timo's pace!) because of the power spread between 4000 and 8000rpm. Complete with a 5.3:1 final drive, top speed was limited to little over 100mph at the 9200rpm limit, but acceleration from 0-60mph was accomplished in only 6½ seconds.

replaced under warranty,' reported Maurice. Furthermore, 'Betweeen 20,000 and 40,000 miles the car overheated on long fast trips. A new head gasket was fitted...Then another! Eventually the cylinder head was resurfaced and the problem was then cured'.

This time suspension components waited until 55,000 miles before requiring replacement, along with a rear exhaust silencer box. The front wheel bearings were replaced at 45,000 miles but Maurice suspected, 'the Dunlop SP Super 205/60 x 13 were probably the cause,' meaning that he tended to fly round corners with even more Welsh abandon than usual. Those Dunlops were terrific; I extracted a set to put on my Lancia with very similar results for suspension and bearing longevity...

In June 1980 our friend celebrated the cessation of RS 2000 production by acquiring a Diamond White Custom RS 2000 from Grays of Guildford for £5034, which was sold to City Speed in Gloucester for £3500, after it had covered but 48,000 miles... Low by LAT Photographic standards! This RS had: 'clutch judder from new; replaced under warranty at 5000 miles. The juddering was still present and persisted throughout ownership of the car. New struts, springs, shocks were fitted at 40,000 miles, plus a new rear silencer box and clutch'. Mr Selden went for the same oversize 205/60 x 13 radials as before, but this time they were P6s. The replacement wheel bearings came at 42,000 miles, just as sun follows moon! There were also 'many small electrical problems. For example I had four rear screen heater switches; the wipers were erratic and the brake warning light flashed for no apparent reason,' reported Maurice Selden of his last RS 2000. Sadly he felt he had to buy Japanese to find a reasonably reliable and affordable rear drive alternative: a Colt Mitsubishi Lancer Turbo.

Overall I thought this record said more than I ever could about the long term reliability of the RS 2000 under duress, for Maurice was then fulfilling mostly a rally photographic brief and the cars tended to cover stage mileage a little bit faster than the back marker competitors!

Aside from the road test RS 2000s, I also experienced temporary ownership of an Escort Harrier. That was was introduced in December 1979 and I had one passed on to me within the Standard House system that was comparatively youthful, by 13 January 1981. I only retained it until April of that year, having covered some 2000 miles more, because a new carburated Escort XR3 came to me.

Testing for the 1976 Tour of Britain. You can see the chunky Dunlops we fitted to the RS 2000's homologated 6inch rims.

The Harrier was not a bad car. It allied a dressed-up Escort Sport 1600 with desirable extras such as FAVO wheels and plain but effective buckets seats and an RS steering wheel. Yet, by 1981, the rear drive Escort felt and look dated for road use compared with the front drive models, which really did offer an exceptional speed and economy balance for the public.

My chief memory of the Harrier was of its efforts to emulate its aeronautical name sake on a particularly snowy Mintex International Rally. I was properly co-driven by the car's former keeper, Steve Fellows of *MN,* and every brow over the Northumbrian/Yorkshire main road network had to be taken flat, or screams of rage came from the left-hand seat, along with tales of *MN* Championship derring-do. Inevitably, Steve goaded us into flight over the one brow where the road did change direction and there was a long silence as we skated into an opposite lock landing on icy grass. However, the Harrier was so well balanced and so short on power that liberties such as these were taken without crumpling any panels. It was certainly fun to drive sideways, but that boxy body needed at least three-quarters throttle to punch it through the air at an indicated 90mph.

That was the last Mk2 road car I drove regularly, but there are some outings in competition cousins to recall.

RS 2000 rallying

Falling under the spell of rallying's slippery attractions I procured one of the original press fleet RS 2000s for a 1976 season that was finally abbreviated by reaching a pre-set overdraft limit. It was fun while it lasted, however...

The car was prepared by Reed Rallysport at Paignton in Devon, a Ford dealership. Basically, the car covered three club events without any engine preparation, but gradually incorporating the Group 1 running gear, such as the close-ratio gearbox and 2.5 turns lock-to-lock steering rack.

Before it tackled even testing, Tony Pond's mechanic of the period, 'Demon' Dick Prior at Uxbridge, ensured that it had the right Bilsteins, a full roll cage, harness and other basic rally equipment. I did go testing at a military establishment with Mr Pond and he spent a lot of time nodding in nervous sagacity...He was too polite to tell *me,* but he advised one of my journalistic colleagues, 'He'll be quite quick while he is on the road, but the bank isn't going to love him when he's off... Again!'

It was a prophetic summary. Sharing with Roger Jones, who later went on to become a national champion alongside Bill Dobie in the *Autosport* series and was familiar co-driving Jeff Churchill and Trevor Smith, most memories are of bridge parapets dissolving in destructive stone showers, or laburnum bushes parting to reveal immovable tree trunks...There was, however, a place inside the top 15 on the Hadrian Centurion, a combination of Kielder forest and Otterburn ranges, the latter's 100mph brows tackled with a shortage of wheel nuts. There was a similar result on a West Country Club event – despite an interlude holding an uprooted gearlever – and I felt justified in tackling the 1976 BRSCC *Motor* Tour of Britain. This was the last such race and rally multi-day wonder held in Britain at Press time – run as the Autoglass-backed 1989 revival – and I honoured the presence of racing circuits with a 160bhp AVJ at Pershore, Worcs, Group 1 motor (new exhaust, multiple downdraught Webers and a replacement camshaft) that was a stunner. It would idle through traffic or outdrag a notoriously effective 3-litre race Capri around Silverstone's simple Club racing triangle.

Although we had contrived at Reeds to set the car up completely 'arse about face', with the front raked down and the rear raised, the elephant-decorated bonnet of the RS 2000 emerged second from a Silverstone race. It was completely revamped up front by the presence of Roger Clark's works struts, when his clutch went pop at Snetterton. The result was super top ten time on the next Mickey Mouse stage around a young forest (full power first; handbrake; full power first; second, handbrake...and so on), but the excitement of running this far up the order rather overcame me. We compensated for previous progress by three separate accidents, including the final laburnum bush into tree trunk episode, before night fell on the first day!

That was that for active rally participation. Reeds Aly 'Jumbus' Khan generously allowed Gerry and the rest of the boys to rebuild the car over a period of months and I sold it to Dorothy 'Dot' Warner. She rallied from a local Henley base and the car went on reliably picking up club awards literally for years afterwards.

Bill Gwynne's car was compared alongside mine on the road and track at the time and he eventually decided that the proper Group 1 layout was better than the Clubman specification for his needs, but either way he did a lot of winning in the car that was neatly self-prepared and a joy to drive.

There were racing miles apart from those on the Tour of Britain. Inevitably, I did one of those Brands Hatch Celebrity Races against fellow hacks, all of whom had got a lot quicker whilst I had been incarcerated at Ford, either that, or I had discovered mortality and pain. The result was a humiliating sixth after T-boning *Autosport's* Ian Phillips in the Avon-shod 1600 Sport. The cars were interesting to drive with enormous sliding ability on the West Country cross-plies, but the lap times were around a then pedestrian 65s for the Club Circuit. The record belonged to former downhill skier Divina Galicia.

There were plenty of track tests, the best Mk2 I remember being the example loaned to journalist Gordon Bruce sponsored by Toric Safety Belts and raced with success in the Mexico Challenge. As ever, the car was straightforward to drive and could only really be upset by the forcible arrival of other competitors within the coachwork, as Gordon later proved...

Front driving

My first sight of the Escort in its 1980 body was of three transparencies of the new shape proudly shown as a teaser by Ford marketing personnel; it came complete with red paintwork, spoilers and the now familiar XR alloy wheels. As with Lancia's coupé and the RS Capris it was a shape I liked instantly, but it was a surprise to find myself sharing a Ghia five-door pre-production example of the new Escort breed some months before the September announcement. The snag was that the car was laden with three other adults for 90 per cent of the three or four days I was allowed at the Belgian Lommel test track, so I failed to spot the ride problem. Fully laden (the condition specified for Ford ride evaluation at the time) the 1.6 Ghia not only rode with aplomb over simulated Belgian *pavé* and the equivalents to British B-roads, but also handled with a stable responsibility that convinced me every penny spent on that independent rear end was worth it. When I gained a chance to drive the car briefly at Dunton's figure of eight without the whines of on-board humanity being hurled around a test track, the speed of the 1.6 was a genuine surprise.

Then came the first full road test 1.1 Fiesta-motored car to contrast with a 1.3L CVH, both from Ford's press department in the UK. These were production cars rather than the Lommel hand-assembled prototypes, where they had still been finishing off the trim as we drove, so that the cars became a little tidier and more impressive by the day! Both smaller-engined examples displayed all the pitch and bounce that would be a feature of early road tests.

I was fortunate in that I sat next to former Lotus driver and then *Autocar* staffman John Miles on an aeroplane, immediately after having driven the Escort to Heathrow, with a diversion to see if the ride really was that much worse than I remembered in Belgium. John Miles kindly confirmed that they had been writing about the uncomfortable ride in recent issues, with more to come, and my self-doubts about the onset of senile dementia faded.

So far as I am aware, I have driven all the cooking range currently offered, plus the sports cousins that have been produced pre-RS Turbo in production form. It really did take until the Summer of 1983 before the ride became worthy of the immense expense and effort engineering had put into IRS, and it took the Orion to demonstrate it to most of us. I can recall the 1.6GL version of the booted saloon gliding over Sussex lanes with an easy authority that almost made me forget the outrageous thumping and groaning shocks administered by my XRs.

Ride aside the Escort was a good all-rounder originally, with excellent brakes – particularly compared with earlier Ford offerings on all but RS models – and amazing high-speed cruising capability on modest power. The 1.1 indicated 95mph and the 1.3 would shuffle along at 105mph without the deafening wind roar that a poor old Mk2 shell suffered at such speeds. The benefits at a legal 70mph were equally welcome and I see that the four-speed gearbox earned 10/10 on my assessment sheet. The handling, sheer cornering power and accurate steering also earned my appreciation at this stage, along with an interior that displayed Ford were fully aware that some potential customers had been lured away by Japanese equipment and finish.

Aside from ride quality and the engine's hoarse note of mechanical despair when asked to operate much above 5000rpm, Ford seemed to have a very serious Golf/Kadett/Astra competitor; one that was immensely improved by the five-speed gearbox, even though the change action was not so predictable and sweet as that of the original ratio quartet.

Individual model annoyances included the flashing econolights on a 1.1 I drove alongside a Fiesta for a week. With similar powerplants the Escort was severely embarrassed whenever equal acceleration rates were demanded...I am not a fan of the American-style automatic with its thumping engagement of the lock-up top gear and a generally shopping car feel to demands for extra power. Yes, it would cruise at an indicated 100mph in 1.6 litre installation with commendable economy, but anyone switching from a manual should try the automatic over varied going before paying extra.

The RS regularly finished in the top 15 on club events with a standard engine, but the springs and dampers were all changed for reasons you can see ...! I raced and rallied Escorts usually on Dunlop tyres and never had a puncture, despite abusing the covers constantly.

This little flight, captured gleefully by my former colleagues at LAT, did not end our 1976 Tour of Britain, but it was not long afterwards that our run was abruptly terminated.

In summary of the non-sporting models one could only say that they gave sporting drivers a crisp response with obviously thoroughly developed service economy and durability. Ford have managed to provide style and some enjoyable pace outside the XR and RS machinery that seems to set the car apart in the British public and fleet buyer's hearts.

Turbo alternatives

Just as their predecessors attracted all the attention of the conventional tuning business, so the front drive Escorts were quickly put through the mangle to try and avoid the humiliations that Golf GTI owners relished handing out to this overtly sporting newcomer in XR guise. At first some followed the approach found on *Autocar* staffman Peter Windsor's XR: twin, double-choke, sidedraught carburettors. 'Nothing like a pair of Webers,' in the old industry opinion, but the tendency was for fuel consumption to slump alarmingly without much more than a headache to show for the conversion in speed terms. Meanwhile the injected Golfs swept smoothly by in style.

Turbocharging was seen as the saviour in XR's carburettor days (pre-Oct 1982) and continues to be extremely popular today, although the RS Escort Turbo obviously persuaded some of those aftermarket customers away. Unfortunately I have tried only two carburettor-era Escorts with turbocharging. The first was by Janspeed and lacked any of the intercooled sophistication now expected and offered by the Salisbury company. The result was not good in economy, but the performance was spine tingling in mid-range feel, not against the watch. There was talk that I would get another chance at turbocharged Janspeed motoring after a critical *Motor Sport* test had brought their PR company down on my neck. Such a machine did not materialize, however, save for a brief squirt around a Donington handling circuit with a prototype five-speed gearbox installed.

The second car came from Ford Motor Co. and erased all those negative memories because it was so cheeky. JNO 20Y was a plain white Escort carrying Escort 1.6L badges on its unspoiled tail and an intercooled 125bhp punch beneath the bonnet! The carburated engine had an 8.5:1 CR, Garrett TBO3 turbo blowing through the Weber 32/34 DMTL

One of Maurice Selden's smart but well-used RS 2000s gains a rare respite from the rally coverage schedule of its driver.

twin-choke carburettor to provide 130lb ft torque; all part of a kit that was reduced to £1000 in anticipation of the RS Turbo's availability about six months before said 132bhp Escort materialized.

I was extremely impressed with this car, which rode on seven-spoke RS 1600i wheels (185/60 Pirellis), Bilstein dampers, 120lb in. front springs and 200lb in. rears, but even the big brakes failed to impress *Cars & Car Conversions* editor Peter Newton. He shared the car with me to Silverstone and reported better handling packages were available and that the cars Ford had lent them in full regalia scored sub-seven second times for 0-60mph, along with honest maximums beyond 125mph. In other words a 2.8-litre Capri would be left behind under acceleration and could nearly be matched on maximum speed by an Escort of 1.2 litres less...

Using an ordinary overdrive fifth Escort gearbox this '1.6L' Turbo whooshed with a distinguished part throttle whine to 100 indicated mph in third and 120mph in fourth, before settling for a displayed 130mph in top...My, how 1600 Escorts have grown up! The mid-range acceleration using some 8 psi maximum boost was seductive.

The interior was left entirely standard as part of the joke: no tachometer, no boost gauge, no fancy steering wheel. I used it mainly over a Bank Holiday to judge at a popular agricultural show (Wart-hogs are my speciality...) and it returned 20.83mpg; 25.45mpg and 22.03mpg with an average closer to 23mpg. Just about what you'd have expected from a 2.8 Capri in similar circumstances.

Race Escort via Datapost

In stark contrast to the rear drive years, my sole competition Escort front drive experience is confined to Richard Longman's 1983 Championship Trimoco Group A class winner. That was assessed on a blazing hot day with a BMW 635 to follow on the Donington circuit and it has to be said the racing Ford had brakes that were operating at another 105% efficiency over those of the BMW.

Not so the racing engine development programme at that stage. Richard Longman & Co. suffered all sorts of traumas as they tried to overcome power deficiencies with increased compression, but eventually a camshaft profile was found (after trying more than five alternatives) that did the job without such combustion chamber squish violence. When I tried the RS 1600i it had 'somewhere in the region of 155 to 160bhp,' and Richard reported, 'We get 7300 to 7400 in fifth at Silverstone. That's over 130mph, not bad for a 1600...'

The first XR3 I drove regularly was used to cover events for Motoring News *such as Northern Britain's Lindisfarne Rally. After which 'Karcher's' operatives kindly restored it to a semblance of pristine silver. The KC lamps were powerful, but properly installed Cibiés finally replaced them with less range, but a better beam spread.*

The absolute engine rpm limit was 7700 and the power unit was much smoother at these speeds than one would guess from the behaviour of its injected roadgoing counterparts.

This Escort crouched on 300lb in. rate front and rear springs and a very special Group A suspension system. At the front this was straightforward racing MacPherson strut with adjustable camber angle, bearings in the top mounts and rose-jointed lower arms, but the back was far more complex. Here the transverse lower arms featured the damper units passing clean through their fabricated steel embrace to a mounting plate a full inch below the arms. All the Ford-revised floorpan modifications had been made swiftly – front tie bar and inner transverse arm mountings points – and Longman's car had curious check straps that prevented the wheels from going onto full droop at the rear and thus inviting spectacular wheel-lifting displays. This was probably just to frighten the fierce class opposition of 1983/84...

As a front drive Escort, the handling was made even more interesting by the presence of a Ferguson viscous-control limited-slip differential (now part of the RS road car's specification and a feature of 1984 Escort Turbo Rally Championship machines) and wider tyres at the front. Avon 7.5 inch slicks were installed for the test with 7 inch wide rubber at the back, Richard Longman reporting that it took a long time to sort out such a sensitive car in respect of rim width and offset, to the eight inch maximum allowed; rims were normally two inches skinnier for wet conditions and Michelins were frequent wear at such times.

In action, the beautifully presented red Escort racer was summarized thus in the November 1983 issue of *Cars & Car Conversions*. 'That you can climb into a strange car and record a time within 4.21 seconds of a front drive ace on such a short acquaintance (I had six timed laps) says everything about the easy handling and stunning brakes possessed by this vehicle...Overall the handling is just as foolproof as you would expect of a modern front driver – and that is a cause for immense admiration, for many laps experience around Donington in road cars tells me just how much development work the team have had to do to provide such dependable progress.'

A complete contrast was the bestial rear drive Mk3 of Nick Oatway which was laid on at Goodwood later in 1983 by Holman Blackburn, who will be familiar to readers of my companion book on the Capri. In fact there was a Capri connection, for Gartrac at Godalming had inserted the ex-Capri 24-valve Ford Cosworth GA V6 in North-South configuration to drive those 11.5 inch wide rear Gotti alloys. Such engines were Capri racing fare in 1974 and also had a career at their usual 3.4 litres in F5000.

This was just a 'soft' version of the V6 with mild camshaft profiles and an estimated 430bhp at 8000rpm. Enough to shift the *four*-speed Escort to 154mph at 7400rpm at Goodwood, even with a number of skipping airborne moments to be overcome in top gear. Spring rates were 550lb in. front and 700lb in. rear, but since the whole car was of heavyweight construction in anticipation of a life in 2-litre rallycross guise, it was not surprising that the handling was distinctly agricultural. The load on the tiny steering wheel and the attitude of the car was completely governed by that torquey 3412cc, feeding around 280lb ft torque to the rear wheels at 7000rpm whenever the driver was sufficiently brave to utilize it.

I summed up in the January 1984 issue of *C&CC:* 'Although my arms ached for a couple of days afterwards, and the memories of mid-corner madness faded but slowly, I came away with affection for the white Escort, and the voracious beast within the front compartment. That Cosworth-Ford V6 really is a very interesting blend of racing and

The Gartrac Escort V6 conversion of the current body into a rear drive/150bhp roadrunner was enjoyed at Goodwood in 1983 for Cars & Car Conversions. *Rather like all those Mk1s with V6 power, but with injection refinement and speed. There was a definite limit to the braking capabilities with non-ventilated units installed at the front.*

My own XR3i poses with the Gartrac V6 road and race cars at Goodwood, the white Manns Garage car offering over 400 horsepower, enough to provide 154mph at 7400rpm that memorable day.

Unique Escort sight of the transverse engined front drive 105bhp posed alongside the Gartrac rear drive, North-South, V6s of 2.8 litres (centre, ex-Capri 2.8i) and the Ford Cosworth 3.4 litre GAA of the racer, reckoned to produce 430bhp at 8000 rpm.

production technology, with masses of torque and a surprising willingness to go for the high rpm numbers.'

On the same crystal clear Goodwood day I also had a few laps in another Gartrac rear drive Mk3. This road car was loaned by courtesy of professional coachbuilder Clive Mansfield, and was beautifully constructed around a production 160bhp Capri 2.8i powerplant, associated five-speed gearbox and drum-braked back axle. Only the 9.6in. solid front discs of Capri ancestry let this gleaming blue testimony to the best of British ingenuity languish in any department behind a properly developed factory car. Quite an achievement, turning a transverse engine front drive four-cylinder into a front motor, rear drive, six, but this showed it could be done without trace of the 'kit-built kar horror.'

RS and XR action

Both the RS1600i and the XR3i arrived for *Motor Sport* to test in time to be published alongside each other in the March 1983 issue, and I was cunning enough to pinch them both before the staff could justly relieve me of these eagerly awaited Escort newcomers. The RS 1600i was £670 more expensive than the XR at that point, but none of the journalists or traders I let out in both cars opted for anything other than the XR3i...But, as I have observed before, the public bought, and continue to pay premium prices for the RS.

Perhaps the funniest comment I had was from a senior BMW dealership representative who though the RS 1600i was 'diabolically twitchy'. Since I had emerged from a greasy roundabout in his £25,000 BMW 7-Series saloon the previous evening, with it flailing from lock-to-lock in violent fury, I thought he had a nerve throwing stones out of that particular glass house...!

The point, however, was accurate enough: the RS 1600i did flick about all over the place and there was no discernible performance advantage, however many more decals it wore. The wheels were wonderful, the seats superior and the tyres wider and lower. RS 1600i traction was definitely *avant* compared to the XR, thanks to that separated front roll bar system. My conclusion was: 'The RS 1600i is already on advance order status and is only available from RS dealers; it may well be that Ford have to make more than the 5000 needed for their sporting purposes. Personally, I think it is the car's styling and interior changes that the customers are buying, for the road performance is little different (and a lot more harshly delivered) than that of XR3i.

'As to the XR3i, it is now a worthy all-round competitor even for the Golf GTI'... The optimism of a 36 year old! After making such comments, I had to own one myself.

First there was an April 1981 to 27 September 1983 sentence of 26,003 miles to serve in HYM 220W, a brand new four-speed XR3 from the Ford Import/Export emporium in central London. In metallic silver with no options at all, for it was ordered as a staff car at *Motoring News*, it was my absolute running-in pride and joy. I could not believe the low noise levels and 30mpg plus economy at speeds up to 60mph (70mph demanded a busier 4000rpm in fourth) and it enjoyed more attention from bystanders than anything outside the Lamborghini class at that early stage in its career.

Even in that modest mileage the bills were not always as low as I would have hoped – around £100 for an exhaust system and warning light job – and the car spent more time in a garage than a Ford has any right to do. Sometimes this was just a question of personal modification for there were two sets of auxiliary lamps tried – KC from Magard and Cibié – the latter properly installed, with support arms to adjust the beams and hold them without irritating flickers. There was also a Pioneer tape player, and some 25 watt speakers of remarkable quality, which were largely wasted by mounting them in the rear side panels without any front speaker equipment at all.

Ford put a second set of Bilstein legs on the back and this did take some sting out of the ride, but the best change I made was to install the alternative NCTs in standard 185/60 sizing. I have also tried Pirelli P6, Uniroyal 340 rallye and the original Dunlop D3s on XR3/3i, and found the Goodyear best for fuss-free cornering under duress and more than adequate in the wet when worn. Their snag is a high noise level and characteristics which compound that ghastly XR3 ride.

Later in its life, the car benefited from extra underbonnet sound-proofing, with immediate benefit for the 5000rpm/90mph natural cruising gait, but it also started puking its water back in a manner that baffled the local dealer. A change of thermostat helped for a while, but it was doing it again by the time it was traded in: no, there was no sign of the head gasket weeping or allowing any other cooling ailment to develop.

When it was sold, just over two years and 26,000 miles later, it had rusted and corroded with superficial untidiness in the engine compartment, but the external paintwork was better than I have ever seen from Ford and in shining health by any standard, save around the back bumper supports, which had been assaulted by a rampant Volvo Gunship, anyway!

The XR3i was bought secondhand during a Ford delivery drivers' strike that prevented an accurate forecast of delivery dates for new cars. Thus I paid £6130 for a 7940 mile injection Escort, in the silver that always seems to decorate my cars despite a preference for blues ('Sorry Guv, silver's all we can get for the next four months,' is usually how I end up with this Germanic colouring), but this Escort was 'the business' on the extras front. Electric aerial, electric front side windows, tinted glass, tilt and slide sun roof; it was all there, bar the central locking. I took my beloved NCTs and 20,000 plus mile wheels with me, but it was a mistake. The revised camber angles of the XR3i meant that the NCTs quickly wore down to expose the uneven wear pattern they had suffered on the knock-knee carburettor car, and I was forced to buy replacement Uniroyals within 7000 miles...

I completed 21,300 miles in the XR3i and continued to like it very much, although longer acquaintance made me painfully aware that this early German-made 3i thumped its way over bumps with graceless lurches and the injection amplified some mid-range resonances. It was faster than I ever dreamed – I'll never moan about Ford putting together press test specials again – and the economy was stunning. I did 13 checks on my original XR3 and got a high of 34.6mpg and a low of 25.01mpg (it covered the Manx rally four-up) with an average of 29.88mpg. In the XR3i, I have figures, usually over far larger check mileages, from 27.45 to 33.8mpg with an average of 31.46mpg. The only modification, apart from tyres that were not originally specified for the model – although I see Cabriolets on Uniroyals – was a four-spoke TWR steering wheel that fine-tuned the driving position and slow speed shuffling comfort to perfection.

My record, however, is nothing beside the kind of mileage representatives at

They use Escort, too! I spoke to around a dozen policemen about the patrolling merits of Escort: both they and their fleet managers confirmed the reliability that I had experienced, over rather longer mileages.

Haymarket Publishing have piled up, usually reliably, in the XR3i, and their record is endorsed by *What Car?* reader Tim Colman. This Harlow resident piled up 62,000 miles on a car purchased on 23 December 1982 in an astonishingly short period of little over a year. HNO 567Y suffered a lot of warranty work compared with my car – but then it was delivered to the customer with the suspension chocks left in place, so some of the subsequent work was hardly surprising! In fact the worst fault also looked like dealer trouble to this outsider: 36,000 miles – replace rear shoes; 36,200 – 'All the brakes locked up and then released. Local dealer unable to duplicate the fault, but the car still felt wrong.' 36,800 miles – 'Brakes failed down 1 in 8 hill. Despite dual circuit brakes the hydraulic fluid made a hurried exit, and the handbrake was used in earnest. This proved to be wrongly routed brake hose chafing on the front suspension.'

This hard-driven car was equipped with 195/60 NCTs in place of the Dunlops and I could not agree more with this company car driver's comment, 'Ford Stereo Radio Cassette: this proved a totally hapless device, which even when decent speakers were fitted, still distorted.' I miss those Pioneer units and this gent also fitted Pioneer speakers, but allied with Sharp audio equipment.

The XR3i served me well and frugally until May 29 1986, when it was sold at 36,600 miles for £4075 via *Exchange & Mart.* By then it had grown a set of 195/60 BF Goodrich T/A tyres which provided phenomenal grip at the expense of a yet more rocky ride and increased twitchiness over bumpy roads.

Because the Escort had been so good to me in its various forms I decided to buy a 1986 Estate, a brand new car with the uprated 90bhp version of the 1.6 CVH running in the L-trim 5-doors. That was delivered June 4 1986 and had completed just over 31,000 miles in December 1988. Despite a specification (4-speaker stereo, light grey cloth fabric trim) and build/red paint quality beyond that which we expected, it lived a toughish life of muck and bullets variety. Usually covered in mud, but annually in Snetterton's reddish sand storms, the finish internally and externally has remained a reminder that Ford really did improve their standards throughout the front drive Escort run.

In that 30,000 miles all has not been sweetness and light. I was not surprised by the exhaust system replacement at 30,000 + or the useless 155 production tyres, you expect that kind of thing. Anyway the tyres were replaced with a 175/70 Goodrich All Season cover that was successfully blooded on the 1988 RAC Rally snows. What I do object to is the standard of servicing (yes, I have thus far gone to Ford dealerships) and the fact that the pinking suffered during its early life could have permanently damaged the engine. We tried three times to get that uphill problem fixed without success, and the standard of a minor crash repair and routine problem fixing has also been pretty dismal.

I do not have the same troubles at the BMW or Honda dealerships I have dealt with, and my daughter definitely enjoys superior (but *very* expensive) service from the Maidenhead Austin Rover distributor in her Mini. I have had at least one Ford around my life since 1969, but if anything terminates the relationship it will be the niggling everyday problems and dealership response to those snags.

Away from the Fords I pay for, the Freebies tested since the first edition of this book have included: second generation Escort RS turbos, a tuned version of same from Bristol Street Motors, Turbo Technics Garrett-boosted XR3i and the XR3i Cabriolet.

I was slightly puzzled after two outings in the standard turbocharged Escort, for it was obviously a better road car than its predecessor. I particularly liked the anti-lock braking in the snow and the quietly competent way this RS turbo devoured distances at surprising speeds. I knew (from firsthand contacts and the press) that it attracted a lot of adverse comment. Most of this I attribute to looks that were less distinguished from the XR3i than previously, and the comparative lack of apparent performance.

My XR3i went in May 1986 because this Performance Car *XR4x4 was generously allocated for my use. The '3i' was the best second-hand buy I have made, here cheered by 195/60 BF Goodrich tyres shortly before its sale.*

The launch RS Turbo was lent to me for a winter week alongside my 1.6 Estate. The anti-lock brakes worked well and the Custom Pack specification was good company.

Driving the XR3i in the later shape was fun in Finnish snow, but the car had become less competitive in performance terms versus increasing class opposition from other manufacturers. Sales were undiminished . . .

The taller final drive made motorways a doddle, but the RS driver presumably gains most driving pleasure away from the jammed confines of the M1 and M25. Then the later RS and its slightly slower accelerative ability (now well behind the £10,000 plus GTI opposition from VW and Peugeot) does not go down well. No matter that it is less quirky around the corners (better brakes and a reset VC differential help a lot), it just has not got the raw excitement of the first Escort Turbo.

Just before the 1988 Snetterton 24-hour race I was chatting to one of the men who went on to win the event, former Capri stalwart Graham Scarborough. From behind the wheel of his recently acquired C-plate turbo first edition he highlighted what the car meant to the faster driver.

'It's just so exciting. It goes like the hammers of hell, and I love the handling. Just

The Classic *Tony Dron snapped at work on the Summer 1986 launch of the RS Turbo. I enjoyed the shared miles, but the car has yet to match the reputation of its predecessor.*

The XR3i was tried again in Britain to cover a Citroen-sponsored stage rally outside Bournemouth. We had a good day at well over 30mpg, but I did not feel the need to replace my earlier car with the new model.

terrific fun...I'd missed out on one of these the first time around, but I had to have one eventually. I'm really pleased I did.' I have not found anyone that enthusiastic about the second edition and I regret to say that the privately owned example I know best had to be transported to a dealership at just over 5000 miles when the electronic management module packed up: that is what happened to my first road test turbo in 1985 at a similarly youthful stage...

Sticking with the standard cars, I tried a 1986 XR3i for a week as a possible replacement to my Y-plate example. It covered a rally in Bournemouth and exhibited the usual 33 + mpg, but it really was not up to the performance and standards of the similarly priced Peugeot 205s or slightly more expensive 8-valve Golf GTIs. It was not a bad car, but competition is hot, hot in this category. The suspension is still only adequate, rather than rewarding: the steering is as good as ever, but the inside wheel hops under power in tight

This appreciative bovine audience gathered when I decided to go topless in the loan Cabriolet. Raising the hood caused little excitement amongst the hedgerows of Buckinghamshire . . .

The Turbo Technics XR3i of 1988 not only had the choice of 130 or 160bhp from its Garrett AiResearch T25 turbo installation, but also showed the Ford RS body kit to advantage from all angles.

In and around the Bristol Street Motors Group RS Turbo the modifications provided by Mike Spence Ltd made a big difference to acceleration and top speed without diminishing town manners. Massive torque (nearly 230lb ft) and 177bhp made every trip an adventure, whilst a steady bar across the engine bay proved its worth outside competition.

corners. That is tiresome and the grip conferred by 185/60 low profile rubber is now equalled by others.

I felt the 105bhp CVH was too coarse and hoarse beyond 5000rpm without really providing the performance now expected. I have driven XR3i with 108bhp from the factory (electronically achieved). I hope that at least that level of extra performance will be in the consumer's hands around the 1990 time of publication for this second edition.

The XR3i Cabriolet was another treat for a week from Ford. Complete with power top it broke the £12,000 barrier in 1988, but it was an excellent and convenient convertible that gave a computed 33.9 to 34.8mpg. The power top was appreciated and vision was outstanding for this type of car through the glass rear screen, or with a lower level of roof stowage than the equivalent (Mk1) Golf can offer. It would even cruise with civilised draughts of open air at our legal motorway pace. In this case I would buy the Ford happily over a Golf. I see the Cabriolet's production figures were on the up when this was written.

The modified Escorts were much more fun, but do make sure you get some sort of valid warranty. Remember, Ford have mechanical reasons to restrict a standard turbo to 132bhp. My first example was a Turbo Technics XR3i with a 12 month warranty, but it had been turbocharged to provide a choice of power outputs at the flick of a steering column switch.

Position 1 gave 130bhp and the equivalent of RS turbo performance on less (0.45 bar) boost from a T25 rather than Garrett AiResearch TO3 turbocharger. Clicked to the second position, the boost was raised to 0.65 bar and things started happening a lot faster on 160bhp and 170lb ft of torque. Instead 0-60mph in the production XR3i bracket of 9.5 seconds, 6.8 seconds was claimed and the 0-100mph rush effectively halved when compared to a standard XR.

Complete with an RS body kit and over £700 spent on a suspension system that featured a replacement alloy crossmember, this turbocharged XR3i was more expensive than a production RS turbo. Yet it was distinctive and worked with exhilarating speed, even over wet roads on standard Dunlop D8s. The brakes were not so good as those of the latest turbo, but otherwise one could see why TT at Northampton have completed over a thousand such Escort turbo conversions.

Yet better still was a modified second generation turbo from Bristol Street Group in Bromley, Kent. Mike Spence Motorsport outside Reading had reprogrammed the electronic engine management and added a Lancia Thema intercooler to reduce considerably intake charge temperatures beyond that possible with the small production item.

The result was a massive 228lb ft of torque at 4000rpm and 177bhp on 5500rpm. All enough to provide a truly memorable, yet utterly civilized, RS turbo for it ran only 0.6 bar maximum boost. This BSG Escort RS was claimed to have reached 146mph at 6400rpm, and it certainly went with a vengeance.

When I tried it in the Summer of 1987, there was no doubt it was just as quick as the lighter production racing 'Mk1s' I write about elsewhere. Durability doubts pushed firmly to one side, I think that is the kind of specification that would interest me in a modified Escort. Ride and handling were amply improved via Koni dampers and an engine bay brace and the complete car added up an extra £1500 or so, well spent.

Gartrac's Euro-Champ recipe

Although the Gartrac formula proved popular for rear drive in what Henry intended to be a front drive Escort, their ultimate expression of Escort design freedom was in producing a 4-WD rallycrosser of a maximum 560bhp. This massive output and approximately 400 lb ft torque was generated by the proven Zakspeed 1.9-litre turbo, based around a Ford cylinder block and Cosworth BD 16-valve origins.

Creators David Bignold (Gartrac) Mike Endean (Xtrac-Hewland transmissions), and driver/entrepreneur Martin Schanche conceived the basic idea of a 4-WD Escort at the November 1982 British Rallycross GP at Brands Hatch. A year later, Schanche débuted the corporate blue and white Ford with a win. It went on to demolish all opposition – Quattro, Porsche and allcomers – through a 22-win 1984 season that also secured the Norwegian and

My first RS Turbo Escort outing was in a prototype that was a little more dilapidated than this example, but drove beautifully. Handling, traction, ride and superbly-mannered turbo installation were the primary memories.

J.W. driving the Xtrac 4-WD Turbo Escort; the quickest 0-60mph car Motor *had ever tested. It averaged 2.7 seconds to 60mph, and under 7 seconds to 100mph.*

his unique Ford Escort the most prestigious title in this sprint sport: European Rallycross Champions.

Another rallycross champion of 1984 was 35 year old John Welch, a panel shop proprietor, who secured the British title with a rear drive 2.3-litre Escort, complete with Chevy-Cosworth Vega cylinder head. For much of 1984, Gartrac constructed a second Escort of the 'Xtrac' 4-WD formula, and it was this similarly Zakspeed-powered device that I drove early in 1985, when it had still to compete.

Naturally the car was immaculate, but its stunning qualities were the acceleration (0-80mph was measured at 3 seconds for Schanche's car in Norway!), traction that could be dialled to suit any surface, and an overall efficiency way beyond that even exhibited by quadruple World Championship winner Peugeot's 205 T16. This Escort weighed slightly less than the French car 2046lb (930kg) and yet its maximum power was some 210bhp beyond that normally run by Peugeot, in January 1985. A few weeks later I arranged to drive the Welch IRS Xtrac rallycrosser again, and *Motor* measured the performance results, including 0-60mph in an average 2.7 seconds, and 0-100mph in less than 7 seconds! Its 0-60mph performance was still unmatched in *Motor*'s testing experience which included F1 turbo cars and 1000bhp drag racers, before its annexing by *Autocar* in 1988.

Impressive though such comparisons and statistics can be, none of the figures really mattered when driving the car. For it is the ease with which Xtrac Escort delivers slip-free speed that is etched on my memory. There are a lot of cockpit controls: eight dials, including a Jones tachometer that records 9400rpm about as fast as you can read it, plus levers to control power split (from 50-50 front to rear, to 28-72 per cent with that lever fully back); individual cockpit anti-roll bar adjustment; and handwheels for boost (max, 1.6bar/23psi) or front to rear brake bias.

The controls become second nature very quickly, however. Thus one finds the way in which this Escort can turn horizon into NOW, increasingly seductive. The DGB Hewland five-speed (as for an early TAG-McLaren) matches the turbo's astounding 9000rpm to 120mph with equal alacrity. Yet the car is so easy to learn that it can be spun around in 360° circles in first gear with photographic accuracy.

At the serious end of its capabilities the urge of 16-valves, twin overhead camshafts and turbocharging turn long and muddy straights into rapid history. An amazing 9000rpm fourth gear pace is so immediately available, even over *very* slippery surfaces.

Handling? Really the Endean version of 4-WD, that allows you to split power bias front to rear, on the move, works exceptionally well. With the drilled aluminium lever fully forward on the 50-50 setting, standing starts to 100mph are accomplished within split seconds of turbo Porsches with yet another 100 to 150bhp. This Escort, however, has the handling to overtake more basic 4-WD conversions at will. Pulling the lever back provides instant tailslides without the need to left-foot brake in the classic front drive/Quattro manner. So it is actually quite a straightforward car to drive faster than a Quattro on first acquaintance.

John Welch generously allowed me to drive the Xtrac car a total of three times, and each was a pleasure that I will not forget. I think the fact that Jonathan Palmer could switch from Formula 1 Tyrrell to the Escort at the 1987 Brands Hatch Rallycross GP and do so well emphasised the friendly speed these devices provided in an hostile environment. Rallycross novice Jonathan won a tough B-final at international level to endorse my opinion that these were the finest competition Escorts of the front drive era. Even in 1988, still totally without factory support and years after the Zakspeed Capris were obsolete, the Xtrac Escorts were up there with the Evolution RS 200s and the supercars of the Lancia/Peugeot stock.

More competition Escort mileage came in the simplest of specifications, 'showroom' Group N. I think it is possible that I simply drove the same RS turbo in different colours, the first time immediately following the Snetterton 24-hour victory. The Abbott/Smith 24-hour winner was one of two such turbos backed by Ilford and prepared by McCrudden Associates/Tracker Vehicles for 1985/86. In 1987 Richard Asquith Motorsport acquired one of those RS turbos and I also drove that, but this time at Mallory Park.

If it was the same car, it certainly did not feel like it. For the 24-hour winner was on Dunlop D4s and mild boost press elevation brought slightly under 160bhp, whereas the Jones version was sampled fresh and ready for the 1987 season with more than 165bhp present. The 1987 rendering also ran on buffed BF Goodrich TA R/1 tyres and was clearly a lot faster and a lot less prone to understeer than the tired 24-hour winner, which would plough its Dunlops into overheated tantrums if pushed at all hard into the unforgiving

Coram curve at Snetterton. In neither case did the car have anything significant in the way of brakes, but otherwise its stable ease of driving and good power-to-weight ratio would have kept it on the pace versus the BMW and Mercedes 16v saloons (2.3/16 and M3).

The truly European Escort and its transatlantic namesakes have served to remind us of a slice of motoring life that serves households great and small, as well as companies of multi-national muscle, policemen, taxi drivers, driving schools, the handicapped, as well as the enthusiastic owners who tend to buy books such as this one.

Here's looking at the plastic 4-WD Turbo Escort to take us into Year 2000 with 50mpg/150mph and minimal servicing ...!

The Ilford-backed Escort RS Turbo was sampled immediately after the 1985 Snetterton 24-hours in which it finished sixth. A year later an Escort RST won outright from the same team.

John Welch (left) and J.W. discuss a later version of the Xtrac turbo 4x4 rallycross contender. The photo lower overleaf shows the command centre of the car. It deployed its enormous power through a massive Hewland 5-speed gearbox.

According to Ford, 1988 output of Escort reached a record 962,000 Worldwide, so that more than 9 million front drive Escorts had been made, 1980-88. For the Autumn 1989 motor shows Ford announced 1990 specification changes that also embraced performers such as the XR3i (seen here) and the RS Turbo. In Britain the Popular and Popular Plus remained as before, but the L, LX, Sport, GL and Ghias gained small trim changes. These included a load compartment light and passenger grab handle at the lower end of the range. Further up, there was variable intermittent wiping, dual tone horns and extended centre console from GL through to Turbo.

Mechanically, XR3i gained most, picking up some 1990 Fiesta XR2i CVH technology to boost power from 105 to 108bhp. Changes included EEC-IV Ford engine management, revised head porting and inlet manifolding.

Visually both XR3i and Turbo gained "droop wing" rear spoilers, that for Turbo colour coded; it was the third rear spoiler design for XR3i since 1980! Escort XR3i also gained Cosworth Sapphire RS-style alloy wheels (but in 14 inch diameters).

Appendix 1

Production Escort specifications

17 January 1968

Ford Escort 1100 De Luxe & Super
Ford Escort 1300 Super
Ford Escort 1300 GT
Ford Escort Twin Cam (see Appendix II)

Body: Unitary steel, two doors, 8 cu ft rear boot. Length, 156.6in; width, 61.8in; height, 53.0in; wheelbase, 94.5in; front track, 49.0in; rear track, 50.0in. Average turning circle, 29ft. Standard on all models were 9 gallon fuel tank, speedometer (90mph for 1100), distance recorder fuel gauge, and Super had water temperature dial. On GT a rev-counter, battery charge indicator and oil pressure gauge were added. Single-speed wipers; floor button operation for screenwashers; two speed heater fan. De Luxe had 7.0in round lamps; Super, GT and early Twin Cam, 9.0in wide rectangular.

Weights: At kerb, 1100 DL, 1641lb (744kg). 1100 Super, 1658lb (752kg). 1300 Super, 1674lb (759kg). 1300 GT, 1716lb (778kg).

Engines: All models had an inline, water-cooled, four-cylinder with . pushrod overhead valve operation and five main bearings. Ford 'crossflow' Kent series with cast-iron cylinder block, head and exhaust manifolding (GT had tubular steel exhaust); alloy inlet manifold. Rotor type oil pump, 4.7 pint (2.7 litre) engine oil, 5.4 pint (3.3 litre) with filter. See relevant Chapter for October 1970 and subsequent modifications. Engine dimensions: *1100,* capacity 1098cc (80.98 x 53.29mm). Ford single-choke downdraught carburettor, 9:1 CR. Inlet valves 1.41in, exhaust 1.24in. Max power (gross figures), 53bhp @ 5500rpm/62lb ft @ 3000rpm. *1300 Super,* capacity 1298cc (80.98 x 62.99mm). Ford single-choke downdraught carburettor, 9:1 CR. Valve sizes, as 1100. Max power (gross), 63bhp @ 5000rpm/75.5lb ft @ 2500rpm. *1300 GT,* cubic capacity and bore x stroke as 1300 Super. Weber 32 DFE twin-choke downdraught carburettor on usual 9:1 CR. Enlarged 1.50in. inlet valves, normal 1100/1300 exhaust (1.24in.) and tubular four-branch exhaust manifold. Max power (gross), 75bhp @ 5400rpm/91lb ft @ 3800rpm.

Transmission: Front engine, rear drive through live back axle. Single dry-plate, cable-operated clutch, four-speed all-synchromesh gearbox. Clutch plate diameter, 6.5in. for 1100s and 7.5in. for 1300/1300 GT. Gearbox ratios: 1st, 3.356 (GT, 3.337); 2nd, 2.185 (GT, 1.995); 3rd, 1.425

(GT. 1.418); 4th, direct (1.00) all models; Reverse, 4.235 (GT, 3.867). Final drive, 4.125 on all models. Oil capacities, 2.0 pint (1.136 litre), rear axle and 1.6 pint (0.909 litre) gearbox, all models.

Suspension: MacPherson strut front with coil springs and telescopic shock-absorption using hydraulic units; rubber mounted upper bearing; compression strut and track control arm (TCA) lower location. Three semi-elliptic leaf springs of 47in. length plus hydraulic shock absorbers mounted at an inclined, 60.5°, for live back axle suspension. Modified during late run, see relevant Chapter. Body to upper axle twin radius arms provided on GT initially, then discontinued.

Wheels & tyres: Pressed steel, 12in. diameter. Standard on original 1100 and 1300s was a 3.5in. C-rim with 5.50 cross-plies; only GT had standard radials, 155 section on a 4.5in. C-rim. Radials, like front disc brakes, were optionally available on non-GT models.

Steering: Three-spoke plastic dished wheel commanding 16.4:1 ratio rack and pinion through 14.9in. diam rim. *Motor* measured 3.5 turns lock-to-lock.

Brakes: 1100 & 1300 non-GT originally standard with 8.0in diam x 1.5in. lining width, four-wheel drum brakes. Option on 1100 & 1300, standard on GT, front 8.6in discs with usual 8.0in. rear drums; servo-assistance supplied with front disc brakes only. Swept area (drums), 150.8sq in. Discs/drums, 163.4sq in.

Electrical system: Dynamo and engine bay 12v 38 Ah battery.

Servicing: Engine oil change, etc. every 5000 miles.

Prices: 1100 DL, £635. 9s 7d; 1100 Super, £666 4s 2d; 1300 Super, £690 15s 10d; 1300 GT, £764 10s 10d.

23 January 1975

Ford Escort restyled into new bodywork with two, three or four-door alternatives, four basic engines and 18 model choices at launch.

Models: Two-door saloons – 1100, 1100L, 1300L, 1300GL, 1300 Sport, 1600 Sport, 1300 Ghia, 1600 Ghia. Four-door saloons – As for two-door, but no 1300 or 1600 Sport. Three-door estates – 1100, 1300, 1300L and 1300GL.

Bodies: Unitary steel, two, three (estate) and four doors with 10.3cu ft rear boot on saloons

with 31.53cu ft for estate. Length 156.6in. (estate, 160.8in.); width, 60.5in. (estate, 62.8in.); height, 53.8in. (estate, 54.5in.); wheelbase, 94.8in. saloons & estates; front track, 49.3in; rear track, 50.3in. Average turning circle, 29.2ft. Standard features on all models included 9 gallon fuel tank, speedometer (120mph on Sport), distance recorder, fuel gauge and water temperature gauge, plus alternator, two-speed wipers and heater fan, reversing lamps (not on base model), electric screenwash and radial-ply tyres. Square headlamps with halogen bulbs for GL & Ghia; round lamps plus spotlamp auxiliaries for Sport, also with halogen bulbs – Ghia shared auxiliary lamps. Weights: Two-door Ford minimums, 1100, 1844lb (838kg); 1300, 1872lb (851kg); 1600 Sport, 1941lb (882kg); 1600 Ghia, 1987lb (903kg). Estate 1100, 2002lb (910kg)

Engines; All models inline, four-cylinder, water cooled, with pushrod OHV, five main bearings, from the Ford Kent 'crossflow' series. Cast-iron head and block with cast nodular graphite iron crankshafts and aluminium pistons with Heron principle bowl-in crown combustion chambers. Rotor oil pump, warning light triggered below 6lb sq in. (std max pressure blow-off, 35-40lb sq in.) with 21lb sq in. normal at 2000rpm and 80°C. Capacity 4.8 pint 6.5 pint with filter.

Engine dimensions: *1100*, capacity 1097cc (80.98 x 53.29mm). Ford Motorcraft GPD downdraught carburettor, 9:1 CR. Inlet valves 1.41in. exhaust 1.24in. Max power (DIN), 48bhp @ 5000rpm/54lb ft @ 3000rpm. *1300*, for models except Ghia and Sport, capacity 1297cc (80.98 x 62.99mm). Ford Motorcraft GPD single choke downdraught carburettor, 9.2:1 CR. Inlet valves 1.50in. with 1.24in. exhaust as for 1100. Max power (DIN), 57bhp @ 5500 rpm/67lb ft @ 3000rpm. *1300 Sport & Ghia*, capacity, bore and stroke, plus 9.2:1 CR as for ordinary 1300 but carburation by Weber 32/36 DGV twin choke, downdraught. Inlet and exhaust valves as for 1300 but with 272° camshaft duration (versus 256° normal) and tubular four-branch exhaust manifold. Max power (DIN), 70bhp @ 5500rpm/68lb ft @ 4000rpm. *1600 Sport & Ghia*, capacity 1598cc (80.98mm x 77.62mm). Weber 32/36 DGV twin-choke downdraught carburettor, 9:1 CR. Inlet valves 1.54in; exhausts 1.32in. GT cam inlet & exhaust 272° duration as for 1300 Sport, but 54° overlap instead of 50°. Tubular exhaust manifold. Max power (DIN), 84bhp @ 5500rpm/92lb ft @ 2500rpm.

Transmission: Front engine, rear drive through live back axle. Single dry 7.5in. diameter plate clutch with cable operation and four speed, all-synchromesh gearbox. Ford C3 automatic with torque convertor operation optionally available. *Manual 1100 & 1300* gearbox ratios; 1st, 3.656; 2nd, 2.185; 3rd, 1.425; 4th, direct 1.00. Reverse 4.235. *1300 Ghia/Sport & 1600 equivalent* ratios: 1st, 3.337; 2nd, 1.995; 3rd, 1.418; 4th, direct (1.00). Reverse, 3.868. Final drive ratios (mph per 1000 rpm in brackets): *1100,* 4.125 (16.3); *1300,* 3.89 (17.1); *1300 Sport & Ghia* 4.125 (16.3); *1600 Sport & Ghia* 19.0). *Automatic* (not available, 1100 or 1300 S & Ghia): 1st, 2.474; 2nd, 1.474; 3rd, 1.00. Reverse, 2.111. Rear axle ratios, 3.89 (1300) and 3.54 (1600).

Suspension: MacPherson strut front with lower link to triangulated roll bar, hydraulic shock-absorption. Rear live axle unit anti-tramp roll bar and vertical telescopic shock-absorbers; three leaf springs of 2.36 in. width. Spring rates, at wheel: Front of all but 1300 & 1600 Sport, 96lb in. Sports, 109lb in. Rear, 105lb in. for all but Estates & Sports, which were 116lb in.

Wheels & tyres: Pressed steel 4-stud of 4.5in. rim width (5.0in. optional or std for Ghias & Sports); drum-braked models had 12in. diameter, rest 13in. Tyres, 155 SR radials except Sport, 175/70 SR.

Steering: Rack & pinion, 17.91:1 ratio-3.5 turns lock-to-lock.

Brakes: Drums all round std on 1100 only with front discs an option as for rest of range. Sport & Ghia had std servo-assist, option on other disc-braked models; all had divided circuit brake systems. *1100,* front drums 8.0in. diam. x 1.75in. width and rear 8.0in. diam x 1.5in. width drums. *1300,* front 9.6in. diam discs with 1100 rear drums. *1300 & 1600 Sports Ghias,* front 9.6in. diam. discs and 9.0in. diam x 1.7in. wide back drums. All have rear self-adjustment.

Electrical system: Alternator, 28 to 55 amp, according to model with 12v battery and 38, 44 or 55 Ah rating.

Servicing: Engine oil change and major service every 6000 miles.

Prices: Car announced in January, sold from 4 March 1975 in UK. Typical range prices, to nearest £: 1100 two-door, £1440; 1100 four-door, £1497; 1300 two-door, £1502; 1300 four-door, £1559; 1300L four-door, £1648; 1300GL, four-door, £1777; 1300 Sport two-door, £1803; 1600 Sport two-door, £1860; 1300 Ghia four-door,

£2068; 1600 Ghia four-door, £2125; 1300 estate, £1701; 1300GL estate, £1920. Automatic transmission, £146 extra.

In June 1975 Ford lowered the Escort starting price with the 1100 Popular two-door at £1299 and the 1100 two-door Popular Plus at £1399.

3 September 1980

Ford go front drive with new Escort launched in three-door hatchback, three-door estate and five-door hatchback bodies. There are three engine sizes and all-independent suspension. Derivatives also available in the USA as well as normal Ford of Europe markets.

Models: Three-door hatchbacks; 1.1 base, 1.1L, 1.3 base, 1.3L, 1.3GL, 1.3 Ghia, 1.6L, 1.6 Ghia, N.B; XR3 & estate phased-in November 1980 – XR3 detailed in Appendix II; estates detailed in relevant Chapter. Five-door new Escort hatchbacks were available in exactly the same 1.1 base to 1.6 Ghia span as the three-door.

Bodies: Unitary steel, three- and five-door hatchbacks, three-door estates. Rear boot holds 10.3cu ft, shelf fitted, 20.3cu ft without; 48.7cu ft available behind rear seats. Estates quoted at 27cu ft, rear seats upright, 57cu ft with back seats down. Length, 156.3in. (estate, 162.0in.); width, 62.5in (estates, 64,6in.); height, 52.6in. (estate, 54.5in.); wheelbase, 94.4in; front track, 54.5in; rear track, 56.3in. Average turning circle from 32.9 to 33ft. Standard equipment included 9 gallon fuel tank, 7.87in. diam. vacuum servo assistance for front disc, rear drum brakes – servo optional on 1.1 in UK. Speedometer, distance recorder, fuel and temperature gauges augmented by GL/Ghia spec. five light advance warning of: low engine oil level, low coolant level, depleted screenwasher bottle content, worn front brake pads, empty fuel tank, and brake fluid low level. GLs took analogue clock into main instrumentation with Ghia/XR3 digital clock roof mounted and tachometer reading to 7000rpm in main cluster, replacing GL clock. All models had two-speed wipers with intermittent facility on all but base as std; two-speed heater fan only on base, otherwise three-speed. All models except base had reclining seat backrests.

Weights: Ford only quoted 1687lb (765kg) for base three-door. *Autocar* Buyer's Guide: 1.1, as

Ford; 1.3 three-door, 1753lb (797kg); 1.6 three door, 1907lb (867kg); 1.1 & 1.1L estates, 1808lb (822kg); 1.3 & 1.6 estates, 1874lb (852kg). Ford Escort Customer handbook 1980, July, quotes from 1782lb (810kg) for base 1.1 up to 2013lb (915kg) for *all* estates!

Engines: All inline, four-cylinder mounted transversely but 1.1 had Fiesta-derived Kent series of cast-iron construction and pushrod OHV. The 1.3 litre and 1.6 shared new Ford Bridgend Compound Valve Angle Hemispherical Head (CVH) with single belt-driven OHC, hydraulic self-adjusting valve lifters and alloy cylinder head on iron block.

Engine dimensions: *1.1,* capacity 1117cc (73.96 x 64.98mm). Ford variable venturi (VV) single-choke carburettor, 9:1 CR. Max power (DIN PS) 55bhp @ 5700rpm/61lb ft @ 4000rpm. *1.3, 1.3L, 1.3GL, 1.3 Ghia,* capacity 1296cc (79.96 x 64.52mm). Ford Motorcraft VV single choke carburettor, 9.5:1 CR. Inlet valves 1.65in., exhaust 1.34in. Alloy inlet and cast-iron exhaust manifolding all models CVH. Max power, (DIN PS) 69bhp @ 6000rpm/74lb ft @ 3500rpm. *1.6L, 1.6GL & 1.6 Ghia,* capacity 1597cc (79.96 x 79.52mm). Ford Motorcraft VV single-choke carburettor, 9.5:1 CR. Inlet valves 1.65in. as 1.3; exhaust 1.46in. Max power (DIN PS) 79bhp @ 5700rpm/92lb ft @ 3000rpm.

Transmission: Transverse front engine with inline gearbox and drive to front wheels. Single dry-plate, cable-operated, clutch with 6.5in. plate diam. for 1.1, 7.5in. for 1.3, 8.0 in. for 1.6. Gearbox ratios for 1.1: 1st, 3.58; 2nd, 2.05; 3rd, 1.35; 4th, 0.95. Reverse, 3.77. Gearbox ratios for 1.3 & 1.6: 1st, 3.15; 2nd, 1.91; 3rd, 1.27; 4th, 0.95. Reverse, 3.61. Final drive ratios: 1.1, 4.06:1; 1.3, 3.84; 1.6, 3.58. Gearbox oil capacity, 4.9 pints. N.B. five-speed transmissions were phased into the range during 1982 for the UK. Vans carried a 4.06 final drive but were also not part of the original range; it was announced in February 1981 for the UK. Mph per 1000rpm figures: 1.1, 16.68; 1.3, 17.89; 1.6, 19.19mph.

Suspension: Front MacPherson struts with coil springs and telescopic, twin-tube, shock-absorption. Lower link triangulated with tie bar on 1100 and with integral front roll bar on 1300 and 1600. Independent rear with transverse lower arms and separate coil spring mounting inboard of twin tube telescopic dampers; longitudinal location links from lower arms forward. Detail damper, front and rear track control arm bush alterations follow launch press criticism: all Armstrong or Armstrong front/Woodhead rear dampers specified for UK Escorts.

Wheels & tyres: Pressed steel 13 x 4¹/2in. width on base & L, GL & Ghia take 13 x 5 in. rims in steel. Smallest rims take 145 SR 13 radials, 5J fit 155 SR with 175/79 SR also optionally available for 5J x 13 (often fitted UK Ghias).

Steering: Rack & pinion with 19.64:1 ratio giving 3.7 (sometimes specified as 3.69) turns lock-to-lock for average 32.47ft turning circle. Wheel diameter 14.75in on all but Ghias which are specified as 15in. diam.

Brakes: All but base 1.1 (for which it was an option) had 7.87in. diam vacuum servo-assistance; diagonally split twin-circuit; tandem master cylinder and 'g-sensing valve' to sense rear wheel lock up. All models had 9.45in. diam. front discs, but 1.6-litre utilized 29-rib ventilation slots with 2½ times extra thickness in disc. Rears, all models: drums of 7.08 x 1.25in. self-adjusting. Total swept area 608sq in. front and 540.31sq in. rear.

Electrical system: 12v 43 Ah battery; 45amp alternator. Breakerless ignition on CVH engines only; 1.1 ex-Fiesta motor had distributor by Bosch or Lucas. Motorcraft plugs for 1.3, Super AGP 12C or Super AGPR 12 C with the latter preferred for 1.6 Halogen or tungsten bulbs originally specified with 110/120w rating.

Servicing: Engine oil & filter change and service every 6000 miles/6 months.

Prices: Three-door hatchbacks: 1.1, £3374; 1.3, £3543; 1.1L, £3695; 1.3L, £3865; 1.6L, £4021; 1.6GL, £4368; 1.6 Ghia, £4883. Five door hatchbacks: 1.1, £3524; 1.3, £3693; 1.1L, £3845; 1.3L, £4015; 1.3GL, £4361; 1.6L, £4171; 1.6 Ghia, £5033.

January 1989

'Mk 4' Escort range specifications, including March 1986 body and mechanical changes, plus revisions in production to January 1989. Prices, as at December 1988.

Models: In three-door hatchback: 1.3 HCS four- and five-speed; 1.4 CVH five-speed; 1.6 CVH five-speed; 1.8 diesel five-speed. In five-door hatchback: as three-door plus 1.6 CVH automatic. In two-door Cabriolet: 1.6 fuel injected CVH five-speed. In three-door Estate: 1.3 HCS four- and five-speed; 1.8 Diesel five-speed. In five-door Estate: as three-door, plus 1.4 CVH five-speed; 1.6 CVH in five-speed manual or three-speed automatic. Performance XR3i/RS Turbo update in Appendix II but note that Cabriolet now confined to mostly XR3i running gear, including engine and transaxle.

Body/trim: Unitary steel construction in styles listed above. Polycarbonate bumpers. Trim levels developed to a choice of: Popular, L and XR3i in three-door; Popular, L, LX, GL and Ghia in five-door. XR3i motivation and trim levels in Cabriolet. Estates in Popular and L (three-door) or L and GL in five-door. Hatchback rear boot holds 12.7cu ft (seats raised) and 37.1cu ft, seats lowered. Estate equivalent figures: 12.7cu ft and 42.4cu ft. The 60:40 unequal split rear seat standard on all but Cabrios and Populars.

Dimensions: Length 158.3in (Estate, 160.6in); width, 72.2in; height 53.9in (Estate, 54.7in, Cabrio; hood up, 55.2in); wheelbase, 94.5in.

Weights: Ford quoted the following in 1988-89 winter. Lightest, 1.3 HCS four-speed in three-door 840kg (1848lb). Heaviest, 1.8 Diesel five-door Estate and 1.6 auto in same body 955kg (2101lb).

Standard equipment: Locking 10.3gal/47 litre fuel tank; vacuum servo assistance for disc front, drum rear brakes (optional anti-lock SCS on all but automatics). Central speedometer, distance and trip recorders, fuel and water temperature gauges on all, plus rev-counter on all but Popular, and L-trimmed Escorts. Two-speed wipers and intermittent throughout; tailgate wipe on all bar Cabriolet. High security locks revised further in production; door handle trim release rockers (no ledge 'buttons'). Central locking standard on: LX, GL, Ghia, XR3i/Cabrio and five-door GL Estate, but without tailgate action on Estate. Heated rear windows throughout, plus front and rear emergency tow hooks. Halogen headlights, side repeater flashers, rear fog and reversing lamps, hazard warning flashers all standard; auxiliary driving lights only standard XR3i and Cabrio.

Engines: All water-cooled, inline four cylinders mounted across engine bay (transverse). Using petrol and capable of adjustment to lead-free fuels were the HCS (High Compression Swirl) and CVH (Compound Valve angle Hemispherical head) units. The HCS does not use an overhead camshaft, but the CVH does with cogged belt drive. Diesel grew from 1.6 to 1.8 litres in 1988.

Engine dimensions: Also listed in separate and subsequent appendix, bar HCS which is described in Chapter 12. Key figures at Jan 1989 were: 1.3 HCS, capacity 1297cc; compression, 9.5:1; manual choke control of twin-choke carburettor; electronic ignition, no contact breaker points. **Max power:** 63bhp at 5000rpm. **Max torque:** 10.3Mkp/75lb ft @ 3000rpm. **Max safe continuous engine speed** 5450rpm. 1.4 CVH, capacity 1392cc; compression, 9.5:1; manual choke control of twin-choke carburettor; electronic ignition. **Max power:** 75bhp at 5600rpm. **Max torque:** 11.1Mkp/80.3lb ft @ 4000rpm. **Max safe continuous engine speed:** 6200rpm. 1.6 CVH, capacity 1597cc; compression 9.5:1; automatic and twin-choke carburettor; electronic ignition. **Max power:** 90bhp @ 5800rpm. **Max torque:** 13.6Mkp/98lb ft @ 4800rpm. **Max safe continuous engine speed:** 6200rpm. 1.6i CVH, capacity 1597cc; compression 9.5:1; Bosch K-Jetronic fuel injection; electronic ignition. **Max power:** 105bhp @ 6000rpm. **Max torque:** 14.1Mkp/102lb ft @ 4800rpm. **Max safe continuous engine speed:** 6300rpm. 1.8 Diesel, capacity 1769cc, compression 21.5:1; mechanical fuel-injection with compression (sparkless) ignition. **Max power:** 60bhp @ 4800rpm. **Max torque:** 11.2Mkp/81lb ft @ 2500rpm. **Max unladen engine speed:** 5350rpm.

Transmissions: Front drive transaxles in four- and five-speed carried over from earlier models. Change quality improved during 1987, see Chapter 12.

Suspension: Revised in detail over previous model but principles remained. Front: MacPherson strut, Track Control Arm, anti-roll bar forward of axle. Rear: independent via pressed-steel arms, strut damping, concentric coil springs, longitudinal tie bar location.

Wheels & tyres: Standard on all but XR3i/Cabrio were 5x13 inch steel wearing 155 SR on all but Ghia and LX, which used the same wheel and 175/70 13 tyres. Cabrios and XRs had a 6x14in steel as standard, or for £250 an optional alloy in the same sizing. Both wore 185/60 HR 14 low profile tyres.

Steering: Rack and pinion carried over, but 1989 model year (post September 1988) had variable ratio incorporated.

Brakes: Carried over, but Lucas Girling anti-lock option (only initially standard on RS Turbo) at £375 in Jan 1989 available on all manual gearbox Escorts during production run.

Servicing: Every 6000 miles/6 months oil and filter change, later amended to every 12,000 miles/12 months after first 6000 mile service. Standard warranty 12 months/unlimited mileage; 6 year anti-corrosion warranty. Extra cost 3 year/60,000 mile warranties available.

Prices: (bracketed for March 1986 intro cost of equivalent model): Popular 3-dr, £6121 (£4921.27); Popular 5-dr, £6388 (no equivalent); Popular 3dr 1.8D, £6955 (1.6 D, £6078.86); 1.3L 5-dr, £7252 (£5930.12); 1.3L 5-dr, £7519 (£6149.98); 1.4L 3-dr, £7427 (£6140.12); 1.4L 5-dr, £7694 (£6539.98); 1.6L 5-dr, £7926 (£6712.01); 1.8DL 3-dr, £7911 (£6871.51); 1.8DL 5-dr, £8178 (£7091.37). 1.4LX 5-dr, £8112 (None); 1.6LX 5-dr, £8344 (none). 1.4GL 5-dr, £8410 (£6919.35); 1.6GL 5-dr, £8642; 1.8GL Diesel, 5-dr £8894 (£7491.17). 1.4 Ghia 5-dr, £9183 (£7553.64); 1.6 Ghia 5-dr, £9415 (£7746.10). 1.6 XR3i Cabriolet, £11,874 (£9816.55).

Estates: Prices for 1989 only, but note that the March 1986 range of Estates spanned £5373.02 for a three-door to £7563.56 for the 1.6GL of five-doors. As for all other Escorts it should be noted that Ford frequently shuffle extra equipment down range and swop labels, obscuring accurate equipment level comparisons. For 1989 the Estate range lined up as follows: 1.3 Popular 3dr, £6667; 1.8 Diesel Popular 3dr, £7501; 1.3L 3-dr, £7798; 1.3L 5-dr, £8065; 1.4L 5-dr, £8240; 1.6L 5-dr, £8472; 1.8L Diesel 5-dr, £8724; 1.4GL 5-dr, £8956; 1.6GL 5-dr, £9188.

Appendix II

High-performance Escort specifications

The Performers I: 17 January 1968 to 31 December 1974

Ford Escort Twin Cam
Ford Escort RS 1600
Ford Escort Mexico 1600GT
Ford Escort RS 2000

Body: Type 49 unitary steel with production changes: flared front wings; ex-Escort van quarter front bumpers; strengthened chassis rails; stronger flitch plates; reinforced front suspension top mounting plates; pick-up brackets for rear radius arms; rear stone deflector to protect rear valance; revised aperture for remote-control gear linkage, approximately ¾in. rear of standard. From Mid-1969 onward (Ford announced at October Motor Show) seven in. round headlamps, QI bulbs and alternator specified instead of dynamo on TC, fitted to subsequent RS product. Battery originally in boot, moved to engine bay in 1973 allowing vertical spare wheel mounting and restoration of some luggage space; consequent changes in braker servo location etc, see text. All models had standard 9 gallon tank, six dial ex-GT instrumentation (but with speedometers from 110 to 140mph and appropriate tachometer markings). See text for seat/steering wheel combinations and options that included Custom/Rallye/Race and Special Build alternatives on RS product.

Dimensions: Length, 156.6in; width, 61.8in; height, 54.5in; wheelbase, 94.5in; front track, 51 in; rear track, 52 in; ground clearance, 6.3in; turning circle, 30ft. These are the original Escort TC factory figures; only the overall height should show any significant difference on later models, and then I suspect even RS 2000 with decambered rear springs (height, 53.0in.) would only be down to original Boreham build road car height. A sort of production return of status quo...

Weights: Original factory Escort TC, 1730lb (784.7kg). In 1974 the official weights were: Mexico, 1731lb (785kg); RS 2000, 2018lb (915kg), distributed 54 per cent front, 46 per cent rear; RS 1600 (iron block), 1920lb (870kg) distributed, 51 per cent front, 49 per cent rear.

Engines: All inline fours with five main bearings and water cooling via front radiator (electric fan on RS 2000). Iron cylinder block, ex-Ford 1500GT non-crossflow, for Twin Cam, the rest all with taller 1600GT/E crossflow block. *Escort TC:* Alloy Lotus 8-valve DOHC head with chain drive, 1558cc (82.55 x 72.75mm), 9.5:1 CR x 2 Weber 40 DCOE sidedraught twin-choke carburettors. Max power: 115 (gross) or 109.5bhp (net) @ 6000rpm/106lb ft (gross) or 106.5lb ft @ 450-0rpm. *Escort RS 1600:* Alloy Cosworth 16-valve DOHC head with belt drive, 1601cc (80.993 x 77.724mm), 10:1 CR x 2 Weber 40 DCOE 48 or Dellorto DHLAE sidedraught twin-choke carburettors. Max power: 120bhp DIN @ 6500rpm/112lb ft DIN @ 4000rpm. *Escort Mexico:* Cast-iron pushrod OHV 8-valve Ford crossflow head, 1599cc (80.97 x 77.62mm), 9:1 CR x 1 twin-choke Weber 32 DFM carburettor. Max power: 86bhp DIN @ 5500rpm/92lb ft DIN @ 4000rpm. *Escort RS 2000:* Cast-iron SOHC Ford 8-valve with belt drive, 1993cc (90.82 x 76.95mm), 9.2:1 CR x 1 Weber 32/36 downdraught, twin-choke, carburettor. Max power: 100bhp DIN @ 5750rpm/108lb ft DIN @ 3500rpm.

Transmission: Front engine, rear drive, via propshaft with UJ at each end and live rear axle. Single dry-plate clutch of 7.54in. diam. (Mexico) 8.0in. (Escort TC/RS 1600) and 8.5in. (RS 2000). Hydraulic clutch activation on all but RS 2000, which featured cable. Gearbox ratios (TC/RS/Mexico): 1st, 2.972; 2nd, 2.010; 3rd, 1.397; 4th, 1.00; reverse, 3.324. RS 2000: 1st, 3.65; 2nd, 1.97; 3rd. 1.37; 4th, 1.00; reverse, 3.66.

Final drive: For Escort TC/RS/Mexico, 3.77: 1; for RS 2000, 3.54:1

Suspension: Uprated MacPherson strut front with roll bar into lower track control arm (TCA). Multi-leaf rear axle with inclined telescopic dampers until November 1973, when vertically mounted. All models had the top radius arm location. Spring rates varied from 'standard' RS of 100lb in. front/97lb in rear to RS 2000's original 130lb in. front, 85lb in. rear. Did not share later mainstream development of combined anti-roll bar/location links dampers. Gas-dampers a widely specified option, Bilstein source.

Wheels & tyres: From Escort TC onward 165 SR-13 on 5.5 x 13in. steel wheels standard, but wheels patterned with spokes in 1973. Options included Minilites and the later 1971-onward FAVO four-spoke alloy (Minilite are lifed magnesium alloy) with 5½J x 13in. initially available, followed by 6 and 7 in. rim options in the same style and 13in. diameter. Larger section tyres available as these wider wheels released

with 175 or 185/70 sizing likely. Original suppliers on TC included Dunlop (also with India) SP68 pattern, Goodyear GP, Pirelli. RS products most likely on Goodyear or Dunlop.

Steering: Originally three-spoke plastic production wheel in TC, but likely fitment of dished three-spoke or flat design for later RS product. Rack and pinion with 16.4:1 original ratio (some RS product fitted with 6 tooth rack instead of 5 tooth). Usually 3.5 turns lock-to-lock, but competition option of 2.5 turns may be found.

Brakes: Two basic servo-assistance layouts (see text) for front, 9.625in. solid discs and rear 9.00 x 1.75 in. drums. RS 2000 had the same fronts, but 8.0 x 1.5in. back drums. Vented front discs part of RS 2000 Group 1 homologation.

Electrical system: TC, originally dynamo with 15 ACR alternator by October 1969. Mexico, 15 ACR alternator and then 17 ACR. Alternator for RS 1600, 35amp/17 ACR. RS 2000, same specification as RS16.

Servicing: TC, every 2500 miles; RS 1600, every 3000 miles; Mexico and RS 2000, every 6000 miles. Cooling system, TC/RS, 12.5 pints; Mexico, 11.5 pints; RS 2000, 12.2 pints. Engine oil capacity: TC, SAE 10W/30, 7.2 pints. RS 1600, SAE 20W/50, 8 pints. Mexico, 10W/30, 8 pints. RS 2000, SAE 10W/30, 6.7 pints. All gearboxes except RS 2000, SAE 80EP, 1.75 pints no regular change needed: RS 2000, 2.4 pints, no regular change needed. All rear axles, 2 pints SAE 90EP.

Prices: See text for individual launch costs. As of December 1974: Mexico, £1854.48; RS 2000, £2075.67; RS 1600, £2528.94. April 1970 Escort TC price, £1291 3s 11d.

The Performers II: 1975-80

Ford Escort Sport 1300 & 1600
Ford Escort RS 1800
Ford Escort RS Mexico
Ford Escort RS 2000

Body: Pressed steel, two doors (Sport available with four doors in 1600 form for UK, 1975-76 only: LHD 1300 counterpart) with RS models continuing to have strengthened suspension mounting points and chassis rails with pick-up points for radius rods. Matt black bumpers, quarter type at front on all but RS 2000, which had a unique polyurethane plastic 'snout' bolted into re-cut front end steel panels. Tail spoilers in flexible rubber on all but Escort Sport (1979-80 Harrier descendant had this and other features discussed in text). Aerodynamic Cd factors from 0.45 to 0.375 (RS 2000).

Standard equipment included a 9 gallon fuel tank and single-pane viewing panel instrumentation. Sport had 110 mph speedo and matching large 7000rpm tachometer, with vertical scale water and fuel gauges between. RS Escorts also had matching large speedo and tachometer, but with three-dial minor instrumentation for fuel, oil pressure and water temperature. Electrical systems all featured 12v batteries in front corner of engine bay but varied from 1600 Sport's 12v 38Ah to RS 2000's 12v 57Ah. Round lamps of seven inch diameter, and usually Lucas manufacture in UK, on Sport (standard with x 2 halogen auxiliary lights), RS 1800, Mexico. For RS 2000 quadruple Cibie halogen lamps of 220/120w rating were fitted.

Variety of interiors according to model and possible Custom Pack fitments (see appropriate text), but three-spoke steering wheel common with crossed flag motif (Sport) or RS symbol.

Dimensions: For all but RS 2000: length, 156.6in; width, 60.5in; height, 55.5in.;wheelbase, 94.5in.; front track, 50in.; rear track, 51 in. Ground clearance, 5.5in.; turning circle, 31ft 8in. (average for RS 1800).RS 2000, as before, but length increased to 163.1in.

Weights: Some factory figures in text, *Autocar* tests showed RS 2000 at 2075lb (941kg), 56 per cent front, 44 per cent rear; RS 1800, 2016lb (915kg), 53 per cent front, 47 per cent rear; 1.6 Sport, 1914lb (870kg), 54 per cent front, 46 per cent rear. All Kerb quotations.

Engines: All inline, water-cooled, four cylinder, with iron blocks on all but alloy block RS 1800, all five main bearings. *Escort Sport:* 1.3 and 1.6 litre 'crossflow' Kent family with pushrod OHV. Sport 1300; 1297cc (80.98 x 62.99mm), 9.2:1 CR, single twin-choke downdraught Weber 32/32 DGV. Max power: 70 PS @ 5500rpm/68lb ft @ 4000rpm. Sport 1600; 1598cc (80.98 x 77.62mm), 9:1 CR, single twin-choke downdraught Weber 32/36 DGV. Max power: 84 PS@ 5500rpm/ 92lb ft @ 3500rpm. *Escort Mexico:* Single overhead camshaft derivative of Pinto family; 1593cc (87.67 x 66mm), 9.2:1 CR, single twin-choke Weber downdraught 32/36 DGV. Max power: 95 PS @ 5750rpm/92lb ft @ 4000rpm. *Escort RS 1800:* Twin overhead camshaft cylinder head with four valves per cylinder and alloy construction of Cosworth design and Hart development. Belt drive for camshafts, 1835cc, (86.75 x 77.62mm) 9:1 CR, single twin-choke downdraught Weber 32/36 DGAV. Max power: 115bhp DIN @ 6000rpm/120lb ft @ 4000rpm. *Escort RS 2000:* Single overhead camshaft derivative of Pinto family, with toothed belt drive to OHC, as for 1.6 in Mexico. Iron head and block 1993cc (90.82 x 76.95mm), 9.2:1 CR, single twin-choke Weber DD 32/36 DGAV. Max power: 110bhp DIN @ 5500rpm/119lb ft @ 4000rpm.

Transmission: Front engine, rear drive, via propshaft with UJ at each end and live rear axle of similar type used throughout high performance, rear drive, Escort's life. All had four-speed all-synchromesh gearboxes with remote control selection. Ratios, together with differing final drives follow. *Escort Sport:* 1300; 1st, 3.337; 2nd, 1.995; 3rd, 1.418; 4th, 1:1; final drive, 4.125 or LHD option of 4.44.1600, same ratios, but 3.54:1 final drive. *Escort Mexico:* 1st, 3.65; 2nd, 1.97; 3rd, 1.37; 4th, 1:1; final drive, as 1600 Sport, 3.54. *Escort RS 1800:* 1st, 3.36; 2nd, 1.81; 3rd, 1.26; 4th, 1:1; final drive, as 1600S/Mexico, 3.54 *Escort RS 2000:* four-speed ratios as Mexico and final drive as for all save 1600 Sport, 3.54:1. All cable-operated, diaphragm spring clutches, 8.5in plate diameters on RS models.

Suspension: *Sport;* Mac Pherson struts, anti-roll bar, front; multi-leaf live rear axle with one extra leaf per side over non-sporting Escort, and telescopic dampers. *RS Mexico/1800/2000;* 130lb in. front, and 115lb in. rear spring rates with common MacPherson strut multi-leaf rear-end layout and dampers, plus axle location rods.

Steering: Three-spoke steering wheels of 14in. (RS) or 14.7in. diameter with rack and pinion geared 3.5 turns lock-to-lock (3.0 turns for *Autocar* test car).

Brakes: Servo-assisted with 9.63in. solid discs; 9.0 inch. back drums (x 1.75 in. width on all RS models). Vented front discs a popular RS 2000 option from Group 1/X-pack.

Wheels & tyres: *Sport,* steel 5 x 13in. with 175/70 SR; same tyre size originally specified as standard throughout RS range but with 5.5 x 13in. steel on *RS 1800/Mexico* and alloy four-spoke 6.0 x 13in. FAVO wheels production-fitted to *RS 2000;* later there was a steel 5.5 x 13in. cheaper version of RS 2000 and an enlarged range of extra-cost FAVO wheels up to 7.5 x 13in. freely available.

Servicing: Every 6000 miles, including oil and

filter change, all models. Cooling system, 9.5 pints for 1600 Sport, 12.5 pints (RS 1800) and 12 pints (RS 2000). Engine oil capacity: 5.7 pints SAE 20W/50 (1600 Sport); 7.2 pints of same grade for RS 1800, and 6.6 pints of SAE 10W/50 for RS 2000. Gearboxes: Sport, 1.58 pints; RS 1800, 2.4 pints; RS 2000, 2.6 pints, all of SAE80. Final drives: Sport, 1.75 pints; RS 1800, 2.4 pints; RS 2000, 2 pints, all of SAE 90.

Prices: See text for launch costs. In 1976. when all the models listed were available, comparative costs were: Escort 1300 Sport, £2322; 1600 Sport, £2393 (four-door, £50 to £60 extra during year); Mexico, £2443; RS 1800, £3049; RS 2000, £2857.

The Performers III: 1980-Jan 1985

Ford Escort XR3
Ford Escort XR3i
Ford Escort RS 1600i
Ford Escort RS Turbo

Model: Escort XR3

Body: Pressed steel three-door hatchback version of 1980 Escort front drive with aerodynamic additions to reduce Cd from standard saloon's 0.385 to 0.375 (i.e. 2.7 per cent reduction). Changes included: hard matt black plastic for extension lip to spoiler, front and rear wheel shrouds, plus deformable plastic tail spoiler mounted on hatchback. Matt black hatch and rear window surrounds.

Standard 9 gallon fuel tank and four gauge instrumentation with a matching 7000rpm tachometer and 140mph speedometer; fuel gauge and water temperature on vertical scales between. Special XR two-spoke steering wheel of 13.5 in. diam. 'Laser' striped trim and sports front seats. Standard LW/MW push-button radio, with many popular options including combined cassette stereo players with LW/MW/FM radios, central locking, electric windows and glass tilt 'n slide sunroof.

Battery 12v 43Ah with 45amp alternator and 230/110w headlamps plus optional auxiliary driving lights. All these carburated XRS manufactured in West Germany.

Dimensions: Length, 159.8in. (unspoiled Escort 156.3in.); width, 62.5in; height, 52.6in; wheelbase, 94.4in; front track, 54.5in; rear track, 56.3in; turning circle, average, 33ft 9in.

Weight: 1969lb (895kg DIN) or 2040lb (925kg) *Autocar* Kerb weight.

Engine: Inline four-cylinder CVH, transversely mounted and water-cooled with electric fan for front radiator. Single belt-driven overhead camshaft. Hydraulic self-adjusting valve lifters. Iron block, alloy head: 1596cc (79.96 x 79.52mm), 9.5:1 CR, single downdraught variable-choke Weber DFT; contactless ignition. Max power: 96bhp DIN @ 6000rpm/98lb ft @ 4000rpm.

Transmission: Four speed all-synchromesh gearbox incorporated in front drive transaxle with 8.0in. plate to diaphragm spring, cable-activated, clutch. Gearbox ratios: 1st, 3.15; 2nd, 1.91; 3rd, 1.27; 4th, 0.95. Later models had five ratios with 0.76 5th added (see Chapter 12). Final drive, 3.84:1 (17.89mph per 1000rpm); five-speed final drive, 3.58:1.

Suspension: MacPherson strut with lower arm pick-up of anti-roll bar of 22mm and 98.4lb in. front spring rate with Bilstein gas-filled strut inserts. Rear, independent via transverse arms, longitudinal tie bars, coil springs of progressive 128 to 220lb in. rating and Bilstein gas-filled dampers.

Wheels & tyres: Production alloy four-hole fitment, 5.5 x 14in. diam. with UK cars on Pirelli P6 Goodyear NCT or Dunlop D3 of 185/60 HR specification.

Steering: Rack & pinion of 19.55:1 ratio and 3.69 turns lock-to-lock; 33ft average turning circle (Ford).

Brakes: Vacuum servo assistance 7.87in. with direct action in LHD or via transfer bar and linkage (RHD). Ventilated front discs of 9.4in. diameter in cast-iron with sliding piston alloy caliper. Rears are 7.1in. drums with leading and trailing shoes and self-adjustment. Low pad warning filament incorporated in original and recommended front disc pads.

Servicing: Change engine oil and filter as part of 6000 mile maintenance. CVH holds 5.7 pints SAE 20w/50 oil when changing filter. Cooling capacity; 12.9 pints. Transaxle is 'lubricated for life'.

Price: November 1980, £5123 inc £342.68 Special Car Tax and £668.22 VAT in UK.

Model: Escort XR3i

Body: In steel and plastic as for XR3 in all external respects save rear badge. Interior modified in respect of trim fabrics and slightly abbreviated switchgear, plus three-spoke steering wheel of 14in. diam. (1983 onward). Fuel tank now 10.6 gallons. British and German manufacture from January 1983, some initial supplies only from West Germany. Cabriolet available 1983 on, manufactured by Karmann of Osnabruck; Cd 0.39, roof up.

Dimensions: XR3i as XR3. Cabriolet has revised boot and roofline (see Chapter 10).

Weight: 2024lb (920kg DIN); Cabriolet injection, 2134lb (970kg DIN). Autocar XR3i kerb figure, 2027lb (921kg), 60.5 per cent front, 39.5 per cent rear.

Engine: Basic CVH as before, but plus Bosch K-Jetronic fuel injection with over-run cut-off, additional HP electric pump and return line for fuel (Chapter 12) allied to usual 9.5:1 CR. Max power: 105bhp DIN @ 6000rpm/101lb ft @ 4800rpm.

Transmission: Later model XR3 five-speed transaxle with 4.29 final drive (20.29mph per 1000rpm). Ratios: 1st, 3.15; 2nd, 1.91; 3rd, 1.28; 4th, 0.95; 5th, 0.76.

Suspension: Principles of MacPherson strut front and IRS via transverse arms maintained but front anti-roll bar diameter to 24mm from 22mm (as original Estate) with Girling monotube damping front and rear, plus revised wheel angles and reduced suspension ride heights (30mm front, 20mm rear).

Wheels & tyres: Alloy 5.5 x 14in. continued with 185/60s (Cabriolet available with Uniroyal, 1984) but cheaper 6.0 x 14in. steel wheel with slotted plastic hubcap also in production with same size tyres.

Steering: As before, but three-spoke wheel standard 1983.

Brakes: Vented front discs and vacuum servo, as before, but 8.0in. van drum back brakes enlarged over original.

Servicing: Every 6000 miles, as before. Replace spark plugs every 12,000 miles.

Prices: February 1983, £6278, including £419.94 Special Car Tax and £818.88 VAT in UK.

Model: Escort RS 1600i

Body: Three-door unitary steel hatchback as before with unique badging and different aerodynamic aids to XR3/3i and four auxiliary lamps as standard in UK. Extended front spoiler bore the original part number 9057705 + Escort 81 and the lipped rear, 9057708 with branding Escort Motorsport. No rear wheel shrouding was fitted and front was not needed from XR either as covered by larger spoiler; Cd 'unchanged' over XR3/3i owing to wider tyres & wheels.

Standard with 9 gallon fuel tank and built on XR3 base. Unique interior with RS-branded Recaro seats and matching fabric rear seat trim. RHD cars with four-spoke steering wheel, RS-branded. Original LHD with three-spoke RS wheel, also on leather rim. All built in West Germany; RHD conversion and standard equipment levels by RS engineers at Boreham.

Dimensions: Length, 159.53in; width, 62.57 in; height, 52.6in; all courtesy of *auto hebdo*, Paris. Wheelbase, as before.

Weight: 1991lb (905kg) *(auto hebdo)*; 2027lb (919kg) *(Autocar)*.

Engine: Inline CVH four-cylinders 1600 base with replacement SOHC camshaft, mechanical valve lifters to replace hydraulics, revised cylinder head porting and new manifold to mount Bosch K-Jetronic; 9.9:1CR; finned Ford Motorsport rocker cover in alloy; large bore 4-into-1 exhaust manifolding; AFT digital electronic ignition system. Air injection tube layout in an L-pattern completely different to RHD XR3i. Max power: 115bhp DIN @ 6000rpm (limiter operational at 6300rpm)/109lb ft @ 5250rpm.

Transmission: Five-speed transaxle based on XR 3 with an 0.83 fifth gear (instead of 0.76), and 3.84:1 final drive in place of XR3's 3.58 and XR3i's 4.29. 20.6mph per 1000rpm, as for RS1600i. Cable clutch, 8.0in plate.

Suspension: MacPherson strut front and IRS with transverse arms retained but anti-roll bars specified front & rear latter (not always fitted UK). Unique front anti-roll bar layout with aluminium crossmember and ride height lowered 22mm. Koni shock absorbing units front and rear.

Wheels & tyres: Then unique seven-spoke RS 1600i alloy wheels, 6 x 15in. diam UK; 195/50 VR Dunlop D4 tyres. LHD: Phoenix, 190/50 HR.

Steering: Usual Escort rack and pinion with own RS steering wheel.

Brakes: Based on XR3 of period with 9.4in. vented front discs and 7in. diameter back drums, plus vacuum servo assistance with conversion linkage in RHD. Aftermarket Ford 8.0in. back brakes offered widely for XRs and RS 1600i by RS dealers.

Lighting: Augmented by twin Hella rectangular and twin Carello round lamps. UK Lucas H4 headlamp supply.

Decals: Bonnet carried 9-strip decoration with RS 1600i embossed; Escort and RS 1600i each side at rear; double strip sidewinders on doors also carried RS 1600i logo.

Price: Launch cost, see text. February 1983, £6834 in UK with taxes.

Model: Escort RS Turbo

Body: Three-door unitary steel hatchback, as before, but with hard plastic and complete colour coding of body items such as bumpers and XR3/3i back spoiler. Replacement front spoiler, wheel and side sill extensions. Standard equipment included opening rear quarter windows and grille also matched to body colour.

Standard 10.6 gallon fuel tank and XR3i Monza/crushed velour interior trim allied to Recaro front seats with round long range driving lamps also standard.

Dimensions: Length, 160.3 in; width 64.5 in; height, 54.6 in; track, 55 in (front), 56 in. (rear).

Weight: CVH turbocharged engine 120kg. Total: 971 kg *(Motor)*.

Engine: Based on 1600 CVH and two years' UK Rally Championship use of turbo. New pistons, stronger and with lower crown for 8.3:1 instead of 9.5:1 CR. Tapered rings (secondary) for increased oil circulation; bigger gudgeon pins; copper-lead big-end bearing sheels instead of aluminium-tin. Sodium-cooled alloy exhaust valves; revised machining of inlet and exhaust tracts. Electronic ignition by Bosch with electronic wastegate control; fuel cut-off (640-0rpm) and ignition cut-off (6500rpm).

Hydraulic valve lifters retained, but Bosch KE fuel injection is allied to Garrett AiResearch T3 turbo with integral wastegate and air-to-air intercooling; thermostically controlled electric fan for duplex radiator installation. Large bore (2.4in.) tailpipe to stainless steel exhaust system. Turbo boost from 0.25 to 0.55 bar (3.5psi to 7.8psi) according to inlet manifold temperature.

Max power: 132bhp DIN @ 6000rpm/133lb ft @ 3000rpm.

Transmission: Current XR3i five-speed transaxle mated to 4.27 final drive (20.3mph per 1000rpm), uprated clutch and world's first mass production use of Ferguson-principle viscous coupling limited slip differential. Clutch has increased spring clamp loads but retains 7.9in. diam. Gear ratios: 1st, 3.15; 2nd, 1.91; 3rd, 1.27; 4th, 0.95; 5th, 0.76; final drive, 4.27.

Suspension: Based on that of XR3i with Girling

monotube shock-absorption used in MacPherson strut front and transverse arm IRS. Front has tie-bar layout like that of RS 1600i (but cast-iron mountings), anti-roll bar freed from wheel location duty; XR3i springs, softer dampers and solid bushes for inner mountings. Rear is as XR3i plus 12mm Orion anti-roll bar.

Wheels & tyres: RS seven-spoke alloys of 6.0 x 15in. diam. Dunlop D4 195/50 VR tyres on launch, or Michelin MXV.

Steering: Usual Escort rack and pinion plus XR3i three-spoke steering wheel.

Brakes: Heavy duty pad and lining materials, plus spoiler cooling ducts, otherwise as Escort XR3i with vented front discs and 8 x 1.43in. back drums, plus vacuum servo assistance.

Decals: Door and side panel stripes + RS on front wing and Escort RS. Turbo RS layout on left of tailgate.

Price: £9250 + £470 for Custom Pack of: glass sunroof, electric windows, tinted glass and central locking.

Model: 1986-1990 Escort XR3i.

Body: Restyled three-door unitary steel hatchback, body colour polycarbonate bumpers, extended front spoiler depth and additional rear spoiler. Claimed aerodynamic Cd, 0.36.

Standard 47 litre/10.4 gallon fuel tank; two-spoke steering wheel with 'soft feel' sections; 1986 fascia including 0-7000rpm tachometer.

Options gradually incorporated until 1989, model has as standard: auxiliary driving lamps; tilt or slide glass sunroof, electric twin mirror operation, central locking, electric windows, AM/FM radio and quad speakers.

Important options by Jan 1989 were the anti-lock brakes at £375; alloy 6Jx14 wheels at £250; fuel computer (£150); black or metallic paints at £120 or £1490 respectively.

Dimensions: Length 158.3in width, 72.2in; height 53.1in front track, 54.5in; rear track, 56.3in; turning circle (average), 33ft 10in.

Weight: 945kg/2079lb in 1989 Ford brochure; 965kg/3133lb, *Autocar* in October 1986.

Engine: Least changed of 1986 model year Escorts. Power remained at 105bhp @ 600-0rpm; max torque, 102lb ft at 4800rpm.

Transmission: Front drive. Final drive, 4.27:1 (20.3mph per 1000rpm in fifth), transaxle ratio as since start of XR3i.

Suspension: Principles as before: MacPherson strut front, independent rear via swinging arms and longitudinal links, but detail changes. Shared 24mm front anti-roll bar with RS Turbo. 1986 modifications included revised anti-bump-steer steering rack/steering arm location; hard plastic inner TCA joints; revised anti-roll bar location, raised front spring rates; raised +10mm/0.39in front ride height.

Wheels & tyres: Standard on 6Jx14 inch steel wheels, styled hub caps and 185/60 HR 14 tyres. Optional alloys in same dimensions.

Steering: Modified rack position as noted above, plus 1989 introduction of variable ratio to reduce parking effort.

Brakes: As before, but with Lucas Girling SCS anti-lock option.

Servicing: Continued at 6000 mile oil and filter changes. Warranty was 12 months/unlimited mileage plus 6 years anti-corrosion.

Price: £7853.93 at introduction (March 1986); £9896 by November 1988.

Model: 1986-1990 RS Turbo.

Body: Three-door steel hatch as for XR3i, except: two bonnet louvres, side sill and slim wheel arch extensions; colour coded rear spoiler. Aerodynamic Cd, circa 0.36.

Equipment as for XR3i, except twin Recaro seats. Originally marketed with extra cost (£572) 'Custom Pack' that added tilt/slide sunroof, central locking and electric front windows. Summer 1987 saw sales of only Custom Pack RS Turbos.

Dimensions: As 1986 XR3i. Brochure, length given as 159.9 inches.

Weights: Split 582kg front, 383kg rear, total 965kg by SVE without options; 980 kg/2156lb with '50% options.' *Autocar* in 1986 reported 1017kg/2247lb for Custom Pack demonstrator.

Engine: Turbocharged and intercooled 1.6-litre CVH with unchanged 132bhp. Now at 5750rpm, instead of 6000rpm. Unchanged 133lb ft of torque now reported at 2750 instead of 3000rpm. Details changed included 8.2:1 compression pistons replacing 8.3:1 that carried new oil control rings; Garrett T3 turbocharger with water cooling of centre bearings; remapped ignition and fuelling points for Motorola ESC II microprocessor management in conjunction with Bosch KE-Jetronic injection mounted on new inlet manifolding. Turbo has its own cast iron Niresist exhaust manifolding and large bore system. RS has unique water radiator plus XR4i cooling fan and motor, installed beside small intercooler.

Turbo motor retained 1597cc (79.96x79.52mm stroke), but crankshaft fillet rolled for extra strength, exhaust valves were carryover Nimonic 80A Sodium-cooled, spark plugs Motorcraft AGPR 901C1. Recommended 10W 30 oil.

Max boost remained close to 0.5 bar; Jetronic fuel module reduces petrol flow at 6300rpm; Motorola module also carried ignition cutout at 6500rpm, overboost ignition cutout and boost reduction when charge temperature exceeded 63°C.

Transmission: Replacement of 4.27:1 final drive by 3.82:1 (22.59mph per 1000rpm in fifth). Revised settings for viscous coupling limited slip differential. The 220mm/8.7in diameter clutch plate carried over from previous model and XR3i, but with 'increased clamp pressure and Ferodo asbestos-free disc'. Gear ratios, as per XR3i.

Suspension: Now based on XR3i (no front tie bars) and shares 24mm front anti-roll bar, but RS has 16mm Orion rear bar, revised settings for twin tube dampers, spring rates up over equivalent XR3i (by 25 per cent front and 12 per cent rear).

Wheels & tyres: Alloy 6x15 inch alloys and 195/50 VR Dunlop D40; also approved, Goodyear Eagle NCT and Uniroyal Rallye in same sizings.

Steering: As per XR3i.

Brakes: Replacement system featured Sierra XR4i front discs (260mm/10.2in diameter) and 229x44mm back drums (9x1.75in). Revised servo assistance operation with a 25.4mm master cylinder.

Decals: Only 'ESCORT RS turbo' on rear, but production changes.

Service: As per XR3i, but first service at 1500 miles. Spark plug changes needed at every 6000 mile service.

Price: At introduction £10,028 without £572 Custom Pack. Dec 1988, retailed at £11,838 including pack.

Appendix III

Production numbers

From the first Escort produced in 1955 (they made 2553 that year, with production ceasing in 1961, after they had made 50,945 of the first Escort/Squire series), Ford kept varied records of their increasingly multi-national output. Sometimes they do not cross-check against each other, but here is how the company reported production in the primary Escort centres to the close of 1988.

Ford of Britain (Halewood)

Escort Mk1 rear drive		Escort Mk2 rear drive (Brenda)	
1967	8028	1975	156423
1968	161747	1976	188303
1969	145040	1977	177929
1970	156768	1978	132224
1971	128430	1979	185525
1972	189873	1980	119603
1973	147320		**960007**
1974	138956		
	1,076,162		**Total Rear Drive UK 2,036,169**

Escort RS 2000 Mk2 production, Saarlouis, 1975-1980

	German market	RHD & LHD exports	Annual total
1975	176	225	401
1976	3520	3431	6951
1977	1753	2891	4644
1978	1417	3428	4845
1979	1242	5498	6740
1980	212	1845	2057
	8320	**17,318**	**25,638**

These figures were compiled in November 1981 inside Ford to support the commercial cause of

RS models. The RS 2000 in this form sold 10,039 in Britain alone, compared to 3759 of the first RS 2000. Altogether 5334 first edition RS 2000s were made, 1162 of them at Saarlouis in 1973-74. The rarest was the Escort RS1800 with 109 registered in Britain during four sales years. By 1988 over 20,000 RS Escort turbos had been made in both bodies during four years. This compares with over 200,000 XR3i Escorts that were sold between 1982-88.

Escort Mk3 front drive (Erika)

1980	37,466
1981	150,487
1982*	134,400
1983*	116,700
1984	94,359
1985	111,525
1986	111,230
1987	122,222
1988	172,706

1,051,095

* Figures are Ford of Britain, for saloons only, and therefore do not match van-included totals of Chapter 2.

Ford of Germany (primarily Saarlouis)

Escort Mk1 rear drive

1967	5
1968	60,121
1969	120,393
1970	154,436
1971	156,958
1972	124,088
1973	156,098
1974	76,289

848,388

Escort Mk2 rear drive (Brenda)

1974	2315
1975	215,738
1976	160,359
1977	95,801
1978	89,864
1979	83,205

497,282

Total Rear Drive (D) 1345670

NB: Post-1980 German figures are rounded-off Ford totals, to nearest 100.

Escort Mk3 front drive (Erika)

1979	23
1980	135,000
1981	278,100
1982	289,800
1983	259,600
1984	237,539
1985	230,017
1986	237,817
1987	265,699
1988	261,465 (projected)

2,194,960

Ford, Valencia, Spain

Escort Mk3 front drive (Erika)

1981	20,100
1982	50,200

1983	58,500
1984	77,599
1985	52,313
1986	79,343
1987	59,172
1988	68,085 (projected)
	329,046

Karmann, Osnabruck, Escort Cabriolet production

1984	35,346
1985	25,115
1986	11,883
1987	12,504
1988	20,289 (projected)
	105,137

Other sources

The Escort, particularly Erika Mk3, is also made at many other locations: Brazil, USA, Spain, and the Netherlands, with Ireland contributing until 1982. KD (knock-down kit) production for exports from Europe accounted for 35,600 Escorts in 1970 and declined progressively to 3,600 in 1983.

World Number 1 by name production: the 1982 evidence

Country	Escort	VW Golf	Toyota Corolla
USA	265000	84000	–
Canada	88000	–	–
UK	135000	–	–
Germany	290000	495000	–
Spain	50000	–	–
Mexico	–	45000	–
South Africa	19000	15000	34000
Japan	–	–	579000
Australia	–	–	23000
Total, Free World(!)	**847000**	**639000**	**636000**

World figures via Ford of America and Autoweek

The 1986 Escort revisions yielded a World record production figure of 963,000. The 1987 total was slightly down (949,000), but that was enough to stay ahead of the Golf and Corolla. Early in 1988 Ford claimed production of the front wheel drive Escort had exceeded 7 million worldwide.

Appendix IV

Performance figures

	1100L	1300XL	1300GT	1300 Sport
Autocar of:	8/6/74	20/5/71	11/2/71	2/12/71
Kerb w, lb	1702	1803	1702	1769
Max mph	79	86	96	92
Accel, secs:				
0-30mph	5.5	5.0	3.9	4.0
0-40mph	8.8	7.8	6.1	6.4
0-50mph	13.2	11.8	8.5	9.2
0-60mph	19.8	17.6	12.4	13.8
0-70mph	34.5	26.6	18.0	18.9
0-80mph	–	55.0	26.0	30.6
0-90mph	–	–	42.8	–
¼-mile; secs	21.6	20.8	19.0	18.9
4th gear, 50-70mph, secs	27.3	18.7	11.3	15.9
Overall mpg	29.4	26.7	25.4	25.0

	Mk2 1100 Popular	Mk2 1300GL	1300 Ghia	Mk2 1600 Sport
Autocar of:	12/7/75	1/5/76	22/3/75	2/4/77
Kerb w, lb	1848	1937	1971	1915
Max mph	79	86	93	97
Accel, secs:				
0-30mph	5.5	4.6	4.0	3.7
0-40mph	8.8	7.4	6.4	5.9
0-50mph	13.2	10.6	9.0	8.6
0-60mph	20.8	16.4	13.5	12.3
0-70mph	32.2	24.8	18.6	16.7
0-80mph	–	48.8	29.9	24.0
0-90mph	–	–	–	38.4
¼-mile; secs	21.3	20.7	19.9	18.6
4th gear, 50-70mph, secs	21.3	18.5	14.0	11.8
Overall mpg	32.1	27.6	29.3	34.3

	Mk1 Twin Cam	**Mk1 RS 1600**	**Mk2 RS 1800**
Autocar of:	6/6/68	30/4/70	26/7/75
Kerb w, lb	1872	1920	2016
Max mph	113	113	111
Accel, secs:			
0-30mph	3.8	3.4	2.9
0-40mph	5.2	4.8	4.7
0-50mph	7.2	6.8	6.6
0-60mph	9.9	8.9	9.0
0-70mph	13.0	12.4	12.4
0-80mph	16.8	16.1	16.6
0-90mph	24.2	22.6	22.0
0-100mph	33.6	32.3	32.9
¼-mile, secs	17.2	16.7	16.9
4th gear,			
50-70mph, secs	9.9	9.5	8.9
Overall mpg	21.5	21.5	26.5

	Mk1 Mexico	**Mk1 RS 2000**	**Mk2 RS 2000**
Autocar of:	10/12/70	11/10/73	17/1/76
Kerb w, lb	1964	1978	2075
Max mph	99	108	109
Accel, secs:			
0-30mph	3.9	2.9	3.0
0-40mph	5.8	4.8	4.7
0-50mph	7.9	6.9	6.4
0-60mph	10.7	9.0	8.6
0-70mph	14.5	12.8	12.7
0-80mph	20.2	17.2	16.9
0-90mph	30.8	24.2	23.1
0-100mph	–	34.5	33.6
¼-mile; secs	18.0	17.1	16.7
4th gear,			
50-70mph, secs	9.4	8.8	8.4
Overall mpg	27.5	26.6	24.7

	Mk3 1.1L 4-speed	**Mk3 1.3GL 4-speed**	**Mk3 1.6GL 5-speed**
Autocar of:	27/9/80	13/2/82	13/3/82
Kerb wt, lb	1830	1825	2032
Max mph, mean	92	96	95
Accel, secs:			
0-30mph	4.4	3.7	3.7
0-40mph	6.8	5.8	5.6
0-50mph	10.6	8.3	8.0
0-60mph	15.5	12.5	11.1
0-70mph	22.7	17.5	16.3
0-80mph	40.4	24.7	22.4
0-90mph	–	43.9	34.6
¼-mile, secs	20.2	18.9	18.6
Top gear,			
50-70mph, secs	19.7	14.2	18.2
Overall mpg	36.9	31.8	32.1

	Mk3 1.6 GL Auto 3-speed	Mk3 1.6L 4-speed
Autocar of:	9/4/83	10/1/81
Kerb w, lb	2032	1852
Max mph, mean	101	103
Accel, secs:		
0-30mph	4.0	4.0
0-40mph	6.1	6.2
0-50mph	8.8	8.4
0-60mph	12.2	11.9
0-70mph	17.1	16.7
0-80mph	25.6	22.9
0-90mph	37.3	37.6
1/4-mile; secs	18.8	18.7
Top gear,		
50-70mph, secs	8.4 in 2nd	12.6
Overall mpg	25.6	32.1

	Escort XR3 4-speed	Escort XR3i 5-speed	Escort RS 1600i 5-speed	Escort RS Turbo 5-speed
Autocar of:	15/11/80	5/2/83	5/2/83	23/3/85
Kerb wt, lb	2040	2027	2027	2136
Max mph, mean	113	116	116	126
Accel, secs:				
0-30mph	3.5	2.9	2.9	2.8
0-40mph	5.1	4.6	4.4	4.2
0-50mph	6.9	6.1	6.2	5.6
0-60mph	9.2	8.6	8.7	7.8
0-70mph	13.0	11.3	11.8	9.9
0-80mph	16.9	15.0	15.0	12.9
0-90mph	22.7	19.4	20.3	16.4
0-100mph	31.8	26.5	27.9	21.8
0-110mph	–	39.0	39.5	30.9
¼-mile secs	17.0	16.7	16.7	16.0
Top gear,				
50-70mph, secs	9.0 = 4th	10.3 = 5th	11.6 = 5th	5.9 = 5th
Overall mpg	27.9	30.5	28.3	26.7

For comparison *Motor Trend,* May 1983, tested a 2016lb kerb weight Escort GT of 82 fuel injected bhp and found: 0-30mph, 3.8s; 0-60mph, 12.1s; 0-70mph, 16.5s; standing ¼ mile in 18.6s @ 73.6mph with US mpg average.

1986 onward 'Mk4' Escort

	1.3	1.4	1.6*	XR3i	RS Turbo
Source:	Motor	Autocar	Motor	Autocar	Autocar
Issue:	3.1.87	19.3.86	6.9.86	8.10.86	27.8.86
Weight, lb	1848	1918	1958	2133	2247
Max mph	94	101	108.3	118	125
Accel, secs:					
0-30mph	4.3	3.8	–	3.3	3.0
0-40mph	6.7	5.8	–	4.7	4.7

0-50mph	9.9	8.4	–	7.0	6.1
0-60mph	14.3	12.4	10.1	9.6	9.2
0-70mph	20.4	17.0	–	12.5	11.4
0-80mph	30.9	25.2	–	16.5	14.1
0-90mph	–	39.1	–	21.9	18.5
0-100mph	–	–	–	30.9	23.0
0-110mph	–	–	–	–	31.0
1/4-mile, sec/mph	19.6/–	18.5/73		17.0/81	18.8/85
Top gear, 50-70mph, secs	20.9	23.0	16.8	12.8	8.4
Overall mpg	33.8	34.6	32.7	30.8	27.4

* The 1.6 Escort GL was a five-door saloon that formed part of a *Motor* Group test, thus full figures were not published.

Appendix V

Competition Highlights

Rallying

Rallying has been the Escort's most successful career in worldwide sporting terms, although its record in Hot Rods was that of total dominance for a period in Britain. Only in rallycross has the Mk3 upheld the original rear drive Ford Escort's international repute as a winning car, but the older rear drive machines continue to pick up awards in all corners of the world.

In World Championship rally terms the original Escort saloon won ...

1968	International (later World) Rally Championship of Makes for Ford of Britain.
1969	International (later World) Rally Championship of Makes for Ford of Europe Incorporated.
	Individual events then, now recognized as World Championship classics, that the original Twin Cams, RS 1600s and cousins won were as follows ...
1968, 69	editions of the Austrian Alpine.
1968	Greek Acropolis Rally.
1968-70,73,74	Finnish 1000 Lakes.
1972-74	RAC Rallies of Great Britain, inc a 1-2-3 result in 1973. The equivalent record for the second generation Escort RS 1800 read ...
1979	World Rally Championship makes for Ford
1979	World Rally Championship for drivers for Bjorn Waldegard of Sweden in and RS prepared and entered from Ford at Boreham
1981	World Rally Championship for drivers for Ari vatanen of Finland in an RS prepared by David Sutton Cars at Acton, West London and entered for Rothmans International
	Individual World Championship class events won were as follows ...
1975-79	RAC Rallies of Great Britain with a 1-2-3 result in 1978; a 1-2 the following year and second places recorded in 1980/81.
1976,77,81	Finnish 1000 Lakes with second and third places in 1979 and simply second, 1980.

1977,79-81	Greek Acropolis Rallies with a 1-2 result, 1977
1977	East African Safari Rally
1978	Swedish Rally: the Mk2 was also second in 1979 and 1981
1979	Rallye de Portugal, a 1-2 result: Escort was second, 1977-78
1979	Motorgard Rally of New Zealand; Escort also won in 1978, but the NZ event had temporarily lost championship status.
1979	Canadian Quebec Championship round.
1981	Brazilian Championship round.

As can be seen the Escort has won world class events in most corners of the globe, but it is also worth recalling it also won (in 1.85-litre pushrod trim) the 1970 World Cup marathon rally, which had no affiliation to a recognized championship, but attracted high quality opposition from Mercedes, Triumph and Citroen. The Ford Escort has won neither Monte Carlo nor Mediterranean neighbour San Remo of the World Championship events. Mk2 Escorts finished second on both; Monte in 1979 and San Remo, 1980.

International Championship Rallying
Naturally the Escort has won a number of internationally recognized events outside the World Championship series. Before listing some to show the car's immense versatility, here are some of the national/international titles the car has helped win ...

1971-75	inclusive RAC British National series.
1976-78	inclusive RAC Home International series developed by Sedan Products and Rothmans latterly when the 1980 title went to Ari Vatanen in a Sutton Escort.
1978,79,81	Saw RAC Castrol *Autosport* (later Pace-backed) Championship go twice to Malcolm Wilson and later to Bill Dobie, both in RS 1800s.
1979-83	Kyosti Hamalainen won the Finnish National Championships with Escort, Group 2 class from 1981 onward.
1979-82	Sarel van der Merwe won the South African National title against increasing opposition.
1979-83	inclusive Ford Escorts won the New Zealand National Rally Championship for Paul Adams, Jim Donald (1980/81); Tony Teesdale (1982) and Malcolm Stewart (1983).
1979,1983	Escort took West German Championships with Group 1 RS2000 for Reinhard Hainback in 1979 and Walter Smolej with an RS1800 in 1983.
1979	New Zealander Rod Millen won the American NARRA series in Escort RS and finished second in better known SCCA series.
1980	International Codasur Champion was Federico West (RS 1600)
1980	European Champion Antonio Zanini mainly used Porsche 911, but won Portuguese Algarve Rally in Escort RS. The Course Car on that event was Hannu Mikkola's prototype Audi Quattro, which was considerably quicker, but ineligible for any awards ...!
1981	Scandinavian International Champion Jouni Kinnunen used Escort.
1981	Scandinavian Nordic Champion was Ari Vatanen in Sutton Ford.
1980	Luxembourg Champion Aly Kridel drove an Escort.
1981	Norwegian Group 1 Champion Terje Sveinsoll used an Escort.
1981	Finnish Group 1 Champion Antero Laine used an Escort.
1982, 83	Portuguese national Champion was Joaquim Santos in an Escort RS.
1983	Norwegian Rally Champion was Escort RS driver Valter Jensen.
1983-88	Rear drive Escort still competitive in UK national events. Sample: July 1988 Cellnet/Autosport Championship (Round 4) Kayel Graphics was the 1st national Group N (production) win seen in the UK, achieved by the Ford Sierra RS of George Donaldson/Al Foubister. Yet third and fourth overall went to Ford Escort RS 1800s and 25 per cent of the top

twenty used the decade-old Ford. That third-place RS was registered STW 201R, a plate first used in 1977 to win the East African Safari Rally (Bjorn Waldegard). Subsequently used by the David Sutton/Rothmans équipe, Malcolm Wilson/Terry Harryman recording third on the 1981 Manx home international.

1988	James Renwick (Escort RS1800), third overall in Cellnet Autosport National Rally Championship.

Obviously it is not possible to record every national and international win for Escort outside the World Championship, but the following will give a good idea of the car's versatility, whether works-prepared, or worked over by a private specialist ...

1968,69,78	Dutch Tulip Rallies won with Escort TC in sixties and RS 1800 in seventies. European Championship status.
1968-70,75-78	were the years of factory Ford wins on the Circuit of Ireland European Championship round, but the event was also won by Ford Escorts between 1970 and 1974.
1968,72,73,75,76, 78, 80	were factory Ford winning years on the Scottish, usually European Championship 1973: All-Escort top ten!
1969,72,74	Wins on Belgian Ypres European Championship event.
1969,70,83	Victories in Czechoslovakian International, renamed Skoda by 1983 win for Robert Droogmans' rented Escort.
1969,70,72	Wins on Tour de Belgique for Escort.
1974-76	Escort RS 2000 in Group 1 trim wins Tour of Britain.
1978	Escort wins Tour of Luxembourg.
1970,73,77,78	Escorts from Boreham win Arctic Finnish European Championship-status rallies. Competitive in private hands for many years, e.g. Hamalainen second, 1983 (G2 RS).
1975,76,79	Factory-backed Ford Escort wins on Manx island European Championship round.
1975	Escort won Boucles de Spa European Championship event.
1971,78-80	Escorts win Cypriot European Championship Rallies.
1972	A trio of factory Escorts finished 1-2-3 in Hong Kong.
1975,76	Escorts won the Taurus rallies in Hungary.
1977,83	Walter Smolej took the last of two German national wins on Rally Westfalen.
1979	Ulster home international on tarmac won by Escort.
1978	Escort wins in Turkish and Polish internationals.
1980	European Championship wins on Algarve (Portugal) plus Lucien Bianchi.
1981	International wins as different as Reno, Nevada and Mintex Yorkshire-based forest event in UK.
1983	European Championship results included four outright Escort wins for obsolete Ford: Volta (Portugal) for Borges plus three victories for Droogmans in Czechoslovakia, Martigny and Belgium.
1983	The Escort, obsolete for four years inproduction, was still winning national Championship events in Britain, Australia, New Zealand, Cyprus, Kenya, Norway and Finland. Finally the Escort Twin Cam, obsolete since 1970, notched up a 1983 victory in Zimbabwe's national championship ...!

Notable Escort Saloon car racing results

1968	RAC British Saloon Car Championship. Overall title, Frank Gardner (1.6 Alan Mann Group 5 Escort Twin Cam/Cosworth FVA Formula 2 engine).
1969	RAC British Saloon car Championship. 2000 and 1300cc class titles to

Chris Craft & John Fitzpatrick (1.8 and 1.3 Broadspeed Group 2 Escort TC and 1300 GT Escorts).

1969　Belgian Championship, Yvette Fontaine. Plus the national titles of Denmark, South Africa & Germany.

1970　RAC British repeat of class titles, same team and drivers.

1970　Belgian Championship, Alain Dex. Plus national Ice Racing Championships of Finland (up to 1600cc, Timo Makinen; over 1600cc, Hannu Mikkola); Norway (Trond Schea); Sweden (E.Berger).

1971　RAC British 2000cc class title, John Fitzpatrick (1.8 Broadspeed Group 2 Escort RS 1600). Using a similar Broadspeed RS Fitzpatrick beat the best in BMWs and Capris outright in two European Touring Car rounds: Austria's Salzburgring and Spain's Jarama, the latter co-driven by Jochen Mass.

1971　Dutch Championship, Han Akersloot, Group 2 Escort.

1972　RAC British 1301-2000cc class title, Dave Matthews (2.0 Broadspeed Group 2 Escort RS 1600). First British Production Racing (then Group 1) class titles to Janspeed Escort 1300 Sports of Jeremy Walton (Castrol) and Ivan Dutton (Britax); in 1973 Dutton won both titles outright in his self-prepared 1300 Sport.

1972　Dutch National Championship, Han Akersloot; Danish title to Erik Hoyer

1973　Three RAC British class titles, but not overall, 2000cc, 1300cc, 1000cc for Andy Rouse, Vince Woodman and Les Nash (all Group 2 BDA-engined Escorts).

1973　German Championship, Dieter Glemser (2.0 Zakspeed Group 2 Escort RS 1600).

1973　Finnish Ice Racing Championship, Timo Makinen; second Danish title to Erik Hoyer; multiple class championship wins in Finland (Kemilainen/ Virtanen, +1600cc/-1600cc) Sweden (Bo Emanuelsson) and Holland (Ernst Berg).

1974　FIA European Touring Car Championship, Makes (2.0 Zakspeed Ford Group 2 Escort RS1600) & Drivers (Hans Heyer of Germany). Heyer/Klaus Ludwig also took the Zakspeed Ford to outright victory in the July European qualifying Round (Nürburgring 6-Hours) after Capris and BMWs wilted.

1974　German Championship, Dieter Glemser (2.0 Zakspeed Escort) Plus 2 class titles in Sweden.

1975　German Championship, Hans Heyer (2.0 Group 2 Zakspeed RS 1600/ 1800)

1976　German Championship, Hans Heyer (2.0 Group 2 Zakspeed RS 1800)

1983　RAC British Championship, second overall and under 1600cc class winner: Richard Longman (1.6 Longman Group A RS 1600i)

1984　RAC British Championship, under 1600cc: Longman, as above.

1985　RAC British Saloon Car Championship, second overall and 1601-2500cc class: Richard Longman (1.6 Group A Escort RS Turbo). Winner under 1600cc class, Chris Hodgetts (1.6 Brooklyn Group A RS 1600i). Separate Makes Championship title went to Ford Motor Co for Escort RS 1600i.

1986　Uniroyal Production Saloon car Championship, Willhire 24-hour race, Snetterton, Norfolk. Outright winners: Lionel Abbott/Mike Smith (1.6 Group N Ford Escort RS Turbo).

1987　RAC British Championship, 1601-2500cc class winner, Mark Hales (1.6 Drury Group A Escort RS Turbo).

Karl Jones (1.6 Asquith Motorsport Group N Escort RS Turbo), class and outright Uniroyal Production Saloon Car Champion.

| 1988 | David Shead (1.6 Bristol Street Group N RS turbo), class winner Monroe Production Saloon Car Championship. |

International Rallycross results
European Rallycross Championship title wins

1973	John Taylor	Escort RS 1600
1978	Martin Schanche	Escort RS Mk2
1979	Martin Schanche	Escort RS Mk2
1981	Martin Schanche	Escort Mk2 Turbo
1984	Martin Schanche	Xtrac 4-WD Mk3 Escort Turbo

RAC British Rallycross Championship

1976	Trevor Hopkins	Escort Mk2
1977	Trevor Hopkins	Escort Mk2
1978	Trevor Hopkins	Escort Mk2
1979	Bruce Rushton	Escort Mk2
1980	Graham Hathaway	Escort Mk2

From 1980-83 title won by BDA Ford Fiesta for Keith Ripp

1984	John Welch	Escort Mk2 Turbo
1984	John Welch	Escort Mk2 turbo
1984	John Welch	Escort Mk2 turbo (RWD)
1987	John Welch	Xtrac Escort Mk3/4 turbo (4-WD)

World Hot Rod Championship
Held at Ipswich and promoted by Spedeworth

1972	Bob Howe	Escort Mk1
1973	Barry Lee	Escort Mk1
1974	Barry Lee	Escort Mk1
1975	Derek Fiske	Escort Mk1
1977	Barry Lee	Escort Mk2
1978	Barry Lee	Escort Mk2
1979	Gordon Bland	Escort Mk2
1980	Mick Collard	Escort Mk2

1976 series won by George Polley, Ford Anglia ...

European Hot Rod Championship title wins.
Run by Northern Hot Rod Promoters Assoc. (earlier by Spedeworth)

1974 Kalderkirchen (D)	Barry Lee	Escort Mk1
1975 Wimbledon (UK)	Barry Lee	Escort Mk2
1976 Wimbledon (UK)	Pete Winstone	Escort Mk1
1977 Wimbledon (UK))	Pete Winstone	Escort Mk2
1978 Hednesford (UK)	Stuart Jackson	Escort Mk2
1979 Hednesford (UK)	Gordon Bland	Escort Mk2
1980 Northampton (UK)	Mick Collard	Escort Mk2
1982 Ballymena (Ulster, UK)	Pete Stevens	Escort Mk2
1983 Warneton Speedway (B)	Pete Stevens	Escort Mk2

Appendix VI

Works rally car specifications & competition Performance figures

Model	Escort Twin Cam	Escort RS 1800	Escort RS 1700T	Escort RS 1700T
Type	Group 2, 1968	Group 4	Road car	Group B, evolution
Year	1968/69	1975-81	1983	1982 prototype
Layout	DOHC, 8-valves, carbs; 4-sp front gearbox Live axle, 2-link	DOHC, 16-valves, most carbs; 5-sp front gearbox; Live axle, 5-link;	DOHC, 16-valve, inj, intercooling, electronic management, turbocharged; 5-sp rear transaxle, independent rear suspension	
Body	2-dr steel; (Gp6, no bumpers, perspex windows, few glass-fibre panels)	2-dr steel; Glassfibre wheel arch extensions; fully strengthened body	3-dr steel hatchback; modified XR3 shape with lightest weight exterior; Kevlar panels for evolution car	
Cd	Circa 0.42	Circa 0.45	0.397 to 0.406, depending on equipment	
Weight, kerb	Circa 2200lb	1950-2420lb (2310lb, 1979)	2334lb	2395lb
Engine	Boreham Lotus TC, 1594cc	Hart Cosworth BDA, 1993cc	JQF Cosworth-BDT, 1778cc	Schrick/Cosworth/Ford, dev. max, 1785.7cc x 1.4 turbo = 2498cc
Bore x stroke	82.6 x 72.7mm	90.4 x 77.62mm	85.4 x 77.62mm	85.57mm bore allowed
Power, bhp	152 @ 7200rpm	255 @ 8500rpm ('79)	200 @ N/A	320-350 @ 8-9000rpm
Gearbox:	Ford Bullet	ZF	Ford-Hewland	Ford-Hewland
1st	2.30	2.30	2.69	2.69
2nd	2.01	1.80	1.82	2.13
3rd	1.70	1.36	1.32	1.71
4th	1.0	1.14	1.04	1.27
5th	–	1.0	0.78	1.18
Final drive	4.9	5.3 (typical '79)	4.375	4.375 or, 3.44/4.25
Brakes	Disc/drum	259mm disc	279mm disc	283mm disc, all vent
Suspension	Struts/leaf-sprung axle	Struts/most leaf-sprung (some coil)	All independent system based on strut front, triangulated-link rear	
Wheelbase, in	94.5	94.8	96.5	96.5 (started on 2-WD, 94.
Max mph	99 @ 7500rpm	108 @ 8500 (5.3 diff)	135-140mph	123 @ 8500 (4.4 diff)
0-60mph, secs	7.9	6.5 (1975)	6.5s, Ford est	4.2, Ford figs
0-100mph, secs	21.0 (99mph)	18.0	N/a	N/a
Overall mpg	18-21 *Autocar*	8-15 (stage/road)	N/a	From 3mpg, on stage

Rally/rallycross performance figures

Mph	1973 works RS 1600	1976 works RS 1800	1985 4x4 Welch Zakspeed RS turbo
0-30	2.9	2.5	1.1
0-40	3.9	3.4	1.4
0-50	5.5	4.4	2.0
0-60	7.0	6.1	2.7
0-70	9.0	8.0	3.6
0-80	11.9	10.2	4.3
0-90	14.9	13.5	5.4
0-100	20.3	16.6	6.6
0-110	–	21.8	8.7
Max mph @ rpm limit	108 @ 8500	108 @ 8500	116 @ 9000
Mpg	8-10	10-12.5	4.3
Bhp	200	250	560
Figures courtesy of	*Autocar*	*Autocar*	*Motor*

Racing performance figures

Mph	1971 Broadspeed RS 1600 (1700cc)	1972 Zakspeed RS 1600 (1785cc)	1976 Zakspeed RS 1800 (1965cc)
0-50	3.8	3.8	3.8
0-60/2*	4.8	5.6	5.1
0-100/99*	12.0	13.0	10.5
0-120/4*	17.7	24.1	16.8
Bhp @ rpm	250 @ 9000	236 @ 9000	280 @ 9000
Fuel cons. Mpg	8.5	6.7	5.1

* Second figure translated from closest km/h equivalent. Thus 0-60 mph = 0-100km/h (62mph) and so on. 1971 Broadspeed Escort figures were obtained by the author with John Fitzpatrick driving at Silverstone Club straight using the fifth wheel timing gear of *Motor Sport* magazine. The Zakspeed figures were taken by independent German magazines and published in *Handbuch der Deutschen Rennsport Meisterschaft, 1981.*

Appendix VII

Ford CVH engine range specifications 1980~88

Engine	1100LC	1100HC	1300HC	1600VV	16002V
Bore (mm)	73.96	73.96	79.96	79.96	79.96
Stroke (mm)	64.98	64.98	64.52	79.52	79.52
Displacement (cc)	1117	1117	1296	1597	1597
Compression ratio	8.5:1	9.5:1	9.5:1	9.5:1	9.5:1
Octane Rating RON	88	96	96	96	96
Maximum power (DIN PS)	55	59	69	79	96
(DIN KW)	40	43	51	58	71
At Engine Speed (rpm)	6000	6000	6000	5800	6000
Maximum Torque (mkp)	59lb ft	62lb ft	74lb ft	92lb ft	98lb ft
	(8.15mkp)	(8.6mkp)	(10.2mkp)	(12.7mkp)	(13.5mkp)
At Engine Speed (rpm)	4000	4000	3500	3000	4000
bmep (kg/cm²)	9.18	9.64	9.89	10.04	10.64
Dry weight (kg)	102.9	103.6	106.2	111.2	111.8

Valve gear					
Camshaft timing:	**OHV**	**OHV**	**SOHC**	**SOHC**	**SOHC**
Inlet Opens ATDC	13deg	13deg	13deg	13deg	8deg
Closes ABDC	28deg	28deg	28deg	28deg	36deg
Exhaust Opens BBDC	30deg	30deg	30deg	30deg	34deg
Closes BTDC	15deg	15deg	15deg	15deg	6deg
Duration of Inlet opening	195deg	195deg	195deg	195deg	208deg
Duration of Exhaust opening	195deg	195deg	195deg	195deg	208deg
Tappets (type)	Hydraulic Lifters, self-adjusting (all models)				
Rockers (type)	Pressed Steel, with centre fulcrum (all models)				
Inlet Valve, head diamater	38mm	38mm	42mm	42mm	42mm
lift	9.56mm	9.56mm	9.56mm	9.56mm	10.09mm
Exhaust Valve head diameter	32.2mm	32.2mm	34mm	37mm	37mm
lift	9.52mm	9.52mm	9.52mm	9.52mm	10.06mm

Fuel system

Pump (type)	Mechanical, pushrod operated diaphragm (all models)
Carburettor, make	Ford Motorcraft .... Weber
type	Variable Venturi .... Twin Choke DFT

Construction

Cylinder block	Grey iron sand casting with external ribs, centre distance between bores 91.8mm.
Crankshaft	Cast nodular graphite iron; main bearing dia 57.99mm. Big-end diameter: 1100, 43.0mm; 1300 and 1600, 47.9mm.
Pistons	Permanent mould gravity diecast light alloy with squish-generating sculptured crowns; two compression rings and one micro-land oil control scraper ring.
Cylinder Head	Light alloy die casting with compound valve angles, hemispherical combustion chambers and single overhead camshaft.

Key

LC	=	*low compression*
HC	=	*high compression*
VV	=	*variable venturi (single-choke)*
2V	=	*2 venturi (twin-choke)*

Escort CVH engines, 1986 onward

	1.4	1.6	1.6i	1.6iT	1.9i(USA)
Bore (mm)	77.24	79.96	79.96	79.96	82
Stroke (mm)	74.3	79.52	79.52	79.52	88
Capacity (cc)	1392	1598	1598	1598	1859
Compression 9.5:1	9.5:1	9.5:1	9.5:1	8.2:1	9:1
Fuel system	2V carb	2V carb	K-jetronic	K-jet + turbo	Bosch electronic injection
Max power (bhp)	75	90	105	132	117
@ rpm	5600	5800	6000	5750	5200
Max torque (mkp)	11.1	13.6	14.1	18.4	16.6
@ rpm	4000	4000	4800	2750	4400
Unleaded fuel capability?	Yes	Yes	Yes	No†	Yes

†Super unleaded (98 octane)

Index